P11H12

4.50

In this book—the first exposition of the entire range of James's philosophy—the reader will become acquainted with every passage of prime importance in *all* of James's writings. Moreover, the reader will also find in the accompanying exposition by Dr. Young, the articulation of James's philosophic system as-a-whole, an achievement which James himself did not present in his own writings.

This book is of major importance to all those interested in American philosophy, religion, and literature. Its appeal cuts across all professional and academic lines, for it is of equal value to philosophers, clergymen, writers, and to the general cultivated reader.

The Philosophy of Henry James, Sr.

The Philosophy of Henry James, Sr.

by

Frederic Harold Young

Bookman Associates : New York

The author wishes to acknowledge, with gratitude, the following permissions to use copyrighted material in this book:

Columbia University Press, for use of quotations from Herbert W. Schneider's *A History of American Philosophy;* also, from Joseph Blau, Editor, of *American Philosophic Addresses,* 1700-1900.

Greystone Press, New York, for excerpts from Sri Aurobindo's *The Life Divine.*

Harvard University Press and Prof. Ralph Barton Perry, for quotations from Prof. Perry's *The Thought and Character of William James.*

Henry Holt and Co., Inc., N. Y., for material from Marguerite Block's *The New Church in the New World.*

Mr. M. A. DeWolfe Howe, for an anecdote about James, from Mr. Howe's *Memories of a Hostess.*

Alfred A. Knopf, Inc., for quoting from F. O. Matthiessen's *The James Family.*

Mr. Paul Reynolds, in charge of the James Estate, New York, for permission to quote from Henry James, (the 3rd)'s, *The Letters of William James.*

Charles Scribner's Sons, New York, for quotation from W. R. Inge's article, "Neo-Platonism," in Hasting's *Encyclopedia of Religion and Ethics.*

Swedenborg Publishing Society, of Brooklyn, N. Y., for quotation from Walter M. Horton's address, "The Significance of Swedenborg for Contemporary Theology."

TO

Valesca

Preface

IN WRITING THIS book as the first treatment of the senior James's philosophy in its entirety, I was guided by two purposes: first, to give quotations of all the key-passages from James's writings, which are extremely inaccessible to general readers, in order to allow James to speak for himself as much as possible; secondly, to render a systematic exposition of the entire range of the sources and products of his thought. As to the first, the reader may be certain that he will become acquainted here with every passage of prime importance in James's works. As to the second, the reader will find, in the accompanying exposition, a presentation of James's philosophy which, in its wholeness, constitutes a remarkably unified system; but this system in his thought-as-a-whole had to be discovered and articulated as such by the present writer. The task of exhibiting James's system as an interrelated totality was complicated by the fact that the literary unit of James's expression of his thought is not the sentence, nor the book-length, but rather the "essay" (or, "letter"), as one who consults the full titles of his works will readily discover; moreover, there are no indexes in any of his books.

James's philosophic vision is one of imposing vitality and possesses a kind of architectural grandeur. This vision is garmented in the sinewy yet graceful English of a prose master. It is hoped that James, Sr., long eclipsed in fame by his sons William and Henry, may come now into his own as a recognized brilliant thinker and author in the epic of American thought and literature.

* * *

When it comes to expressing my appreciation of the various persons and institutions to whom I am directly and indirectly indebted for aid in the composition of this work, I find it, as is usual in such under-takings, quite impossible to do exact justice to all who have assisted in the completion of this enterprise.

To Professor Herbert Wallace Schneider of Columbia University, I am under a most basic and happy kind of obligation. His scholarship in the field of American philosophy and religion is too well known for me to make further comment, except to add that his fine knowledge and critical standards were always at my service. In writing this book I consulted him more frequently and directly than any other person.

My debt to Professor Ralph Barton Perry of Harvard University, the pioneer scholar on Henry James, Sr., is very great indeed. From his *The Thought and Character of William James,* I have drawn more heavily than from any other source on the elder James. Moreover, Professor Perry was responsible for discovering the James-Emerson correspondence (now in Widener Library at Harvard University), and for obtaining permission to publish it.

To Professor Austin Warren, another early scholar of James, I am indebted for the excellent bibliography in his book, *The Elder Henry James.* With his bibliographic foundation I went on to complete what I believe to be an exhaustive bibliography of and about James.

Various persons in the Departments of Religion, English, and Philosophy at Columbia University aided me in a very definite way by their critical reading of the first drafts: Marguerite Block, whose thorough knowledge of Swedenborg was invaluable; Quentin Anderson, with his significant studies of the senior James's influence upon the philosophy in the novels of Henry James, Jr.; Joseph Blau, who discussed material sources and suggested collateral sources to consult.

It is a pleasure also to extend my appreciation to Professor Gustav E. Mueller, of the Philosophy Department of the University of Oklahoma, for his reading of this book in typescript and for his pertinent criticisms.

Professor Harold A. Larrabee, of the Philosophy Department at Union College (James's *Alma Mater*), aided me considerably with numerous suggestions, and I here express my gratitude.

From Professor F. O. Matthiessen of Harvard University I received, by correspondence, the value of his keen judgment on various details; also, helpful courtesies from the present William James.

Other individuals whose names could not possibly be omitted, because of their immeasurable and sometimes indefinable aids, are: my wife, Valesca Herzog Heidt Young, who performed with me the arduous labor of checking all quotations and notes besides proof-reading the whole, in addition to rendering many other services; my stepson, William J. Heidt, II, who contributed many keen suggestions; and my father, the Rev'd Harold E. Young who supplied encouragement. To each I express my lasting and affectionate gratitude.

Among the institutions to whose staffs I am under a permanent obligation, are: Columbia University Library, Union Theological Seminary, Princeton Theological Seminary, the Library of the Academy of the New Church at Bryn Athyn, Pennsylvania; the Newark, New Jersey, Public Library; the New-Church Press and Library of Brooklyn; the Swedenborg Foundation of New York City, the New York City Public Library, the Houghton Library at Harvard University, and lastly, the Library of Congress at Washington, D. C. I am also obligated to the University of Chicago, Butler University in Indiana, and the University of Pennsylvania, for the use of unpublished material. Each of the above-named institutions was most gracious in their cooperation, some of them allowing me a greatly extended time limit for the use of sources which, in certain instances, were absolutely irreplaceable. My regret is that I cannot name here, all the individuals on these library staffs who were generous with their time and talents far beyond one's normal expectations.

While gladly acknowledging the high excellence of the assistance of the previously mentioned authors, it should be said that the responsibility for the systematic interpretation of James's thought in the following pages, rests with the author.

F. H. Y.

Upper Montclair, New Jersey
11 November, 1950

Contents

Chronology of James's Career

1811	Born June 3 at Albany, New York.
1830	Graduated from Union College, Schenectady, New York.
1835-37	Student at Princeton Theological Seminary.
1837	Visited England with a letter of introduction from Joseph Henry to Michael Faraday, through whom James derived his interest in Sandemanianism.
1838	Edited and prefaced Sandeman's *Letters on Theron and Aspasio*.
1840	*Remarks on the Apostolic Gospel*. Non-extant. Married Mary Robertson Walsh.
1842	William James, born January 11.
1843	Henry James, Jr., born April 15.
1844	Visited England again, passed through "spiritual crisis," and was introduced to Swedenborg's works; met James John Garth Wilkinson.
1846	*What Constitutes the State*. (*WCS*)
1847	*Tracts for the New Times*. (*TNT*)
1848	Translated, edited, and prefaced Victor A. Hennequin's *Love in a Phalanstery*.
1850	*Moralism and Christianity*. (*MC*)
1852	*Lectures and Miscellanies*. (*LM*)
1853	*Love, Marriage, and Divorce*. (*LMD*)
1855	*The Nature of Evil*. (*NE*)
1856	*The Church of Christ not an Ecclesiasticism*. (*CCNE*)
1857	*Christianity the Logic of Creation*. (*CLC*)
1861	*The Social Significance of Our Institutions*. (*SSI*)
1863	*Substance and Shadow*. (*S and S*)

1869   *The Secret of Swedenborg.* (*S of S*)

1879   *Society the Redeemed Form of Man.* (*SRFM*)

1882   Died December 18 at Boston, Massachusetts, and was buried at Mt. Auburn Cemetery, Cambridge. Mrs. James had died in February of the same year.

1885   *The Literary Remains of the late Henry James,* edited by William James. (*LR*)

PART ONE

The Roots of James's Philosophy

Chapter One

The Intellectual Career of Henry James, Sr.

A visitor at the home of Tolstoy reports that the Count has one short shelf of precious books, and among them are the volumes of the elder Henry James. With a gesture of pleasure, Tolstoy pointed out the volumes, saying that this Henry James is the most suggestive writer that America has produced.

—EDWIN MARKHAM[1]

I have often tried to imagine what sort of a figure my father might have made, had he been born in a genuinely theological age, with the best minds about him fermenting with the mystery of the Divinity, and the air full of definitions and theories and counter-theories, and strenuous reasonings and contentions, about God's relations to mankind. Floated on such a congenial tide, furthered by sympathetic comrades, and opposed no longer by blank silence but by passionate and definite resistance, he would infallibly have developed his resources in many ways which, as it was, he never tried; and he would have played a prominent, perhaps a momentous and critical, part in the struggles of his time, for he was a religious prophet and genius, if ever there were. He published an intensely positive, radical, and fresh conception of God, and an intensely vital view of our connection with him. And nothing shows better the altogether lifeless and unintellectual character of the professional theism of our time, than the fact that this view, this conception, so vigorously thrown down, should not have stirred the faintest tremulation on its stagnant pool.

—WILLIAM JAMES[2]

· 1 ·

THE ELDER HENRY JAMES was and remains a unique figure in the history of American thought and culture. That a man such as he should appear in a lusty young nation absorbed in material expansion and inflated with the gases of heady, if thin, idealisms—that even one man of James's kind should appear is not altogether accidental, of course, but it is nonetheless remarkable.

A philosopher who was passionately religious, and at the same time a religionist who was as passionately philosophical; a devout Christian believer in spirit and in truth, who was yet a radical opponent of every kind of clericalism and ecclesiasticism in the institutional aspects of Christianity; a superb individualist who yet dreamed of a Spiritual Socialism comprehensive of all humanity; a thinker with flavors of mysticism, secularism, and neo-Gnosticism compounded in his own specific fashion—such is the complex and stimulating character with which we are to become acquainted in this study. However contradictory or mutually exclusive such reality-and-life views may seem among themselves, abstractly or logically considered, they were nevertheless combined in his singularly vital personality with a fusion inimitable in itself, and very delicate to describe. He was indeed lord of these counter-positions by virtue of his profound spiritual intensity and integrity.

Poetic metaphysician of a spiritual philosophy, prophet, heretic, spiritual theist and theo-humanist—any or all such labels may be applied to him; but the man himself is greater than them all, and in the end he somewhat eludes the awkwardness and limitation of every attempt to label him.

James's contribution to philosophic and religious thought was all but completely ignored in his own day. Only three or four men and two women are on record as having made a thoroughgoing effort to comprehend, with substantial and critical depth, James's thought;[3] and each of them, however much they differed in detail from each other and from James, held for him and his thought the highest respect. By this same token of unmerited neglect he becomes all the more precious to us today as we attempt a rounded and vital comprehension of his spiritual philosophy. Not only so, but by virtue of his intellectual impact on his celebrated sons—William James the psychologist-philosopher and Henry James the novelist-critic—we are dealing perforce with a man who determined much of the direction of important streams of cultural thought in America until the present moment. He alone does not, of course, fully account for the genius of his sons;

yet after a thorough study of the intellectual history of the Jameses, it is transparently evident that there was a powerful cause-and-effect relation operative in the association between these three. If the sons proved themselves eminently worthy of such a father, the father was quite as worthy of such sons. F. O. Matthiessen reports George Bernard Shaw's opinion on this matter as follows: "When Bernard Shaw indulged his love of trying to shock by declaring to Henry Junior that the most interesting member of his family was neither himself nor his brother but their father, he found that no praise could have been more welcome." And then Matthiessen adds an opinion on his own account: "Put beside either son, the father displays, in his maturity, a unique spaciousness and serenity."[4]

II

The biographical externals of James's life are as meagre and as undramatic as the intellectual life is rich and rewarding. He was born at Albany, New York, June 3, 1811, son of William James, who was a wealthy merchant and leading public citizen of that city. The elder William James came by his wealth as a result of combined energy and foresight. The latter quality was demonstrated notably in his support, politically and financially, of the proposed Erie canal, from investments in which he realized a handsome fortune that was comparable in those days only to that of the Astors and a few others. Having arrived in America from County Cavan, Ireland, at the age of eighteen in 1793, he left at his death in 1832 an estate valued at three million dollars. With such a munificent financial flooring assured, Henry James, the senior, was free to choose his own way of life. The remarkable thing about his decision—or, more accurately, series of decisions—is that probably no other American of the period, given a similar capital and the current opportunities for increasing the same, would have chosen to spend his life trying to tease out of his soul and brain a satisfying religious metaphysics of creation! Such an intellectual evolution in James's case is striking enough testimony to the vigor and independence of his mind: but we are getting ahead of a few more details of his biography which are important for our understanding of him.

At the age of thirteen he suffered an accident in putting out a stable fire, which event, after two years' confinement in bed, led to the amputation of the injured leg in a time when anesthesia was unknown. This tragic and devastating experience could not but have a permanent effect upon his thought and life, especially in deepening a tendency to introspection in a lad who was, on his own account, very buoyant and expansive with animal spirits. Despite this unfortunate occurrence, he prepared for Union College, entering that institution at Schenectady in 1828 and graduating with the class of '30. It appears that Dr. Eliphalet Nott, the President of Union, was the dominant influence of James at this stage of his intellectual career, for Nott was not only a shrewd administrator but, for the times, a genuinely stimulating and liberalizing intellect. At age nineteen James graduated. Two years later his father died and young Henry was confronted with making a decision about a profession—at least, he *thought* he was, for as it turned out, he lived most of his life following no profession, unless one were to describe him as a free-lance-professional-metaphysician! At any rate, the richly religious vein in his nature suggested the choice of the ministry. Raised as a Presbyterian, his natural preference for a theological seminary was Princeton. He matriculated there in 1835 with a class of fifty-eight men, but he was not destined to graduate. After remaining for two and a half years he left the Seminary, with both head and heart in revolt against the doctrines of orthodox Calvinism. James never admitted in any of his literary remains to any particular value in his seminary experience but for one touching exception. In his book, *The Nature of Evil*, he steps outside the tenor of a tightly-reasoned discourse to express a tribute to one of his professors, "Good old Dr. Miller, of Princeton. . . . A less mercenary, or more guileless piety than Dr. Miller's, I never knew, and he would have been universally reckoned a pattern of Christian manhood. . . . God love and bless his honored head for ever!"[5] Obtaining a six months' leave from Princeton to go to England, he took farewell of the Seminary forever, though he was not conscious at the time that it was a final separation. Arriving in England in the autumn of 1837, he visited not only in that country, but sojourned with an uncle at Bailieborough, County Cavan, Ireland, the birthplace of his father. Otherwise we know nothing in particular of his travels, for his career is intellectual and spiritual throughout rather than geographical, temporal, or personal. There was indeed a spiritually important result from this trip, for, holding a letter of introduction from Joseph Henry to the great scientist Michael Faraday, he came into contact, through Faraday, with Sandemanianism, of which somewhat more will be said in a later connection.

In 1840, he married Mary Walsh, sister of his dear friend Hugh Walsh, of the same class as himself at the Seminary. All evidence on the basis of remarks made in letters by James, as well as in letters of their sons, indicates that Mary James was a quiet-mannered person who radiated a steady, intelligent love into her family's life. James's regard for her was so deep that when she died he lost all interest in living, and survived her by only a few months. At first they resided at 21 Washington Place, New York City—now 41 Washington Square South—where William was born in 1842, and where Emerson was taken upstairs to see the newborn child. Henry was born the next year. Between these years and 1866, when the family made their permanent residence at Cambridge, Massachusetts, they made many trips to Europe, remaining abroad for the education of the boys for years at a time, punctuated with several years of living at Newport, Rhode Island.

During their stay in New York, James corresponded in the early '40's with his old friend, the famous physicist Joseph Henry; while on March 18, 1842, according to Emerson's *Journal,* the Concord sage and James met for the first time.[6] Although they were to remain lifelong friends, there is not to be found any more pentrating criticism, so far as it goes, of Emerson's incompleteness as a philosopher than that penned by James.[7] When James went to England in the fall of 1843, Emerson gave him letters introductory to Carlyle and John Sterling. At the Carlyles' home he met James John Garth Wilkinson, the brilliant Swedenborgian scholar and interpreter, John Stuart Mill, Tennyson, George Lewes, Arthur Helps, Spedding, Baldwin Brown, and Frederick Denison Maurice, noted clergyman and Christian Socialist of the Church of England.[8] Toward the last of his life, James gave, in an interview to the Boston *Sunday Herald,* his blunt estimate of this group: "They were cynical—all cynical but Sterling and Mill. . . . Their talk was depraving to the last degree."[9] Allowance may be made for the circumstances of an interview, but such vigor of opinion was entirely native to him throughout his life. He judged very sharply because of the loyalty he had to his own central and persistent convictions. Of Maurice he said: "Maurice disappointed me very much. I wanted to talk with him, but he wouldn't talk. He perhaps felt that my views were pestilent. He seemed narrow outside the pale of the church."[10] Of Mill and Sterling he was superlatively commendatory: "Mr. Mill was the best of the lot, except Sterling, who was the truest man I ever met."[11] Of Carlyle he observed: "He scoffed with hearty scorn at the contented imbecility of

Church and State with respect to social problems, but his own indifference to these things, save in so far as they were available to picturesque palaver, was infinitely more indolent and contented."[12] Or again: "Carlyle was, in truth, a hardened declaimer. He talked in a way vastly to tickle his auditors, and his enjoyment of their amusement was lively enough to sap his own intellectual integrity."[13]

While still in England on this particular trip, James experienced a profound conversion, a conversion exemplified in the two major aspects of such an experience—that is to say, the turning away *from,* and the turning *to.* This inner event was preceded by a period of exhausting nervous debilitation, best described by the term "vastation" as his new-found master, Swedenborg, had already named such an experience. The term literally means "an emptying," and is ideally precise to express just what happened to James. This crisis of James's innermost being reminds one of the classical "four steps" of the "Mystic Way": *awakening, purgation, illumination*—though James never quite achieved the fourth step—*union* with the Divine. James had been "awakened" for many years by intensive and extensive study, as also by the discipline of writing out his thoughts, theological and philosophical. He was now being "purged," or "vastated"; he was next to be "illuminated." Between the purgation and the illumination, however, was a somewhat prolonged interval of more than two years. James describes the vastation phase with extreme intensity, and as one reads it, he cannot help but be reminded of the very parallel experience of William James when he was about twenty-eight. James graphically verbalizes this inner upheaval:

> One day . . . having eaten a comfortable dinner, I remained sitting at the table after the family had dispersed, idly gazing at the embers in the grate, thinking of nothing, and feeling only the exhilaration incident to a good digestion, when suddenly—in a lightning-flash as it were—"fear came upon me, and trembling, which made all my bones to shake." To all appearance it was a perfectly insane and abject terror, without ostensible cause, and only to be accounted for, to my perplexed imagination, by some damned shape squatting invisible to me within the precincts of the room, and raying out from his fetid personality influences fatal to life. The thing had not lasted ten seconds before I felt myself a wreck, that is, reduced from a state of firm, vigorous, joyful manhood to one of almost helpless infancy. The only self-control I was capable of exerting was to keep my seat. I felt the greatest

desire to run incontinently to the foot of the stairs and shout for help to my wife,—to run to the roadside even, and appeal to the public to protect me; but by an immense effort I controlled these frenzied impulses, and determined not to budge from my chair till I had recovered my lost self-possession. This purpose I held to for a good long hour, as I reckoned time, beat upon meanwhile by an ever-growing tempest of doubt, anxiety, and despair, with absolutely no relief from any truth I had ever encountered save a most pale and distant glimmer of the Divine existence,—when I resolved to abandon the vain struggle, and communicate without more ado what seemed my sudden burst of inmost, implacable unrest to my wife.

Now, to make a long story short, this ghastly condition of mind continued with me, with gradually lengthening intervals of relief, for two years, and even longer....[14]

James then narrates how he consulted physicians who recommended a water-cure treatment, upon which advice he acted. At the water-cure resort, however, he became weary of "diet, and regimen, and disease, and politics, and parties, and persons,"[15] and found himself clinging to only one main thought which he italicizes for stress:

> *The curse of mankind, that which keeps our manhood so little and so depraved, is its sense of selfhood, and the absurd abominable opinionativeness it engenders. How sweet it would be to find oneself no longer a man, but one of those innocent and ignorant sheep pasturing upon that placid hillside, and drinking in eternal dew and freshness from nature's lavish bosom!*[16]

The "natural" man's repose in the adequacy of his moral and intellectual powers to search for God, and by searching, find Him, was now permanently shattered in James. He reacted with the fury generated by his inner convulsion: "Truth indeed! How should a beggar like me be expected to *discover* it?" (Italics supplied.)[17] Then he states the solution:

"Truth must *reveal itself* if it would be known, and even then how imperfectly known at best!"[18] (Italics are James's.) Thus the "illumination" was drawing nigh.

It came through the mediation of a lady at the water-cure resort who possessed "rare qualities of heart and mind."[19] She described his spiritual and organic *malaise* by the Swedenborgian term, "vastation," and directed him to the study of Swedenborg. James betook himself to London and secured Swedenborg's treatise on the *Divine Love and Wisdom*, and *Divine Providence*.[20] In London he soon made acquaintance with Dr. James John Garth Wilkinson, who was a really extraordinary man in his own person, quite aside from the fact of his being the English translator of some of Swedenborg's major scientific works. Wilkinson was a name not unknown to James before this meeting, for in 1841 James was cognizant of Wilkinson's publication of Coleridge's "Original Comments" on Swedenborg, at the end of which Wilkinson had added some critical notes of his own. The friendship now begun, flourished rapidly, so much so that when James's third son was born in 1845, he named him "Garth," after Wilkinson. Inasmuch as there will be discussion of James's relation to Swedenborg's philosophy in a later section of this study, suffice it here to state that the works of the Swedish theologian were shipped with the other effects of the family on all their subsequent journeys.[21]

From 1845 on, James emerges as a man who has found himself and his philosophy. In December of this year he gives a lecture to the Young Men's Association in Albany, entitled *What Constitutes the State*. This was to become his first acknowledged publication, he having previously written an unsigned "Preface" for the 1838 American edition of Robert Sandeman's *Letters on Theron and Aspasio*, and *Remarks on the Apostolic Gospel* (1840), the latter being, so far as is known to scholars of the elder James, non-existent today. With the appearance of *What Constitutes the State* in 1846, James's period of literary productivity begins, and there is a fairly steady stream of works from his pen until within a few months of his death in 1882.

Not so long after the Albany Address he became impressed, through his friend, Parke Godwin, with the doctrines of the French socialist, Fourier. Thereafter he came into personal contact with the "Brook Farm" leaders, including George Ripley, John S. Dwight, Charles A. Dana, and other "Associationists" like Albert Brisbane, Horace Greeley, and William Cullen Bryant. But although such expressions as "Society the Redeemed Form of Man," and "man's associated destiny" occur abundantly in James's writings, he never participated actively in, nor identified himself with, any social experiment among the many utopian ventures of his time. The impact of Fourierism on James will be traced in another context, when we consider his doctrine of Society and Redemption.

The years from 1846 to his death in Boston on December 18, 1882, were occupied with travelling, corresponding with friends here and abroad, educating his sons, and above all, with writing and re-writing his gospel of Spiritual Creation and "Spiritual Socialism,"[22] as Schneider so defines it. Though he and his gospel were but a voice in the wilderness of other gospels, he was not any the less loyal to it. He still expounded and preached it with the old-time vigor when men who also had had visions in their youth—Dana, Ripley, Greeley—had become silent because of the spiritual recoil that sprung from disillusionment. James verbally proved the faith that was in him to the very last; but, as a reader of James has observed: "He never went even *wading* in reality," for he never developed his spiritual philosophy to the actual test of social reform, and so never ran an equal risk with Dana, Greeley, and company, of disillusionment!

NOTES

1. Edwin Markham, "Distinguished American Family," *Cosmopolitan*, Vol. L (Dec. 1910), p. 145.
2. William James, in his "Introduction," as editor of his father's *Literary Remains*, p. 12.
3. These students and critics of James's philosophy were: James Freeman Clarke, J. J. Garth Wilkinson, Charles Sanders Peirce, George H. Howison, Mrs. Julia Kellogg, and A. Orr (Mrs. Sutherland). With some of their evaluations of James's doctrines we shall become acquainted in the course of this study. Probably it should be added here that William James and Henry James, Jr., were no cursory students of their father's philosophical and theological ideas.
4. F. O. Matthiessen, *The James Family*. (Alfred A. Knopf, New York, 1947), p. 7.
5. *NE*, 124-126.
6. Emerson's *Journal*, Vol. VI, p. 163.
7. "The Radical Dogmatics," in *Radical*, II (1867), pp. 87-91.
8. Austin Warren, *The Elder Henry James*. (Macmillan Co., N. Y., 1934), p. 51.
9. "Henry James, Sr.," an interview related in the Boston *Sunday Herald*, Apr. 17, 1881.
10. *Ibid.*
11. *Ibid. Cf.* also James's tribute to Mill in *Substance and Shadow* (1863), p. 322.
12. *Literary Remains* (1884), p. 425.
13. *Ibid.*, pp. 432-433.
14. SRFM., pp. 44-46.
15. *Ibid.*, p. 47.
16. *Ibid.*, pp. 47-48.
17. *Ibid.*, p. 49

18. *Ibid.*
19. *Ibid.*
20. *Ibid.*, p. 51.
21. Henry James, Jr., *Notes of a Son and Brother.* (Scribner & Sons, 1913), pp. 158-159.
22. Herbert W. Schneider, *A History of American Philosophy.* (Columbia Univ. Press, 1946), pp. 301-312.

Chapter Two

James and His Cultural Environment

EVERY THINKER, HOWEVER individual his special emphasis and modes of expression, stands in relation to the total complex of cultural forces in his epoch, whether it be that he placidly reflects those forces in his own thought, or dynamically revolts against them. Even in radical reaction against contemporary currents of thought, the thinker uses the ideological elements of his time as the leverage by which he diverges. There is a strictly commensurate ratio between acceptance and rejection in the interaction of thinker with environment; and neither he nor we could take the measure of his own contribution unless there were a given constellation of basic presuppositions, both implicit and explicit, in the society and culture of the thinker's era.

James, though a highly individual thinker, is no exception to this general principle. Before entering upon a critical inquiry concerning the major thought-currents operative upon and more or less decisive in his intellectual development, it is apropos to approach him in terms of the general religious and secular ideological movements dominant in his time. In the following account, the purpose is merely to sketch briefly these movements and James's relation—which is usually one of revolt—to them.

The chief thought-movements of the period in America were Calvinism (though on the wane), Unitarianism, Transcendentalism, and Socialism. James was affected by all four with varying degrees of depth, and he was not least affected when he became a radical critic of, or a revolutionary against, any or all of them. Yet the most determined rebel cannot reject every shred of influence from the forces which he so ardently indicts. The critic who finds that which is really worth criticising, is perforce going to appropriate whatever real values there may be in a given tradition to a far greater extent than your docile acceptor, even though the critic himself is quite unconscious of it, and indeed, even vigorously asserts the contrary! Moreover, the rebel usually presents the ironical aspect of fighting the supposed enemy with weapons of the same type. If one would fight the rationalist, for example, one must out-rationalize the rationalist! Reason must be used to overthrow reason, and faith to overthrow faith!

Now it is illuminating to apply these reflections to James, for savagely as he criticised Calvinism, Unitarianism, Transcendentalism, and Socialism, he imbibed definite values from each on the way to the crystallization of his own philosophy. Let us examine his relation, positive and negative, to these movements in this light.

Calvinism was the first great system of thought by which James was stamped. Reared in a Presbyterian family, the father of which was a strict Calvinist, James, with his sensitive and eager intellect, could not escape taking deep draughts from this well. As we have seen, he went so far as to spend two and a half years in preparation for the Presbyterian ministry at Princeton Theological Seminary, and it took him precisely that period of time to decide that it was not for him. It is curious to note that in all his books he never makes a direct frontal attack upon Calvinism as a whole. He retained a basic lifelong respect for much of its thought. Although he highly transformed Calvinist doctrines concerning the sovereignty of God, justification by faith, and the problem of evil, through his constant re-statements on these themes, the point is that their importance was ingrained by his Calvinistic inheritance regardless of ultimate difference in formulation. That he did hold his intellectual respect for Calvinism despite his thorough emotional separation from it, is indicated in a striking passage from a letter to Emerson under date of May 11, 1843:

> You don't look upon Calvinism as a fact at all; wherein you are to my mind philosophically infirm—impaired in your universality. I can see in Carlyle the advantage his familiarity with it give him over you with a general audience. What is highest in him is built upon that lowest. At least so I read; I believe Jonathan Edwards redivivus in true blue would, after an honest study of the philosophy that has grown up since his day, make the best possible reconciler and critic of this philosophy—far better than Schelling redivivus.[1]

James had cut his theological teeth on a substantial ring! He wrote this letter in less than a decade after leaving Princeton, at a period when his reaction against Presbyterian orthodoxy might have been expected to be still very intense.

Throughout his writings, James, however he formulated them, asserted and reasserted the sovereignty of the Divine, the priority and superiority of Revelation over Reason, a theologically objective conception of Christ's redemptive work, and the profound importance of the problem of evil. All this is evidence of the indelibility of the Reformed theology upon his mind and spirit. Ralph Barton Perry comments upon the persistence of this strain in James:

> But though James insisted upon the unreserved lovingness and lovableness of God, and upon the solidarity of mankind, his personal religious experience was profoundly Calvinistic. It is Calvinistic in this very idea of human solidarity. For is it not a first premise of Calvinism that the sin of Adam is communicated to his whole progeny, so that the race is like an organism which, being stricken in one of its members, must suffer in all? James was Calvinistic, too, in his unreserved acceptance of the view that man is estranged from God. Religion begins with despair. This is not an accident, but a necessary condition; there can be no upward path that does not start from the depths. He was Calvinistic in his acceptance of the doctrine of justification by faith, salvation being an unmerited bounty, proceeding from indulgent love to its unworthy object.
>
> ....But the depth of his Calvinism only makes the more astonishing his radical departure from it—a departure so radical that it might be termed an inversion. For Calvinism, men fall collectively, and are saved individually. . . . But that which is the mark of salvation for the Calvinist, that sense of the special favor of God which expresses itself in a preeminent capacity for righteousness, is for James the very moment of the fall. The biological man is innocent. It is when he presumes to claim individual superiority, whether on the score of his prerogatives or on that of his exceeding piety, that he is most completely alienated from God. What he must repent is his pride, and the beginning of his salvation appears when he identifies his own hopes altogether with those of the race. In short, for James men fall individually, and are saved collectively![2]

Perry rounds out the picture of James's reaction-pattern against Calvinism:

James's repudiation of orthodox Calvinism—and he kept repudiating it heartily for many years to come—evidently was an occasion of scandal, as well as of evangelical anxiety, to the Presbyterian friends of his youth. As late as 1859 his former Princeton roommate wrote to admonish him, and elicited the following reply:

Newport, May 12, [1859]

My dear Sir,

. . . . It is obvious from certain expressions in your letter that your good heart is pained by what you conceive my renunciation of the gospel, meaning thereby my rejection of Calvinism. I can't offer one word in alleviation of that pang. I reject Calvinism, it is true, with a good-will for which Webster's dictionary is poor in terms of expression, but I do so only in the sovereign interests of Christianity, very heartily worshipping the man Christ Jesus as the only God of heaven and earth; seeing, in other words, no divinity above the conditions of my own nature. You, I imagine, can hardly conceive the completeness of my contempt, on the one hand, for all those monstrous and odious caricatures of the Divine name which make our Calvinistic literature a sickening abomination to the heart, more even than a falsity to the intellect. . . .[3]

This division between his heart and his head, in their almost separate reactions to Calvinism, is one that runs throughout his entire intellectual and spiritual history. With his heart he rejected Calvinism with a passionate finality, but with his intellect he spent a lifetime trying to re-forge the Calvinist doctrines. His feeling against Calvinism was complete, while his intellectual respect for it he never lost. Running throughout this study we shall come upon many evidences of the tremendous influence of Reformed theology upon the temper, method, and content of his theological speculations, no matter how much he may have inverted this or that doctrine from its original Calvinist formulation. Perry, conscious of this fact, sums it up very tersely in a sentence:

This Calvinistic reaction against Calvinism was the main generating force of James's lecturing and writing, and all his later doctrines have this Calvinistic-anti-Calvinistic core.[4]

We shall be able to analyze his relation to Calvinism in detail when we study his Sandemanianism; meanwhile, we must survey other influences.

With Unitarian rationalism, James was, at least intellectually, more out of accord than with Calvinism. Its confident rationalism, and the accompanying "moralism" in the Unitarian movement were abhorrent to James's spiritual genius. It was a genuine case of *à rebours*. Accurately identifying Unitarianism with "natural religion" in general—for that matter, he identified even Calvinism with natural religion in the sense we shall later come to understand—he inveighed heavily against it. Over against its "reason," he insisted on Revelation—with a capital "R"; against its moralism he asserted the profound spiritual danger implicit in moral self-confidence as a claim upon the Divine regard. James considers Unitarianism as the third main division within Christendom because it is the representative of pure rationalism in religion:

> We are all of us more or less involved in some branch of the reigning ecclesiasticism, Catholic, Protestant or Unitarian. . . .[5]

Further:

> Romanism, Protestantism, and Unitarianism or Rationalism, are only so many variations of one and the same original air, the second being simply a florid reaction or return upon the first, and the third a still more florid reaction upon the second.[6]

Again:

> This is the exact infirmity of Unitarianism, that it baptizes nature, that it pours consecrating oil upon the natural selfhood, and bids it aspire to immortal bliss. It is thus preeminently an obscuration of Christian truth. There can be no question that the ranks of Unitarianism include as much moral or personal worth as those of any other sect, and none of the sects indeed are deficient in such worth. But the extremest moral or personal worth is quite consistent with an intense hostility to the Divine Name, and Unitarianism viewed simply as an intellectual system, seems to me preeminently adapted to obviate all suspicion of this truth, and lull the soul nursed in social decorum to the most fatal of slumbers. Viewed intellectually, it is a religion adapted only to cultivated people, people in whom their essential nakedness is effectually veiled by the fig-leaves of natural good, and who worship God on the same impulse of aesthetic obligation, and with the same sense of vital aloofness, as characterize their admiration of a fine landscape or a beautiful flower.
>
> Thus, we have seen, Romanism defeats the gospel of Christ, by imposing the burden of an ecclesiastical righteousness on the soul. Protestantism in its turn defeats it by imposing the previous obligation of an *inward conversion from evil to good in the substance of the selfhood*: a conversion which is not only impossible in the nature of things, or which, if it were possible, would turn the human selfhood into God, but is also void even of an apparent war-

rant in Scripture. . . . And finally, Unitarianism defeats it by exhausting its necessity, or denying any insuperable discrepancy between the Divine and human natures; so turning the gospel into a mere sentimental or expurgated edition of the Law, an edition with the terrible music of Sinai left out. And thus viewed altogether, these three ecclesiastical diversities combine in one great anti-Christian unveracity, which brings good tidings to many a fold unblessed of the Divine Shepherd, and offers a message of peace in many places where the gospel itself would only prove a cartel of defiance.[7]

James rounds off his critique of Unitarianism in particular with a blow aimed at the very heart:

Thus Unitarian Rationalism approximates man to God, by vacating Christianity as a *supernatural* method of salvation; or what is the same thing, by reducing Christ to merely human dimensions, and so reconstructing a purely natural basis of intercourse between God and man. This is tantamount to curing hunger by pronouncing starvation impossible, and the demand for nourishment premature and illusory. Unitarianism is thus a fearful anachronism. It is nothing more nor less than a revivification of the old Paganism, with its sentence of death suspended, and the hue of a wan and wintry life substituted instead. Paganism is good in its place, because it looks assiduously forward to something better to ensue. But take it out of its place, give it the name and the dress of that better thing which is to come, and it becomes to all who fixedly persuade themselves of its truth, a most hurtful masquerade, palsying the Divine grasp of the soul, or chilling the energy of regeneration at its very source.[8]

Transcendentalism fared hardly better under James's searching criticism as he turned through all points of the contemporary theological compass. He castigated the "subjectivism" of its philosophical grounds and methods, its inevitable affinity to pantheism, with its resultant blithe disregard of the gigantic problem of evil.[9] His strictures on Transcendentalist philosophy are usually directed to its great leader, Emerson, as in this instance:

In fact, this was my friend's inveterate limitation in philosophy, that he never raised his eyes above the basement story of creation, but was content to remain an obdurate naturalist till the end of his intellectual days. The feebleness of the naturalist point of view inheres in this, that nature falls entirely within consciousness and does not directly connect with God therefore. . . . And Mr. Emerson had no spiritual insight into creative order, because he had no adequate doctrine of consciousness.[10]

James is even sharper in this choice diatribe:

> I wish very much by the way that our Unitarian and Universalist philosophers would take a look in this direction, and give up their sentimental shrieking at the devil regarded as a vital element of human consciousness. Because in that case our insane and inane Transcendentalism, against which the prevalent so-called Spiritualism is a maudlin protest and reaction, would fail of its backbone, and human thought would again recover its tonic quality, and we should all get deliverance from that puerile Pantheistic gabble which is fast strangling the higher faculties of the mind under the grasp of an all-devouring Imagination, and in comparison with which as it seems to me unmitigated Atheism would be manly sincere and evangelical.[11]

His relation to Fourieristic or Associationist Socialism, was of the same pattern as that to the aforementioned movements—the pattern of both acceptance and rejection. There were, in his day, many kinds of socialism: Christian, Fourierist, Owenite, and Marxist, along with minor variations of each. Inevitably they overlapped at various points and with varying degrees. James never mentions Marx in all his fifteen volumes, seventy-odd articles, and correspondence. Writing to the New York *Tribune,* he says:

> I distinctly aver that the proper earthly issue of Christianity is— I was very near saying Socialism. But Socialism means the doctrine of Fourier, or St. Simon, or Comte—means some specific theory or other in regard to the organization of society. And Christianity does not properly issue in any doctrine or theory, but only in life— a regenerate natural life of man.[12]

Despite his deep sympathy with both Fourierist Socialism and Christianity, and his attempt to fuse them both with Swedenborg, he would *not* use a term already in circulation in England by F. D. Maurice, namely, "Christian Socialism." Actually he left his particular brand of Christianity-Socialism-Swedenborgianism unnamed, and Schneider is acute in labeling it "Spiritual Socialism." At any event, James did not and would not identify himself actively with any concrete Socialist program, any more than he would make a public commitment of himself to membership in a church or a sect. His own "Spiritual" Socialism was not a program at all: it was rather an apocalyptic vision. One of the many paradoxes in the life of this man was that, however much he preached man's "associated destiny," he refused to become "associated" actually with any party in Church, School, or State! No Thoreau or Nietzsche could excel the actual, practical aloofness of this super-individualist who was preaching a spiritual Socialism! The result, practically speaking, was that, as Schneider so tersely expresses it, James's contemporary influence amounted to no more than that of "a mild gad-fly."[13]

This all-too-telescopic survey of the relation James bore in general to the religious, social, theological, and philosophical thought movements in his day, was presented as preliminary to a detailed examination of what, after his Calvinist inheritance, were the three most formative forces in the evolution of his philosophy. These were: Sandemanianism, Swedenborg, and Fourierist, or Associationist, Socialism. Each, in the next three chapters, calls for special and critical inquiry.[14]

NOTES

1. The correspondence between James and Emerson—thirty-four letters by James, thirty-two by Emerson, is preserved at the Widener Library, Harvard University.
2. Ralph Barton Perry, *The Thought and Character of William James.* (Little, Brown & Co., copyright now with Harvard Univ. Press, 1935.)
3. *Ibid.,* pp. 13-15.
4. *Ibid.,* p. 15.
5. *NE,* p. 11.
6. *Ibid.,* pp. 164-165.
7. *Ibid.,* pp. 173-175.
8. *Ibid.,* pp. 172-173.
9. *Vis-à-vis* the changes that Unitarianism and Transcendentalism were making in New England orthodoxy, James has the following pungent comment to make:

   "I am aware that a certain diligent transmutation of orthodoxy is going on in New England, by which it is eviscerated of its immemorial contents, and yet avouched to be the same gospel. But somehow, in spite of the extreme zeal and good faith embarked in this enterprise, no dispassionate observer of the process can help feeling that the solid nutmeg aroma of the old orthodoxy is rapidly dissipating into a thin flavor of basswood." (LM, p. 159.)

   Now that the reader has savored James's literary style, it is apropos to cite here some of the opinions of contemporary writers concerning it. His son William says:

   "It would indeed be foolish to seek to paraphrase anything once directly said by him. The matter would be sure to suffer; for, from the very outset of his literary career, we find him in the effortless possession of that style with which the reader will soon become acquainted, and which, to its great dignity of cadence and full and homely vocabulary, united a sort of inward palpitating quality, gracious and tender, fierce, scornful, humorous by turns, recalling the rich vascular temperament of the old English masters, rather than that of an American today." (*LR,* p. 9.)

Of the varied estimates passed by reviewers on James's style of writing, I find only one who had anything but high praise for it. John Albee, in reviewing *The Literary Remains,* and in obvious direct rebuttal to William James's remarks just quoted above, says:

"We see nothing ourselves to remind us of old English masters, and much that does indicate the American of today whose literary token is an effort to make himself heard by a diction out of proportion to the thing said. American writers have not yet attained poise and repose, but are unduly stimulated by the immense material activities which surround them, and the vast spaces over which they strain to make themselves heard."

(John Albee, "Review of *The Literary Remains,"* in the *Journal of Speculative Philosophy,* XIX (1885), p. 436.)

As applied to James, such criticism is palpable nonsense. No man ever wrote among us who was *less* stimulated by the immense *material* activities around him!

10. *LR,* pp. 267-268.
11. *S and S,* note, p. 253.
12. Letter to New York *Tribune,* Sept. 22, 1855, p. 5.
13. Herbert W. Schneider, *op. cit.,* p. 302.
14. Aside from the particular study James gave to Sandeman, Swedenborg, and Fourier, he was widely read in philosophy, theology, literature, and sociology. In philosophy he is obviously read in:

   Plato, Aristotle, St. Augustine, Francis Bacon, Calvin, Boehme, Pascal, Descartes, Leibnitz, Berkeley, Locke, Hume, Kant, Sir William Hamilton, Schelling, Fichte, Hegel, Schopenhauer, J. S. Mill, Spencer, Cousin, Comte, Taine, Maine de Biran, Jouffroy, Janet, Saisset.

   In physical science:

   Darwin, Huxley, von Humboldt, Agassiz.

   In social science and economics:

   Fourier, St. Simon, Owen, Cabet, Bastiat, Buckle, Carey.

   In literature:

   Beyond the recognized masters—particularly Homer, Virgil, Horace, Cicero, Dante, Shakespeare, Goethe, Schiller—he was especially fond of William Blake, and disliked Dickens intensely. He was personally acquainted with Emerson, Carlyle, Thackery, and Howells.

Chapter Three

Sandemanianism and James

ROBERT SANDEMAN (1718-1771) was born at Perth, Scotland. He studied medicine at St. Andrews but became a linen manufacturer instead of a doctor, and finally became a preacher through the influence of his father-in-law, the Reverend John Glas, 1695-1773. Glas had developed an independent position against "National" Churches in his most famous treatise, *The Testimony of the King of Martyrs Concerning His Kingdom,* published in 1727. Because of his teaching Scriptural authority for Independency, Glas was at first suspended and then deposed in 1730. He carried his parish at Tealing with him, and went on to organize a sect which grew to embrace parishes at Dundee, Edinburgh, and Perth. Although the General Assembly later revoked his deposition, he continued independently to the end of his career.

When Sandeman became connected with the Glasite movement, its main characteristics in doctrine, discipline, and worship were already matured. The worship was an attempt to reproduce the primitive customs of Apostolic Christianity, such as the kiss of peace, celebration of the *Agape* as a common meal with broth, and occasional ritual washing of one another's feet in imitation of the Lord's example. With Sandeman's appearance, if not under his direct guidance in each case, other features were added: weekly observance of the Lord's Supper, and the requirement of unanimous attendance at the love-feast, or *Agape.*

Discipline and government involved the designation by parish vote of elders, pastors, and bishops who were, despite their hierarchical titles, entirely equal in authority. No one could attain, or retain, such entitlement if they married a second time. Candidates for such posts were chosen without regard to education or occupation. Sandemanians disbelieved in a paid clergy. General regulations for the sect as a whole prohibited the consumption of anything strangled, or of anything with blood. Other prohibitions included the forbidding of playing games of chance, particularly those with dice, since lots were held sacred. The private accumulation of wealth was under ban. Property of individuals in the sect was liable to be conscripted at any time for sharing with the poor or for meeting financial needs of the church. Unanimous decisions were required at church meetings.[1] A plurality of bishops, pastors, and elders was established as necessary for official business at church meetings of the individual parishes; furthermore, the presence of two elders at any decision involving discipline, as also at the administration of the Lord's Supper, was requisite.[2]

Before considering the doctrine, with which we are here especially concerned, it is apropos to relate briefly the subsequent history of Sandeman and the sect. In 1757 he published his best known work, *Letters on Theron and Aspasio,* in rebuttal to the Reverend James Hervey's *Theron and Aspasio.* This book of Sandeman's spread the movement to England. In 1764, however, he and James Cargill came to Boston, and soon thereafter, to Danbury, Connecticut, a headquarters from which he founded about a dozen churches in New England. Because of their Loyalist leanings as the American Revolution approached, they lost ground heavily, and by about 1890, the last existing parish closed its doors. Sandeman himself died in Danbury in 1771. The following excerpt from the epitaph inscribed on his gravestone at Danbury is a convenient point of departure for a scrutiny of the doctrinal views of the Glasites and Sandemanians:

> Here lies, until the resurrection, the body of Robert Sandeman, a native of Perth, North Britain, who, in the face of continual opposition from all sorts of men, long boldly contended for the ancient faith, that the bare word of Jesus Christ, without a deed or thought on the part of man, is sufficient to present the chief of sinners spotless before God.[3]

The major theological positions of the sect had been developed by Glas in his published works.[4] From a study of his *Works,* the leading principles are, negatively, opposition to philosophical theology[5] and mysticism[6]; positively, affirmation of justification by faith alone, "faith" being a simple, immediate, intellectual apprehension of Revelation and grace, and not a "saving faith" which Glas associated with emotionalism.[7] To the notion of faith as defined should be added the doctrine that truth for the Christian is "given," to which the concept of the sovereignty of grace in Christ is the objective complement. The believer is thus posited as completely passive, though it is difficult to see how "intellectual" comprehension of one's justification in Christ can occur "without a thought on the part of man," as Sandeman maintains. From these premises, it is understandable that Glas was opposed to missionary propaganda and effort.

Sandeman accepted these views *in toto,* but he developed the doctrine of "justifying faith" to an even more radical extent than Glas, going so far indeed as to bring upon himself and the sect the charge of antinomianism. Sandeman not only wrote with a narrower range of scholarship and a more contracted theological horizon that Glas, but he also wrote with greater asperity toward clergy of the other churches. Despite his ability, so far as it went, he was considerably less balanced in theological grasp than his father-in-law. The latter had tried to protect himself and his churches against the possible charge of antinomianism by his recognition of a place for "works" as a result of one's having the true faith, works having no merit unto salvation of themselves, but valuable simply as external signs of a believer's faith.[8] Sandeman became fanatical on this issue, as already suggested by the word "bare" in the quotation above, taken from his epitaph. In his *Letters on Theron and Aspasio,* of which James brought out an edition in this country in 1838, based on the fourth Edinburgh edition and with a two-page unsigned preface by James, Sandeman offers his definition of "faith":

> The apostles used the word *faith* or *belief* in the same sense we do to this day in common discourse. We are properly said to believe what any man says, when we are persuaded that what he says is true. There is no difference betwixt our believing any common testimony and our believing the gospel, but what arises from the nature of the testimony. . . . *If we receive the witness of men, the witness of God is greater;* so must produce greater certainty or firmness of persuasion.[9]

In the "Appendix" of the same work, the author goes from the subjective aspect of faith in the above definition, to a statement on the objective side:

> The apostles maintained, that Christ did enough to save sinners in his own person, without their concurrence, and that all who were *so persuaded,* accordingly found salvation in him.[10]

This is what Sandeman meant by the "One Thing Is Needful" on the title page of his book.

Dickinson renders the gist of these definitions very well when he says:

The Sandemanians allege, that faith is called receiving the love of the truth; and the Apostle often speaks of faith and truth to the same purpose, as in John XVI, 13, the Spirit of truth; 2 Cor. iv, 13, the Spirit of faith. . . . The scriptures consider faith, not as a work of ours, nor as any action exerted by the human mind; but set it in direct opposition to every work, whether of body or mind. . . . This contrast excludes every idea of activity in the mind, from the matter of justification; so that we cannot speak of preparatory works of any sort, without making the gospel a law of works. . . .

Every doctrine, then, which teaches us to do, or endeavour any-thing towards our acceptance with God, stands opposed to the doc-trine of the Apostles, which, instead of directing us what to do, sets before us all that the most disquieted conscience can require, in order to acceptance with God, as already done and finished by Jesus Christ.[11]

James, too, as we shall discover very often, frequently identifies "faith" with "truth," as he certainly does in his long article on "Faith and Science."[12]

Let us pause to reflect upon the implications of this Sandemanian doctrine. The first observation that one may properly make is that a subtle shift of theological focus has occurred in the thought of Calvinist churches, in the development from official Presbyterianism in Scotland to the independent kind of Calvinism exemplified in the rise of the Glasite-Sandemanian sect. This shift in focus may be described as a shift, in Sandeman, from the classical Calvinist doctrine of the sover-eignty of God to what amounts to the sovereignty of Christ; or, from a theo-centric to a Christo-centric focus. And, though Sandeman would doubtless have been horrified at the mere thought of it, is not the way open for the next shift in focus to the sovereignty of *faith, in the be-liever?* Obviously, no one of these emphases is theoretically exclusive of belief in the others, but practically speaking, which is the real point involved here, these theological "climates," so to term them, fade over the horizon as new ones emerge, as stars in their courses change their positions to an all-night observer.

As one reads through Sandeman's *Letters,* he finds there much talk, to be sure, about justification through Christ's work alone, but the burden of the argument is *not* the object of faith, but the *how* of faith in the believer. This argument is addressed to the theme of demonstrating how men should properly appropriate the objective core of salvation. This stress upon the correct *manner* of believing is the opening wedge for further theorizing in this direction. The appeal cannot be made to faith as exclusively belief—that is to say, wholly intellectual—without stimulating the human mind to increased intellectual activity! If faith is to be identified entirely with intellectual assent, and if the emotional side of faith, usually known as "trust," is to be ruled out along with the doing of good works, the door is open, if only by a crack, for an intense preoccupation, intellectually, with one's beliefs. James did not hesitate to open the door wide, exploiting the opportunity for a lifetime of soaring speculation in religious metaphysics hardly distinguished at more than one point from a neo-Gnosticism, or a kind of theosophy. If truth is "given" in radical objectivity by Revelation through the Bible alone,[13] and is received passively and exclusively in the intellectual part of the believer's nature, what is to prevent the momentum of human thought from speculating more and more on the phenomenon of belief itself, especially when the intellectual element alone is given such sheer and single priority? Did not Glas and Sandeman write, between them, nearly ten volumes about the right *method* of "belief"? It is giving hostages to theological fortune to practically identify truth and faith, to open the door to intellectuality in religion, and then expect to leave it at that! Once started, there can be ultimately no authority other than intellect itself to say: "thus far and no farther." Once pin the human consciousness down to a passive reception of divine truth, at the same time barring the emotional element of trust and asserting the invalidity of the practical element of good deeds, and it is inevitable that the force of human thought will break through the dyke and find its revenge in turning passive intellectualism into dynamic intellectualism, which is precisely what James, after he discovered Swedenborg, did.

In striking the account of James with Sandemanianism—so suggestive, in one or two basic aspects, of Barthianism today—it is obvious that he acquired from it his lasting anti-ecclesiasticism, as well as his strong antinomian strain. These characteristics of his thought endure permanently, as will be apparent when we come to the treatment of the specifically Jamesian philosophy.[14] His eventual apologetic for Spiritual Socialism is, on its "spiritual" side, a growth from the Sandemanian emphasis on lay "fellowship." This egalitarian, spiritual laicism fostered the radically social-democratic conception which James eventually expressed in language that is Whitmanesque in passion and in flavor of utterance. One soon perceives, however, that James is entirely concerned with spiritual social-democracy rather than with political:

> Man has derived no original boon from legislation. The service it has rendered him has been purely ministerial, consisting in a very slow denial of the chance supremacy of one race over others, or of one class over others. The utmost it has done, has been to clothe the instinct of human unity in progressive but temporary formulas. It has by no means *created* the unity it has acknowledged. It has merely developed the essential unity which all men have in God, their infinite source.[15]

More tersely:

> No law can ever say what man *is*. It can only say what he *is not*.[16]

James based his vision of a great spiritual social-democracy of "universal man" on the spiritual possession of "conscience" by all men, irrespective of social, cultural, economic, or racial distinctions. We are not concerned here to go into the complex meanings which he came to associate with the concept of "conscience," for that will be part of our task in the chapter on his Doctrine of Spiritual Evil; but we are concerned here to see that he derived his basic notion of conscience from Sandeman and that he came to develop the idea in terms of striking parallelism to Sandeman's treatment of "faith." First, let us see what Sandeman thought about conscience (incidentally, there is the germ here of what, coupled later to Fourierism, led James to his denunciation of "civilization"):

> The meanest day-laborers have full as great sensibility of conscience as those who are wholly employed in learning; yea, we may perceive this sensibility more evident in the poorest villages, than in cities furnished with all the branches of education.[17]

But just how did Sandeman conceive of the conscience? He has not left us in doubt:

> Not to be tedious, I think we may freely say, that the proper excellency of man above other animals, lies in his conscience, or what he knows without reasoning.[18]

What man "knows without reasoning"—that is the essence of the matter for Sandeman. Note the parallelism of exposition of the concept of "conscience" to that of "faith" (or belief) in Sandeman. Just as belief is passive intellectual acceptance of salvation through Christ only, so conscience is exclusive of "reasoning" or "any thought on the part of man" also; and conscience is, therefore, the passive, spiritual organ of perception for distinguishing between good and evil.

Now James later developed the concept of conscience far beyond that of Sandeman, but it is pertinent for present purposes to observe how he assumes, for his fundamental axiom, the same intuitionist theory that Sandeman held; and in a moment we shall consider briefly some of the critical difficulties inherent to intuitionistic theories of conscience. In addition to the fact that James held generally to the intuitionist view, it is important, for seeing the lasting Sandemanian aspect in James's thought, to observe how, though James himself *never* speaks of faith as "without a deed or thought on the part of man," he develops "conscience" in terms remarkably similar to Sandeman's treatment of "faith"; the point, for the moment, being that a Sandemanian habit of mind is carried over by James, but applied, not to "faith," but to "conscience." To trace this process is illuminating of this fact. Of conscience, James says:

> For conscience is *not* what it is commonly reputed to be, a mere miraculous endowment of human nature, liable therefore to all the vicissitudes of men's hereditary temperament, much less is it a mere divine trust to the intellect of men, liable, therefore, to all the vicissitudes of our natural genius and understanding. On the contrary, and in truth, it is *the divine natural humanity itself*....[19]

Further:

> Thus the seat of conscience is neither the affections nor the intellect, but the life. Its primary office is not to tell us what is good and true, or teach us how to feel and think, but to tell us what is evil or false, or teach us what to avoid.[20]

It clarifies things somewhat if we understand that when James says "life," he is using the word in Swedenborgian sense of "love" or sometimes "will," which is the organ in man, following Swedenborg, for the reception of love; hence, his use is richer in meaning than any ordinary employment of the term, as also of the word "will."

Analytically speaking, therefore, James isolates "conscience" from our "temperaments," from our "intellect" and "opinions" and "understanding," from our "affections" and from our "sentiments," as radically and extremely as ever Sandeman isolated intellectual belief from trust, thoughts, and deeds "on the part of man." In this respect, James reminds us also of Kant's isolation of "duty," "conscience," and "moral law" from thought and "inclination." It is very clear, then, that the Sandemanian roots in James's methodology in treating conscience, show up vigorously. He attempts to isolate and objectify conscience as Sandeman had isolated and objectified the "bare" act of faith. The logical result of such a theory of faith is religious individualism, with its attendant corollaries of antinomianism and anti-ecclesiasticism.

Mention was previously made of critical difficulties on any intuitionist theory of conscience. It is pertinent at this junction to take notice of the logical problem involved. In effect, Sandeman makes "faith" *and* "conscience" to be, in each case, its own criterion. This criticism was levelled at Sandeman, for, as the critic put it, Sandeman, by reducing faith to bare intellectually-passive assent (and *somehow* with "no thought on the part of man"), reduces Christian life and character by such a procedure "to the mere point of credence of the truth—and is literally making that credence the evidence of itself."[21]

* * *

The period of James's most active interest in Sandemanianism, begun in association with his friend Michael Faraday in 1837, extended to the publication of his small book, *Remarks on the Apostolic Gospel,* in 1840. Apparently it was printed exclusively for private distribution, since there is no record of publisher included with the title as listed in the bibliography of James's literary works, printed a few months after his death. In that same bibliography there was a sub-title description of the *Remarks* as follows: "A Pamphlet maintaining the absolute divinity of Jesus while denying the doctrine of the Trinity."[22] Unfortunately, no copy of this work seems to have survived which otherwise might have thrown further light on the sources and the early form of James's philosophy.

Concentration in this chapter has been centered upon James's derivations from Sandemanianism.[23] He always retained the Sandemanian emphasis upon faith over works, with the attendant antinomian strain likewise remaining powerful. Despite the vast Swedenborgianized superstructure of thought which James reared upon the Calvinist-Sandemanian foundation, the latter yet functioned always as *the foundation.*

NOTES

1. Article, "Glasites (Sandemanians)," *Ency. of Religion and Ethics.* (Scribner's N. Y., 1928), Vol. VI, p. 231.
2. John Hayward, *op. cit.,* p. 127.
3. John Hayward, *op. cit.,* p. 396.
4. John Glas, *The Works of Mr. John Glas* in 4 vols. (Edinburgh; 4th edition, 1861).
5. John Glas, *Works,* Vol. I, pp. 102-103, 137.
6. *Ibid.,* Vol. II, p. 69.
7. *Ibid.,* Vol. IV, p. 386.
8. *Ibid.,* Vol. IV, p. 402.
9. Robert Sandeman, *Letters on Theron and Aspasio* (Boston, 1838), p. 257.
10. *Ibid.,* p. 415.
11. Rodolphus Dickinson, *Field's Works* (Greenfield, Mass., 1818), pp. 22-23.
12. "Faith and Science," *North American Review,* Vol. CI (1865), pp. 335-378.
13. John Glas, *Works,* Vol. II, p. 69.
14. Since illustrations for all these tendencies in James's thought will be abundantly cited when the body of his philosophy is considered in later chapters, it has seemed unnecessary to cite references from James in the context of this section—as, for example, with regard to his antinomianism.
15. *LM,* p. 23.
16. *Ibid.,* p. 32.
17. Robert Sandeman, *op. cit.,* p. 181.
18. *Ibid.,* p. 146.
19. *S of S,* p. 160.
20. *Ibid.,* p. 159.
21. "Sandemanian Theology," in *Eclectic Review,* Vol. LXVIII (1838), p. 528. An able, unsigned article.
22. *Cf. The Literary World,* Vol. XIV (1883), pp. 9-10.
23. For the general bibliography on Sandemanianism, the reader is referred to the section devoted to the subject in the bibliography at the end of this book.

Chapter Four

Swedenborg and James

. . . I cannot help cherishing an opinion that there is some validity in these experiences [of Swedenborg] in spite of all the absurdities involved in the stories about them, and the crazy and unintelligible ideas which deprive them of their real value.
—IMMANUEL KANT[1]

Note (b), pp. 4-6, [of Swedenborg's The Worship and Love of God] would of itself suffice to mark Swedenborg as a man of philosophic genius, radicative and evolvent. Much of what is most valuable in the philosophic works of Schelling, Schubert, and Eschermeyer, is to be found anticipated in this supposed dementato.
—SAMUEL TAYLOR COLERIDGE[2]

A colossal soul, he lies vast abroad on his times, uncomprehended by them, and requires a long focal distance to be seen; suggests, as Aristotle, Bacon, Selden, Humboldt, that a certain vastness of learning, or quasi-omnipresence of the human soul in nature, is possible.
—RALPH WALDO EMERSON[3]

The gigantic reach of the man's mind . . . his vast erudition, untouched by pedantry . . . his guileless modesty . . . the free, unconscious movement of his thought, reflected from the great calm realities with which he was in habitual contact; his unstudied speech, bubbling up at times into childish naïveté and simplicity,—all these things, while they take his books out of the category of mere literary performances, and convert them into an epoch, as it were, of our associated mental history,—into a great upheaval or insurrection of the human mind itself,—yet assuredly reduce the feats of our sincerest theologians and philosophers to the dimensions of ignorant prattle, and turn the performances of our ordinary literary posturemongers into stale and mercenary circus tricks.
—HENRY JAMES, SR.[4]

A MAN OF James's intense vitality could not long remain satisfied spiritually or intellectually with the horizons of Sandemanianism. Althought he gave himself to Sandemanian doctrine with zeal, he could not long have remained within its extreme biblicism, accompanied as it was by a literalistic hermeneutics in the interpretation of Scripture, nor long have remained content with its "bare" Solifidianism which defined faith as being exclusively exhausted in its intellectual form of "belief," and even then, denying any room whatever for "any thought on the part of man." Faith confined to a single proposition—even to such a great and important proposition as justification in and through Christ—was hardly sufficient to do duty for a full-blooded and full-minded religion in the soul of a man on his way to construct a Philosophy of Creation!

Four years after writing the *Remarks on the Apostolic Gospel* under the Sandemanian influence, James, in 1844, was approaching the psychological crisis so vividly described by himself in the quotation presented in a previous chapter of this work. It was the discovery of Swedenborg through Mrs. Chichester's mediation at the water-cure resort during his visit to England in 1843, which gave him the greatest deepening, heightening, and broadening of his intellectual and spiritual life that he was ever to experience.

In 1771, the same year that Sandeman was buried at Danbury, the last volume written by Swedenborg, *The True Christian Religion,* was published. Until he was nearly fifty, Emanuel Swedenborg (1688-1772) had devoted his life to science, having produced approximately seventy-seven scientific works, mostly in Latin. His scientific achievements were remarkably anticipative of later developments. Among other attainments deservedly credited to him are: the introduction of the calculus to Sweden; psychological theories that are highly suggestive of Freud[5]; the identification of lightning with electricity before Frankin; the advocacy of the nebular hypothesis of the origin of planets from the sun, and the derivation of planetary motion from the same source. In his nebular theory he pre-dated both Kant and Laplace, since his *Principia* appeared in 1734, while Kant's pamphlet *Theories des Himmels* came out in 1755, and Laplace's *Exposition du Monde* in 1796.[6]

But scientific eminence was compounded with an astounding psychological phenomenon in this man, when the scientist with a European reputation turned in mid-career to theology—a type of theosophy is probably a more exact term—and produced about the same number of works in his new field as he had authored in science. Kant, who had praised him abundantly for his scientific genius, now ridiculed him with a book of sarcastic title,[7] apparently because Kant could not reconcile himself to a man's conversing with angels (as Swedenborg claimed to do, in full waking consciousness), without violating his intellectual integrity. It was a natural enough reaction on the part of a critical empiricist and rationalist.

Swedenborg resigned his position with the Royal Mines in 1747 and began the period of his theological compositions. Unusual books, these! One after another appeared. Europe's thinkers blinked, for they had not seen their like, nor have since, from an equally distinguished scientist and philosopher.[8] Their author was entirely above any reproach of vainglory or insincerity, inasmuch as he signed his name to none of these volumes until the *Conjugal Love* in 1768; moreover, he bore the expenses of publication throughout—a not inconsiderable amount— from his own resources, which were never opulent.

A word should be said about his theory of the Church before we inquire into his main theological teachings. The true church is invisible; it is constituted in the minds and hearts of men by a love for goodness and truth. He made no attempt to organize a church, though his idea of the spiritual "New Church" led others to found a visible church in his name and to use his writings as authority; and this action led to the inevitable attempts to define "orthodoxy" and "heresy." The conflict between the liberal and "orthodox" wings of the New Church group in this country is lucidly traced in Marguerite Block's *The New Church in the New World*. Although the problem of whether or not to sanction a new sect did not come up in Swedenborg's time, it is probable, from internal evidence of his writings, that he would have refused such sanction. In any case, this attitude was heartily endorsed by James, and much as he attacked older ecclesiasticisms, his repudiation of the Swedenborgian sect was particularly virulent because the sect violated, according to James, the very genius of the *spiritual* Church which Swedenborg conceived and taught.

In coming to a consideration of the cardinal ideas in Swedenborg's philosophical theology, it quickly becomes evident that they fall naturally under three main heads: God, the World, and Man; or, as he often calls the first two, "The Divine" and "Nature." Before proceeding to an inquiry on these heads, it is helpful to clarity of understanding if a certain mist about Swedenborg's theology in general is cleared away. Despite Emerson's selection of Swedenborg as the type of "The Mystic" in his *Representative Men,*[9] one finds after reading somewhat at length in the Swedish thinker's works that James was partially justified in holding the contrary view. On even a superficial perusal of his writings there is no ground given for seeing in them either mystical intentions, ideas, or characteristic mystical language. He dryly reports his visions *of* spiritual beings and *of* the spiritual universe of which the natural universe is an inversion, as in a mirror. Swedenborg displays very little, if any, of the mystical nisus toward *union* with, at least in the sense of *identity* with, God, as in the *Vedanta,* for example. Where is the strain of the mystic's effort to express the ineffable? Instead we find a series of thirty-odd volumes of what at times is "tedious" (the word is James's) reportage on the structure and administration of the celestial universe, written in a style almost as dry as that of government documents. Men of vision—whether they be in science, ethics, or religion— are usually realistic and objective in temperament, even though the "object" be an idea or pertains to the future and so unrealized as yet. The seer is so concentrated on *what* he sees that he is unlikely to identify even his innermost being with what he sees in vision. He usually devotes his will and his intellect in loyalty to his vision, but *vision of* is a long way indeed from ontological *identification with.* The seer—*literally* the *see-er,* is what might be called a spiritual perceptualist, an analogue to the sensory perceptionist in the empirical theory of knowledge. That Swedenborg was a seer is unquestionable; that he was a mystic in his seeing appears to us questionable. Every angel and every devil, in heaven and hell respectively, retains always his own identity just as much, no more and no less, as Swedenborg retains his own identity throughout all his visions. James says plainly enough that Swedenborg was "no mystic"[10] or "religious specialist," but a "universalist."[11]

James's observations on Swedenborg as being non-mystical, throw light on James himself as to whether he was a mystic or not. Rarely, very rarely indeed, does he ever use the word, and it is very plain from his own standpoint that he never considered himself to be mystical in either temperament or philosophy. A fuller treatment of this point will be developed when it comes to a specific evaluation of James's general type of thought. James was certainly not "mystical" in his estimate of Swedenborg:

> As I have already said, his books are singularly void of literary fascination. . . . Certainly the highest truth never encountered a more lowly intellectual homage than it gets in these artless books. . . .[12]

He rises to even stronger language:

> There is actually no writer worth naming, after Matthew, Mark,
> Luke, and John, certainly no living writer, whose personality, both
> moral and intellectual, is so little grandiose as Swedenborg's, i.e.,
> so little melodramatic or impressive; none who exerts so little
> voluntary influence upon his reader. In fact the total fashion of
> the man's mind is in this respect so evangelic or celestial—it con-
> trasts, for example, so vividly with my own depraved intellectual
> habit—that if it were not for the things he incessantly says, which
> are manifestly underived from himself, and the clear prophetic
> glimpses he perpetually gives us into the very heart of creative
> truth—truth that none of our poets, or visionaries, or sages, or
> philanthropists begins even as yet to babble—the perusal of his
> books would be extremely difficult to me, would be in fact little
> short of a downright penance.[13]

On the other hand, when James indulged in positive appreciation of
his favorite philosopher, who was of course Swedenborg, he quickly
reaches the level of rhapsody:

> The gigantic reach of the man's mind, too, in bringing back every
> subtlest ineffable splendor of heaven, and every subtlest ineffable
> horror of hell, to the purest phenomenality, to the mere shadowy
> attestation, positive and negative, of a *Divine Natural Manhood,*
> which they are both alike impotent to create, or even by themselves
> to constitute; his vast erudition, untouched by pedantry, and never
> for an instant lending itself to display; his guileless modesty under
> the most unexampled experiences; his tender humility and ready
> fellowship with every lowest form of good; the free, unconscious
> movement of his thought, reflected from the great calm realities
> with which he was in habitual intellectual contact; his unstudied
> speech, bubbling up at times into a childish *naïveté* and simplic-
> ity,—all these things, while they take his books out of the category
> of mere literary performances, and convert them into an epoch,
> as it were, of our associated mental history,—into a great upheaval
> or insurrection of the human mind itself,—yet assuredly reduce
> the feats of our sincerest theologians and philosophers to the di-
> mensions of ignorant prattle, and turn the performances of our
> ordinary literary posturemongers into stale and mercenary circus
> tricks.[14]

James never knew either the art of understatement, or of any balancing
point between extreme praise and radical censure. Often the rhapsody

and the criticism were applied to the same man; and when it came to his own writings and ideas, he often forgot himself into rhapsody, only to turn anon and quite as ruthlessly apply criticism to himself. This is what makes James appear to be one of the most contradictory of thinkers, at once so stimulating and yet the despair of the impatient to interpret.

Now that the more peripheral aspects of James's conception of his relation to Swedenborg have been surveyed, the way is clearer to a study of the ideas which James derived from his Swedish mentor. What, then, and in brief, are the dominant doctrines of Swedenborg concerning God, the World, and Man? This is important to our study of James because, however much he modifies that theologian's doctrines in statement and application, he is continually referring to Swedenborg in every book he wrote from 1845 to 1882, when he was at composition on his last, unfinished work, *Spiritual Creation,* included posthumously under the title *Literary Remains.* Not only so, but James believed himself to be teaching the same basic principles in philosophy and religion that the great Scandinavian taught, and he gave his life to the effort of expounding these principles.

In moving from Sandeman to Swedenborg, James passed from a very restricted theological scope to a tremendous horizon. If spatial language were adequate at all to convey spiritual experience, one would have to say that the change in location was astronomical! A stranger and vaster contrast can hardly be conceived between two men within the area of religious philosophy than that between the crabbed, brittle, one-doctrine, arid intellectualism of the Scotchman and the many-storied, dynamic, theology of the Swede! No wonder James had a powerful and enduring conviction of personal release, spiritually and intellectually, into direction and redemption!

Because Sandeman was so paltry in theological range, and Swedenborg so immense, there is no value in trying to compare them any further, except in regard to Sandeman's main doctrine—that salvation is possible only through bare and passive intellectual belief in justification through faith alone. It happens that Swedenborg directed some of his strongest attacks upon this doctrine; indeed, next to his criticism of the orthodox doctrine of the Trinity, he may, with a great deal of evidence, be said to have directed his most sustained attack upon this particular tenet. A criticism more thorough than Swedenborg's can hardly be imagined or desired. We preface his reasoned assault with a spicy, sarcastic passage:

> It is wonderful that the doctrine of justification by faith alone, although it is not faith, but a chimera, should gain every point in Christian churches, that is, that it should reign there amongst the clergy, almost as the only essential of theology. It is that which all young students in theology eargerly learn, imbibe, and suck in at the universities; and which, afterwards, as if inspired with heavenly wisdom, they teach in the churches, and publish in books; by which also they seek and obtain the name of superior erudition, fame, and glory; for which also degrees, diplomas, and rewards are conferred. . . . [15]

From the satirical mood he passes to the reasoned siege of the dogmatic citadel:

> God cannot spiritually regenerate man, except so far as man, according to his laws, naturally regenerates himself. God is in the perpetual effort of regenerating, and thus of saving man; but this He cannot effect, except as a man prepares himself a receptacle, and thus prepares the way for God, and opens the door. . . . [16]

As against Glas's disbelief in "saving faith," Swedenborg holds:

> God from Himself, as Order, in order and into order, created the universe, and likewise man, in whom He fixed the laws of his order, by which he became an image and likeness of God; which laws, in the sum, are, that he should believe in God and love his neighbor, and as far as he does those two things by natural power, so far he makes himself a receptacle of the divine omnipotence, and so far God conjoins Himself to him, and him to Himself; thence his faith becomes living and saving, and his practice becomes charity, also living and saving. [17]

Of the notion that faith is arbitrarily granted, by God's inscrutable election, to certain persons—and hence a "faith" for which all men cannot but wait for passively, in hope and despair alternately—of this Swedenborg makes short business:

> From perception concerning the faith which exists at this day, it can not be known, that faith, in its comprehensive sense, is a complex of truths, and still less, that man can do something to procure faith for himself; when yet faith in its essence is truth, for it is truth in its light; and thus, as truth can be procured, so also can faith. [18]

His tying together of faith and works, amounts in the following to an explosive blast:

> Now, as it is impossible for God to condemn any one who lives well and believes aright, so, on the other hand, it is impossible for God to save any one who lives wickedly, and thence believes falsely. . . . Every one who knows anything concerning the essence of God, and concerning the free agency of man perceives this. . . .[19]

It is extremely doubtful that Swedenborg ever heard of Sandeman, though they were contemporaries for many years; yet one would think from reading the following passage that he was parrying Sandeman word for word, blow for blow. Is it possible for two antagonists, from all evidence available totally unknown and unrelated to each other, to lock forensic horns any more tightly than this:

> That the church, at this day, should separate faith from charity, by saying that faith alone, without the works of the law, justifies and saves, and that thus charity cannot be conjoined with faith, since faith is from God, and charity, so far as it is actual in works, from man, never came into the mind of any apostle, as is very manifest from their epistles. . . .[20]

And the *coup de grâce* is given to the whole chain of assumptions in the doctrine of the Lutheran and Reformed Christianity, as expressed in the *Formula of Concord,* which he quotes first before delivering his own thrust:

> *That man, as to what is good, is utterly corrupt and dead; so that, in the nature of man, since the fall, before regeneration, there remains, or is left, not even a spark of spiritual strength, by which he can, of himself, be prepared for the grace of God, or apprehend it, when offered, or, of and by himself, be capable of retaining that grace; or, in spiritual things, understand, believe, embrace, think, will, begin, finish, act, operate, cooperate, or apply, or accommodate himself to grace, or do any thing towards conversion, wholly or by halves, or in the least degree. And that man, in spiritual things, which respect the salvation of the soul, is like the pillar of salt of Lot's wife, and like a stock or a stone without life, which has not the use of eyes, mouth, or any of the senses. That still he has the power of moving from place to place, or he can direct his external members, come to public assemblies, and hear the Word and the Gospel.[21]*

To which Swedenborg replies:

> But who, that possesses reason and religion, would not hiss at those things, as absurd and ridiculous? For he might say with himself, "If it were so, for what purpose, then, is the Word, for what purpose is religion, for what purpose is the priesthood, and for what purpose is preaching, but something vain, or sound without sense?"[22]

It was precisely the "priesthood" and "preaching" that Sandeman and James disliked!

Swedenborg would have an end of this whole kind of faith:

> . . . For if faith is spoken of, and imputation is not added, faith is merely a sound; and if imputation is spoken of, and faith is not added, it is also merely a sound; but if those two are spoken of conjointly, something articulate is produced, but as yet without meaning. Wherefore, that the understanding may perceive something, a third must necessarily be added, which is, the merit of Christ; thence a sentence is made, which a man can speak with some reason; for the faith of the present church is, that God the Father imputes the righteousness of His Son, and sends the Holy Ghost to operate the effects of it.[23]

Swedenborg proceeds to say, that these three—faith, imputation, and the merit of Christ—are "not Christian, for the merit of Christ is not imputable."

Probably before this, the reader has been asking himself: what relation does this profound conflict between Sandeman's theology and Swedenborg's, have to do with James? It is most pertinent to ask this question, but curiously and disappointingly enough, James never directly expressed himself on the matter. There is in none of his eleven main books (this leaves out only his two "Prefaces" and the unavailable *Remarks*) a single reference to Sandeman, much less is there offered any consciously composed contrast between Sandeman and Swedenborg. Yet in all of James's major books, Swedenborg is not only mentioned frequently, but more often than any other name. From this we derive the conclusion that Sandemanianism faded greatly from James's "conscious" reflections, but it lingered on in his "subconscious" very definitely. It is very evident from the foregoing passages that Swedenborg was opposed violently to justification by faith alone, but it will also become increasingly evident that he was a supreme moralist in the large place which he gave to "works." In this respect James did not follow Swedenborg but rather retained a strong Sandemanian flavor in his anti-moralism. James also diverged from Swedenborg in his comparative lack of interest in eschatology. Nevertheless, Swedenborg's impact upon James was much greater than Sandeman's, and although James differed from Swedenborg in many important respects, it will become very obvious, as our study of both Swedenborg and James proceeds, that James derived the basic structure and much of his philosophical terminology from the Swedish thinker. What then were the salient principles and concepts in Swedenborg's philosophy of religion?

In his great systematic opus, *The True Christian Religion, Containing the Universal Theology of the New Church*, Swedenborg gives a summary of the entire corpus of his theological reflections for the last thirty years of his life. The fourteen chapter headings give a clear idea of the range of topics treated:

Concerning God the Creator.
Concerning the Lord the Redeemer.
Concerning the Holy Spirit, and Concerning the Divine Operation.
Concerning the Sacred Scripture, or Word of the Lord.
The Catechism or Decalogue Explained as to its Eternal and Internal Sense.
Concerning Faith.
Concerning Charity or Love toward the Neighbor; and Concerning Good Works.
Concerning Free Agency.
Concerning Repentance.
Concerning Reformation and Regeneration.
Concerning Imputation.
Concerning Baptism.
Concerning the Holy Supper.
Concerning the Consummation of the Age; Concerning the Coming of the Lord; and Concerning the New Church.[24]

It may be added, as a clarifying comment, that when Swedenborg said "concerning," he meant, given the context of his own exposition, that he was thoroughly in belief of each of the above headings. This outline of *The True Christian Religion* will now serve very conveniently as a means of designating at the outset the chief points of Swedenborg's system, adopted, half-adopted, modified, distorted, or neglected by James. As one runs through the captions of the chapters given above, and then reads James's major books, he is impressed with how many aspects of Swedenborg's theology James omitted altogether. In performing such a review, we find that James's philosophy of religion—hereby James is ascertained to be a philosopher of religion, and then only of certain aspects, rather than a systematic theologian—deals (sticking entirely for the present purpose to Swedenborg's terminology), very largely with God the Creator, and with the Lord as Redeemer; hardly at all with the Holy Spirit (though he does employ considerably the concept of "Operation," but frequently calling it "Use"); somewhat with Sacred Scripture; hardly at all with the Decalogue; much with Faith (of which "Truth" and "Revelation" are very close to being perfect synonyms); little with Charity; somewhat with man's Free Agency; very little if at all with Repentance; little with Reformation, but much with Regeneration; nothing, except minor criticism, with Imputation; little with Baptism; little with the Lord's Supper; considerably with the Consummation of the Age (though with a decidedly differing doctrine of his own, exhibiting a blend of Fourier's socialism with Swedenborgian eschatalogy); and finally, next to nothing about either the Coming of the Lord or the New Church.

To have shown by this schematic contrast the lack of any interest by James in Swedenborg's theological system as a whole, is not to imply thereby that James was not profoundly concerned with, and agreeable to, the philosophical roots explicit and implicit in his Swedish master. Indeed, James sometimes develops these roots more at length than Swedenborg himself, for as to relative predominance of intellectual traits, Swedenborg was far more of the scientist than James, and James was more of the philosopher strictly speaking than Swedenborg, the one using scientific facts, especially physiological facts, as analogues for theological reflection; while the latter used philosophical reflection and analysis as data for his religious speculations.

For our purposes, it is the philosophical roots and tendencies in Swedenborg that we shall here attempt to expound. In the exposition of these, we shall confine ourselves mostly to references from Swedenborg, since the parallels in James's thought will appear in connection with the presentation of his philosophy in subsequent chapters. The immediate intention is so to achieve an adequate understanding of Swedenborg as will throw the whole pattern of James's major concepts into clear perspective, for if we achieve such an understanding, the whole task of penetrating to the meaning of his thought will be made easier and ever so much more intelligible. If James were a strictly systematic thinker—which he is not except within terms peculiar to himself—the procedure would be to inspect his system directly, and place his connections with

Swedenborg in footnotes. But since it is the latter who is the more systematic thinker, the writer has decided that, for the sake of a true apprehension of James himself, it is wise to enter upon an exposition of those parts of Swedenborg's philosophy and theology which have a bearing upon James.

Swedenborg's philosophy is God-grounded from first to last. It begins and ends with God. Although there are many propositions about Nature, Humanity, and History in his system, yet their ground, meaning, and object (or "End") is based always in the nature, purpose, and power of the Divine (both Swedenborg and James often use the adjectival form instead of the substantive "God"). Perhaps the most exact term that is applicable to him, in view of the large place of the "Divine Wisdom" in his thought as compared with traditional and ecclesiastical theology, is "theophilosophy," or to use the Greek word, it is literally *theosophia,—i.e.,* Divine Wisdom. At least the term is worthy of attention in describing a man who, though having deep affiliations with dogmatico-theology, yet differs from it as remarkably as he may agree in other respects.

In thoroughly systematic fashion, he distinguishes God as to His (A) *Divine Esse,* the attribute of which is Infinity subdivided into immensity and eternity); as to (B), His *Divine Essence,* the attributes of which are Divine Love and Wisdom; as to (C), His *Divine Existere,* the exemplifications of which are Creation, Redemption, and Regeneration. Modern theologians tend to identify these differentiated attributes respectively as (A), Metaphysical; (B), Moral (or spiritual); and (C), Dynamical.

Before considering in order the Divine Esse, Essence, and Existere it is necessary, because of its bearing on James's acceptance of a unitarian doctrine of God and his rejection of the dogma of the Trinity, to treat of a basic presupposition constantly and consciously held by Swedenborg throughout his philosophy: namely, the unity of God. The first seventeen sections of *The True Christian Religion* are devoted to this theme of God's unity; and when he is discoursing on this subject, he is speaking not of a unity *within* God—since to conceive otherwise were preposterous, but of the oneness of God viewed *ab extra,* or by the spiritual perception of man. That there is a God, and that by logical and metaphysical necessity He is the only and one God, are fundamental to Swedenborg's thought, though he is quite aware that there is nothing distinctive or original in such propositions merely as stated. The oneness of God is more prominent in his thought than arguments for His "existence"; in fact, God does not "*ex*-ist" at all; He simply IS. He disdains, therefore, arguments for His existence, in the kind of thought involved in the ontological, cosmological, and teleological "proofs" of the existence of God. It is when he stresses the oneness—since to have two or more gods is to have no *real* GOD—and unity of God, that he is led to express a vigorous polemic against the orthodox dogma of the Trinity which maintains God to be one in substance and three in persons. Swedenborg ridicules this; nay, indicts it severely as the cause of more atheism, because of the confusion it raises in religious and theological comprehension, than any other cause in Christian history. It is to him the very worst of all heresies. His quarrel is with the Nicene and Athanasian Creeds, not with the Apostles' Creed:

> That the apostolic church did not know anything at all concerning a trinity of persons, or concerning three divine persons from eternity, is very evident from the creed of that church, which is called the *Apostles' Creed.* . . . . There is no mention made of any son from eternity, but of the Son conceived by the Holy Spirit and born of the Virgin Mary; they knowing from the apostles that Jesus Christ was the true God, I John, v. 21; and that in Him dwelt all the fullness of the Godhead bodily, Col. II, 9. . . . [25]

He comes to his own doctrine of "triune" God:

> The general essentials of one man are his soul, body, and operation. . . .
>
> That those three essentials, viz. the soul, body, and operation, were and are in Lord God the Saviour, every one acknowledges. That his soul was from Jehovah the Father, can be denied only by Antichrist, for in the Word of both Testaments He is called *the Son of Jehovah, the Son of the Most High God, the Only-begotten;* therefore the Divine of the Father, like the soul in man, is his first essential. That the Son, whom Mary brought forth, is the body of that divine soul, follows from this, that no other than the body, conceived and derived from the soul, is prepared in the womb of the mother; this, therefore, is another essential. That operations make the third essential, is because they proceed from the body and soul together; and those things which proceed are of the same essence with those which produce them. That the three essentials, which are Father, Son, and Holy Spirit, are one in the Lord, like the soul, body, and operation, in man, is very evident from the words of the Lord, that the Father and He are one, and that the Father is in Him and He in the Father; in like manner, that He

and the Holy Spirit are one ,since the Holy Spirit is the Divine, proceeding out of the Lord from the Father, as was above, n. 153, 154, fully demonstrated from the Word. . . .[26]

This is all cognate to James, for we recall that the sub-title of his non-extant *Remarks on the Apostolic Gospel* carried this announcement: "A Pamphlet maintaining the absolute divinity of Jesus while denying the doctrine of the Trinity."

Given the Swedenborgian doctrine, James's announcement (which would seem to the uninitiated odd or even perverse), in asserting the "absolute divinity of Jesus" while at the same time "denying the doctrine of the Trinity," is cleared up. There is difficulty, however, in trying to prove that James derived such a doctrine from Swedenborg alone, for the *Remarks* was published in 1840; yet, on James's own account, it was not, as we have seen, until 1843-44 that he came to know and to study Swedenborg. It would seem necessary to hold, therefore, that James had come independently to the same position with regard to Christ as God Himself in His only person, at the same time denying the Trinity, as Swedenborg did, yet without Swedenborg's influence. His unitarian trend of thought might be accounted for partially by contact with Unitarians from New England; yet this theory does not account for his utterly non-Unitarian assertion of the "absolute divinity" of Jesus.

Another point to be noted, by way of both similarity and contrast, between Swedenborg and James, is their common reference to the apostolic period as the standard type of Christianity; but, whereas Swedenborg refers to the Apostolic *Church*, James—reflecting Sandemanian-ism here—speaks of the Apostolic *Gospel*. The Swede was always more of a churchman by temperament and vision than James; after all, Swedenborg was the son of a bishop! James's attitude toward any kind of churchly or ritual observances whatever, came out very strongly only a week before his death:

> Tell him [evidently the clergyman-to-be in charge of his funeral] to say only this: "Here lies a man, who has thought all his life that the ceremonies attending birth, marriage, and death were all damned non-sense." Don't let him say a word more.[27]

To return to our main theme: the task of elucidating Swedenborg's doctrine concerning the Divine Esse is now before us. He says:

> We shall treat first of the Divine Esse, and afterwards of the Divine Essence. It appears as if these two were one and the same;

but still *esse* is more universal than *essence,* for an *essence* supposes an *esse,* and from *esse, essence* is derived. The Esse of God, or the Divine Esse, cannot be described, because it is above every idea of human thought, into which nothing else falls, than what is created and finite, but not what is uncreated and infinite, thus not the Divine Esse. . . .

That *Jehovah* signifies I AM and To BE, is known. . . . Since God is *Esse,* He is also Substance, for an esse, unless it be a substance, is only an ideal entity (*ens rationis*); . . and whoever is a substance is also a form, for substance unless it be a form, is an ideal entity; wherefore both can be predicated of God, but so that He may be the only, the very, and the first Substance and Form.[28]

To *Esse* he proceeds to add *Existere*:

That God is not only Esse in itself, but also Existere in itself, is because an esse, unless it exist, is not any thing; and in like manner, an existere, unless it be from an esse. . . . The reason why *Esse* and *Existere* are here used, and not *Essence* and *Existence,* is because a distinction is to be made between *Esse* and *Essence,* and thence between *Existere* and *Existence,* as between what is prior and what is posterior; and what is prior is more universal than what is posterior.[29]

In the "Preface" to *The True Christian Religion,* the translator includes this clarifying comment, though not an unexpected one to those acquainted with the classical terminological tradition in western philosophy:

Esse properly means "to be," but it is used to denote "BEING itself, in the abstract," or "the inmost essence of things"; and *existere* properly means "to exist," but it is used to denote "BEING as it is manifested," or "the sensible existence of things."[30]

Swedenborg extends his analysis of *Esse*:

To this they added, that the Divine Esse is a DIVINE ESSE IN IT-SELF, not from itself; because *from itself* supposes an Esse in itself, from another prior; thus it supposes a God from God, which is not possible. What is from God is not called *God,* but is called *Divine;* for what is a God from God?[31]

Now that Swedenborg has presented the concept of Esse, he introduces us to the major attribute, and the secondary sub-attributes of Esse. The one great, inclusive attribute of Esse is Infinity, which in turn embraces the sub-attributes of Immensity and Eternity. We shall find that James uses the word "Infinite," or "The Infinite," practically as often as he uses the term "God," or "The Divine." It becomes for him essentially a synonym for "God."

From contemplation of the Divine Esse, Swedenborg turns to reflection upon the Divine *Essence*:

> We have distinguished between the Esse of God and the Essence of God, because there is a distinction between the infinity of God and the love of God: and infinity is applicable to the Esse of God, and love to the Essence of God; for the Esse of God ... is more universal than the Essence of God: in like manner, the infinity is more universal than the love of God; wherefore, *infinite* is an adjective belonging to the essentials and attributes of God, all which are called infinite; as it is said of the Divine Love, that it is infinite, of the Divine Wisdom, that it is infinite, and of the Divine Power, in like manner; not that the Esse of God existed before, but because it enters into the Essence, as an adjunct, cohering with, determining, forming, and, at the same time, elevating it.[32]

Swedenborg has raised the profound question of the relation of the metaphysical, sheer *is*-ness of God, to the differentiated attributes of His Essence *i.e.*, Love and Wisdom, while "infinite" is stretched to embrace both Esse and Essence. He proceeds to define Essence more specifically:

> Now, because God is the very, and the only, and thus the first Substance and Form, whose essence is love and wisdom; and because out of Him all things were made, that were made; it follows, that He created the Universe, with all and everything of it, out of love by wisdom; and that thence the Divine Love, together with the Divine Wisdom, is in all and every created subject.... These things may be illustrated by innumerable things in the world; as by the HEAT and LIGHT from the sun, which are the two universals, by means of which all and every thing, upon the earth, exists and subsists: these are there, because they correspond to the Divine Love and the Divine Wisdom.... They may also be illustrated by the two essentials and universals, by which human minds exist and subsist, which are THE WILL and THE UNDERSTANDING; for of these two the mind of every one consists.... The reason is, because the will is the receptacle and habitation of love, and the understanding of wisdom; wherefore those two faculties correspond to the Divine Love and Wisdom, from which they originate. Moreover, those same things may be illustrated by the two essentials

and universals, by which human bodies exist and subsist, which are
THE HEART and THE LUNGS. . . . [33]

From this basis a parallel series of emanations and correlations may be
constructed from Swedenborg's pattern, ranging from God's Essence
to human physiology:

LOVE.......>..GOOD..................WILL........>.......LIGHT........>.... HEART
WISDOM........TRUTH........>...UNDERSTANDING. CHARITY........... LUNGS[34]

Besides sweeping the distance from God's essence to human physiology in these series, he makes certain further identities and correlates:

> It is said in John, *The Word was with God, and the Word was
> God; in Him was Life, and the life was the Light of men, I: 1,4.*
> By *God*, there, is meant the Divine Love, and by the *Word*, the
> Divine Wisdom. . . . Life in itself is the very and the only life, from
> which all angels and men live. Human reason may see this from
> the light which proceeds from the sun of the natural world, in that
> this is not creatable, but that forms, receiving it, are created; for
> eyes are its recipient forms, and the light, flowing in from the sun,
> causes them to see. It is similar with life, which, as was said, is the
> light proceeding from the sun of the spiritual world, that it is not
> creatable, but that it flows in continually, and, as it enlightens, it
> also enlivens the understanding of man; consequently, that, because
> light, life and wisdom are one, wisdom is not creatable; so neither
> is faith, nor truth, nor love, nor charity, nor good; but that forms
> receiving them are created; human and angelic minds are those
> forms.[35]

From discussion of God's essence as Love and Wisdom, he proceeds to
treat of the essence of love in particular:

> Spiritual and celestial love is love toward the neighbor and love
> to the Lord; and natural and sensual love is love of the world and
> love of self.[36]

Constant preoccupation with love of self and the world leads, spiritually
speaking, to making the will and understanding the abode of "infernal"
love, and this constitutes "hell."[37] These teachings, as well as all the
foregoing, will be found scattered throughout James's writings.

Associated with the Divine Love and Wisdom are correlated—as were
infinity, immensity, and eternity with Esse—the attributes of omnipotence, omniscience, omnipresence.[38] With these "predicables" of God,
as derived from Divine Love and Wisdom, we are not further concerned

here, since they do not appear to any appreciable extent in James's thought. Neither can we go into Swedenborg's treatment of the concept of "Order," upon which he lays much stress, and which reflects his scientific habit of mind. It shows up in James when he combines "Order" with "Spontaneity," thus yielding the concept of spontaneity-in-order. This respect of Swedenborg as scientist for "law" and "order" accounts for his more critical analysis of "miracle" than James. Miracles, according to Swedenborg, happen with regard to Divine *order*, and they are no longer either necessary or desirable, since they "force," and so destroy, man's free agency, for which Swedenborg had a higher regard than James.[39]

Having treated of the Divine *Esse* and the Divine *Essence*, Swedenborg dwells next on the Divine *Existere* as it exhibits itself in the dynamic, active, "operational" aspects of the Divine Reality. We recall that he made reference to the *Existere*, or the being of God as manifested in and to sensible existence, but in that context, the reference was merely in passing. When, however, he comes to the dynamic aspects of the Divine, he considers the *Existere* necessarily, for in existence, God manifests Himself under three great processes: Creation, Redemption, and Regeneration.

With these aspects of the Divine, James's philosophy is preeminently concerned; so much so, in fact, that one might well be justified in calling his speculations, *James's Philosophy of Creation*, "creation" often including redemption and regeneration, in his widest use of the term. To put it in other words, and to use Swedenborg's own terms, James is almost wholly concerned, not with the Esse or the Essence of God, but almost exclusively with His Existere. To understand James's philosophy of Creation and Redemption, it is highly necessary to continue our systematic exploration of Swedenborg.

Swedenborg renders his general concept of the Divine Existere, as exhibited in Creation, Redemption, and Regeneration, in his reinterpretation of the orthodox Trinitarian formula:

> . . . By three persons, I understood three proceeding divine attributes, which are Creation, Redemption, and Regeneration; and that those are attributes of one God; and that, by the birth of the Son of God from eternity, I understood his birth foreseen from eternity, and provided in time; and that it is not above what is natural and rational, but contrary to what is natural and rational, to conceive that any Son was born of God from eternity. . . . [40]

In other words, Swedenborg's doctrine of a triune God applies only to His *existere;* secondly, creation-redemption-regeneration are dynamic phases of the one God throughout as His activity goes forth into the entire realm of existence. To put it in other words, his view is that of a functional rather than a substantial, a dynamic rather than a mythological, tri-unity of attributes rather than of "persons."

Swedenborg discusses creation, redemption, and regeneration *seriatim.* As for creation, he begins first by reminding us of the "uncreatables," which are: Life, Love, Wisdom, Good, Truth, Heat, and Light.[41] That which is creatable are "forms," or receptacles, for receiving the uncreatables which proceed into the forms by influx from God. In this "procession" of the uncreatables into forms as receptacles, we detect the Neo-Platonic doctrine of emanation. The creative activity is confined, therefore, to producing Forms for the uncreatables. Swedenborg, and James after him, are opposed to the doctrine of creation by God *ex nihilo;*[42] creation is expressed first as a process of *Form-ation,* as James calls it. The receptive forms in man—the *will* for receiving the Divine Love and the Good, the *understanding* for receiving the Divine Wisdom and Truth—are passive; but when infilled with life, love, good, wisdom, and truth, they become spiritually alive and activated, having entered into active response to the streams of love and wisdom from God. This process of Formation is one of "perpetual creation" to both Swedenborg and James. As Swedenborg expresses it:

> Since the universe was created by it [the *Word,* or wisdom], therefore, also, the universe is preserved by it; for, as subsistence is perpetual existence, so preservation is perpetual creation.[43]

The "end" of creation—"end" in the logical and teleological sense of "purpose"—was the creation of man, in whom are concentrated mineral, vegetable, and animal existence, with the crowning possibility of spiritual (angelic) existence, or, by default of realizing this, infernal (diabolic) existence. Some of James's most beautiful writing, to be quoted at length later, will center on this theme of man as God's climactic act in creation. Swedenborg is more prosaic, but just as definite, on this head:

> Thence it is evident, that the universe was created by God, that uses might exist; wherefore also the universe may be called a *theatre of uses;* and because man was the principal end of creation, it follows, that all and every thing of order was brought together into him, and concentrated in him, that God might do primary uses through him.[44]

The next attribute of the Divine Existere, after Creation, is Redemption. The meaning of Redemption for Swedenborg centers in the Divine Esse's descent to assume the "Human" (Swedenborg regularly prefers the adjective to the usual substantives such as "Incarnation," or "Humanity.") This assumption of the Human is what is meant by the "Son of God," not as a separate "person," but as Jehovah God (*esse* plus *essence*) in union with man.[45] Historically, the being who thus resulted from this union of the Divine and the Human was Jesus Christ. By His enfleshment, "God became Man, and Man God, in one person."[46] His life on earth was a "progression" to the perfect union of his Divine and Human, possible only after the Passion. This progressive phase was His "humiliation." The completed union itself, for which the Passion was undergone, was His "glorification."[47] We shall see subsequently that the Passion was *not* the means of redemption of man, but for the completion of the at-one-ment of God with His Human. This element of "progression" in perfecting the union of the Divine and the Human seems to preserve the historical reality of the God-man in Swedenborg's theology; for if the union with the Human was perfect from the moment of Christ's conception, it would have ruled out progressive development of the historical Jesus; and without that, how would there be, or how could there have been, any *real* Incarnation of the Lord, in and of the Human?

Swedenborg explains the Incarnation of God thus:

> ... By the Son of Mary is meant the merely Human, is manifest from the generation of men, that the soul is from the father, and the body from the mother; for the soul is in the seed of the father, and it is clothed with a body in the mother; or, what is the same, all the spiritual that man has, is from the father, and all the material is from the mother; as to the Lord, the Divine which He had was from Jehovah, the Father, and the human was from the mother; these two united are the Son of God.[48]

James appropiates this view as to the Lord (both James and Swedenborg usually say "Lord" as referring to "God-in-His-Human" rather than "Jesus Christ"), but generalizes the father's role as transmitter of the spiritual, and the mother's as donor of the material, into a doctrine of paternity-maternity to be later expounded.

We now come upon Swedenborg's distinctive doctrine regarding the relation, or rather the non-relation, of Redemption and the Passion of the Lord upon the cross. The Passion is not, he says, the means of redeeming men:

That the Lord alone had merit and righteousness by the obedience which He yielded to the Father, and especially by the passion
of the cross, is said and believed at this day in Christian churches;
but it is supposed, that the passion of the cross was the very act
of redemption, when yet that was not the act of redemption, but
the act of glorification of his Human. . . . The acts of redemption,
by which the Lord made Himself righteousness, were that He executed a last judgment, which was done in the spiritual world, and
then separated the evil from the good, and the goats from the
sheep, and expelled from heaven those who made one with the
beasts of the dragon, and of the worthy He founded a new heaven,
and of the unworthy a hell, and successively reduced all things
in both to order. . . .[49]

On reading him further we find that Swedenborg fixes the historical-
spiritual locus of the acts of Redemption in the Lord's temptation
experience, when he subjugated the wild beasts which are symbolic of
"infernal spirits" sallying forth to attack Him from hell; also, Redemption is performed for the whole order of men and angels when He
calmed the sea by saying "Peace, be still"; and finally, His redemptive
power operates at this day in aiding men and angels to fight off the
diabolical assaults of hell in the ceaseless drama of their choosing either
for spiritual-heaven or spiritual-hell.

In passing, it should be remembered that, to Swedenborg, angels are
none other than former human beings passed from this earthly life
to a spiritual state nearer to God. There are three degrees of heaven
which, in ascending order toward God, are: "spiritual-natural," "spiritual," and "celestial." Each man passing from this earth goes, after an
intermediate period for his finding out to which degree of heaven he
belongs, to the heaven with which he had spiritually identified himself
while on earth.[50] The same is true, by correspondence, of the hells:

. . . That there are three heavens, and these distinct according to
three degrees of height; that there are three hells, and these also
distinct according to three degrees of height or depth; that the hells
are opposed to the heavens in each and every particular; also that
the lowest hell is opposite to the highest heaven, and the middle
hell to the middle heaven, and the uppermost hell to the lowest
heaven. . . . The heavens and hells are thus opposite, because their
loves are opposed. In the heavens, love to the Lord, and consequent
love to the neighbor, constitute the inmost degree; in the hells,
love of self and love of the world constitute the inmost degree. In
the heavens, wisdom and intelligence, springing from their loves,

constitute the middle degree; in the hells, folly and insanity, springing from their loves, and appearing like wisdom and intelligence, constitute the middle degree. In the heavens, the results from the two other degress, either laid up in memory as knowledge, or determined into actions in the body, constitute the lowest degree; in the hells, the results from the two other degrees, which have become either knowledges or acts, constitute the outermost degree.[51]

In commentary on this passage it should be added that to Swedenborg, love constitutes the inmost, the essence, of man; and a man is rated spiritually, for his befitting heaven or hell, according to his type of love. The receptacle of love in man is the will, and because man is in "equilibrium" between spiritual heaven and spiritual hell as he decides to resolve the profound ambiguity inherent in the exercise of his will, he therefore has freedom of will:

> In the natural world, that which acts, and which re-acts, is called force, and also endeavor; but in the spiritual world, that which acts and re-acts is called life and will. Life in that world is living force, and will is living effort, and the equilibrium itself is called freedom. Spiritual equilibrium therefore, of freedom, exists and subsists between good acting on one part, and evil reacting on the other part; or between evil acting on one part and good reacting on the other part. The equilibrium between good acting and evil re-acting exists with the good, but the equilibrium between evil acting and good re-acting exists with the evil."[52]

In this identification of the origin of evil with man's spiritual misuse of his freedom of agency, Swedenborg stands in the tradition of the Old Testament, St. Paul, St. Augustine, Pascal, Calvin, Kirkegaard, and, let us add, James. All this is basic to our later understanding of James's profound conception of "spiritual evil" in his *The Nature of Evil*.

To return, after this apparent digression, to the passage quoted about the correspondent heavens and hells, we can now clarify what he means by the lowest degree of heaven and the outermost degree of hell as consisting in "memory and knowledge." Love to the Lord and the neighbor is characteristic of the will at the highest or celestial level; the love of wisdom, is characteristic of the will at the middle or spiritual level; but, the *mere memory of,* or *knowledge about,* what should really determine and direct the will, is characteristic of those in the spiritual-natural heaven and the outermost hell. Such people belong, according as the scale slightly tips the balance, to either the mildest heaven or the mildest hell.

It is necessary to ask the reader at this juncture to return further back yet, as we raise the question: what has all this to do with the meaning of Redemption? Plenty! For it is now clear what Redemption is to Swedenborg:

> The Lord came into the world principally for these two purposes, that He might remove hell from angel and man, and that He might glorify his Human. For before the coming of the Lord, hell had grown up so as to infest the angels of heaven, and, by interposition between heaven and the world, to intercept the communication of the Lord with the men of the earth; whence no divine truth and good could pass through from the Lord to men; thence a total damnation threatened the whole human race, nor could even the angels of heaven have long subsisted in their integrity. Therefore, that hell might be removed, and thus that impending damnation be taken away, the Lord came into the world and removed hell and subjugated it, and thus opened heaven. . . .[53]

This Divine action was Redemption, illustrated concretely whenever the Lord while on earth met temptation, rebuked the violence of natural elements, or drove demons out of the souls of deranged men.

What, then, was the meaning of the Passion? It was that second of the two purposes spoken of in the last quotation, namely, the "glorification" of His Human:

> What REDEMPTION is, has been shown in the preceding articles, as that it was a battle with the hells, a subjugation of them, and afterwards an establishment of order in the heavens. But glorification is the unition of the Human of the Lord with the Divine of his Father. This was done successively, and was fully completed by the passion of the cross. . . . But although redemption and the passion of the cross are two distinct things, yet they make one with respect to salvation; since the Lord, by union with the Father, which was completed by the passion of the cross, became Redeemer to eternity.[54]

Thus there were two purposes involved in the Incarnation: the one, being objective, directed to establishing redemption through conquering hell and setting heaven and earth in proper order; the other, being subjective, aimed at the glorification of his Human, God thus merging Divine and Human into perfect union. Actually, this is the most impressive exhibition of mysticism that ever occurs in Swedenborg's philosophy—this union of the two natures in the Lord. God has become Man; Man has become God—but *only* in the Lord. It is a tremendous, unique, and awesome mysticism, and constitutes for Swedenborg the whole meaning of the Atonement as being the achieved at-one-ment *within* God's metaphysical Esse and His historical Existere as the Lord. Moreover, the Incarnation is *not* an atonement for man's sins.

These two purposes—redemption and glorification of his Human— were achieved by the Incarnation; were, so to speak, totally objective to and exclusive of, any action or merit on man's part. This highly objective theory of Redemption, and the Passion as instrumental to the Lord's Glorification were appropriated by James without modification. James Freeman Clarke, in his brilliant review of James's *The Nature of Evil* writes to this point, and what he says applies equally well to Swedenborg:

> We cannot speak as we should like to do of his doctrine of Christian redemption and salvation. This is especially interesting as the latest result of the tendency which has always existed in the Christian Church to regard the work of Christ as both objective and subjective, laying sometimes more stress on the one and sometimes on the other. In the early centuries of the Christian Church the objective work of Christ was popularized under the form of a battle with Satan, in which conflict Satan was overthrown and his prisoners rescued. In the Middle Ages, the same tendency to exalt the objective side of Christian salvation expressed itself in Anselm's theory of a debt paid to God; which theory maintained its triumphant pre-eminence till the days of Grotius. Since that time the subjective view of human life, awakened by the Reformation, has caused Christ's work to be regarded as mainly one on the human soul. The present reaction in this book toward an extreme objective view is, therefore, somewhat remarkable. But it is so imperfectly developed, that it is not possible fully to understand it, and therefore we cannot pretend to criticise it.[55]

Clarke would have not found the theory of redemption and salvation "so imperfectly developed" if he had been reviewing Swedenborg's *The True Christian Religion!*[56]

The third and last great dynamic attribute of God in His *Existere,* is, in Swedenborg's system, Regeneration. In order to grasp his teaching on this theme, it is desirable to attend to his metaphysics of the Holy Spirit, for it is through the agency of God as Holy Spirit specifically that Regeneration takes on reality. He has constructed his doctrine of the Holy Spirit by aid of an analogy from the triune constitution of man:

> There are general and also particular essentials of one thing, and both together make one essence. The general essentials of one man are his soul, body, and operation. That these make one essence, may be seen from this, that one is from another, and for the sake of another, in a continual series; for man begins from the soul, which is the very essence of the seed: this not only initiates, but also produces in their order those things which are of the body, and afterwards the things which proceed from those two, the soul and body together, which are called operations. . . .
>
> That those three essentials, viz. the soul, body, and operation, were and are in the Lord God the Saviour, every one acknowledges. That the soul was from Jehovah the Father . . . that the Son, whom Mary brought forth, is the body of that divine soul . . . that operations make the third essential, is because they proceed from the body and soul together. . . . That the three essentials, which are the Father, Son, and Holy Spirit, are one in the Lord, like the soul, body, and operation, in man, is very evident from the words of the Lord, that the Father and He are one, and that the Father is in Him and He in the Father; in like manner, that He and the Holy Spirit are one, since the Holy Spirit is the Divine, proceeding out of the Lord the Father, as was above, n. 153, 154, fully demonstrated from the Word. . . .[57]

This type of discourse gives him an opportunity for another attack upon a trinity of persons in the Godhead, and he doesn't miss the chance. We quote it as perhaps the most clarifying passage of all on this subject:

> When it is said, that the Father, Son and Holy Spirit, are the three essentials of one God, like the soul, body and operation in man, it appears to the human mind as if those three essentials were three persons, which is not possible; but when it is understood, that the Divine of the Father, which makes the soul, and the Divine of the Son, which makes the body, and the Divine of the Holy Spirit, or the proceeding Divine, which makes the operation, are the three essentials of the one God, then it falls into the understanding. . . . But if those three divine essentials are called persons, and to each one is attributed his own property, as, to the Father imputation, to the Son mediation, and to the Holy Spirit operation, then the divine essence becomes divided, which yet is one and indivisible; so not any one of the three is God in fullness, but each in subtriplicate power, which a sound understanding cannot but reject.[58]

Now that we are taught to see the one God as a Divine Soul-Body-Operation all fused in the "Lord" as visible to men in Jesus Christ, what function appertains to the Lord in *Operation?* Swedenborg answers in one word: *Regeneration.* But Regeneration is a generic term covering many distinguishable and nameable sub-activities of the Lord's work in men's souls, and he gives us a detailed list in propositional form:

> That the Divine virtue and operation, which are meant by the Holy Spirit, are, in general, Reformation and Regeneration; and, according to these, Renovation, Vivification, Sanctification, and Justification; and, according to these, Purification from Evils, and Remission of Sins, and finally Salvation.[59]

Thus the whole subjective side, denied in his theory of Redemption, is, under the category of Regeneration, taken care of by his theory of these varied activities of the Lord as Holy Spirit.

A word should be said concerning his treatment of "Salvation," for salvation is the culmination of God's activities as oriented toward man, and man's response to them. Salvation is the total complex which eventuates from two great series of contributing factors, objective and subjective, divine and human. Objectively speaking, or from the Lord's side, those factors are summed up in His incarnation involving his acts of redemption, glorification, and constant regeneration of man through love and wisdom. Subjectively speaking, or from man's side, the contributive factors are: repentance, reformation, love, and faith.[60] Every factor on both sides, Divine and Human, is necessary as the two series converge upon the ultimate attainment of Salvation. All this will be found duplicated in James.

To pass in review the theology of Swedenborg as thus far presented, what are some of the general philosophical characteristics by which it may be critically identified and described? There are strong flavors of at least two philosophical traditions—voluntaristic and rationalist. But it appears to this writer at least that the stronger vein is the rationalistic. Despite his assertion of the priority of will (life, love), over the understanding (wisdom, truth, faith), the implication of his writing in his highly intellectualized elucidations of man's religious life commits him willy-nilly, *at least as a theologian,* to the ascendancy of the intellect.

It seems plain that in Swedenborg the *rational* method and philosophy actually predominate. Though he assumes consciously as a presupposition that he is only revealing more clearly the spiritual realities as contained in Scripture and attested by Faith,[61] yet he really uses the rationalistic method in his very interpretation of scripture. He stood strongly within the "wisdom-school," so suggestive of theosophic proclivities, that he can hardly escape the philosophical label of rationalistic metaphysician and theologian. Yet he is far from being an absolute idealist, even though love and wisdom are the essence of God, because the Divine Esse is "beyond thought," is ineffable and unknowable in itself. (Hence, thought and being are not identified nor identifiable to him, as in the Hegelian metaphysics.)

In the dry, rationalistic manner with which he negotiates his exposition, and in respect to methodology and certain concepts, he reminds one of Aristotle more than of any other great philosopher. That this is no accident is because Swedenborg was an Aristotelian before he was a Neo-Platonist, and the influence of Aristotle is very strong within the Neo-Platonic pattern which he later adopted. It is not necessary to trace all the many ways in which this Aristotelian impact on Swedenborg shows itself, but only in those respects in which they are carried through to James's thought. The first point we are concerned with is the relation of Swedenborg's "End-Cause-Effect" triad to Aristotle's "Four Causes." Sewall puts it thus, quoting first from Aristotle's *Metaphysics,* Book I, Section 3:

> "Cause or ground is said to be fourfold. Of these we declare the one to be the essence and the being-somewhat; another the matter and the substance; a third from which is the beginning of the movement; and the fourth the cause underlying this, that on-account-of-which, and the good; for this is the End of the becoming and of all movements."
>
> Inverting this order we have, therefore, in Aristotle the three degrees: 1. End or first cause, which is the "good," and that for the sake of which a thing exists. 2. The efficient cause, or the motion by which the end proceeds to the effect. 3. The matter and substance; and 4. The particular thing realized in this substance.[62]

Aside from Sewall, Swedenborg's own language regarding "End-Cause-Effect" makes the Aristotelian basis clear:

> It is known indeed that end, cause, and effect follow in order, like prior, subsequent, and final; also that the end begets the cause, and, through the cause, the effect, that the end may have form; also about these many other things are known; and yet to know these things, and not to see them in their applications to existing things is simply to know abstractions. . . .[63]

The End-Cause-Effect triad operates, according to Swedenborg, on the Principle of "Discrete Degrees." There is *in*-fusion, or influx, from End through Cause to Effect; there is no *con*-fusion, so avoiding Pantheism. A few more brief citations from Swedenborg under the heads respectively of End, Cause, and Effect, will yield a rounded view of his thought on this subject. First, on "End":

> In all these, the first is singly supreme in the subsequent things; yea, it is the sole thing in them, and because it is the sole thing in them, it is the all in them. That this is so is clear also from these well-known truths; that the end is the all of the cause, and through the cause is the all of the effect; and thus end, cause, and effect are called first, middle, and last end. Further, that the cause of the cause is also the cause of the thing caused; and that there is nothing essential in causes except the end . . .[64]

On "Cause":

> Yet from effects nothing but effects can be learned; when effects alone are considered no cause is brought to light; but causes reveal effects. To know effects from causes is to be wise; but to search for causes from effects is not to be wise, because fallacies then present themselves, which the investigator calls causes, and this is to turn wisdom into foolishness. Causes are things prior, and effects are things posterior; and things prior can not be seen from things posterior, but things posterior can be seen from things prior. This is order. For this reason the spiritual world is here first treated of, for all causes are there. . . .[65]

On "Effect":

> That the outmost degree is the complex, containant, and base of prior degrees, is clearly seen from progression of ends and causes to effects. That the effect is the complex, containant, and base of causes and ends can be comprehended by enlightened reason; but it is not so clear that the end with all things thereof, and the cause with all things thereof, are actually in the effect, and that the effect is their full complex. That such is the case can be seen from what has been said above in this Part, particularly from this, that one thing is from another in a threefold series, and that the effect is nothing else than the end in its outmost.[66]

Swedenborg translates this Aristotelian language into theological application, and here we come into matters that belong, both in terminology and meaning, to the very bases of James's philosophy—a fact that will be quickly and easily recognized in later chapters:

As regards love and wisdom:—Love is the end, wisdom the instrumental cause, and use is the effect; and use is the complex, containant, and base of wisdom and love; and use is such a complex and such a containant, that all things of love and all things of wisdom are actually in it; it is where they are all simultaneously present. . . .

Affection, thought, and action are also in a series of like degrees, because all affection has relation to love, thought to wisdom, and action to use. Charity, faith, and good works are in a series of like degrees, for charity is of affection, faith of thought, and good works of action. Will, understanding, and doing are also in a series of like degrees; for will is of love and so of affection, understanding is of wisdom and so of faith, and doing is of use and so of work. As, then, all things of wisdom and love are present in use, so all things of thought and affection are present in action, all things of faith and charity in good works, and so forth. . . .[67]

This stress upon "Effect," or theologically, upon "Use" (since End-Cause-Effect corresponds to Love-Wisdom-Use in James, as in Swedenborg); this stress is the cue for understanding James's spiritual "positivism" in which he sees the "natural" world as the "effect" and so, "con-tin-ent" (he uses this spelling instead of "containant"), of Love and Wisdom, of the Celestial and the Spiritual Worlds, of End and Cause. Hence, although James is utterly opposed to Naturalism *per se,* he usually capitalizes the term "natural" in the climactic phrase, The Divine-NATURAL-Humanity. This would appear as rank self-contradiction were it not that one had made himself acquainted with the Swedenborgian doctrine of the Natural World as "effect" and so "containant" of End and Cause, Love and Wisdom, from the Spiritual World.

From what has gone before, we are able to discern two major types of triads in Swedenborg, which may be identified as: A. The *Ontological,* or "substantial" triad; *i.e.,* the Celestial-Spiritual-Natural Worlds; and B. The *Functional,* or dynamic triad of End-Cause-Effect. Between these two triads is what may be called: C. the *Structural* triad, consisting of the principles of Order-Correspondence-Discrete Degrees, bearing in general the same relation to Swedenborg's philosophical system that Leibnitz' principle of Pre-established Harmony did to his system. The ontological triad and the dynamic or functional triad cannot be conceived as rigidly exclusive of each other, for in reality they criss-cross each other with tremendous complexity; moreover, the logico-structural triad of Order, Correspondence, and Discrete Degrees constitutes a mediating triad which applies to both the ontological and the functional triads, just as by analogy, "Cause" mediates between "End" and "Effect," or "Wisdom" between "Love" and "Use," or the "Spiritual World" between the "Celestial World" and the "Natural World."

The principle of "Discrete Degrees" is especially important because it enables Swedenborg and James to avoid Pantheism. The meaning of "discrete" may be enhanced to our comprehension by using an example from daily life, *i.e.,* the psychological triad of motive (End), thought (Cause), act (Effect), which is a familiar pattern of experience. Motive remains motive, thought remains thought, and act remains act, even when the motive and the thought in a given situation are enclosed within the act which contains the motive and the thought, as "effects" contain "ends" and "causes" in Swedenborg's metaphysics. This doctrine of Discrete Degrees suggests Aristotle's influence again, for there seems to be a parallel between Aristotle's tension (or discreteness) involved in the struggle of potentiality for actuality, and Swedenborg's principle.

Still another, and for our purposes, the final, resemblance between Aristotle and Swedenborg may be observed regarding the respective contributions of the male and female principles in human generation. For both, the male is the "active and effective principle" (Aristotle), which Swedenborg and James call the "spiritual principle," while the latter also follows Aristotle in considering the "material principle" to be contributed by the female.[68]

The principle of Correspondence of Forms from one discrete degree to another, is that of proceeding from higher to lower, as from the celestial to the spiritual to the natural world; or from within outward, as motive (or "end") to cause to effect; from love through wisdom to use. Henry Drummond's idea of "Natural Law in the Spiritual World" is the very opposite of Swedenborgian-Jamesian *Spiritual Law in the Natural World.*

James relished this Aristotelian realism in Swedenborg's philosophy, and described it with customary and flavorsome **vigor:**

> Thus he had no shred of a tendency to Idealism, but was a realist of the first water, a realist of absolutely no *nuance* whatever, having just as unfeigned a reverence for the senses in their sphere as for

the soul in its sphere, and practically therefore just as incapable of confounding the two spheres as any carman you may meet upon the street.[69]

Since the Neo-Platonic frame into which Swedenborg fitted his Aristotelian methodology of concepts and logical principles was superimposed later, and because treatment of it will be given in connection with James's doctrine of Spiritual Creation, it remains only to draw a few closing observations in this chapter. Perhaps we should not conclude without a comment concerning James's imitation of Swedenborg's use of scatological terms. Doubtless the psychoanalyst could find much in Swedenborg's psychological history to explain his quite frequent and pungent employment of such descriptive terms as "fetid," "excretory," "excrementitious," "putrid," "stinking," and so on; though perhaps the simple explanation is that it arose out of his long scientific study of animal organisms, which experience provided him with strong olfactory metaphorical adjectives for the portrayal of spiritual disorders. A quotation conveys this stylistic trait so much more forcefully than either theory or comment:

> Moreover, evil and the truth of faith cannot be conjoined otherwise than as a stinking with an aromatic substance, as urine with delicious wine; and they cannot be together any more than a putrid carcass with a living man in one bed. . . .[70]

And now from Swedenborg's American disciple, a century later:

> Thus moralism is the parent of fetichism, or superstitious worship, the parent of all sensual and degrading ideas of God, the parent of all cruel and unclean and abominable worship. . . . [It] . . . bids me . . . make myself, in short, under the guise of a voluntary and mendacious humility, perfectly ulcerous with spiritual pride, a mass of *living* purulence and putridity.[71]

This exploitation of scatological discourse seems as innocent of implying morbid psychological states in James as the masculine prose of the lusty Elizabethans fails to mark them as "pathological." Admitting the extraordinary sensitivity of James spiritually, intellectually, and physically, he was nevertheless, by all available evidence, a soundly happy man in his friends, in his writings, and in his family life. Because James was as full-blooded and full-bodied as he was full-minded, he relished Swedenborg's—well, why not coin a phrase, and call it, Swedenborg's "metaphysical physiology":

It has been shown that the entire heaven resembles one man, and that it is in the form of a man, and is therefore, called the GRAND MAN. It has also been shown, that the angelic societies, of which heaven consists, are arranged like the members, organs, and viscera, in man; so that some are in the head, some in the breast, some in the arms, and some in every particular part of those members (see n. 59-72) . . . for instance, the societies which are in the head correspond to the head in man . . . and so in all other cases.[72]

Again:

Hence also it is usual in common discourse to say of one who is intelligent and wise, that he has a head; of one who is in charity, that he is a bosom friend; of one who excels in perception, that he is keen-scented; of one who is distinguished by intelligence, that he is sharp-sighted; of a very powerful man, that he has long hands; and of one who wills from love, that it is from the heart.[73]

James applies physiological symbolism in other directions, but the influence of his master shows clearly enough. To cite only one illustration:

History we may say then is the skin of the mind, its ultimate tissue or common covering, binding in one its several viscera of heart, lungs, and brain: Church, State, and Society being the outward forms under which this great unseen trinity of powers stand cloaked and represented.[74]

Alongside this "realistic" image of History, it is intellectually diverting to compare it with Josiah Royce's definition of History, as "time warmed over." History as "the skin of the mind" and History, as "time warmed over"! Perhaps this is one way—though a whimsical one—to measure the difference between realist and idealist!

The main concepts for which James was heavily mortgaged to Swedenborg have been reviewed. Many other minor considerations could be added, but certainly the later chapters will exhibit ever more broadly the fundamental fact that from the Swedish scientist and theologian, James borrowed more extensively than from any other single source during his intellectual career; but in this extensive borrowing, he sometimes neglected, sometimes distorted, sometimes truly reflected, the various elements that constitute the total structure of Swedenborg's vast speculations.

*   *   *

A review of the intellectual forces that have worked thus far in the development of James's thought, enables us to gain a perspective on our philosopher.

In Sandemanianism, James found antinomian and anti-ecclesiastical views, which rested on the basic Sandemanian doctrines of the supremacy of the Gospel over the Law (both in the Judaic and the moral sense), and the paramount importance of the Gospel as over the Church, respectively. Although Swedenborg had been most vigorously at pains to attack precisely such doctrines as antinomianism and anti-ecclesiasticism, James nevertheless held to these views all his life. It was, therefore, the Calvinist and Sandemanian inheritance in James which was chiefly responsible for James's misinterpretation of Swedenborg at certain basic points.

It will be recalled that, previously in this chapter, a comparison was rendered between the outline of Swedenborg's systematic theology as given in *The True Christian Religion,* and what was appropriated, neglected, and often distorted by James's interpretations—all of which demonstrates that James was as independent in utilizing Swedenborg's thought for his own purposes as he accused Emerson of being. This distortion of Swedenborg's doctrines is in effect a highly arbitrary performance. Certainly it disqualifies him, in any critical sense, as a Swedenborgian scholar, and it is unreasonable to suppose that James actually regarded himself as such. Doubtless he believed himself to be advocating the same principles as Swedenborg—*those* principles, that is, which he chose to expound; but the free style and personal emphasis in his writings about Swedenborg would seem to indicate that he could not have deceived himself so far as to believe that he was a genuine "Swedenborgian theologian" as some writers have asserted;[75] and much less a "leader of American Swedenborgianism."[76]

In his doctrine of Nature, for example, James differs definitely from Swedenborg. For James, "Nature" exists to provide a "logical ultimate or phenomenal background to the human mind. . . ."[77] But Swedenborg sees Nature, not with the idealist tendency of James, but as the *real* theatre for the ultimation (or, to use Whitehead's term, "concretion") of spiritual principles, and as a confirmation of God "from the things visible in Nature."[78] True, this confirmation is of value to the mind of man; but both God and His operations in Nature, as well as Nature itself, are real and independent of their value to man's mind. Probably one very good reason why James misunderstood Swedenborg's doctrine of Nature is because he never read, from any indication in his writings, a single volume of Swedenborg's scientific works. This fact, plus James's lack of any real understanding of physical science, was enought to cause his failure to grasp the "Aristotle of the North" as Swedenborg has been called.

Swedenborg, highly trained and deeply versed in the higher mathematics, anatomy, metallurgy, and engineering, is always the scientist, who knows that one of the essential tasks of Science is to go "behind the senses," to use a Jamesian phrase against James himself, for he held that Science "cannot go behind the senses." Swedenborg's two intellectual loves were Science and Theology, which he related by the "Science" of Correspondences—and not by Philosophy! James, inadequate as a scientist, goes to Theology by way of Philosophy, and in so doing, differs widely from Swedenborg at basic points, as in their respective views concerning Science and Nature. Without this perspective we could as easily misunderstand James as he misunderstood Swedenborg, and put his distortion of his master down to arbitrary and disingenuous caprice, which, obviously, was not James's intention. His depreciation of Science and Nature as compared with Swedenborg, seems most reasonably explained on the ground of his weakness in Science and his inordinate reliance upon Philosophy. By education and temperament, James was incapable of grasping and expounding the scientific presuppositions which lay at the root of Swedenborg's theological conceptions.

It is highly unwarrantable, however, to think that we have achieved any real understanding of James simply by observing his differences from Swedenborg. A thinker must be understood and judged in terms of his own aim and as to how well he succeeds or fails in achieving his own purpose.

In order to comprehend James's aim, it is requisite that we take another and deeper look at the influence of Transcendentalism upon James. Through the leadership of Coleridge and Emerson, there was in the America of 1820-1860 a general interest in "Spirit," including its various expressions as "spirituality" and as popular "Spiritualism." It all started with German Romantic Philosophy's use of "Spirit" in the works of the idealist philosophers. It did not become much clearer when it was imported into England by Coleridge, whence it was in turn imported into America by Emerson. In the briefest possible way of stating it, "spirit" to Coleridge was Kant's "Reason" in man, minus Kant's warning that the Reason could only supply the categorical forms for what was supplied both by the Understanding and by Experience through the Senses; moreover, Reason, according to Kant, had no power to perceive Reality-in-itself. To Coleridge, however, human Reason was able to penetrate to Reality itself because of his belief in a Platonic theory of human knowledge. For Coleridge, with his Platonism, ideas are not merely "regulative" as with Kant, but "constitutive." With pure Rationalism he held that:

> Self-evident propositions are principles not only of thought, but of truth and being. Space and time are forms of sensibility, but not mere forms. Reason and experience coincide; the ideas of the pure reason and the laws of Nature correspond.[79]

Both Coleridge and Emerson derived the idea of "correspondence" between the spiritual and natural worlds, between mind and natural law, from Swedenborg. The end result of their Transcendentalism, however, was a dualism of Spiritual Causation in the spiritual realm and of Natural Causation in the natural realm. It was a case of parallelism between the two kinds of causation, with a pre-established harmony between them ordained originally by Divine Reason.[80]

Now James was concerned with the problem of resolving this dualism of parallel causation, and he did it by his doctrine of spirit as an efficient cause *in* the natural world. This power of spirit to operate in the natural order as an efficient cause, James called "creation" as distinct from the Transcendentalist doctrines of spiritual and natural causation which operated only within their own respective realms, without interaction.

James was at pains to illustrate his doctrine of spiritual creation in the natural order with examples that were homespun and taken from practical life. We will became acquainted later with his illustration of the coat, which involves both cloth and the skill of the tailor; but the "spiritual" being of the coat consists in its "use" and the "power it exerts" as a creative cause over both cloth and tailor, who are merely the constituents which the coat required. Or for another illustration: saltpetre, he says, is "nitric acid 54 and potash 47.2" as to its chemical constituents. They do not "create" the salt; on the contrary, it is the salt which creates them. In James, spiritual causation, or creation, always operates *in* the natural order; creation is always from higher to lower; or, in Swedenborgian terms, from End to Cause to Effect. It is the "superstructure" of a house which *creates,* because it requires, the foundation.

Thus Spirit, on the Jamesian construction, is not an *extra*-natural process as it was for Transcendentalism, but a creative process *in* nature. In a sense, this amounts to saying that James was concerned more at the outset with the germinal idea in Swedenborg's principle of "influx" than he was with Swedenborg's principle of "correspondence" between the spiritual and natural worlds—the principle so beloved by the Transcendentalists. But in all justice to James, it should be said that he developed a highly original doctrine of spiritual causation (or creation), which was remarkably well advanced over Swedenborg's "influx," and he expended on the idea of Spiritual Creation in Nature, a wealth of reasoning and of illustration, of literary and of philosophic power.

This teaching of spiritual causation in nature has an important implication for man's spiritual life in general; for now spiritual life is no longer, under the dissolving impact of James's view, a mere transcendence about which, by definition, man can only have certain abstract notions at best. Spiritual life, interests, and activities are, to James, a dynamic *process in* man, *in* nature, *in* the individual, and *in* the cosmos as a whole. Powerful in its sheer dynamism is the movement of spiritual causation throughout involution and evolution, creation and redemption, in James's philosophy; and it is this dynamical interpretation of spirit which brings James close to the center of the most vital and religious thought of the nineteenth century. There can be no question but that, had he not insisted upon employing his peculiar and unconventional terminology, his contribution to the philosophy of religion with respect to creation, evolution, and redemption would have received the recognition it so much deserved.

In his prolonged effort to construct a doctrine of spiritual creation, James thus differed not only from the Transcendentalists, but from Swedenborg, who, though he speaks of spirit occasionally as causative in the natural world, nowhere expands this single doctrine to anything like the extent that James did.

In his concentration upon the task of framing a "scientific" doctrine of Spiritual Creation in Nature, James owes much to constant challenge and criticism from his close friend, Wilkinson. In England, Wilkinson had been concerned with leading the English Swedenborgians away from too much fascination with popular Spiritualism, with its mediums, seances, and its claims of communications with "spirits" of persons who had departed this life. For this kind of spiritualism, Wilkinson had nothing but contempt. Of course, this popular "Spiritism" pointed for precedent to Swedenborg's reports of intercourse with spirits, but Swedenborg himself was caught in this problem and confessed his difficulty in deciding upon the authenticity of such "communications." At any rate, Wilkinson tried, quite successfully, to steer Swedenborgians away from this side of the master's life. His own particular aim was, on the basis of Swedenborg's scientific works, to establish a kind of "Christian Science." He was always encouraging James to frame a "scientific" doctrine of spirit as against Coleridge's foggy transcendentalism on the one side, and popular spiritualism (or spiritism) on the other. James agreed completely with Wilkinson's contempt for popular spiritualism, and he tried to build a scientific interpretation of Spirit in Nature. But Wilkinson, who asserted that Swedenborg's system had " no place for metaphysics proper," often complained to James that he was "too metaphysical." Wilkinson wanted a "scientific" interpretation, and although he encouraged James to essay such a task, what James produced was, in reality, not a scientific but a philosophic (or, perhaps more precisely, a Gnostical) interpretation of Swedenborg which reflected James's own intellectual presuppositions more than it expounded Swedenborg's.

NOTES

1. Immanuel Kant, *Dreams of a Spirit-Seer explained by Dreams of Metaphysics* (1766), trans. by Goerwitz (London & New York, 1900), p. 162.
2. Samuel T. Coleridge, from *Notes* on Swedenborg's *The Worship and Love of God*, reprinted in *New Jerusalem Magazine*, Vol. XIV (Aug., 1841), p. 474.
3. Ralph W. Emerson, "Swedenborg: The Mystic," essay in *Representative Men* (1849).
4. *S of S*, p. 211. This reference falls in the "Appendix." James's appendices often contain the richest summaries of his thought. There are no Indices for any of his books, thus increasing the difficulties for the expositor.
5. Marguerite Block, *The New Church in the New World*. (Henry Holt & Co., N. Y., 1932), p. 166.
6. T. F. Wright, "Swedenborg," Baldwin's *Dictionary of Philosophy and Psychology* (N. Y., 1928), p. 626.
7. Immanuel Kant, *Träume eines Geistersehers, erläutert durch Träume der Metaphysik* (Königsberg, 1766).
8. For the chief theological works by Swedenborg, consult the appropriate section in the general bibliography at the end of the book.
9. Ralph Waldo Emerson, *op. cit.*
10. "Emanuel Swedenborg," *The Nation*, Vol. IV (1866-67), p. 329.
11. This matter of whether Swedenborg was a mystic or not is really not so easily settled as ⁄ James's overpositive and oversimplified statements would indicate. When Marguerite Block, a thoroughly competent scholar of Swedenborg, read this part of the first draft of this study, she made these important notes: "I think one would call Swedenborg a 'psychic,' rather than a 'mystic.' He seems to have a lot of 'E.S.P.!' [extra-

sensory-perception]. He was an extreme type of 'visualizer' who actually *saw* his ideas in symbolic pictures.... His philosophy was a *mystical philosophy*.... But, his *method* was rationalistic.... That is what makes him so baffling ... mystical content and rational method."

12. *S of S*, pp. 13-14. James's low opinion of Swedenborg's literary artlessness is not shared by Swedish literary critics as, for example, Atterbom who speaks most highly of the literary beauty of *On the Worship and Love of God.*

13. *Ibid.*, p. 211.

14. *Ibid.*, p. 211.

15. Emanuel Swedenborg, *The True Christian Religion* (Lippincott, Philadelphia, 1873), No. 181, pp. 151-152.

16. *Ibid.*, No. 73, pp. 58-59.

17. *Ibid.*, No. 74, p. 60.

18. *Ibid.*, No. 349, pp. 248-249.

19. *Ibid.*, No. 341, p. 244.

20. *Ibid.*, No. 355, p. 252.

21. *Ibid.*, No. 356, p. 253. *Formula of Concord* (Leipsig Edition, 1756).

22. *Ibid.*

23. *Ibid.*, No. 626, p. 420.

24. *Ibid.*, pp. v-xvi.

25. *The True Christian Religion*, No. 175, p. 148.

26. *Ibid.*, Nos. 166 and 167, pp. 143-144. Swedenborg's denial of the orthodox Trinity of Persons is worthy of a brief review of Christian thought on this topic. Denying the tri-personal, tri-hypostatic trinity, in which doctrine there is an attempt to avoid a mere abstract unity in the Godhead, Swedenborg nevertheless asserts in another form, a tri-unity of *attributes* of the *one* person of God. In brief, he conceives a triad of attributes rather than a triad of persons; and his triad is expressed as God's "Love-Wisdom-Power." This is a tri-unity of *essential* attributes.

It is when God engages His Power in creative activity that a second triad appears in Swedenborg's thought: namely, the triad of Divine manifestation (or Revelation) to man, in the threefold activity of Creation-Redemption-Regeneration. This second tri-unity of God's activity has had an equally long history in Christian doctrine with the tri-personal Trinity. It goes back at least to Irenaeus' "dispensational" (*dispositio*) trinity, and to Tertullian's "economic" trinity. The orthodox dogma is a trinity of *essential* distinctions within Godhead, or *ab intra;* while the dispensational trinity is of God's *revelations* of Himself as seen from man's side, or *ab extra.*

Servetus, in his treatise *de Trinitatis Erroribus* (1531), p. 112f., expounded just such a trinity-of-manifestation, but denied the essential Trinity *within* Godhead, for as he phrased it: "There is no other person of God but Christ ... the entire Godhead of the Father is in him." The identity of this view with that of Swedenborg's and James's, is too obvious for comment.

Swedenborg's and James's doctrine of a God of triune revelation as Creator-Redeemer-Regenerator, is really in a main line of Christian thought since Augustine; for as Harnack observes, from Athanasius to Augustine is the record of a gradual displacement of the orthodox, essential Trinity-of-Persons by the "economic" trinity-of-manifestation. Modern Protestantism, quite apart from official Unitarianism, is generally more concerned with the "economic" than with the tri-personal trinity, and so approaches Swedenborg's position.

Another way in which modern Protestantism unconsciously tends to agree with Swedenborg and James is in the results of the argument to God by analogy to man's psychological constitution (this psychological argument was started by Augustine's trinity in man of "memory, understanding, and will"). The result of this line of argument is, curiously, that much, perhaps most, of modern Protestant theology is given to a discussion of *the* personality of God rather than to the concept of personality *in* God, and as though there were only *one* person of God! And this, quite outside of Unitarianism! Thus, much of Protestant Christianity has come, inadvertently, to occupy a position very similar to that of Swedenborg and James; it is an oblique, rather than a direct, denial of the orthodox dogma. There is still, however, one important difference: to Swedenborg and James, God is the Lord, and the Lord *is* God; while much of Protestant theology still discusses the issue of the "likeness" (*homoiousion*) of Christ to God. It is interesting to observe that the issue has turned full circle from the question of Christ's "God-likeness," to God's "Christ-likeness." With our two thinkers, there is no problem, either way, of "likeness."

27. Henry James (the third). *Letters of William James* (Atlantic Monthly Press, 1920), Vol. I, p. 16.
28. *The True Christian Religion*, Nos. 18 and 19, p. 16. Also, No. 20, p. 17.
29. *Ibid.*, No. 21, p. 18.
30. *Ibid.*, p. iv.
31. *Ibid.*, No. 25, p. 21.
32. *Ibid.*, No. 36, p. 33.
33. *Ibid.*, No. 37, pp. 33-34.
34. *Divine Love and Wisdom* (Agar's trans., N. Y., 1943), pp. 442-515.
35. *The True Christian Religion*, Nos. 39 and 40, pp. 35-36.
36. *Divine Love and Wisdom*, Sec. (21), p. 450.
37. *Ibid.*, No. 395, p. 445.
38. *The True Christian Religion*, No. 49, p. 45.
39. *Ibid.*, Nos. 52-70, pp. 47-55; also, No. 501, p. 351.
40. *Ibid.*, No. 26, p. 22.
41. *Ibid.*, No. 472, p. 336.
42. *The True Christian Religion*, No. 76, p. 62.
43. *Ibid.*, No. 224, p. 180.
44. *Ibid.*, No. 67, p. 53.
45. *Ibid.*, No. 81, p. 71.
46. *Ibid.*
47. *Ibid.*, No. 81, Proposition VII, p. 71.
48. *Ibid.*, No. 92, p. 77. Swedenborg and James derived their theory of genetics from Aristotle.

49. *Ibid.*, No. 95, p. 79.

50. *Heaven and Hell* (Penguin, 250th Anniv. Ed., London, 1938), pp. 288, 298.

51. *The Divine Love and Wisdom*, No. 275, pp. 287-288.

52. *Heaven and Hell*, No. 589, pp. 313-314.

53. *The True Christian Religion*, No. 579, p. 392.

54. *Ibid.*, Nos. 126 and 127, pp. 107-108.

55. James Freeman Clarke, "James on the Nature of Evil," *The Christian Examiner*, Vol. LIX (1855), pp. 134-135.

56. In the last sentence of the quotation from Clarke, there is incidentally, a perfect *apologia* for the present writer's extended exposition of Swedenborg. James "imperfectly develops" so many concepts which he acquired from Swedenborg.

57. *The True Christian Religion*, Nos. 166 and 167, pp. 143-144.

58. *Ibid.*, No. 168, p. 144.

59. *Ibid.*, No. 142, p. 123.

60. *Ibid.*, No. 142f.

61. T. F. Wright, "Emanuel Swedenborg," Baldwin's *Dictionary of Philosophy and Psychology* (1928), p. 628. This account of Swedenborg, though highly compressed, is an excellent summary.

62. Frank Sewall, *Swedenborg and Modern Idealism* (London, 1902), p. 19.

63. *Divine Love and Wisdom* (Agar's trans., N. Y., 1943), No. 189, pp. 180-181.

64. *Ibid.*, No. 197, p. 186.

65. *Ibid.*, No. 119, pp. 113-114.

66. *Ibid.*, No. 212, p. 202.

67. *Ibid.*, Nos. 213-214, pp. 203-204.

68. Aristotle, *On the Generation of Animals*, Book *I*, Sections 20-21.

69. *SRFM*, 124.

70. *The True Christian Religion*, No. 383, p. 275.

71. *MC*, 160.

72. *Heaven and Hell*, No. 94, p. 49.

73. *Ibid.*, No. 97, p. 51.

74. *S and S*, p. 463.

75. Woodbridge Riley, *American Thought* (N. Y., 1941), p. 329.

76. J. S. Bixler, "William James," *Encyclopaedia of Religion* (Philosophical Library, N. Y., 1945), p. 385.

77. *S of S*, p. 191.

78. Emanuel Swedenborg, *The True Christian Religion*, No. 12, p. 9.

79. M. J. Ryan, article, "Coleridge," in Hastings' *Ency. of Religion and Ethics*, Vol. III, p. 711.

80. Wilkinson, although criticising Coleridge in the following, might well have written these words as a friendly warning to James:

"Two different schemes of philosophy, new at least in their form, are at present in the world—the Synthetic, which constructs the mind from the pure being of consciousness and conscience, and discards all adjuncts and imagery, as only referring to the senses and sensual mind, but having no relation to the Reason.... Allowing no conceptual limits, except to *things*, it does not distinguish between the human spirit, in the highest sense, and the Creative Spirit. Man has in himself ... an ultimate ground of reality ... God and the Soul are identical—consequently, the

soul is creative—in other words synthetic. The idea of man's immortality
is convertible into that of his instant eternity. These doctrines are rapidly being adopted by the modern intellectual world;—perhaps they are
the natural outgrowth of its religion;—perhaps an abstract RIGHT of
private judgment amounts to self-deification;—perhaps justification by
faith, followed by the imputation of infinite attributes to human beings,
is the theological complex of the idea;—in fine, perhaps Protestantism
and Rationalism are one." (*The Monthly Magazine* (London: June,
1841), Vol. V, p. 616).

Doubtless it was Wilkinson's hammering which forced James to clarify
his stand against "Idealism" and "Rationalism."

Chapter Five

Socialism, Associationism and James

To conclude, Socialism promises to make God's great life in man possible, promises to make all our relations so just, so beautiful and helpful, that we shall be no longer conscious of finiteness, of imperfection, but only of life and power utterly infinite . . . Every one who trusts in a living and therefore active God, . . . in short every one whose hope for humanity is alert, behooves to acquaint himself forthwith with the marvelous literature of Socialism, above all with the writings of CHARLES FOURIER.

—HENRY JAMES, SR.[1]

. . . the penetrating, celestial Swedenborg . . . the gigantic and earthborn Fourier. . . .

—J J. GARTH WILKINSON[2]

THE CRITICISM OF "Civilization" in European social philosophy may be said to have made itself effective with the publication of Rousseau's *Emile* and *The Social Contract,* both in 1762. From that date, the current of literary, political, religious, and philosophical critiques of civilization swelled in volume like a mighty river fed by many tributaries, until in Karl Marx and Engels this new stream may be said to have cut its own channel and found its own banks across the ideological map of Europe. The period from 1762 to 1867, the latter date being that of the publishing of Marx's first volume of *Das Kapital,* was *the* century of social visions and protests, compared to which the three-quarters of a century since 1867 is, in quality of social aspiration, speculation, and protestation, as the fitful flashes of a lighthouse beacon at night compared to the light of the sun at noonday.

The intellectual-spiritual life of this great movement between *Emile* and *Das Kapital* reflected many and complex currents-counter-currents in thought and method, but not in spirit and goal. From the groping sentimentalities of Rousseau's works, to the powerful engine of criticism in Marx's great work, is a long and intricate record of kaleidoscopic intellectual climates and dynamics. But did the common, underlying Romantic spirit in them all really change? Marx's dream of the classless society is partly in the true Romantic tradition of social philosophy, and the goal was still the same—that is, *basically* the same—the birth of a just, free, and happy Society. The critical side of this tremendous century from Rousseau to Marx—and we might well add Nietzche—was, in the end, for the sake of the great ideal of a transformed—or as James puts it, a "redeemed"—Society, which would transcend the inequalities and iniquities of "Civilization."

How came it about that "Society" superseded "Civilization" as the overmastering concept in the social thought of this epoch? Had not men been accustomed to think of "Society" as made up of Church and State, and that that was all there was to society? We may find an answer if we allow ourselves a telescopic survey of western social philosophy from Aristotle to Rousseau, without any pretext either of completeness or of scientific generalization, but simply for descriptive purposes. We note first that in the Greek city-states no distinction was made in either social theory or practice between ethics and politics on the one hand, or between politics and "sociology" on the other. A science of Society, aside from the State, was as undreamed of in Aristotle's time as a science of Ethics for the individual apart from Politics. The first great division within the body social-and-politic was into Church and State after Christianity became the state religion under Constantine. "Society," as such, distinguished, or distinguishable, from Church and State was unthought of. During the high mediaeval epoch the Church was dominant. But with the breakdown of feudalism and the rise of national states, the State became dominant. Yet the State was in turn challenged by revolutionary leaders and thinkers. Especially in England, from the time of *Magna Carta* on, the State was clipped in power, both in theory and in fact, from absolute monarchy to an increasingly constitutional-parliamentary monarchism. Hence arose the Anglo-American political tradition as freedom *from* government and statism, insofar as possible. *Laissez faire* and free trade expressed this philosophy in economic policy. Locke was its classical philosopher, as Adam Smith was its economist.

On the Continent, the development regarding the philosophy of the State was the reverse of that in England. Hegel conceived the goal and meaning of history to be "Freedom" indeed, but freedom, *not from* the State, but freedom *through* the State; and, one might add accurately enough from various Hegelian contexts, freedom *by, for,* and *in* the State. Although Hegel appears to make the State paramount, as against the Anglo-American concept of "Society" as greater than the State, it must be recalled that Hegel's concept of *Gesellschaft,* which is the sphere of private-vital interests within the "whole of life," is parallel in a real sense to western "Society," while the State to Hegel was a "limited-finite" form of "wholeness" within the life of history. Even so, it can be seen that Hegel's doctrine of the State is philosophically different, and eventuates in different practical applications to government, than the Anglo-American theory and practice.

This new consciousness of Society (which at best is somewhat of an ideal concept rather than a scientific one), produced new leaders very soon after Rousseau. Robert Owen (1771-1858) appeared in England, and St. Simon (1760-1825) in France, soon followed in the same country by François Marie Charles Fourier (1772-1837), the founder of "Associationism," with whom we are particularly concerned in this chapter.

Nine days after Swedenborg died in 1772, Fourier was born. With biographical details and even with the technical details of Associationist Socialism we are not, for our purposes, concerned. Suffice it to say that his socialistic philosophy spread to America through the medium of Albert Brisbane's *Social Destiny of Man,* published in 1840. Brisbane had spent considerable time studying Fourierism in France, and after the publishing of *Social Destiny of Man,* he followed that with *Association; or, A Concise Exposition of the Practical Part of Fourier's Social Science,* in 1843. Brisbane was abetted in his cause by Horace Greeley, editor of the New York *Tribune,* who allowed the advocates of "Association" to purchase a column in that organ for the propaganda of their social principles.

Associationism was the second socialistic ripple to break on American shores from the tidal wave of social visions, critiques of civilization, programs of reform, and philosophies of revolution that emanated from Europe. The first was the Owenite Socialism, arriving here in 1824, through Owen in person. The focal year of its greatest strength was 1826, at which time eleven socialistic communities were in existence in the United States, all more or less due to the excitement raised by Owen.[3] The second was Fourierism, publicized by Brisbane and Greeley in 1842, and achieving its focal year of greatest vitality in 1843, with thirty-four communities established at or near this date.[4]

Fascinating as it would be to investigate the history of these communities during what is perhaps, considering the rich ferment of social-religious-philosophical and even medical idealism of these years, the most amazing decade (1840-1850) in the variegated record of American social thought—such an investigation is not pertinent to our study. What is pertinent, however, is (1) the impact of Fourierism on the famous Brook Farm Community at West Roxbury, Massachusetts, plus James's contact with the leaders of that community; and (2) the cross-breeding of Associationism with Swedenborgianism.

Brook Farm, founded in 1842, was originally the child of New England Unitarianism by suggestion of the noted Dr. William Ellery Channing; Noyes quotes Emerson's lecture on Brook Farm to this effect.[5] Channing himself stood rather midway between Unitarianism and Transcendentalism, and the community reflected these two strains in its intellectual physiognomy. *The Dial* and *The Present* were started as its first organs of public expression; but by the winter of 1843-44, the community was led by another Channing—William H.—to embrace Associationism. *The Dial* and *The Present* gave way to the *Phalanx,* which in its turn gave way to the *Harbinger,* the latter being an English equivalent of Fourier, which in French means a "harbinger" or "purveyor."[6] Brook Farm now became "the chief representative and propagative organ of Fourierism" in this country.[7]

At this point James enters the picture; I say "enters" advisedly, lest the reader expect that James is actually going to join Brook Farm, for it is quite impossible to catch him in the act of "joining" any Society, Phalanx, Church, or Club—except "The Saturday Club" in Boston. James was to the last, the radical individualist, though preaching a spiritualistic Socialism as man's redemption all the while! Yet James enters the Socialist picture to this extent: Noyes states that James contributed thirty-two articles, essays, and letters, signed as "Y. S." ("your servant"), to the *Harbinger.*[3] Nevertheless, James characteristically denies his sympathy with Brook Farm in a Postscript addressed to Mr. Hepworth Dixon, author of the sensational book, *Spiritual Wives* (London, 1868):

for example, Mr. Dixon condescends, *inter alia,* upon my unworthy name in connection with the Brook-Farmers, a community with which, while it existed, I was in no relation whatever either of knowledge or of sympathy.... He first gives me the title of "reverend," and calls me a "Brook Farm enthusiast"; the facts being that I never belonged to any ministry ordained or unordained, and that I almost never heard of the Brook Farm Association till it failed to exist.[9]

James's contributions to the *Harbinger*—I can find no record of his having contributed to the *Phalanx*—were submitted after the *Harbinger* removed to New York in 1847 (to cease publication in 1849). These articles, essays, and letters reveal the Swedenborgianized Fourierism that James was beginning to write in this period, and this leads to an inquiry concerning a general movement to fuse the philosophy of Swedenborg with the social science of Fourier, of which movement James was only one individual participant. It happens that Noyes saw this attempted fusion very clearly, and wrote a series of articles in either 1868 or 1869—he does not say which in his *History*—entitled "Swedenborgiana," in the *Circular,* which was the organ of the Oneida, New York, Community of which Noyes himself was a leader and from which place he wrote the *History of American Socialisms.* In that book he devotes a chapter to "Brook Farm and Swedenborgianism," and quotes himself from his articles on "Swedenborgiana":

> The foremost and brightest of the Associations that rose in the Fourier excitement, was that at Brook Farm. The leaders were men whose names are now high in literature and politics. Ripley, Dana, Channing, Dwight, and Hawthorne, are specimens of the list. Most of them were from the Unitarian School.... The movement really issued as much from transcendential Unitarianism as from Fourierism. It was religious, literary, and artistic, as well as social.... But the remarkable fact ... is ... it brought upon the public mind, not only a new socialism but a new religion, and that religion was Swedenborgianism.
>
> The proof of this can be found by any one who has access to the files of the *Harbinger.* ... The simple truth is that Brook Farm and the *Harbinger* meant to propagate Fourierism, but succeeded only in propagating Swedenborgianism. The Associations that arose with them and under their influence, passed away within a few years, without exception; but the surge of Swedenborgianism which they started, swept on among their constituents, and, under the form of Spiritualism, is sweeping on to this day.

Swedenborgianism went deeper into the hearts of the people than the Socialism that introduced it, because it was a religion. . . . Swedenborg's offer of a new heaven as well as a new earth, met the demand magnificently. He suited all sorts. The scientific were charmed, because he was primarily a son of science, and seemed to reduce the universe to scientific order. The mystics were charmed, because he led them boldly into all the mysteries of intuition and invisible worlds. The Unitarians liked him, because, while he declared Christ to be Jehovah himself, he displaced the orthodox ideas of Sonship and tri-personality, and evidently meant only that Christ was an illusive representation of the Father. Even the infidels liked him, because he discarded about half the Bible. . . .[10]

Noyes concludes his portrait of Swedenborgianism:

After 1847 Swedenborgianism proper subsided, and "Modern Spiritualism" took its place. . . . Spiritualism is Swedenborgianism Americanized.[11]

That James was not at all in sympathy with "Swedenborgianism Americanized" is evident from his attacks upon Spiritualism.[12]

As for James, his contact with "Swedenborgiana" doubtless began, thought it seems to be impossible from the sources to demonstrate it with absolute certainty, by influence of his old friend of Princeton Seminary days, Parke Godwin. In 1844, Godwin published his able little volume on the doctrines of Fourier, in which we read:

Thus far, we have given Fourier's doctrine of Universal Analogy; but it is important to observe that he was not the first man of modern times who communicated this view. Emanuel Swedenborg, between whose revelations, in the sphere of spiritual knowledge, and Fourier's discoveries in the sphere of science, there has been remarked the most exact and wonderful coincidence, preceded him in the annunciation of the doctrine, in many of its aspects, in what is termed the doctrine of correspondence. These two great minds,—the greatest beyond all comparison in our later days,— were the instruments of Providence in bringing to light the mysteries of His Word and Works, as they are comprehended and followed, in the higher states of existence. It is no exaggeration, we think, to say, that they are THE TWO commissioned by the Great Leader of the Christian Israel, to spy out the Promised Land of Peace and Blessedness.

But in the discovery and statement of the doctrine of Analogy, these authorities have not proceeded according to precisely the same methods. Fourier has arrived at it by strictly scientific synthesis, and Swedenborg by the study of the Scriptures, aided by Divine Illumination.[13]

James's first book over his own signed name, *What Constitutes the State* (1846), a lecture delivered in Albany in December 1845, shows the yeast of Associationism plus Swedenborg, as exemplified in Godwin, already at work. He came into further contact with Swedenborgianized Associationism through his friendly commerce with George Ripley, Charles A. Dana, John S. Dwight, William H. Channing, and Horace Greeley; the first four having come to New York to live after the failure of Brook Farm. James was very intimate with them all from 1847 onward. Moreover, it seems highly likely that he read not only Brisbane but also Dr. Charles Julius Hempel's book, *The True Organization of the New Church as Indicated in the Writings of Emanuel Swedenborg and Demonstrated by Charles Fourier,* which appeared in 1848. Since James's own views on Socialism will be offered in the chapter in "The Doctrine of Redemption and Spiritual Socialism" in this study, let us pause to take a more than cursory look into Hempel's work, first because it is a remarkable book in its own right, but mainly because it will greatly broaden our understanding of James.

Hempel devoted, as he says, ten years of studious preparation to the writing of this book, and with the express purpose of interlocking the philosophy of Swedenborg and the social science of Fourier, as stated definitely enough in his "dedication":

> I dedicate this work to the adherents of Fourier and Swedenborg.
> The doctrines of these two great men cannot remain separate.
> Their union constitutes the union of Science and Religion. . . .
> And, of Swedenborg, I have shown that the doctrine of Fourier
> is an application to life of Swedenborg's theories.[14]

The reference to "the union of Science and Religion" is illuminating *vis-a-vis* James's use of the term "Science," for all these writers of the Associationist School, including James, use the term very rarely if ever as applying to the mathematical or to the physical sciences, but always to "social" science. They take this for granted without direct explanation because it becomes so obvious to their readers. One other refinement in definition might well be noted: by "social science" they did not mean an academic theory or course of study at a university, but rather a practical, politico-social program, and hence the name "Socialism."

Further on in his book, Hempel says he prefers Swedenborg's term "consociation" to "Association." Playing a variation on the two terms respectively, he asserts that *"cum-*sociation" has a more "internal" meaning than *"Ad-*sociation," and this is the reason for his preference of "Consociation."[15]

Once again, as we saw in his free-lance interpretation of Swedenborg, James nowhere gives the systematic structure that lies behind and within his own developed "spiritual socialism," and for this reason it is desirable to present in outline this structure *via* Hempel's exposition, for he is the most systematic expounder of what results from the cross-fertilization of Swedenborg with Fourier. Godwin devotes only a few paragraphs to the connection between them, but Hempel proceeds throughout 454 pages to draw analogy after analogy between the Swedish and French thinkers. An examination of the most relevant passages is now presented. Firstly:

I. The Grand Man of Swedenborg's vision of the organization of all the angelic societies, is none other than Fourier's *Series of Groups* applied to heaven, a sort of series of phalanxes.[16]

II. The "love-principle" in Swedenborg is what Fourier calls "Passion."[17]

III. Fourier's Divine Being is a Trinity of three principles:

   (1) The Creating Principle, or Father.
   (2) The Created Principle, or Son.
   (3) The Neuter or Mathematical Principle, or Holy Ghost.

Fourier's "Trinity" is "correspondent" to Swedenborg's three great "degrees," thus:

   (1) The Celestial, as from God, in the first degree.
   (2) The Spiritual, as being from the Celestial, in the second degree.
   (3) The Natural, as being from the Spiritual, in the third degree.

Hempel presses home a further "analogy" between these ontological levels of reality, and the principles of knowledge in the human mind:

   (1) The Celestial Principle—The Pure Passion Principle.
   (2) The Spiritual Principle—Divine Truth.
   (3) The Natural Principle—The Scientific Principle.[18]

The three "principles" of the above, as given in the right hand column, may be seen in turn to correspond with Swedenborg's "Love-Wisdom-Use" triad.

At this point in our exposition, it seems that one is entitled to a little *divertissement*. For such a purpose there is nothing more delectable to one's humor, or more healthy for one's imagination, than to indulge them by quoting a few of the *curiosa* to be found in Hempel. Here are a few choice specimens which no gracious soul can read without being both amused at the naïveté and yet touched by the quaint pathos of these visions; and, truth to tell, we may be unable to help ourselves from being secretly and wistfully envious of an epoch that produced men capable of such a combination of innocence and yet audacity in thought and hope:

> But Industrial Armies [idea borrowed by Bellamy in *Looking Backward?*] cannot of themselves achieve the regeneration of the globe. . . .
> And Fourier supposes furthermore, that this agent, when the earth shall have been fitly prepared for its reception, will manifest itself at both poles in the shape of a ring which Fourier proposes to name the *"Boreal Crown."*
> The Boreal Crown will be the chief means by which the physical disorders of the globe are to disappear, the ice of the poles, and the sands of the desert.[19]

But we do not have to wait for the fulfillment of such apocalypses in the future to note the miracles that have already happened:

> Why was it that Swedenborg should have been born in Sweden? The sublimest tendencies of the soul having their organs on the top of the head, it was necessary that the architect of practical Christianity should have been born in the country which typifies the head.[20]

After all, Plato had a kind of literary world-physiology after the physiological and human-cosmic image in the *Timaeus,* and he is a rather respectable thinker!

Not only for "practical Christianity" do we have the consolation that its architect was born in the country signifying the head, but Swedenborgian "physiology" also has something to say about political dynamics as well:

> Why should the French manifest so frequently and so intensely a desire to invade Germany? [This was in 1848!] Because in the

unborn foetus ... the blood, instead of being sent from the right ventricle to the left by means of the pulmonary artery, rushes through the foramen ovale *directly* from the right ventricle into the adjoining left. ... The invasion of Germany by the French being a phenomenon of fetal circulation—in other words, a phenomenon of social subversion—those who at present advocate the propriety of such an invasion, advocate the continuance of the fetal life of Humanity. . . .

The invasions of England into France were highly subversive, because in true circulation, England should receive venous blood from France, as the right lobe of the lungs receives the blood from the right ventricle through the pulmonary artery. . . .

The violent and thorough agitation which the blood receives in the right ventricle, points to the special destiny which France has to accomplish. It is destined to be the fountainhead of the science of Gastronomy. . . .

Sweden and Norway will lead an eminently spiritual existence; they will regulate the religious unity of Humanity. Through Scandinavia the earth will be in direct communion with heaven.[21]

From the physiology of religion and politics he passes to "Gastronomical Harmonies," and he gives us directions about "the nature and object of a truly Christian meal [as] indicated in the following passages from the Heavenly Arcana of Swedenborg, No. 7996."[22]

It is an indication of James's robust sanity that, in the midst of such heady speculations and apocalyptic phantasies as the above— and even an intellect of Fourier's capacity could indulge them—James kept his balance so that we find nothing of this sort in him. Though he often becomes hyper-visionary, it is with the profound and moving dignity of a Hebrew prophet. There was too much of the philosopher in him for such indiscreet flights. It should be remembered that he lived and wrote in the midst of amazing social-intellectual-religious fermentation. The '40s to the '60s were not only the decades of Transcendentalism and Socialism, but of theories and cults of phrenology, gastronomy, vegetarianism, mesmerism, homeopathy, hypnotic healing, and spiritualisms of various kinds. In his sympathy with Associationism, James came closest to the spirit and thought of a contemporary philosophico-religio-social movement; but his intellectual stamina, humor, and sense of proportion saved him from any real flinging of himself into the whirlpool of social nostrums. To some, this was moral cowardice and intellectual equivocation; to this writer it seems to have its admirable aspect, though he is quite ready to admit that admirations are often gauged to one's own rationalized prejudices. Nevertheless, it would seem a well-taken judgment that a man as intellectually daring as James, should be given all the more credit for not losing himself in the headstrong vagaries of a seething period of speculation, the like of which this country has never seen, before or since.

Hempel's attack upon civilization, however, was more serious than his phantastical excursions, and this did influence James, as did also the strictures of Brisbane, Godwin, Dana, and company. They challenged James's thought and helped to shape his views on labor, government, women's rights, love, marriage, divorce, and crime prevention. Fourier himself had set the example for Associationists in his trial of civilization before the bar of socialism's ideal:

> The present Social Order is a ridiculous mechanism, in which portions of the whole are in conflict with, and acting against the whole. We see each Class in Society desire, from interest, the misfortune of other classes, and place in every way individual interest in opposition to public good. The Lawyer wishes litigations and suits, particularly among the rich; the Physician desires sickness (the latter would be ruined if everybody died without disease, as would the former, if all quarrels were settled by arbitration;) the Soldier wants a war, which will carry off half his comrades, to secure him promotion; the Undertaker wants burials; Monopolists and Forestallers want famines, to double or treble the price of grain; the Architect, the Carpenter, the Mason, want conflagrations, that will burn down a hundred houses, to give activity to their branches of business.[23]

Hempel delivers himself of the same theme:

> Civilization is like unto the seed which hides a new principle of life within its bosom. When this new form of life has broken through the enclosing wall, the body from which it has drawn substance and strength, decays, and finally crumbles into dust. It is thus with Civilization.[24]

To Parke Godwin, however, falls the credit of penning a truly powerful indictment of the same great enemy, for "the present state of society" means what Fourier and Hempel mean by "civilization." To read it is to have one's mind stabbed awake, as by a "shock" treatment. It is curious how realistic, from certain angles of analysis, these idealists can be!

That the present state of society is utterly and abominably false, and needs a thorough organic renovation, is further evident since it imposes a restraint upon the practice of the *absolute* duties of life, almost as rigid and grievous as that which it lays upon the indiscriminate indulgence of the subversive passions. It is almost a matter of doubt, whether the world would be more disturbed and injured by the unbounded freedom of the passions, or by the un-flinching assertion of all the virtues. Suppose that Truth and Justice were at once applied to the existing ways and relations of Mankind! ... What a universal uproar and distress among the plots of public men, the frauds of merchants, the tricks of politicians, the innumerable basenesses of industry, of legislation, of the press, of the pulpit, among secret dislikes and dissimulations in families, between man and wife, parents and children, the deceptions of Love, the ignoble conventions of politeness and law upon which society rests! Or, let Justice be done among men, and what devastations, what exposures, what overturnings, what horrors, would be the wild and cruel result?[25]

For the cure of this horrible mess of civilization Godwin postulated the superiority of Associationism to every other plan for society's greatest welfare because it combined the advantages of all the systems that had been either tried out or thought out:

Individualism denies the authority of any power but its own will, and therefore leads to Disorder; Absolutism denies the will of the individual, and therefore leads to Oppression and Tyrany; and so of the other forms. But in Association, which denies none and accepts all, the liberty of the individual is conciliated with the order of the state, distinctions of rank harmonized with the guarantied rights of the masses. There is *absolute* unity of purpose and movement; hierarchical or *feudal* graduations of honor; the *guarantied* minimum and freedom of all classes; and the utmost *individuality* allowed to every person.[26]

Given this Swedenborgianized Fourierism on the ideological side, the practical motive, as related to the ideological, emerges as nothing less than the regeneration of all men in the ideal Society wherein will reign "Harmony" and "Attraction." James, unlike Fourier, concerned himself not with any specific program for this regeneration, but confined himself to composing the vision of such a state. We would like to know how it will be brought about? He never tells us *how;* he merely tells us *what* it will be. All we know is that, as he writes the score for his symphony of the ideal society, it is orchestrated with the dynamics of "celestial Swedenborg" and "gigantic, earthborn Fourier" in a happy marriage of spontaneity and order, of spiritual individuality and social equality; or, in effect, a synthesis of Transcendentalism's Moral Individualism with Swedenborg-Fourier's implicit Spiritual Socialism.

The mention of the Socialist principle of "Harmony" above, leads us to a consideration of the relation between Fourierist Harmony and Jamesian "Spontaneity." "Harmony" and "Attraction" were used by Associationists as practically synonymous, while James prefers "Spontaneity" on the whole, though the term is often found in Socialist literature of the period, while, on the other hand, the terms "Harmony" and "Attraction" are also found in James; but the latter's preference for "Spontaneity" is still a fact ("Spontaneity" will appear as a distinctive concept in William James's philosophy also). Quotations from both will demonstrate that the difference is mostly a matter of vocabulary rather than of ideological content:

> In the society to be discovered, Reason and Passion will be in perfect accord [James's "Intellect" and "Heart"]; duty and pleasure will have the same meaning; without inconvenience or calculation, man will follow his bent; hearing only of Attraction, he will never act from necessity and never curb himself by restraints; and, consequently, he will find a charm in all his functions.[27]

A little further on, Godwin combines Attraction with the concept of "Order"; just as in James we shall find the combination of "Spontaneity" with "Order":

> Now, Fourier promises to men a social system, in which Order will be produced by the free action of the passions.[28]

This is an inversion of the conventional view—at least conventional in that period—that Order must be *imposed* upon the free exercise of the passions; to hold, therefore, that "Law and Order" could and should be produced by freedom *for* man's passional nature, was rank heresy to most people, and so exposed Fourierists to the charge of "free love" —a charge quite oversimplified and wide of the mark, since Fourier conceived that there were at least twelve major passions. It is always the intellectual line-of-least-resistance to focus attack on some one item in a new philosophy which disturbs one's most habitual prepossessions. It is similar, in this instance, to the popular oversimplification of "sin" as being basically something of a sexual matter, whether referring to

Adam's "original sin" or to the "unpardonable sin" of the New Testament.

Hempel expresses the same fusion of order and spontaneity as Godwin:

> Man's freedom and happiness increase in proportion as he succeeds in realizing an *orderly* but *spontaneous* development of his passions, or his *inborn, genuine tendency to action.*[29]

James might have written that sentence word for word! The congruence of Swedenborgian and Fourierist terms is noteworthy. "Order" is a concept common to both philosophies; so is "Spontaneity" or, as Swedenborg usually calls it, "freedom." Finally, the definition of "passions" as springing from the "tendency to action," reminds one of the equivalence of "action" for the Associationists (and James) with Swedenborg's realm of "effect" and "use."

If we bear in mind the citations just given, as we now take a passage from James, the resemblance will be strikingly evident:

> A true fellowship or society then among men has an internal ground or origin, springs from their spontaneous sympathies and attractions.[30]
>
> Exactly such is the fate of all our social institutions. None of them is adequate fully to express man's spiritual unity, since the only adequate expression of that is the organization of the whole race in perfect fellowship, an organization not by human legislation, not by police, not by convention, but by God's legislation which is SCIENCE [Fourier's "Social Science"], and primarily by that method of science which has been termed *the law of the series,* and applied to the human passions.[31]
>
> It is society alone which perpetuates these brutal relations between man and man, relations of force, of obligatory courtesy, which keep us forever incredulous of any spontaneous and lasting harmony.[32]

Enthusiastic as James was, as also his friend Godwin, about "Science," these men were, however, deeper-rooted in their Calvinism than ever they became in "Science." Let Godwin speak:

> Never shall we obtain true happiness, never shall we gain true Liberty, until we shall have elevated all men to Happiness and Liberty. We are members one of another, parts of one great whole, living links in the great living organism of Humanity.

. . . Surely, those old dogmas of the Church heretofore so mysterious, relating to the *federal* headship of Adam, to the imputation of sin, to the Eucharist and communion of saints, may have a profound significance![33]

Godwin, in a non-liturgical communion, knew the "social" interpretation and the "corporate" values of the Eucharist as well as a Christian Socialist like Maurice in the Anglican Church! This view of Godwin's flowered in what might be called a Calvinist Socialism:

Let us descend into our own hearts; do we not feel that we abandon with regret the earth which science can render so beautiful? Do we not feel happy that we are bound up with its fate, connected with the fate of all men, that we must suffer with our brothers, but like them, too, be called to the enjoyment of all bliss? Are not these the very conditions on which we should have requested our life, while we should have refused it on the slightest chance of an eternal damnation?[34]

What such men as James and Godwin did was to turn Calvinism's dark side up—toward the sunlight, shall we say? Where Reformed theology was negative, they made it positive; where it was individualistic, as in the doctrine of election, they socialized and universalized it; where it was sombre, they made it joyous. But they knew their rootage and respected its tough fibre and austerity of spirit, however much they passionately revolted against it in doctrinal details.

The flowering of Calvinist thought began a century before James in the person of Jonathan Edwards. Quite aside from metaphysical theology there is a parallel in Edwards' love of nature to James's love of society. It is something to give us pause for meditation, that Edwards' glorious love of nature and James's transfiguring love of society flourished, if not *because* of, at least *out* of, a theology as sternly logical and as spiritually melancholy as Calvin's. Few modern men will ever know the despairs and the ecstacies of spirit, the sense of tragedy or the release of vision, which men such as James and Godwin experienced as they stood within-against the Calvinist philosophy of their fathers. Theirs was the Augustinian experience of the "illumination" of the soul struggling with the dour rationalism of what William James would call the "tough-minded" Calvinist theology. A passage from the senior James demonstrates the radical intensity of reaction that occurs when men wrestle in their souls with such a theology, and conquer it not by superior logic, but by hearts overflowing with profound love:

> In short, we practically affirm the literal verity of the Divine Incarnation in every form of human nature, the unlimited indwelling of the infinite Godhead in every man of woman born; so turning every man by the sheer pith of his manhood into mitred priest and crowned king, or avouching ourselves finally to our own consciousness and the world's willing recognition as a faultless human society, instinct with God's unspeakable delight and approbation.[35]

Would we be far wrong in supposing, given the intensity of their social passion, that James and Godwin really felt themselves "elected," with all the strength of sublimated Calvinist conviction, to extend "election" to the whole race of man, or "universal man," as James was fond of saying? Thus a theology generates its complement; a gospel, its other half.

*   *   *

Though later James became critical of Associationism and Socialism in general, because of his underlying and undying Calvinism, it left its mark nevertheless on his spiritual and intellectual evolution. A great ferment had entered his soul and mind, and even after the first flush had passed, one can easily identify thereafter the socialist vein in his thought like a geological stratum. The contact bore results that were deep and lasting. As Calvinism, Sandemanianism, Swedenborg, and Associationistic-Socialism boiled together in his intellectual alembic, James eventually produced that philosophy whose content in part, whose architecture in whole, were James's specific creation— that really unique blend, in the history of American thought, of Spiritual Creationism and Spiritual Socialism.

In closing this chapter it is only fair to the movement from which James received so much stimulation, to quote a passage in which James reaches a lyric level. The gospel according to philosopher James here expresses itself with the passionate spiritual hunger of a Hebrew prophet and with the poetic radiance of the Psalmist. With no benefit of Church, Clergy, or Liturgy, but with only a doctrine and a rare man behind it, Spiritual Socialism here reaches the level of poetry, prophecy, prayer:

> But the really strange thing to me is how any creature of God should wish anything else than the knowledge of His love. Thou,

O God, art my inmost life and being; I am but the shadow and semblance of thee. Shine thou through me and I shall be clear. . . . Wherefore reveal thy law . . . that spiritual law which shall be written, as thou hast said, on our very hearts and minds, or what is the same thing, in the infinite harmonies of our passional and intellectual natures![36]

This occurred at the end of a "review" of *Vanity Fair!* Truly, James was a God-enravished soul.[37]

NOTES

1. Henry James, Sr., *Moralism and Christianity*, pp. 92-93.
2. J. J. Garth Wilkinson, "Correspondences," *Aesthetic Papers* (Boston, 1849), p. 134.
3. John Humphrey Noyes, *History of American Socialisms* (Philadelphia, 1870), pp. 13-14.
4. *Ibid.*, p. 14. This book is a clear and intelligent account of the socialistic experiments in America during this remarkable decade. *Cf.* also Morris Hillquit's *History of Socialism in the U. S.* (New York, 1910).
5. *Ibid.*, p. 104.
6. Parke Godwin, *A Popular View of the Doctrines of Charles Fourier* (New York, 1844), p. 28.
7. John Humphrey Noyes, *op. cit.*, p. 107.
8. *Ibid.*, p. 212.
9. *S of S*, p. 241.
10. John Humphrey Noyes, *op. cit.*, pp. 537-539.
11. *Ibid.*, p. 540.
12. "Spiritualism Old and New," *Atlantic Monthly*, Vol. XXIX (1872), pp. 358ff. *Cf.* also "Spiritualism: Modern Diabolism," *Ibid.*, Vol. XXXII (1873), pp. 219ff. It is anticipating a bit the subsequent discussion, a few pages on, of the Associationist doctrine of "Harmony," but this seems to be the best place to mention this item. After Associationism had failed in America, "Harmony" was carried forward as a doctrine in the "Spiritualism" movement, with the result of an inversion of the doctrine. From being a social, objective, and extrovertive principle, it became individual, subjective, and introvertive, as illustrated by "Social Science" becoming "Psychic Science." Up-to-the-minute evidence of this came to my attention just recently in reading the "Church News" page of the Newark *Evening News* (New Jersey), for December 13, 1947, p. 6. The combination of Swedenborgian terms ("Spiritual," "Divine Revelation," and "Psychic") and Fourierist terms ("Harmony," "Promotion," and "Universal") is very instructive:
    "Church of Spiritual Promotion and Harmony."
    "Universal Temple of Divine Revelation."
    "Roseville Temple of Psychic Science."
    "Church of Spiritual Harmony."
    "The Little Spiritual Church."

13. Parke Godwin, *op. cit.*, p. 106.
14. Charles Julius Hempel, *The True Organization* ... (New York, 1848), p. 12.
15. *Ibid.*, p. 20.
16. *Ibid.*, p. 18.
17. *Ibid.*, p. 23.
18. *Ibid.*, p. 30.
19. *Ibid.*, p. 233.
20. *Ibid.*, p. 354.
21. *Ibid.*, pp. 354-359.
22. *Ibid.*, p. 402.
23. Albert Brisbane, *Association; or a Concise Exposition of the Practical Part of Fourier's Social Science* (New York, 1843), p. 33.
24. Charles J. Hempel, *op. cit.*, p. 76.
25. Parke Godwin, *op. cit.*, pp. 113-114.
26. *Ibid.*, p. 72.
27. Parke Godwin, *op. cit.*, p. 42.
28. *Ibid.*, p. 42.
29. Charles J. Hempel, *op. cit.*, p. 75.
30. *MC*, p. 108.
31. *Ibid.*, p. 126.
32. *Ibid.*, p. 178.
33. Parke Godwin, *op. cit.*, p. 28.
34. *Ibid.*, p. 95.
35. Joseph Blau, Editor, *American Philosophic Addresses*, 1700-1900 (New York, 1946), pp. 249-250. James's July 4, 1861, Address at Newport on "The Social Significance of Our Institutions," from which this reference is taken, is probably the most remarkable July Fourth Address ever given on this continent, in many senses of the word. It is instructive to compare it with Webster's *Bunker Hill Address* which, though not given on a July Fourth occasion, was in recognition of a patriotic event. The comparison reveals among other things, the basic difference between a mind steeped in philosophical reflection and one accustomed to a far narrower range of ideas, though using those few with a better eye for effect.
36. "Vanity Fair, or rather Becky Sharp," *Spirit of the Age*, Vol. I (1850), pp. 50-51.
37. *Cf.* the bibliography on Fourier and Socialism at end of this book.

PART TWO

James's Spiritual Philosophy

Chapter Six

The Doctrine of Spiritual Knowledge

Full however as his books are on this account of the profoundest philosophic interest, they naturally contribute almost nothing to one's scientific advantage. You need never go to them for any direct help upon existing social or scientific problems. You might as well go to a waving wheatfield to demand a loaf of bread. Just as in the latter case before getting one's loaf, one would be obliged to harvest his wheat and convert it into flour, and then convert the flour itself into dough, and afterwards allow the dough to ferment before putting it in the oven and baking his bread: so in the former case before getting the slightest scientific aid from Swedenborg, he will be obliged first of all intellectually to harvest his spiritual principles, and then gradually bring them down through the hopper of his imperious daily needs, and under the guidance of the great truth of human equality or fellowship, into social and personal applications wholly unforeseen I doubt not and perhaps undreamt of by the author himself.

—HENRY JAMES, SR.[1]

I

IF JAMES HAD presented his philosophical theology in systematic fashion as Swedenborg did in *The True Christian Religion,* we should follow that for the remainder of this study. Since he did not, we are compelled to establish some method for organizing and presenting the body of his thought in this and subsequent chapters. There is not the slightest aim or desire to impose a system as such on James; indeed, quite the opposite. In a critical exposition of a thinker whose major doctrines are so many-faceted and interlaced, and whose literary expression is apparently simple in its forthrightness, and yet tantalizingly elliptical, the scholar is driven more than ordinarily to the choice of a method of organization. The outline now to be given of the remaining chapters seemed the most natural order to the writer, from the standpoint of methodological convenience, and as a guide to clarity of exposition.

Had James desired any *one* systematic rendering of his thought, he himself would have imposed upon his works such a systematic form. Upon his expositor, therefore, falls the risk and responsibility of selecting some principle of order in the presentation of James's main doctrines, and the writer does so now in full consciousness that there is an arbitrary element involved; but he is assured that that must needs be true of any scholar of James. So long as writer and reader are together conscious of the situation, there is little danger of seriously misapprehending James at the truly vital points in his thought.

As we plunge now into the task of comprehending the chief conceptions in James's hierarchical Spiritual Philosophy, we are bidden to walk many a mental tightrope between supernaturalism and naturalism, pantheism and theism, realism and idealism, monism and pluralism, orthodoxy and heretical radicalism, positivism and pan-psychism, spirtualism and secularism, neognosticism and atheism, individualism and socialism, spontaneity and law. Reverberations of all these thought-currents are found in his philosophy because of, as we shall learn in the chapter on "The Doctrine of Spiritual Creation," James's *Trinal Monism*, which operates in Reality, in Process, and in Dialectic throughout.

II

The wise words that James penned regarding the best way to engage in a profitable study of Swedenborg, quoted on the page fronting this chapter, apply so precisely and abundantly to James himself that it would almost seem as though he must have been giving, if obliquely, a suggestion about how to get the most out of his own writings. In any event, no wiser words could be written for the purpose of indicating the most fruitful method of studying James's major doctrines. We shall try, then, to harvest his "spiritual principles" first, and then "gradually bring them down through the hopper" of our understanding.

James is obligingly explicit in giving us his theory of spiritual knowledge, and once we acquire this as a foundation, the subsequent doctrines should be somewhat easier to grasp. He exhibits his conception of the types, or, as he calls it, the "hierarchy of knowledge," in a passage found in the "Appendix" to his July Fourth Address at Newport:

> There are three realms of life in man, one exterior or physical, one interior or psychical, one inmost or spiritual; or one realm of body, one of mind or soul, and one of spirit; and each of these realms claims its proper unity or organization, the first being *sensibly* organized, the second being *scientifically* organized, the third being *philosophically* organized. Now each of these organizations or unities demands of course its own appropriate light. The sun is the light of sense. Reason is the light of science. Revelation is the light of philosophy. Each of these lights is absolute in its own sphere, and good for nothing out of it. The light of the sun is essential to my bodily health, the light of reason to my mental health, the light of Revelation to my spiritual health. But if I attempt to make one light do another's duty, I infallibly reduce my intelligence to fatuity on the one hand, or exalt it to madness on the other. For these various realms of life in man agree not directly, but by inversion; their accord is not one of continuity, but of correspondence; and if, accordingly, I use the light of one realm to illumine the objects of another one, I shall only be able to see things upside down, and hence hopelessly falsify my own understanding. Thus our senses make us acquainted with finite existence, and demand only the light of the sun, the moon, and the stars; science makes us acquainted with relative existence, and demands, therefore, a purer light than that of sense, the light of reason; but philosophy alone makes us acquainted with infinite and absolute existence, and it demands, consequently, not merely a subtler light than that of nature, but a more penetrating and less flickering one than that of reason, even the serene and steadfast ray of Revelation.[2]

There is much in that passage indeed, but we are concerned only with the central point, which is James's morphology of knowledge. The hierarchy of knowledge is three-storied: sensible, scientific, philosophical; to which the sun, reason, and Revelation are the corresponding illuminators. The former—sense, science, philosophy—may be said to constitute the subjective aspect of knowledge; the latter—sun, reason, Revelation—may be regarded as the objective factors in knowledge, or more accurately, knowledges. The subjective-objective factors in knowledge, as will be seen when James's full doctrine of knowledge is before us, are united in a "marriage."

Although James is preponderantly concerned in the entire range of his philosophy with the spiritual level—*spiritual* knowledge, *spiritual* creation, *spiritual* evil, *spiritual* incarnation, *spiritual* redemption, *spiritual* socialism—he gives, nevertheless, considerable attention to sense and reason if only to put them in their proper hierarchical niche and to exhibit them all the more strongly by contrast with the supremacy of spiritual knowledge as the climax of human knowledges. Sense, Science, and Philosophy, or as he sometimes puts it, Sense, Reason, and Revelation, are now to be considered in turn.

Of "Sense," James naturally has less to say than about Science and Philosophy; however, what he does say is important. In *Substance and Shadow,* which is technically the most philosophical of his books (with *The Secret of Swedenborg, Society the Redeemed Form of Man,* and *Christianity the Logic of Creation* coming next in this respect), there are amplified passages devoted to the realm of sense:

> Sense is perfectly competent to attest facts of simple or disunited existence, facts of body in other words: and within all this range consequently her testimony is absolute over all but metaphysicians and madmen. But the moment she attempts to suggest a fact of life or soul, which is a composite fact, a fact of relation and therefore of order, she makes herself simply ridiculous. She reveals to us sun, moon and stars existing each in visible contrast or oppugnancy to the others; but if she goes on to allege the scientific order which nevertheless binds these discordant bodies in the unity of a pervasive soul or life, she is sure to turn the truth literally and exactly upside down.[3]

Sense is thus innocently effective in its mode of acting directly upon its objects, but it is ignorant of "relation." No conceptual complications cross its naive responses. James would have us see both the strength and weakness of Sense:

> Sense takes for granted the essential finiteness of all existence. It supposes the horse to be the horse in himself, and irrespectively of his relations to other existence; the sheep the sheep, and the rose the rose, in themselves and without reference to the relation of unity they bear to the rest of Nature: it supposes that pleasure is pleasure in itself and irrespectively of pain, light light irrespectively of dark, bitter bitter irrespectively of sweet, good good irrespectively of evil, high high irrespectively of low, and

so forth: so that Natural Religion which is the child of sense by Faith, in order to conceive of Divine things has only to intensify these finite existences indefinitely.[4]

Sense and Science are often included in the same denial of their finality before the bar of philosophy's judgment:

Properly speaking, the senses are completely subterranean to the sphere of our characteristic human life . . . as distinguished from our animal affections and thoughts. And one would as soon think therefore of consulting a grubbing mole about the approaching occultation of Jupiter, as of consulting our best scientific men (purely as such) in regard to the existence of spiritual or celestial realities. Men become acquainted with these realities, as it seems to me, not through any docile hearing of the ear merely, still less through any wearisome ratiocinative balancing of probabilities, but purely in the way of an exquisitely inward or aesthetic craving, that is, in the way of a gradual expansion or education of the heart to them. And in my opinion consequently any man must be still unacquainted with them who needs the testimony of his senses to assure him of their existence. For this would imply that they were not spiritual but material realities, existing in space and time.[5]

There is, however, no great danger to spiritual philosophy from the side of sense alone. The race's extended experience in its climb out of the pit of superstition has disillusioned it of the sovereignty of sense:

In the earliest literature of the race, which is always symbolic or sacred, sense is denominated the *serpent,* because cradling as it does man's infant intelligence it takes him captive unawares, and makes him think that its own good and evil, its own true and false, its own pleasure and pain, are the measure of all Divine or spiritual reality. There is not much danger of this effect now, for owing to the race's long experience sense is pretty well unmasked, and has had its poor rampant and innocent head quite sufficiently bruised indeed under the heel of men. That is to say: the humbuggery of sense and its promises is now perfectly understood in theory, and the human race once having learned is not likely soon to unlearn the lesson, however indifferent to it any number of individuals may continue to show themselves in practice.[6]

The proper humility of Sense before Science is advised, with Jamesian flavor in the phrasing:

Science accordingly, as concerned only with the higher phenomenon of life or the relative, takes existence or the finite for granted;
using the materials which sense supplies without the least distrust
of their absoluteness. But let sense beware how she presumes
upon this good-natured attitude of science! Let her take good
heed lest she desert her own humble province, which is that of
attesting the finite exclusively, and assume on that experience to
attest the relative as well! For science in that case must instantly
pronounce her a false witness.[7]

Science is a far more insidious and subtle opponent to Philosophy
than Sense, unless it can be taught to see itself for what it is, namely,
a mediator between Sense and Philosophy. The most salient passages
on James's attitude toward Science are expressive of both his respect
for, and fear of, Science. Its first debit, spiritually and philosophically
regarded, is that it is homo-centric rather than theo-centric, and so is,
to Spiritual Philosophy, as outmoded as the Ptolemaic astronomy is
to the Copernican. It is plain that James, with Swedenborg ever in the
background of his mind, finds most modern science as unhappily pre-
Swedenborgian as Ptolemaic astronomy was pre-Copernican. Ironically
enough, says James, soon after Copernicus freed men from the geo-
centricity of an outdated astronomy, Kant came along—with still
more irony in that he had ambitions to effect a "Copernican revolution" in philosophy—and became mostly responsible for "making us
the centre of intellectual movement, and all other things circumfer-
ential to us; while the rectification which Copernicus operated in the
popular astronomy altogether consisted in placing us in the circumference of physical motion, and removing its focus to the greatest
possible distance from us."[8]
The result is:

Sense, which is individual observation, so long as it is unchecked
by science, makes the sun revolve about the earth. And science,
which is associated observation, so long as it is uncorrected by
Revelation, makes God revolve about man, the creator about the
creature, the infinite about the finite, turning Him into a mere
rewarder of our merit towards Him and a punisher of our demerit.[9]

Given this tension between Science and Philosophy—unless indeed
Science is willing to recognize the superior place of Philosophy—there
is another tension between Science and Sense, in the opposite direction.
Science progresses only by its denial of sense as conclusive in itself,
science thus treating sense as philosophy has to treat science:

Reason however antagonizes sense. It denies the essential finiteness of natural existence, by affirming its strictly rational character; inasmuch as everything that exists does so only by virtue of its implication in other things. But then, although it denies finiteness to natural things by thus endowing them with an exclusively relative character, it goes on itself to make this relative character of all existence absolute in God's sight, so affirming a purely rational or moral Deity. Reason conceives that the difference we see between horse and rose, between pebble and mountain, between high and low, light and dark, good and evil, bitter and sweet, painful and pleasant, are absolute differences, characterizing God's vision as well as our own. . . .

If science consequently had the least legitimate pretension to furnish the final evolution of the mind, or, what is the same thing, if reason should constitute the true basis of intercourse between God and man, hope would be limited in the human bosom to the lowest or most conceited persons; i.e. to such as could most easily assure themselves of their own superior merit to others; while despair would be the lot of all those whose natural modesty, or cultivated sweetness, might lead them to prefer others to themselves. A scientific religion indeed, that is to say, a religion which claims exclusively rational sanctions, is a philosophic absurdity. It may be tolerated as a criticism upon established superstition; but it will never succeed in enlisting the disinterested respect, much less the enthusiasm, of its followers; because it subjects the heart to the inspiration of the head, and makes worship a prompting of duty rather than affection; an affair of the lips and not of the life.

Science is thus . . . nothing more than an indispensable middle-term between Religion and Philosophy. . . . [10]

James did not intend to suffer any secularized version of the doctrine of "election" to arise! Science's *self-election* as man's sole reliable guide, was as odious as the arbitrary election by God of individuals for salvation or damnation in Calvinism.

Discord in the hierarchy of knowledge breaks out when Science, in its revolt from the overlordship of Sense, comes to take itself too seriously and assumes airs of finality. Still, even if Science is naive as to her larger function and unwitting of her ministerial role to Philosophy, it is nonetheless serving the cause of spiritual knowledge profoundly:

Science accordingly, as the bridge of transition from one to the other, is bound, first, to chase God out of Nature (so relating herself negatively to Religion) by, secondly, bringing Nature itself within man (so relating herself positively to Philosophy). . . . Philosophy is a demonstration of the Infinite within the finite, of the Absolute within the relative; but this demonstration will be perfect, of course, only in so far as the infinite and relative have been previously ascertained by an analysis of Nature so thorough and unsparing, as shall forever suppress all doubt upon the subject. Now science is the instrument of this analysis. . . . What science sees in nature accordingly is never God but man; that is to say, it decrees the universality of law . . . and the consequent exclusion of the infinite; thus making it incumbent upon Philosophy to give the religious instinct a higher intellectual evolution, or else leave it barren forever.[11]

Science is so close to Philosophy, even if unconsciously, that it should become conscious of this inner bond, and in effect, should be ashamed for not lining up with Philosophy as closely as possible, for at bottom Science is a moral phenomenon which means that the divorce from Sense is already a *fait accompli*. Divorced from Sense, Science should marry itself to Philosophy as its completion:

Philosophy makes the characteristic sphere of human life to be spiritual, and is manifestly therefore in no danger of yielding to sense in regarding man as primarily a subject of nature. But science ought also to be above any such temptation, inasmuch as she herself makes morality the true characteristic of human nature, so endowing man with an individuality unknown to all earth's tribes, and insuring him the unlimited dominion of nature. She thus most distinctly reverses the order which sense establishes between man and nature.[12]

It is obvious that James sees no reason for anything but profound amity between Science and Philosophy (or, in theological terms, Spiritual Religion).[13]

What happens when Science places its final faith in "laws of Nature" as the ultimate level of knowledge obtainable by man? James answers in language of robust picturesqueness:

Sea-sickness is but a type of the loathing and dejection which beset the philosophic stomach, when set adrift upon this restless heaving ocean of knowledge, with no more commanding foothold of doctrine, than is supplied by what men call "the laws of nature." These so-called laws of nature, far from inhering in nature, exert a controlling power over her, and hence can only be conceived of as reflected from some higher source, which is the mind of man. Mere men of science themselves, like Comte, are beginning to reverberate this philosophic instinct. They too declare that these so-called "laws of nature" are not any substantive forces or entities discoverable in nature, but only certain convenient harbors or anchorages which the mind itself constructs against the dreary and disgusting diffuseness of natural fact.

But in truth what we call "the laws of nature" are the mind itself in its most general or bodily form, i.e. its least individual and spiritual form. For the mind has a generic unity as well as a specific one; a common form as well as a particular one; a public evolution as well as a private one; a natural existence as well as a spiritual one: and this common or public form must be wrought out to its full measure of expansion, before the individual or private form can perfectly realize itself, or become adequately empowered for its own spiritual functions. The various sciences, each aiming in its own sphere to express or bring out the spiritual unity which underlies all natural variety, are only so many partial embodiments of this great mental corporeity of the race, which will be completely illustrated only by the great-science which litters all the special sciences, namely: the science of human society or brotherhood. Any attempt accordingly to explicate Nature by what we call "the laws of nature" is sheerly preposterous. It in fact suspends such explication upon a previous knowledge of the human mind: i.e. postpones its only accurate issue to the advent of a true philosophy of history, which alone exhibits the perfect structure of the mind. To investigate Nature by her own light consequently, or without some previous and commanding doctrine of Man connecting her with God, is like putting to sea without a compass.[14]

James would save Science from her "ontologic craze" of holding that it had discovered "laws of Nature" when it has in fact only revealed the laws of man's mind for understanding Nature, which (because Science has insufficient resources within itself), must be supplemented by the critical vision of spiritual philosophy:

But I am forgetting my purpose, which was to show a certain ontologic craze on the part of science. . . . This craze consists all simply in looking upon nature as a fixed or finite existence, thus as materially constituted, as being in short a strict phenomenon of space and time. It is all very well, mind, nay, it is a matter of stern necessity, to regard nature as materially or outwardly constituted *to our senses*. For inasmuch as nature is a purely metaphysic quantity [i.e., as James says in other connections, there is no *sensible* object identifiable as "Nature"; James hated abstractions *per se* as much as Berkeley], it is evident that she can only be reflected to our understanding through the obedient mirror of physics. . . . But this is not what science, at least in the person of her more renowned modern adepts, means. She does not hold that nature is dependent, for her intellectual recognition by us, on a certain objective or material imagery addressed primarily to our senses, and through them to our understanding. By no means. She holds that nature is actually identical with this physical imagery, and has neither conceivable being nor existence apart from the unconscious forms which to a more instructed eye simply reveal her perfections. This is why I have called this illusion a craze on the part of science. . . . These objective or material facts, which so gravel and impede the onward march of science, are nothing, as we have seen, but *ultimates* of Divine order, in the sphere of sense; just as bricks and mortar are ultimates in the same sphere of architectural order. You would not rate very high a man's genius who should pretend to deduce the architectural order of the Parthenon from the stone and lime and water which nevertheless gave it its sole material basis?[15]

Science makes no mistake if it rests content in the *constitutive* order of "seeming" instead of the *creative* order of "being"; but too often it is not thus content and is bitten with a "desire to dogmatize" beyond its proper function:

Thus where Swedenborg says that all natural existence is created by a soul of use behind it—use to other and higher things—our modern science affirms that all natural existence is constituted by some primary natural substance, say protoplasm, and that there is an end of the matter. There can be no objection of course to the scientific man's attempt to reduce if he can all organized existence to a common basis; but the objection comes when he attempts to make any formula of his on this grossly gratuitous and impertinent subject, of vital concern to philosophy. For in doing this he at once betrays his crass ignorance of what philosophy means, confounding, for example, every concept that is proper and dear to it with its exact opposite, *individuality* with identity, *life* with existence, *form* with substance, *cause* with condition, *creation* with constitution. Philosophy is perfectly indifferent to what naturally *constitutes* existence or gives it outward body, but reserves all her interest for what spiritually *creates* it, or gives it inward soul.[16]

Having maneuvered into view the heart of the argument of Philosophy with Science, James has high sport with T. H. Huxley:

"Pursue," says Professor Huxley, "the nettle and the oak, the midge and the mammoth, the infant and the adult, Shakespeare and Caliban, to their common root, and you have protoplasm for your pains. Beyond this analysis science cannot go; and any metaphysic of existence consequently which is not fast tethered to this physical substance, which is not firmly anchored in protoplasm, is an affront to the scientific understanding. . . . "
I have no doubt, on his own showing [says James], that the initial fact in all organization is protoplasm. But at the same time I avow myself unable to conceive a fact of less vital significance to philosophy. *Philosophy cheerfully takes that and every similar fact of science for granted.* The initial fact in the edifice of St. Peter's at Rome was a quantity of stone and lime. This fact was assumed by the architect as necessarily included in the *form* of his edifice, about which form alone he was concerned. The identity of his edifice, or what it possessed of common substance with all other buildings, interested him very little; only its individuality, or what it should possess of differential form from all other buildings, was what exercised his imagination. To conceive of Michael Angelo concerning himself mainly with the rude protoplasm, or mere flesh and bones, of his building, is at once to reduce him from an architect to a mason. And, in like manner, to conceive the philosopher intent upon running man's immortal destiny, or spiritual form, into the abject slime out of which his body germinates, is to reduce him from a philosopher to a noodle.[17]

James's insight into individuality as a distinguishing concept in Philosophy as contrasted with Science's "Identity," reminds one of the profound dictum of Goethe that "Nature is most careless of the individual, but Individuality is what Nature is aiming at." But Science cannot concentrate upon individuality except incidentally to its main task of noting traits-in-common among whatever objects it may investigate, with the end in view of establishing scientific "laws."

After having thus surveyed the limitations of science, James makes a rhetorical summary of the function of science as basis for philosophy:

Now science cannot go behind the senses [this is precisely what Swedenborg maintained Science does]. She is the first dry land bred of their watery and wide-weltering chaos, and her obvious *raison d'être* is to furnish a kindly fixed earth to men's feet, while they are trying to realize a worthier life for themselves than sense and science both are capable of ministering. . . . Beginning in sense and its necessities, she must always report herself to the guardian- ship of sense to have her labors identified and acknowledged. . . . Science consequently . . . is nothing more than a living *memory* of the race, organizing the facts of universal experience and observa- tion which are requisite to base its future intellectual and spiritual unity.[18]

James is now prepared to give his full-blown conception of Philos- ophy. It has been transparently clear, from his strictures on Sense and Science as confusing themselves with each other, or both with Philos- ophy, that he has supreme regard for Philosophy—and not for just any Philosophy, but "spiritual" Philosophy dependent upon Revelation as her "light." He almost attains the level of rhapsody when he descants upon the role of Philosophy:

Philosophy is this superior and reconciling form of Truth. She neither inflames finite against relative, nor relative against finite; she affirms neither religion alone nor science alone, neither sense alone nor reason alone; but sense and reason, finite and relative, religion and science, both together one and indissoluble in the unity of a new or regenerate mind of the race. Philosophy dares not with religion affirm God alone; nor with science dares she affirm man alone; she says neither infinite by itself nor finite by itself; neither absolute by itself nor relative by itself; but both alike blent in living and indistinguishable unity.[19]

Elsewhere James speaks of philosophy as "the science of belief," though he does not develop the statement, and passes on to his deeper notion of the gnosis upon which philosophic belief must rest. James is surely gnostic, not in the sense of being identified with classical Greek Gnosticism as an historical movement of thought, but in the sense of what *gnosis* came to mean as a word—"knowledge of the Divine." He puts the relation of knowledge to belief negatively in the following passage only because he has just been attacking the Kantian "blight" on philosophy:

Philosophy *a fortiori* exposes our most assured beliefs to an utter downfall; for belief rests upon knowledge as a house rests upon its foundation.[20]

James continues, in an extended section, to belabor Kant and Sir William Hamilton for their philosophic "sins," and in so doing, shows us his own view of philosophy:

> It is true that Kant devolves upon the moral instinct, as Sir William Hamilton devolves upon a blind faith, the duty from which they severally absolve Philosophy, that of conducting men to the Infinite in knowledge. But what is this but to exhibit Philosophy transferring to other hands her own appropriate office of mediating between heaven and earth, between religion and science, between truth and fact, between life and existence, while she herself urges upon us instead a lesson of abject helpless scepticism with reference to both interests?[21]

This task of Philosophy as "mediator" is central in James's thought:

> For the sole legitimate pretension of any philosophy, is, not to intensify the discord which both sense and reason, both faith and science, allege between infinite and finite, between absolute and relative; but forever to reconcile them in a unity so perfect that neither will care thenceforth to know how much belongs to the one element, or how much to the other.[22]

The heart of Philosophy in the economy of knowledge is summed up in one sentence:

> Philosophy deals only with the essence of things, that is with the spiritual realm, the realm of life—of consciousness—of creative substance in a word—where science never penetrates—to which indeed she is incapable of lifting an eye.[23]

James nowhere gives a technical philosophical term for his epistemology. The closest he ever came to using strictly philosophic terms is in a passage from *Society the Redeemed Form of Man*:

> Idealism seems in fact a gross but inevitable husk of the mind's critical advent. But its role is essentially critical: that is, it is not the least rightfully dogmatic. And nothing can be more insane, therefore, than to regard the new dogmatism as constituting the positive boon to the intellect which it ignorantly assumes to do. Our intelligence is built not upon negation but affirmation, and the current scientific idealism is at best but a transition point between the once active but always baseless and now defunct metaphysics of theology, and that philosophic naturalism or realism which is even now looming in our intellectual horizon, and ready to avouch

itself the fixed immovable earth of the mind, the adamantine rock of man's spiritual faith and hope.[24]

How we wish he had elucidated the meaning, to him, of "philosophic naturalism or realism"! It is an illustration of James's stimulating, but at the same time, tantalizing impotence to handle traditional philosophic terms with critical and historical consistency, or to attain a position that is susceptible of positive philosophical identification. We are, for example, conscious of how, to him, Nature—philosophically regarded—is ministerial to Spirit. Considered from the angle exclusively of a doctrine of Nature alone, his view of Nature seems *at times* describable as "philosophic naturalism or realism"; but it must be held in mind that nature to him, though *act*-ual in its "degree" and "kind," is not *re*-al, as compared with reality of Spirit or the even "more" ultimate reality of the Divine Esse beyond thought and discourse.

Having presented James's theory of the structure of knowledge in his own terms, the query arises: what is the most appropriate technical term for his concept of "spiritual" knowledge, as contrasted with "sensible" and with "rational" knowledge? The word "spiritual" which qualifies every major doctrine in James's thought is far from being self-explanatory, and it is our task in the next chapter to essay the range of meaning involved in that immensely significant adjective. But it would seem to the writer that exploration of the word "spiritual" would not help us so much in an epistemological context as in connection with a consideration of his ontological doctrines.

As has been said, James never gives a technical philosophical theory of knowledge. The present writer, however, offers in a tentative frame of mind, the term "Spiritual Realism." With reference now to the relation of this term to the passage from James last quoted, we can possibly say that his ultimate Spiritual Realism holds within itself a Naturalistic Realism also, but enclosed by the former. Certainly it is surprising, and difficult to account for otherwise, that he said "philosophic naturalism or realism" rather than "philosophic spiritualism or spiritual realism." His adjective "philosophic" is itself ambiguous: if we take it to mean "spiritual knowledge," as we must on James's own grounds and explicit exposition, and apply the adjective "spiritual" to the above terms used by him, we would have "spiritual naturalism," which might mean a naturalistic theory of revelation, or, in other words, a naturalistic supernaturalism. At all odds, there is much difficulty, on the showing of James himself, in placing his thought epistemologically speaking within its proper technical, philosophical designation. But to this writer's discernment, Spiritual Realism seems to be the most satisfying label. James's Spiritual Realism reminds one strongly of Berkeley's empirical idealism. The reader must have perceived the strong Berkeleyan flavor in James's epistemology of "living" knowledge. That James himself was conscious of his closeness to Berkeleyan idealism, but only in the epistemological sense, is very obvious from his note, "Berkeley and His Critics," pendant to his lecture on "The Laws of Creation" in *Lectures and Miscellanies*:

> I do not think that the Bishop's statement was calculated to obviate all misconception, but I am surprised that any candid inquirer should long fail to supply his omissions. Evidently he intended nothing more than to discriminate between being and existence, between substance and form. He wishes to show that the sensible world was simply formal, existential, or phenomenal, and that if you took away therefore that thing which determined its form, its existence, its phenomenality, you necessarily took away itself. . . . For its selfhood was not absolute, but relative, or conditioned upon a certain limited intelligence. Hence if you destroy its relation to this intelligence, you necessarily destroy itself. He did not mean of course that you would alter its sensible qualities, that you would remove it from time and space, that you would reduce it to physical nonentity. For his whole proposition was, that its sensible qualities were inseparable from it, that it could *not* conceivably transcend the limits of time and space, that its entity was under all circumstances *physical* only. It is not being, he said, but only the appearance or manifestation of being, and hence if you destroy its sensible qualities, those qualities which make it appear, which give it visibility, you destroy its very self. . . .
>
> . . . Berkeley had no intention to affirm the *sensible* non-entity of matter, but only its *supersensuous* or logical non-entity. . . . At all events, whatsoever may have been his theory of creation, he declared that matter existed *only* in forms appreciable to sense, and challenged his opponents to abstract it from these forms, and put it into logical or supersensuous ones. . . .
>
> The mind of man is so immersed in sense that he deems the sensible world the real world, and the natural life his essential life. Hence when Berkeley declared that this sensible world was a pure surface . . . and that if you abstracted the senses therefrom, it would disappear *in toto*, they supposed him to mean that it would perish *in se* or *as to those sensible properties which he all the while declared inseparable from it.* . . .

Thus you perceive that Berkeley did not mean to say, that when men sleep or die, either one or all men, the earth becomes defunct *in se,* or goes into sensible annihilation. He merely meant to say that it became incognizable to any higher intelligence. His idea was that it was a mode of existence known only to a finite intelligence, an intelligence bounded by the bodily senses, and that consequently, when you should unbind or *in-*finite that intelligence by the sleep or death of the body, it would become utterly unknown.[25]

James proceeds to say that he has no objection to accepting Berkeleyan epistemological idealism:

Thus guarded from misapprehension, it seems to me that Idealism is not to be resisted, at least my understanding fully affirms it, for Idealism does nothing but assert the purely phenomenal nature of material things. I must hold to this conclusion, because I insist upon God's essential *humanity,* and upon man consequently as His only creature.[26]

Immediately following the selection just quoted, James breaks forth with an orchestration of Berkeleyan *esse* is *percipi,* and *percipere,* which would have warmed the Bishop's heart and mind. The parallelism between Berkeley's famous "choir of heaven and furniture of earth" passage, and James's, is so remarkable that it can be enjoyed best only by quoting Berkeley and James in succession:

Some truths there are so near and obvious to the mind that a man need only open his eyes to see them. Such I take this important one to be, viz. that all the choir of heaven and furniture of the earth, in a word all those bodies which compose the mighty frame of the world, have not any subsistence without a mind; that their *being* is to be perceived or known; that consequently so long as they are not actually perceived by me, or do not exist in my mind, or that of any other created spirit, they must either have no existence at all, or else subsist in the mind of some Eternal Spirit: it being perfectly unintelligible, and involving all the absurdity of abstraction, to attribute to any single part of them an existence independent of a spirit.[27]

And now James, with characteristic Swedenborgian and Socialist accompaniment:

Whatever exists else, exists only in subordination to man, is included in his existence. Thus the entire realm of nature, or the universe of time and space, is involved in his proper subjectivity. I wish to be taken literally. I wish to be understood as saying, not only that every mineral, every vegetable, and every animal existence, but also that every star whether wandering or fixed, every sun and every system of suns, within the flaming walls of space—whatso'er the heaven of heavens embosoms, or the misconceived depths of hell—is contained in man, and draws its nutriment only from the paps of his great destiny.[28]

James does indeed come very close to Berkeley's theory of knowledge, but not to his general metaphysical Immaterialism, for James strives, however inadequate his exegesis of Swedenborg may be, to follow his master in holding to *some* reality for Nature beyond pure phenomenalism. How explain otherwise his references to "material substance," and his insistence upon God's working through spiritual causation *in* Nature, and his capitalization of the middle term in the Divine-NATURAL-Humanity?

James's theory of knowledge also resembles somewhat, in its basic principle, what Inge says of Plotinus', that is, a "real-idealism." Since Inge's description of Plotinus' theory of knowledge was colored, as was James's and Swedenborg's, by the Cambridge Platonists, it is not surprising that the following analysis by Inge of Plotinus is a good statement as a background for understanding James's epistemology:

> The organs which perceive the world under these three aspects are the bodily senses, the discursive reason (*dianoia*), and spiritual perception . . . (*noesis*). It is only when we exercise the last—the highest faculty of our nature, a power "which all possess but few use"—that we ourselves are completely real and in contact with reality. This reality is neither an independently existing external universe nor a subjective construction thrown off by the mind. It is constituted by the unity in duality of the spiritual faculty and the spiritual world which it beholds in exercising its self-consciousness. . . . If the spiritual world may be called the self-externalization of the spirit, spirit may with equal propriety be called the self-consciousness of the spiritual world. Plotinus is not an idealist in the post-Kantian sense, though he argued against Longinus that "the spiritual world is not outside spirit." . . . In saying this, he did not mean that all reality is mental, or that apparently external objects are created by the mind which perceives them; he only meant to deny one interpretation of Plato's Ideas—that which made them independently existing entities, which the mind contemplates as something other than itself. The

noeta are not outside *nous*; but they are certainly not created by *nous*. . . .

Reality is constituted by the trinity in unity of the perceiving spirit (*nous*), the spiritual world (*ta noeta*), and the spiritual perception (*noesis*) which unites subject and object in one. This correspondence and mutual dependence of subject and object holds good all down the scale.[29]

In summary, it seems that whether we call James a realist-idealist, or a spiritual realist, in his theory of knowledge, we are not as close as might be desired to his philosophical terminology, which was independent of both realism and idealism in their Platonic and Hegelian meanings. Moreover, James—whether it was his doctrine of Nature or of Knowledge—was concerned in the end only with their bearing on man's redemption, and not with their pure scientific or philosophical classification.

III

It would be most inappropriate to conclude this chapter without a consideration of James's view of the relation of philosophical knowledge, or gnosis, to "Revelation." This connection must be investigated if we are to complete our study of his theory of knowledge. It is therefore inevitable that we should inquire: what is the relation of Revelation to the hierarchy of human knowledges in James's philosophy?

James, as we have seen, considered "Revelation" to be the "light" of Philosophy, as the sun is the light of Sense, and reason the light of Science. But he didn't leave the matter with this simple declaration. He developed his concept of Revelation both negatively and positively. As to the negative side, this subdivides into two kinds: (1) An attack upon those who do not hold to the reality and validity of Revelation; and (2) A critical examination of the limits of Revelation itself.

To James, a faith in Revelation as the light of Philosophy was a logical result from his thoroughly objective habit of mind, nourished by Calvinism, Sandemanianism, and Swedenborg. Despite the vast differences between any one of these three forces in his intellectual development and the other two, they agree in at least this fundamental point: that Revelation is the highest vision and method of receiving, Truth, that lies open to men. Bred and trained to revelationism, James never deviated from it as a theoretical postulate. The question will not down, however, whether James's revelationistic postulate is, when examined with regard to his actual practice, much more than a postulate; for it is readily recognized that he rarely quotes the Bible as compared, not only to Calvin, but also to Swedenborg. The latter cites Biblical passages much more considerably, both in number and extent, than James. Moreover, Swedenborg engaged in an extended effort to work out a hermeneutics which he hoped would prove to be a final exegesis of Sacred Scripture; but in James there is no such attempt at systematic S̃criptural interpretation. From these facts, it may seem to be an accurate statement that James's clinging to "Revelation" was at bottom a philosophic conviction, nothing more and nothing less. The mere assertion of faith in revelationism seemed to be sufficient for him, in view of his failure to construct a doctrine of Revelation on the basis of Scripture like a Biblical theologian; and in view of the fact that he *never* claims to have any direct revelations in his own experience, as Swedenborg did. Nonetheless, he defended the philosophic *theory* of Revelation with typical vigor, unable as he was to desert the habit of mind established in him by his early Calvinistic training. It was the objective-social-public implications of the doctrine of Revelation that held his intellectual loyalty to the last, and it is because Transcendentalism lacked these qualities—it being subjective, individualistic, privately authenticated—that he attacked it unmercifully. This animus against the transcendental principles came out most sharply in his charges against Emerson:

> Mr. Emerson's utterances, accordingly, are never dogmatic but at most poetic. . . . They are exceptional or occasional, having no relation to the common habit of men, nor even to the individual's most objective self-forgetting states, but only to his intensely subjective moods, when he seems to himself identified with the universe, and even with its creator. Thus the law of the religious life with Mr. Emerson is not any sincere, veridical, outward Revelation, but an inward, particular intuition; not intelligence, but sentiment; not publicly authenticated truth but privately authenticated fancy; and hence he feels himself free as no mere prosaic mind can, to magnify the Rig-Veda above the four Evangelists, and to accept any of our modern coldblooded self-conscious visionaries-by-profession, as of like telescopic reach with the beatified all unconscious seer of Patmos. . . .[30]

The second kind of negative treatment of the concept of Revelation is found when James comes to examine the doctrine on its own grounds. With a startling inversion of customary thought, James defines Revelation negatively as an "obscuration," a "veiling over." He never fails in his genius to perplex!:

> Every revelation of God to man capable of winning his assent, must take place within the intelligible limits of his own nature. The validity of the revelation is rigidly contingent upon its familiar adaptation to the intelligence it would enlighten. . . .
> Revelation always implies a descent of Divine truth, a coming down on its part to a lower plane of intelligence than is primarily its due, in short a humiliation or obscuration of its legitimate splendor, in order not to harm the dim and feeble intelligence which still aspires to know it.[31]

But although Revelation involves "obscuration" when compared to the *full* light of its Divine Source, it conversely means a removal of obscuration when related to man's mind as the receptacle for receiving it. Still, though Revelation is the greatest method for unveiling Truth to men, it is not to be confused with the Truth itself:

> But revelation does not constitute truth. It only and at best bears witness to it, by revealing it,—that is, by *unveiling* it, or removing a dense obscuration which it encounters in the natural mind of men. Thus the Christian revelation finds men ignorant of the highest truth,—that of their *natural* relation to God, which dominates all their possible spiritual relations with him; and it accordingly *unveils* these true natural relations by removing the masses of erroneous tradition with which man's absurd pride and jealousy had overlaid it.[32]

With this critical examination of the negative aspects of his theory of Revelation in mind, we are in position to consider the positive side of his doctrine, for James has a powerful emphasis on Revelation as a constructive method. One of his most perceptive students has summarized what Revelation does for us according to James:

> Experience gives us self-knowledge; revelation, divine knowledge. An unrevealed God is practically no God at all to the human understanding. . . . Revelation is an inverted image of the truth; information, a direct image. If a direct knowledge of God were imparted to us it would leave the mind no chance to grow; hence revelation is symbolic, thus shielding and fostering human freedom. The religious history of the race is the veritable history of the human mind, and this history involves the doctrine of a Divine revelation.[33]

The inmost meaning of Revelation to men, therefore, is its guarantee and protection of human freedom, and he says in one connection that the "total problem of Philosophy is, to reconcile freedom with dependence; or to show how finite may be incessantly vivified by infinite, without necessary inflation to the lower interest or necessary collapse to the higher.... "[34] This is, however, a bit of typical Jamesian exaggeration, for he says, as we shall learn in the next chapter, that the "sole problem of Philosophy is creation." Yet there is no serious inconsistency in the two statements, though both are stated in the superlative degree, since the chief problem of creation by God was to combine freedom and dependence—or "necessity" as he often calls it—in the making of man.

The further development of this notion that Revelation is the basic guarantor of human freedom is found in *Christianity the Logic of Creation,* where is discovered his most extended definition of Revelation. He sharpens the contrast between information and revelation, and proceeds to state this contrast in still other terms:

If now these things be so: if we have no sensible knowledge of spiritual existence: if from the very necessity of the case, our senses give us no authentic information either as to our origin or our destiny: then clearly all our rational convictions upon the subject must be strictly contingent upon some supernatural illumination, upon what men have called REVELATION, in order to distinguish it from mere information. Revelation is commonly conceived of as if it were only information of a higher grade.... But this is an absurd use of the word. What is meant to be said in either case is, that the person in question gives us *information* of a certain character, and the character being unusual, it is supposed to be entitled on that account to the more dignified name of *revelation.* But revelation is not a mere elevated information, because, strictly speaking, it is not information at all. Information always means *imported* knowledge, knowledge which is not involved in our consciousness, but which comes up to the soul from the senses, or is derived *ab extra.* Revelation, on the contrary, means *exported* knowledge, knowledge which belongs wholly to the sphere of consciousness, or comes down to the senses from the soul, thus *ab intra....* Information is *subjective* knowledge; that is to say, it embraces whatsoever lies *below* myself, whatsoever is contained in the sphere of sense, and excluded from the consciousness. Revelation, on the other hand, is *objective* knowledge; that is to say, it embraces all that is *above* myself, whatsoever is included in the sphere of consciousness, and excluded from that of sense. . . .

It is indeed manifest from all that has gone before, that only this revealed or *mirrored* knowledge of spiritual substance is possible to us. God, or perfect Love and perfect Wisdom, is the sole and universal spiritual substance; is what alone gives being and gives form to all things; in other words, is sole Creator and Maker of the Universe. But we cannot know God intuitively, for in that case we should require to *be* God: we can only know Him experimentally, that is in so far as we become subjectively conscious of being animated by perfect Love and perfect Wisdom. . . .[35]

The last paragraph is especially interesting, for it definitely disconnects intuition from Revelation. This is entirely logical, of course, since, if our knowledge of God were *in*-tuitive it would not need to be *re*-vealed; and, as James says, if we had intuitive knowledge of God, we would *be* God, for only God can have truly *in*-ward knowledge of himself. Years later, in his last and uncompleted essay on *Spiritual Creation,* James began to use the term "intuitive" as a positive attribute of man's philosophic knowledge, as contrasted with his scientific knowledge, which is "reflective," "reverberatory," and only "probable." But his use of "intuitive" in his last essay is vague and lacks the more masterful analysis of his intellectual prime. For example, on the very next page from which the single words, quoted two sentences previously, were taken, James speaks of faith, or "conscience," as "perception." And spiritual perception is not the same as intuition; so that, his use of intuition in his later writings is not clear enough to draw any important deductions therefrom. [36]

But what, the reader may well ask, has all this to do with "freedom"? Simply this: that Science operates on the basis of information which carries with it coercion on the mind and the sense of obligation to accept factual data. This is the level of "necessity" in man's consciousness. But through Revelation, man's inmost life—James in expansive moods, uses "life," "spirit," "consciousness," "personality," and even "conscience" as practically synonymous—discovers its true meaning in relation to the Divine, and is "free" to accept and reject that meaning as he is not when dealing with facts of the physical order. This is the level of "freedom."

Alice Seechrist summarizes the two realms of freedom-necessity, as conceived by James, substantially thus:

Information . . compulsion . . necessity to act;
Revelation . . . impulsion . . . freedom to choose or reject.[37]

By the light of Revelation we acquire freedom *vis-a-vis* Nature because we can see her for just what she is, real enough to sense, but presupposing a spiritual world, both as her own ground, and as having meaning to human consciousness:

> Books pre-suppose wit in the reader, as the looking-glass pre-supposes all the beauty it reflects. JUST SO THE NATURAL WORLD, *which is the world of appearances or phenomena,* PRESUPPOSES THE SPIRITUAL WORLD, *which is that of substance or reality,* AND IS UTTERLY UNINTELLIGIBLE WITHOUT SOME LIGHT OR "REVELATION" THENCE DERIVED.[38]

Science can give us neither inner freedom from the compulsion of external facts, nor give us true insight into Nature—which are two different ways of saying the same thing, for if we cannot see the world of external nature correctly as phenomenal and limited to sense rather than as having any meta-physical validity or existence, we are indeed un-free:

> Science is conceived of, by all her professed partisans, as furnishing final and positive *body* to the mind, while theology and metaphysics supply it at best with a mere tentative organization. And as Swedenborg exactly reverses this process of mental growth, making philosophy and science both strictly ancillary to religion, merely scientific men conceive a prejudice to him. . . .
>
> I call the scientific intelligence in men *reflective,* that is, re-verberatory, because it systematically discards the witness of man's inward or living consciousness in formulating its inductions, and depends altogether upon outward or sensible observation. Thus it is not a free, but rather a servile intelligence, acknowledging in outward fact the authority that belongs only to inward and invisible truth—so leaving out what is characteristically human or individual in men, namely, freedom, and staying itself instead only upon what is organic or universal, namely, force.[39]

There is another aspect to Revelation in James's thought which is important: namely, that though revelation comes to men individually, its import and content is social and universal. The prophet and seer, of which Swedenborg is the greatest type in modern history, is "individual," but the content he receives by revelation is to become "universal." In passing, it is well to comment that James himself never claimed to be a prophet or seer, any more than he claimed to be a mystic. His role was rather that of the philosophical critic and expounder of what his own great seer-guide, Swedenborg, had bequeathed to him. On the whole he is the stimulating and independent expositor of one "greater than he."

To return to the "social" meaning in Revelation: James not only refers in innumerable passages to the social message of the Hebrew prophets, but identifies the progress or delay of Revelation in history with the parallel advance of retrogression of society itself:

> Revelation then regarded as a full and impartial voucher of the divine name, is restricted to the same negative law of growth or evolution which society itself obeys, since it is identical with the very personality of society.[40]

Doubtless the most appropriate conclusion to this section on Revelation is James's view of the practical side of this doctrine. If he was concerned to elucidate Revelation theoretically, he was equally concerned for its practical application. James was very much the "spiritual" pragmatist. We recall the passage previously quoted in which he asserted that we know God "experimentally" rather than "intuitively." This is James's spiritual empiricism, and it shows distinctly enough in the "Appendix" to his Newport Address:

> Certainly no one knows better than I do that this reputed light of Revelation is professedly very much honored throughout Christendom. But it is only the comparatively worthless body we honor, not its Divine and life-giving spirit. For practically how stands the case? What practical use do we apply Revelation to? ... Revelation was given to us for use, not for show; and its use plainly is, to give light where no other light is practicable, namely, in relation to the principles of the Divine Administration in human affairs, or the meaning of Providence in history. ... Surely no light is designed to attract attention to itself, but only to dissipate surrounding darkness. . . . For what would we think of a man who, after lighting his lamp in the evening, should continue steadfastly gazing into its flame, instead of diligently availing himself of its light to go about his business?[41]

Of the *content* of Revelation there has been no mention in this section, but only an exposition of James's *rationale* of Revelation. The content is bound up with those great spiritual truths of Spiritual Creation, Spiritual Redemption, and the Divine-Natural Humanity; but of these high themes, there will be subsequent consideration.

NOTES

1. *Substance and Shadow*, p. 105.
2. *SSI*, pp. 43-44. *SSI*, in Blau's *Philosophic Addresses* does not contain the Appendix Notes. These were given to me in photostat by Professor Blau, and they follow the paging of the original book by James.
3. *S and S*, p. 363.
4. *Ibid.*, p. 450.
5. *SRFM*, pp. 352-353.
6. *Ibid.*, p. 360.
7. *S and S*, pp. 362-363.
8. *Ibid.*, p. 286.
9. *Ibid.*, p. 119.
10. *Ibid.*, pp. 451-452.
11. *Ibid.*, pp. 453-454.
12. *Ibid.*, p. 355.
13. Benjamin Peirce, renowned professor of mathematics at Harvard and father of the great philosopher, Charles Sanders Peirce, and a contemporary of James, would agree with James in general on this point, as in the following:

    "Science and religion are born of the same house, and that house is not divided against itself. There will be at times an apparent conflict between them arising from defects of human nature; but all this confusion is of human origin, and it originates in the deficiency of our knowledge, not in the greatness of it." ("The Conflict between Science and Religion," *Unitarian Review*, Vol. VII (1877), p. 656.)

    Peirce goes on to say that when the writer of *Genesis* spoke of God's creating the "firmament," his conception of "firmament" was only the "science" of the time; hence, on Peirce's view, modern science's quarrel is not with the religion of *Genesis* so much as with the poor science!
14. *S and S*, pp. 525-526.
15. *SRFM*, pp. 237-238.
16. *Ibid.*, pp. 241-242.
17. *Ibid.*, pp. 242-244.
18. *Ibid.*, pp. 358-359.
19. *S and S*, p. 334.
20. *Ibid.*, p. 98.
21. *Ibid.*, pp. 98-99.
22. *Ibid.*, p. 261.
23. *Ibid.*, p. 305.
24. *SRFM*, p. 246.
25. *LM*, pp. 333-337.
26. *Ibid.*, p. 339.
27. George Berkeley, *The Principles of Human Knowledge*, Part I, #6.
28. *LM*, p. 339.
29. W. R. Inge, Article, "Neo-Platonism," Hastings' *Encyclopaedia of Religion and Ethics*, Vol. IX, pp. 310-311.
30. *The Radical*, Vol. II (1867), pp. 87-88.

31. *S and S,* pp. 159, 160. James's view of Revelation as a "descent of Divine truth ... a humiliation or obscuration," is Swedenborg's doctrine of the "accommodation" of truth to the "human receptacle."
32. *LR.,* p. 399.
33. Julia Kellogg, *The Philosophy of Henry James,* pp. 17-18.
34. *S and S,* pp. 102-103.
35. *CLC,* pp. 29-31.
36. *LR,* pp. 330-331.
37. Alice S. Seechrist, "Henry James the Elder," *The New-Church Messenger,* Vol. CXXXIX (Sept. 3, 1930), pp. 203-206.
38. *CLC,* p. 26.
39. *LR,* pp. 329-330.
40. *S of S,* p. 74.
41. *SSI,* p. 45.

Chapter Seven

The Doctrine of Spiritual Creation

The sole problem of Philosophy is creation: is to ascertain how the infinite creator imparts finite form to the creature; a form which shall be the creature's own and separate him to all eternity from the creator.

—HENRY JAMES, SR.[1]

Mr. James looks at creation instinctively from the creative side, and this of itself has a tendency to put him at a remove from his readers. The usual problem is: Given the creation, to find the Creator; to Mr. James it is: Given the Creator, to find the creation. God is; of His being there is no doubt, but who and what are we?

—JULIA A. KELLOGG[2]

And first, we are struck, in reading the book [Substance and Shadow], *with its foreign, antique, Oriental, or inverted style of thought. It seems not to have been written in New England, but in Egypt or Persia,—not in the nineteenth century after Christ, but the nineteenth century before him,—not by one inheriting the training of American Orthodoxy, but by one fed on the vast abstractions of the Valentinian Gnostics, reinforced by the Antinomianism of Marcion. He everywhere moots theosophic questions, not psychological ones,—thus ignoring his own century and its tendencies, and taking up the problems of the early East. The great question with us is the "origin of evil"; the vast difficulty with the Gnostics was the existence of the universe. How can God, being infinite and absolute, create a finite world? The solution to this, they deemed, would also carry with it a solution of the existence of evil.*

—JAMES FREEMAN CLARKE[3]

I

THAT THE DOCTRINE of Spiritual Creation is James's central doctrine is not, as he uses the term, difficult to maintain; it would indeed be preposterous to contend otherwise, for he stretches the term "Creation," on numerous occasions, to include the doctrine of "Redemption" as well. Creation and Redemption are distinguishable functionally, but basically they add up to *perpetual creation* for James. It is instructive to note the frequency of the creation *Leitmotiv* in the entire range of his thought. If one were to enumerate the book titles, plus the chapter and page headings in James's works, which involve a statement in one form or another of this overmastering concept of Creation, the list would easily reach well over a hundred titles! The mere knowledge of this frequency is evidence enough to us of James's lifelong preoccupation with an attempt to construct a satisfying Doctrine of Creation.

Certainly not in the history of philosophic speculation on the American continent, has any one significant thinker devoted so much intense and persistent reflection to the concept of creation. James saw and thought of everything in existence *sub specie creationis*.

II

With the preliminary study of Swedenborg in Chapter IV as our intellectually established headquarters, so to speak, it is now possible for us to explore James's Doctrine of Spiritual Creation with increased comprehension. On the metaphysical side, we understand "Spirit" as the *causal* aspect of reality and process, operating, in the Swedenborgian triads, from the Spiritual World upon the Natural World, as cause *between* End and Effect; or, as Wisdom *between* Love and Use. If stated psychologically from man's side, "Spirit" is the Understanding operating *between* Will and Action.

Our understanding of spirit as causality receives confirmation of its correctness by James's efforts to convert "cause" as a merely scientific concept, into a thoroughly philosophical and theological category. This attempt to transform "cause" as commonly used and understood in science, to a concept in line with its loftier meanings in a spiritual philosophy, will became steadily more apparent as the reader follows the selections from James. Before coming to the constructive aspect of his creation doctrine, James begins negatively by attacking the doctrine of creation *ex-nihilo*:

Orthodoxy alleges that God makes all things out of nothing, out of absolutely no material whatever; so that if they turn out ill, the responsibility of their aberration in no way attaches to themselves: for by the hypothesis they have no selfhood or character but what God imposes upon them, being summoned into instant consciousness by the creative fiat: and so attaches wholly to their maker. . . .

Natural religion conceives that there was originally a space *where,* and a time *when,* creation was not. It conceives accordingly that these two great idle wildernesses of time and space were inhabited by a mute inactive Deity alone; and that this extraordinary Deity, tired at last of slumbering in eternal sloth, sent forth a great creative shout, or succession of shouts, which made the existing cosmos suddenly appear as if it had always been.[4]

James continues his attack on creation *ex nihilo*:

Nothing [*i.e.,* no-thing] does not and cannot exist. There never was a time when things were not, nor a space where they were not; because things exist only to a rationally and sensibly finited intelligence: time and space being the mere universals of such an intelligence, its constitutional implication and attestation. It is thus supremely childish to cogitate creation as an incident of time and space, however brief or however protracted. If you allow it only this force you reduce it at once to actual nullity or leave it only an ideal truth, by making it a mere phenomenon of the human mind. Space and time are really mental substances, having no other function than to compel all the objects of Nature and all the events of History into the compass of the human form. In this state of things it is of course preposterous to imagine a space where and a time when creation did not exist, but was summarily mechanized into being. . . . Not scepticism indeed, but the frankest possible denial, is properly incumbent upon every candid mind, with respect to these mere *enfantillages* of cosmological inquiry. . . .

Nothing does not exist, since all existence is made up of persons and things; and to say that God gives being to what does not even to its own apprehension exist, or possess at the very least a fallacious consciousness, is to leave no ground of discrimination between creature and creator, and to end by organizing a nauseous Pantheism. Nothing means on its face as in its bosom no-thing, non-existence. It means what neither is nor appears to be, what has neither being nor the semblance of being, neither substance nor form, neither real nor conscious existence. All finite existence is of two kinds, personal and real, moral and physical. Whatsoever transcends both of these categories is spiritual and infinite; whatsoever falls below them is not to be conceived, does not exist, is no thing even.[5]

Before diving straight into his concept of spiritual causation as over against creation *ex nihilo,* James makes oblique approaches to it through a treatment of subsidiary concepts: that is *via* "constitution," and "existence." Of "constitution" he says:

> The common sense of mankind affirms with no misgiving, that every thing we see is created by God. . . . No doubt the common sense of the race begets very crude very superstitious very unworthy conceptions of this great theme, and as a general thing degrades the creative process from a purely spiritual to a purely physical and even mechanical one. For this reason the philosopher has been from time immemorial very shy of the vulgar conclusions upon the subject: but Philosophy herself has never demanded that these conclusions should be ignored, but only that the popular conceptions should be chastened and elevated. Least of all has she ever been willing to sink the idea of spiritual creation in the purely scientific and preparatory notion of material constitution. She equally disavows the ancient philosopher who sought to run creation into a scheme of physical order; and the modern philosopher who seeks to run it into one of logical order; because they both alike deny creation in any intelligible sense of the word, and so vacate Philosophy as a substantive vocation by attempting both alike to account for existing things on scientific principles, or without the allegation of spiritual substance.[6]

From this it is evident that, to James, Nature ("the physical order") is *constitutive;* Reason ("the logical order") is *regulative;* while Spirit (the "active, *form*-ative, causative order") is *creative.*

The constitutive order which Nature presents is otherwise designated as the "principle of identity" by James, whereas the creative order exemplifies the "principle of individuality":

> The least attention to the foregoing criticism will show, that Kant's philosophic weakness lay in his habitually confounding that which constitutes a thing or gives it identity, with that which creates it or gives it individuality. He invariably confounded the subjective constitution of existence, or what gives it phenomenal consciousness, with its objective reality, or what gives it spiritual and unconscious being. . . . Nature finites or fixes me, that is,

gives me bodily identity or consciousness. God alone in-finites or unfixes me, by giving me spiritual individuality or unconscious being. In a word: whatsoever falls within the realm of consciousness, or is embraced within the sphere of our subjectivity, possesses a merely con-stitutional force, and denies itself any creative significance.[7]

He presents an even more graphic exhibition of the difference between "constitution" and "creation" in what might well be termed a philosophic parable:

> Every coat of course logically pre-dicates a tailor and a piece of cloth, but you convey a very inadequate notion of the actual garment by enumerating these purely constitutional elements of it. I utterly refuse to conceive the coat upon such niggardly terms. I am free to admit that the tailor and the cloth are necessary *data* of the coat, are logically implied in its constitution: but this sort of knowledge is purely scientific as interesting only the tailor and manufacturer, and not philosophic as interesting all mankind. . . . The coat itself or spiritually, *i.e.* in the use or power it exerts, is something very different and superior to the material elements which go to constitute it: it indeed involves (or presupposes) these elements, and can therefore never be involved in them. The coat when truly conceived, when conceived as a finished garment, causes both the tailor and the piece of cloth to disappear in the bosom of its own unity or individuality, whence they never reappear till the coat itself disappears or falls to pieces. . . . But obviously the coat is not merely a visible existence, it possesses also an invisible or spiritual BEING in that distinctive use or power which it exerts over other existence, and which accordingly constitutes its true individuality. . . .[8]

In his article on "Swedenborg and James," Kimball has caught this meaning in James's parables for illustrating his theory of creation, and restates it in his own language:

> . . . A true conception and discussion of the great problems of God's true creation have no direct reference to crude physical constitution, any more than the art-conception of the artist has reference to, or involves the constitution of the quarry whence his material is derived.[9]

It is Science, observes James, that asks: "What *constitutes* a thing as being precisely what it is?" But Philosophy has another and a different task:

Philosophy has nothing whatever to do with the constitution of things or their production to sight, that is, with the material realm, the realm of organization or body; and it is science alone accordingly which teaches the chemist that a neutral salt is the product of an acid and an alkali. . . . Philosophy deals only with the essence of things, that is with the spiritual realm, the realm of life—of consciousness—of creative substance in a word—where science never penetrates, to which indeed she is incapable of lifting an eye.[10]

There is another concept which philosophers play with, says James, to avoid facing up to constructing a doctrine of creation: that is, the concept of "existence." But "existence" is an ineffectual dodge of the real problem, for it is every way an inferior concept to that of creation:

Existence is presupposed in life, the finite is presupposed in the relative, just as sense is presupposed in consciousness: and for that very reason there can be no direct but only an inverse accord between them, precisely like that which exists between a house and its foundation, or between substance and shadow.[11]

Kant, James holds, inverts the true relation:

Precisely this however is Kant's mistake. He makes life evolve existence not involve it; the child evolve its parents instead of involve them; and by a necessary fatality turns consciousness from a purely spiritual force to a material one, so converting infinite into finite, personality into mere reality, or man into a thing. Never was a grosser violence done to Philosophy. The finite is one with itself or identical: how is it possible to allege therefore within its proper limits the logical contradiction of subject and object, of the me and the not-me? The finite is the exclusive realm of the me, *i.e.* of subjectivity; the infinite of the not-me, *i.e.* of objectivity. Every thing in nature says me with equal pertinency though with unequal emphasis. The mineral says it by its gravitation or *vis inertiae;* the vegetable by its sensibility; the animal by its volition; man by his spontaneity. . . . But these are all merely various grades of the Finite, not with reference to the infinite, but within itself; for the greatest conceivable intensity of the finite constitutes, not the greatest nearness to, but the greatest remoteness from, the Infinite.[12]

This alleged Kantian confusion of infinite with finite, of essence with existence, led him, in James's opinion, to the most egregious blunder of all—that is, the postulation of "things-in-themselves" or noumena, which is the same thing as saying, "existence, or existents, in-themselves." This notion, obviously, is irredeemably repugnant to James. The doctrine of "things-in-themselves" cuts directly across the absolutizing of experience, but it also conflicts with a doctrine of *spiritual* creation. James indulges a lusty rhetoric in an all-out attack on "noumena":

> Of course Kant is inhibited by the nature of the case from dogmatizing on the subject of *noumena*. He does not even pretend to affirm that they so much as exist even. He only insists that the phenomenal quality of existence affords no guarantee of its essential quality, and forbids you to infer the substance of things from their form: but as to whether or not any such essence or substance of things anywhere actually exists, he will not allow himself even an opinion. He is like a man who disputes the title-deeds of an estate in the interest not only of an unknown but of an essentially unknowable and possibly altogether imaginary tenant, and without being too sure indeed that the estate itself exists *in rerum natura*: all he is sure of being, that if the estate itself be not an imaginary quantity, and if there be any legitimate title to it such title cannot by any possibility vest in the apparent incumbent.
>
> Don Quixote was but the faintest type of this "metaphysic wit"; for the Dulcinea he served, though she was not the lofty lady his chivalrous imagination painted her, was as yet a veritable flesh and blood damsel, known and loved of all the fragrant kine at least whose distended udders used to yield up their grateful morning and evening sacrifice to her tender priestly manipulation. But this noumenal divinity for whom Kant pants, and in whose honor he lays his logical lance in rest, is destitute of any substance whatever, even a lying substance. She is not only not a decent milkmaid, she is the most trumpery verbal abstraction ever palmed by logical impudence upon human patience, representing no valid existence nor yet the ghost of such an existence, her gaunt insensate bowels yearning with no maternal tenderness; her fleshless breasts having never heaved with one throb of wifely affection or maiden modesty.[13]

After venting himself rhetorically with very questionable justice to Kant, James settles down to a more philosophical presentation of the same theme:

> What Kant and Sir William Hamilton call "real" things, "noumenal" things, or "things-in-themselves," are in truth things which

involve their own substance, those which are self-existent or infinite and hence uncreated. It would be sheerly idle then to predicate creatureship of "real" or "noumenal" things, because in the first place we can never know whether or not they so much as exist; and in the second place if they do exist they will be sure to exclude creation: since created things never involve their own substance or selfhood, but on the contrary evolve it by diligently acknowledging what is not themselves. . . .

Has the phenomenon any surer title to creation than the noumenon? If we abandon "real" existence to Kant as uncreated, shall we not, a fortiori indeed, be obliged to abandon phenomenal existence to the same ruthless negation? Unquestionably. . . .

Or to express the result more succinctly. "Real" things, considered as involving their own substance, do not exist, being prevented doing so by their very reality. And phenomenal things, being by this definition unreal, are only the more forcibly forbidden to exist by their own unreality. For if we cannot admit "real" things to exist, it would be highly indecorous to admit "unreal" ones to that distinction; unless indeed we wish to prove creation itself a sham. In either case alike then we get rid of existence, and hence of creation, as an "imbecility" of the uncultivated understanding; and become qualified at last with Sir William Hamilton to turn Philosophy herself as the voucher of creation, into a snivelling idiot whining over "doubt as the beginning and end of knowledge."[14]

James turns next to examine the concept of "Cause":

The question of cause rightly regarded opens up to the philosophic mind the largest realm of knowledge, the spiritual realm, the realm of soul, of use, of power; and utterly disdains the merely material realm, the realm of body, inertia, of death.[15]

Thus, "Cause" is the bridge-concept, in a manner of speaking, between Philosophy and Spiritual Truth, thrown across the stream of thought from Philosophy's side of the river. But it must not be supposed that speculations on "Cause" can any way displace or equal the validity of Revelation as the light of Philosophy; the concept of Cause is simply the best that human thought, unaided by Revelation, can do. Granting it to be the highest concept native to Philosophy per se, it must be borne in mind that "cause" is, as he tells us on the very next page to that from which the last excerpt was taken, "strictly ancillary to that of creation." Inevitably, James sees most of modern philosophy as misconceiving and mishandling the true meaning of causation. In his attacks upon philosophers' theories of causality, James distinctly shows what, to him, cause is *not*. Sir William Hamilton is the butt of these remarks:

> Who but a philosopher-beside-himself would ever dream of asking the cause of a mere fact of existence? Suppose Sir William Hamilton going into a chemist's shop in Edinburgh and demanding with a grave face "the cause of saltpetre." Would not the chemist reply at once, with a smile at the simplicity of his questioner, "that the cause of saltpetre as a fact of existence was doubtless one with the cause of all other facts of existence, and that he, as a chemist, would be sorry to obtrude so far upon the domain of Philosophy as to attempt teaching the philosopher himself how Divine that cause was: but that if, as was probable, by the cause of saltpetre he meant not its cause philosophically speaking, he should be happy to inform him that it was nitric acid 54 and potash 47.2. . . .
>
> When for example you announce the constitutional formula of saltpetre as nitric acid 54 and potash 47.2, you simply mean to say that if you fulfill this prescribed conjuration the salt itself will appear: *i.e.* these servile constitutional elements will disappear in their own creative substance, will become glorified into a higher form of life, into a superior personality, than they themselves have any intrinsic title to. Plainly then the acid and the alkali do not create the salt: at most they phenomenally constitute it . . . the acid giving it paternity or soul, the alkali giving it maternity or body. It is the salt on the contrary which creates them by exacting them as the invariable purchase of its own phenomenality.[16]

The significant differentia between "cause" and "creation" are noted by James:

> The conception of cause obviously differs from that of creation in this respect, that the former always presupposes existence, while the latter is always presupposed by it. Cause is a demand which is made by my intelligence in order to explain an otherwise inexplicable change which has come over the face of existence. . . . But creation is demanded by existence itself: not by existence regarded as a changeable phenomenon, but as an orderly permanent quantity. . . . No new fact of existence attracts my attention, but only some change which has come over the face of the old facts. . . . Causation is thus a direct confession of Nature's insufficiency to herself, a direct disclaimer of her power to originate any of her own phenomena: and hence it involves an indirect attestation to the spiritual substance from which all natural existence flows.[17]

In view of the divergence in meaning between causation and creation, and yet at the same time the value of causality to serve as a hand-maiden to the greater concept of creation, it is true that:

Philosophy alone is competent to say where and what cause is: to fill the conception out with its eternal substance. . . . The scientific recognition of cause has always been of this purely educative efficacy, as gradually leading the mind forth from the thraldom of nature, from the iron bondage of Fact, into the enlargement and freedom which flow from the presence of rational supersensual Truth. It has never been anything but the fruitful seminary or matrix of a superior philosophic idea, which is that of creation.[18]

That causality is not found within phenomenal existence as such, but by implication, is the reason why James speaks of causality as only the threshold to "creation"; it is the John the Baptist going before the true philosophic Messiah—that is to say, the Doctrine of Spiritual Creation.

In analyzing "constitution," "existence," "noumena," and "cause," James has been leading us with diminishing obliqueness to the very idea of creation itself as he conceives it. In *Christianity the Logic of Creation,* he gives probably his clearest presentation of what he means by "to create" and by "creation." This passage takes us right to the heart of his thought:

Let us then boldly reverse our point of view. Let us cease to regard creation as an historical incident, as an event in time and space, by learning to regard history itself, or all the events of time and space, as mere incidents of creation. . . .

Let me beg of you then distinctly to rememeber that I use the word *create* with strict scientific accuracy, as always meaning *giving being.* To create a thing means to give it inward or substantial being; he who creates a thing *himself constitutes the substance* of that thing. . . . Creating or giving being is an exactly inverse process to that of making or giving form. When I say God creates me, I suppose myself already formed or existing; I take my existence for granted, or as inseparably implied in my proposition. Existence is an absolute and indisputable fact, and unless we had this preliminary basis of sensible experience, we should be utterly void of supersensuous experience of every sort, whether belief, or hope, or aspiration. Accordingly, in alleging my creation by God I do not refer to any mere fact of existence, to any sensible operation of God, but wholly to a spiritual and invisible operation; one which utterly transcends the realm of time and space, because it falls altogether within that of affection and thought [James often uses the last two nouns as synonyms for the Swedenborgian "Love" and "Wisdom" respectively]. In other words, in alleging my creation, I do not project myself back in imagination to some period more or less remote, when an exertion of voluntary energy on God's part resulted in my physical genesis or formation—resulted in giving me existence. Far from it. I take my physical formation or existence *pro confesso,* as an indispensable platform of the creation which I allege. For I say that God creates *me,* and obviously by *me* I mean my human form . . . my conscious personality. It would be absurd of course to allege any abstract creative energy on God's part, to say for example that He creates what has no existence, or what is unconscious and invisible: because, as we have already seen, that would only be saying in a roundabout way that He creates nothing, or that He is no creator. We can never conceive of creation except as proceeding on the basis of some existing selfhood, as involving some subsidiary sphere of formation, as predicable in short of certain conscious or visible existences.[19]

That entire passage is worth many readings and re-readings, for it contains the very core of what James specifically means by "creation." Negatively, creation of James does not mean life, matter, or our physical natures; for these, following Swedenborg, he asserted to be un-creatables. They are merely imparted or "communicated" to the postulated, already-given "existence" of the creature. Positively, creation to him means the giving of consciousness to the creature in a process to be described in the chapter on Spiritual Man.

The distinction between "formation" and "creation" in James's thought is very important: the former applying to a "sensible operation" by God in preparing us, from the given materials of physical selfhood, to be proper receptacles for the reception of our spiritual creation which consists in God's giving us "inner being" through sharing with us His Divine Love and Wisdom. This wholly spiritual operation is executed by God strictly within the sphere of "affection and thought" which are the human analogues, in Swedenborgian terms, to the Divine Love and Wisdom. In general we see James's hierarchical conception of reality, Celestial-Spiritual-Natural, at work here: "formation" occurs wholly on the level of the natural world and is a mere preparation for creation; while "creation" occurs wholly on the level of the spiritual world, though directed *upon* and *into* the natural world. Since man is in part a citizen of both worlds, it requires the two processes, Formation and Creation to account for his total natural-spiritual being.

Although spiritual creation, as applied to man, means the reception of Life-Love-Wisdom-Consciousness-Personality from God, James does not mean to imply for a moment that God creates "life" itself, because God Is Life; therefore, He rather communicates or imparts it to man through Divine Love, since it is the essence of true love to ever seek an object other than itself to love. This "communication" *by* God is "creation" *to* man.

James enlarges his creationist philosophy in relation to three propositions in Swedenborg, which James puts in his own phrasing:

1. God's perfection is such that He cannot create life, but only communicate it;

2. It is of prime necessity therefore that a suitable form exist prepared to receive such communication;

3. This form, thus necessary to enracinate creation or separate between creator and creature, must be itself natural.[20]

Of the first proposition—the uncreatability of, but the communicability of, Life—we have already spoken above; communication of life to a crea-*ture* is indeed crea-*tion*. In comment on this proposition, James remarks:

To create means to give being or communicate life to what assuredly is not oneself; and if this be so the creator is bound in order to impart His own being or communicate Himself to the creature, above all things else to posit the creature, or afford him some adequate and veracious ground of self-consciousness. Thus selfhood, which is one's ability to feel one's life as one's own and not as another's in him, is the inexpugnable necessity of creation. . . . The creature must be absolutely and unchangeably himself, must possess identity, or real and conscious distinction from his creator: otherwise creation in any honest sense of that word must confess itself an unqualified sham, and tumble off into the bottomless abyss of Pantheism.[21]

In explication of Proposition 2, James restates the distinction between Formation and Creation:

By the sheer necessity of the case, then creation involves in order to its own functioning a distinctively formative sphere of experience on the part of the creature, by means of which the creature who is Divinely vivified, may come to self-consciousness, to the formal recognition of himself as so vivified. Let us rather say that the creative *nisus* totally emerges in this preliminary process of formation, so that God actually creates or gives being to things only in so far as He first gives them subjective form.[22]

Why should the created form be of necessity natural? Why must it needs involve the relation between a common nature and an individual subject of that nature? Why might it not be a purely spiritual form, *i.e.* retain the individual element and exclude the communistic one? I shall try to make my answer full and clear. . . .

Spiritually viewed creation means the eternal conjunction of creator and creature; but what sort of conjunction would this be, if the creature were without any identity, forever discriminating him to his own perception from the creator? Evidently no conjunction at all, and consequently no creation. The whole stress accordingly of the creative Providence is exerted to secure a permanent and ample base for creation, in endowing the creature with selfhood or subjective constitution. . . .

For it is obvious at a glance that if life were conferred upon the creature immediately by God; if it were conveyed to him by some direct exhibition of the Divine power, and without any constitutional reaction on his part; it would be nothing short of an imposition. And the creature in that case would be so far from any capacity to appropriate it, or feel it to be his own, that he would not be able even to perceive it. He would be less in sympathy with it spiritually than the stone is in sympathy with the genius of Shakespeare.[23]

The spiritual end of creation as meaning "the eternal conjunction of creator and creature" is, as we shall soon learn, an almost exact duplication of Swedenborg's thought, almost to the self-same wording.

Once the "preliminary process of formation" and the subsequent "spiritual creation" have occurred, are there any moments of respite in, or from, the Divine activity? No: the word "occurred" is not even quite accurate, much less "respite"; for "occurred" is too suggestive of an event happened once and for all, and creative Divine activity is an eternal process; and as for "respite" from such activity within Divinity itself, or from the creative process on the part of man, there is none such. James's God is, as he says, not a "holiday" God in the least, but rather a "working" God. But what will existing religion say to James's view? He has no optimistic illusions:

What will our existing religion and science say to these things? Neither of them is likely to admit with any too-ready complacency, that neither our finite nor our rational parts, neither our bodies nor our souls, neither our substantial identity with, nor our formal diversity from, all other existence, has the least basis outside of consciousness. Yet the truth is philosophically indisputable. Body and mind are both alike an unceasing spiritual communication—a perpetual living operation or miraculous creation—of God in our nature.[24]

As for redemption, *sub specie creationis*:

> Thus our spiritual creation is only the truer or philosophic name for our distinctively NATURAL REDEMPTION: since nothing short of this redemptive work can establish the Divine claim to be a universal creator.[25]

The word "universal" provides a connecting link between James's concept of redemption as "our Spiritual Creation" and his conception of *Society the Redeemed Form of Man,* which was the title of his last full-length book. In other words, redemption as "the Divine claim to be a universal creator," and the social, "associated" destiny of man are simply two ways of stating the same proposition; as seen in the former, it is stated from God's side, and as seen in the latter, it is stated from man's side.

This doctrine of "perpetual creation" reminds one of Mâlebranche's doctrine of God as the only real and constant causation of all that is; but although Divine creation, in theory, is, to Mâlebranche, perpetual in the sense of an unending series of successive acts of creation, it is *not as strictly perpetual* as James's "Body and mind are both alike an unceasing spiritual communication—a perpetual living operation or miraculous creation—of God in our nature." This observation would hold also as between James and other thinkers who, with Mâlebranche, held the "successive-acts-of-creation" view, such as St. Augustine, St. Bonaventure, and Descartes.

In the chapter on "Swedenborg and James," it was indicated that the Neo-Platonic metaphysics which was later superposed by Swedenborg upon his Aristotelianism, would be considered in connection with James's Doctrine of Spiritual Creation; it is therefore necessary for us to treat of this important matter now, as it is impossible to realize a full understanding of James without such an inquiry. In Neo-Platonic thinkers like Plotinus and Erigena, a great dual movement is hypothecated, in the first of which there is a series of emanations from God outward and downward into all the given Universe, and in the second half of which there is a return movement of "ascent" back toward God. In Lovejoy's *The Great Chain of Being,* the dual aspects of this one great movement are identified by the terms "descendentalist" and "ascendentalist" respectively. The most recent philosophy which evinces a strong suggestion of this Neo-Platonic pattern is to be found in Whitehead's doctrine of the "primordial" and the "consequent" natures of God. A single instance from Swedenborg, out of ever so many possible quotations, is sufficient to see how much this Neo-Platonic framework is present to his thought. In the concept of influx from the Celestial to the Spiritual to the Natural World, we have the "downward" movement; in the "ascent" from the world of "outmosts," or Nature (sometimes referred to as "lastmosts" or as "effects") through "man to God," we have the "upward" movement:

> The universal end, that is, the end of all things of creation, is that there may be an eternal conjunction of the Creator with the created universe; and this is not possible unless there are subjects wherein His Divine can be as in Itself, thus in which it can dwell and abide. In order that these subjects may be dwelling-places and mansions of Him, they must be recipients of His love and wisdom as of themselves; such, therefore, as will elevate themselves to the Creator as of themselves, and conjoin themselves with Him. Without this ability to reciprocate no conjunction is possible. These subjects are men, who are able as of themselves to elevate and conjoin themselves. That men are such subjects, and that they are recipients of the Divine as of themselves, has been pointed out many times. By means of this conjunction, the Lord is present in every work created by Him; for everything has been created for man as its end; consequently the uses of all created things ascend by degrees from outmosts to man, and through man to God the Creator. . . .[26]

One of our modern American theologians, in an address commemorative of the two hundred and fiftieth anniversary of the birth of Swedenborg, speaks of the resemblance of Swedenborg's—and so, James's—philosophy, as having the "closest" analogy to that of Neo-Platonism, a conclusion which the writer, after reading the *Divine Love and Wisdom,* had arrived at independently before seeing Horton's paper:

> In my former study of Swedenborg, I had the impression that he was himself an idealist like Berkeley and Kant, and a mystic like

Meister Eckhart or William Law. There are certainly close affinities between Swedenborg's thought and that of the idealist and mystics, which have caused his works to be more popular in their circles than elsewhere; but much correspondence with Swedenborgians and closer reading of the texts have convinced me that his philosophy is neither Berkeleyan idealism nor Kantian idealism, and it certainly does not point the soul to that ecstatic absorption into remainderless union with God, in which the classical type of mysticism culminates. Perhaps the closest analogy to Swedenborg's philosophy is to be found in the teachings of the Neo-Platonists, who constantly made use of Plato's famous suggestion (in the parable of the Cave in the *Republic*) that there is a glorious Sun in the world of the Ideas, beside which our earthly sun and all that it illumines are but shadows. Plotinus called this Spiritual Sun the divine *Nous* or Intelligence, the first emanation of the supreme, unknowable Deity; and he thought of the visible world as an effluence from this invisible creative Source, proceeding from it by a series of successive emanations, each derived from the last, like a succession of rocket-bursts dividing and sub-dividing. There is a certain resemblance between these stages of emanation and Swedenborg's discrete degrees; but there are important differences as well. Swedenborg's degrees are more sharply discontinuous than Platonic emanations. Matter, for the Neo-Platonists, is the principle of non-being and evil; for Swedenborg, the natural world is *real* and *good,* the necessary "matrix" and fixed "support" of all spiritual life. With his doctrine of constant "influx" from the spiritual into the natural world, Swedenborg bridges the gulf between God and man as completely as any idealist or mystic; but he leaves man distinct from God, a free and responsible denizen of an objective material universe—thus, like the Scotch realists, getting "the best of both worlds."[27]

We are now perpared to observe this Neo-Platonic pattern of thought in James himself. He starts in by using the verbs *"in*-volves" and *"e*-volves" before he turns them into the corresponding nouns "involution" and "evolution," which correspond to the downward and return movements respectively, or as James often says, the "descending" and the "ascending" movements. Let us now trace James's thought in this matter by illustrative quotations:

Whatsoever creates a thing, gives it being, *in*-volves the thing, not the thing it. The Creator involves the creature; the creature *e*-volves the Creator. . . .[28]

James supplements man's evolving of God with the idea of nature's evolving of man:

> In one word Nature is rigidly involved in man or the spiritual creation; and instead therefore of her herself involving him, she does nothing but systematically and untiringly evolve him.[29]

The full meaning of "in-volving and e-volving" is vividly depicted by James in the following passage:

> In a word, according to Swedenborg, God creates us or gives us being only by thoroughly incarnating Himself in our nature; but inasmuch as this descent of the creator to creaturely limitations incidentally involves of course, on the part of the creature, the strictest inversion of the creative perfection, or a spirit of the utmost pride rapacity and tyranny, so it must itself necessarily provoke a corresponding ascending movement on God's part, giving us spiritual extrication from this infirmity. Otherwise creation would remain utterly inoperative save in a downward direction. . . .
>
> Let us clearly understand then that the Divine operation in creation is made up of two movements: one strictly subjective or creative, which is a movement of humiliation consisting in giving us natural being or identity; the other strictly subjective and redemptive, which is a movement of glorification consisting in giving us the amplest individual or spiritual expansion out of that base root. The prior movement, the descending, statical, and properly creative one—gives us natural selfhood or consciousness, a consciousness of separation from God, of a power inhering in ourselves and independent of Him. The posterior movement—the ascending, dynamical, and properly redemptive one—gives us spiritual consciousness, a consciousness of union with God, and makes us abhor and recoil from nothing so much as the spiritual filth of all sorts—the exuberant pride, inhumanity, and concupiscence—which lies concealed in every motion of our moral power. . . .
>
> His [man's] proper life of selfhood must in order to his imaging God involve two movements, one statical, the other dynamical, and constitute their unity. That is to say, his existence must be both natural and spiritual, both common and proper, both public and private, both universal and particular, both generic and specific, both broadly identical with all other existence, and yet intensely individual and distinct from it.[30]

With the main essentials of James's doctrine of creation now before us, an extract from Peirce's review of *The Secret of Swedenborg* is admirably apropos:

An appearance is only in consciousness. To create, therefore, or cause an appearance, is to awaken a consciousness, to vivify. To give being is to give life, or being is life. God's being, then, is creation; is vivifying other things, is living in others. Now, to have one's life in others is to love. So the essence of God is love. The creature's being also lies in another, namely, in God; and, therefore, his life too is love; only as he does not confer this life upon that other, but receives it from him, it is receptive or selfish love, while the Creator's is perfect and unselfish love. Since, therefore, the Creator is perfect love, the creation is to be explained on the principle of love.

The creator, then, cannot have made his creatures for his own sake (for love does nothing for its own sake), but for theirs. Accordingly, he must seek to make them, as much as possible, independent. As long as their being is in God, it is true that any independence they can seem to have will be a mere illusion, but that illusion God must grant. So he gives them a world of phenomena in which and relatively to which they have a reality and a self-determination.

But as all removal from God, all disparateness to his being, is mere self and nothingness, the Creator could not be satisfied with a creation which should stop short at this point, but must institute another movement in creation whereby the creature may be brought back into harmony with him, and thus really appropriate his Creator's being. This return movement is called redemption. The machinery of this process is man's history, and is, therefore, naturally extremely complex. It has two parts, the redemption of the race, and the redemption of the private man. The redemption of the race is effected by the history of the race, by the breaking down of governmental forms, the development of the family relationship, and above all by the vicissitudes of the Church which culminate in the incarnation of our Lord. By these means a brotherhood is produced among men, such that every man without constraint obeys the laws of society. The redemption of the individual man is produced by his life and the influence of conscience, which lead him to a perception of the truths of religion. In this redemption creation reaches completion.

Swedenborg holds time to be an illusory appearance, and therefore it does not follow that God cannot be without at the same time creating.[31]

Peirce's remarks on man's social and private redemption anticipate somewhat our chapter on "The Doctrine of Redemption and Spiritual

Socialism," but they were included here because they summarize so beautifully the whole circle of the creative-redemptive, the involution-ary-evolutionary, movements in James's philosophy.

It is worth an effort to define James's creationism in relation to creationist views held by other thinkers, or by the Church, in western thought. It is obvious that he does not agree with Traducianism, which maintains that the soul of a new child is generated from the souls of its parents; nor with Pre-existentialism, which holds to the previous existence of the soul, because this only leads to an endless regress; nor with Special Creationism, which holds to the view that the soul is infused by God into the foetus of every newly-conceived child at the moment of conception, because James is opposed to the idea that God creates—*i.e., shares* His life—at specific, ascertainable *times*. What, then, may we call James's doctrine? It is really very difficult to say, and perhaps no term precise enough can be found. Although the term "emanation" appears rarely in James's writings, it is obvious that the hierarchical structure, substantial and functional, with the attendant principle of "influx" from Celestial to Spiritual to Natural, along with the Neo-Platonic dual movement enclosing the whole—it is obvious that this is basically an emanationist creationism. Yet it is difficult to have emanation and *real* creation at the same time. The problem of holding an emanationist philosophy at the same time with a creationist doctrine is permanent in all types of Neo-Platonic thought, and it is perhaps beyond the reach of a fully satisfactory "solution" in terms of human discourse.

It seems most fitting, as a general conclusion to this chapter, to give the reader a glimpse of how James broadly applied his Doctrine of Spiritual Creation in written debate with Francis Ellingwood Abbot, whose theory of a "self-existent Universe" was dubbed a virtual atheism by James. He says:

> In short, you are a materialist of the most unflinching pattern; for while the ordinary adherent of that faith is content to affirm the "eternity" of matter, you stride a myriad leagues ahead of him to endow it with "self-existence" also. And eternal self-existence is precisely what all theists ascribe to God.... So why not drop "God" as an embarrassment to your cosmology? ... By the way, as selfhood is in use by all reflective people to express the indi-vidualizing principle in existence, or what distinguishes particular from universal, is it not, to say the least, somewhat crude in you to make your "universe" self-existent? ... What you call "the uni-

verse" is no thing at all, is not the least a sensible reality, but only and at most, a mental organization, whereby, in our ignorance of spiritual creation, we have been wont to bestow a provisional unity, an hypothetic being, upon the contents of our senses; and then convert that supposititious being or unity into an indurated ontologic or material existence. . . . "Universe" is not really *existent* save to thought.[32]

And then he attacks Abbot in terms of the "whole-parts" concept, again from the perspective of "spiritual creation":

You habitually speak of logical *universals* as generated by their respective particulars, or make the *parts* of a thing to constitute its *whole* . . . but actually, or in the order of life, the process is inverted; that is, more than reversed. For, in truth, not only do the parts constitute not the whole, but the whole creates the parts. . . . It would be a manifest license both of thought and speech to say, that its parts *created* it, or gave it *being* . . . but it is no license either of thought or speech to say that the *whole creates the parts*. For each special part taken by itself, and all the parts taken together, exist by and for the whole, and by and for it alone. And that thing by which and for which other things exist, may be said so far forth to create those things, or give them being.[33]

James received keen and generous criticism regarding his doctrine of creation from his oldest son William, who was destined to be a distinguished philosopher in his own right. There are fragments of a fascinating philosophical correspondence between these two in the Appendix to Volume II of Perry's great work, *The Thought and Character of William James,* from which we now take two excerpts. It is unnecessary to quote the elder James, since the burden of his letters to William, who was studying in Europe at the time, is so similar to the views on creation with which the reader is now acquainted. In the first passage, William James shows that he is conscious of the philosophical tightrope his father is walking in the attempt to keep clear of pantheism:

Berlin, Oct. 28, 1867.

My dear Father,

I acknowledged your metaphysical letter last week. . . .
But there occurs an objection at the very threshold which seems to me more important. It refers to the whole conception of creation, from which you would exclude all arbitrariness or magic.

Now I don't see what the word "creation" can mean if this be totally excluded, or what there is to justify its discrimination from pantheism. Creation, emanation, have at all times been opposed to pantheism, immanence; and it is evident from the scorn with which you always mention pantheism that you, too, place a broad gulf between them. The essence of the pantheistic conception, if I understand it, consists in there being a necessary relation between Creator and creature, so that both are the same fact viewed from opposite sides, and their duality as Creator and creature becomes merged in a higher unity as Being. Consequently a conception really opposed to pantheism must necessarily refuse to admit any such ratio as this,—any such external ratio,—so to speak, between them; must deny that each term exists only by virtue of the equation to which it belongs; the Creator must be the all, and the act by which the creature is set over against him have its motive within the creative circumference. The act must therefore necessarily contain an arbitrary and magical element—that is, if I attach the right meaning to those words—undetermined by anything external to the agent. Of course it is impossible to attempt to imagine the *way* of creation, but wherever from an absolute first a second appears, *there* it must be;—and it must be magical, for if in the second there be anything coequal or coeval with the first, it becomes pantheism.

So much for the way in which I apprehend the terms, and you will see how I fail to understand why on the one hand you have such an aversion to pantheism, and yet on the other to arbitrary creation. . . .

Ever your loving son,

Wm. J.[34]

In the second extract, William James states his logical objections to three major premises in his father's doctrine of creation. The passage displays that logical perceptiveness, though not in terms of technical logic, which William James exhibited so brilliantly in his philosophic career:

You posit as preliminary to your construction these three premises:

(1) The creature cannot possibly have a real distinctness or separateness from the Creator;

(2) Yet he must somehow have a logical distinctness, to identify him as created;

(3) He must also be "worthy" of his creative source, or reflect in some way its likeness.

The objections I now have to make are purely logical ones—you have as yet no right to bring in any data from feeling (or psychological ones) to aid in rebutting them.

I say, first, that, though to reconcile (1) and (2) your introduction of the concept *"appearing* to exist" seems quite legitimate, yet you are wrong in claiming this to be synonymous with "appearing *to himself* to exist *as non-created"*; since (in the absence of any third spectator) the appearance may logically be an appearance to the Creator as well as to the creature; and an appearance of createdness as well as uncreatedness. Hence the deduction of your first step is not logically cogent.

Your final step, that after which the process of creation is complete, results in the existence of a creature appearing to himself as such. You assume all along that such a consciousness-as-creature is impossible save with the preliminary experience of a consciousness-as-free, to serve as a foil, or ground to rise from. This seems to me an unnecessary assumption, for the moment you admit any qualitative determination at all of the creature's being, consciousness-as-created would seem as admissible as anything else to be its primitive form. . . .[35]

Whatever the logical difficulties that his son or anybody else seemed to find in his creation doctrine, James kept on expounding it with undiminishing faith and vigor to his last writing day. William and friends outside the family circle were one in recognizing that the real basis of his religious and philosophic doctrines was James's own radiant consciousness of the Divine in man; in other words, the basis was what William might well have called, "temperamental." Much as James tried to express his innermost faith in the language of philosophical discourse, he never pretended for a moment, despite the positive intensity with which he held to his doctrines and the assertive vigor with which he expressed them, that his thoughts were logically articulated in all their jointure, or that they made up a finished system of speculation. He would gladly sacrifice abstractly-logical consistency of statement in a twinkling, rather than exhibit a theological body of thought which, though perchance logically chaste, was, with regard to a dynamic religious *Weltanschauung,* too suggestive of Lord Bacon's charge against the "final cause," when he complained that it was *sicut virgo, Deo consecrata, sterilis.*

The man who wrote against the cold, aloof Deity of Calvinism and of Deism in the following language can never be justly accused, whatever his logical shortcomings, of being "as a virgin, consecrated to God, sterile"! :

> I am free to confess for my own part that I have no belief in God's absolute or irrelative and unconditional perfection. I have not the least sentiment of worship of His name, the least sentiment of awe or reverence towards Him, considered as a perfect person sufficient unto Himself. That style of Deity exerts no attraction either upon my heart or understanding. Any mother who suckles her babe upon her own breast, any bitch in fact who litters her periodical brood of pups, presents to my imagination a vastly nearer and sweeter Divine charm.[36]

NOTES

1. *Substance and Shadow*, p. 384.
2. Julia Kellogg, *op. cit.*, pp. 4-5.
3. James F. Clarke, "Henry James on Creation," *Christian Examiner*, Vol. LXXV (1863), p. 216.
4. *S and S*, pp. 68-69.
5. *Ibid.*, pp. 405, 407.
6. *Ibid.*, pp. 352-353.
7. *Ibid.*, pp. 274-275.
8. *Ibid.*, pp. 288-289.
9. W. H. Kimball, "Swedenborg and James," *Journal of Speculative Philosophy*, Vol. XVII (1883), p. 117.
10. *S and S*, pp. 304-305.
11. *Ibid.*, p. 362.
12. *Ibid.*, p. 374.
13. *Ibid.*, pp. 336-338.
14. *Ibid.*, pp. 270-273.
15. *Ibid.*, p. 332.
16. *Ibid.*, pp. 304, 307.
17. *Ibid.*, pp. 307-308.
18. *Ibid.*, p. 324.
19. *CLC*, p. 175 ff.
20. *S and S*, p. 397.
21. *Ibid.*, pp. 400-401.
22. *Ibid.*, pp. 402-403.
23. *Ibid.*, pp. 408-410.
24. *Ibid.*, p. 434.
25. *SRFM*, p. 145.

26. Emanuel Swedenborg, *Divine Love and Wisdom*, No. 170, pp. 159-160. Toksvig, in *Emanuel Swedenborg: Scientist and Mystic* (Yale, 1948), traces the Neo-Platonic element in Swedenborg to his reading of the Cambridge Platonists during his numerous and extended visits to England.
27. Walter Marshall Horton, "The Significance of Swedenborg for Contemporary Theology," pp. 18-19. A pamphlet printed by The Swedenborg Publishing Association (New York, 1938).
28. "The Works of Sir William Hamilton," *Putnam's Magazine*, Vol. II (Nov., 1853), p. 479.
29. *S and S*, p. 417.
30. *Ibid.*, pp. 396-397, 425-426.
31. Charles Sanders Peirce, "James's *Secret of Swedenborg*," *North American Review*, Vol. CX (1870), p. 464.
32. "Knowledge and Science Contrasted," *The Index*, Vol. VII (1876), p. 172.
33. "The Philosophy of the Heart," *Ibid.*, p. 231.
34. Ralph B. Perry, *op. cit.*, Vol. II, pp. 711-712.
35. *Ibid.*, p. 715.
36. *SRFM*, pp. 333-334.

Chapter Eight

The Spiritual Meaning of Nature

...Both naturalist and supernaturalist agree upon its [Nature's] absoluteness to the extent of allowing it, the one a power of really separating man from God, the other a power of really conjoining them [e.g., Emerson]. The pretension is perfectly idle on either side.

—HENRY JAMES, SR.[1]

For if you consent to make Nature absolute as well as contingent ...if you thus operate a real or spiritual disjunction between God and man, you can never hope to bring about that actual or literal conjunction between them which Swedenborg affirms in his doctrine of the Divine-Natural-Humanity, save by hypostasizing some preposterous mediator as big as the universe and as ancient as the world.

—HENRY JAMES, SR.[2]

We cannot know Divine goodness and truth in a direct or presentative way, but only in an indirect or re-presentative one ...And Nature is the proper theatre of this stupendous Divine abasement and obscuration,—of this needful revelation, or veiling over, of the Divine splendor, in order to adapt it to our gross carnal vision. Throughout her total length and breadth, accordingly, she is a mere correspondence or imagery of what is going on in living or spiritual realms; but a correspondence or imagery which is vital nevertheless to our apprehension of creative order.

—HENRY JAMES, SR.[3]

WITH THE EXPOSITION of the Doctrines of Spiritual Knowledge and Spiritual Creation in mind, it is comparatively easy to grasp James's spiritual interpretation of Nature, though the word "easy" is not to be taken absolutely, for there are profound ideas involved in this particular doctrine. James entertained a healthy respect for Nature; this we would expect from an intellect so objective in its determinations; but there is in his philosophy none of the Transcendentalist ecstacy about "Nature" such as one finds in Emerson or Thoreau. Carlyle never had to administer to James the witticism which he directed to Margaret Fuller's remark that she "accepted" the Universe, when he said: "Be-gad, she'd better!" Nor would one have said about James what was said of Thoreau, that he spoke of Nature as though he had "invented" her!

James had a qualified regard for Nature, or rather for the "actuality" of Nature as he sometimes expressed it. The word "actuality" is used advisedly, though James himself is no more strictly consistent in his use of terms here than elsewhere; nevertheless, it is possible to discern a basic propriety, from our study of James, in understanding "reality" as applicable in relative strictness to the Divine or Celestial World; "ideality" as referable to the Spiritual World (*in* man—the exclusive realm of "consciousness"), and "actuality" to the Natural World. These three terms—reality, ideality, actuality—are the ontologic and epistemologic pointers in Jamesian discourse for referring to the three great levels of being: Divine, Spiritual, Natural, on the one hand; and on the other hand, to the hierarchy in man's knowledges—Revelation and Philosophy (*real* or spiritual knowledge), Science (ideal, rational, knowledge-of-relations), and Sense (actual, sensible, perceptual, phenomenal, "apparent" knowledge). Nature's function is to "appear" and "act" out what spiritual causation determines. It is therefore *act*-ual rather than *re*-al. It is appearance-as-such, generated from the real world of spirit, which in turn is generated from the Divine.

Having said this, however, it must be admitted that there is another current of thought in James which, at first sight, seems to be the reverse of his trichotomous differentiation into real-ideal-actual, with no remainder of "reality" left to Nature. For it was a view of Swedenborg, re-echoed in James, that the "Effect" was the continent (James uses "con-tinent"; modern translators of Swedenborg generally use "containant"), of the "End" and the "Cause." It would appear, then, that Nature, being, in Swedenborgian terms the "lastmost," the "outmost," and the "ultimate" of creation, should be regarded as in this sense, the *most real* in the hierarchy of being. In consonance with this theory is the fact that when James speaks of Swedenborg's doctrine of the Divine-Natural-Humanity, he almost always capitalizes the middle term thus: The Divine-NATURAL-Humanity. But we are checked from adopting this interpretation as final, because of the realization that "ultimate" as applied to Nature means the terminus of the "downward movement" from the Divine through the Spiritual to the Natural; hence, it *is* ultimate in the involutionary order, while it is the reverse of ultimate in the evolutionary order. The ultimate "ultimate," so to speak, is found only at the consummation of the "upward or return movement" which is redemption as the eternal conjunction (in James it amounts to identification), of the human race, or Society, with God. In terms of creation, the Divine and the Spiritual orders are "ultimated," as Swedenborg and James put it, in the Natural; but in terms of redemption, Nature is only the "flooring" from which Spirit recoils for its backward journey to God.

Apropos of this general theme, there is another related observation that may be made regarding the "metaphysical physiology" of Swedenborg and James, as the writer has decided to term it. When, as we shall see later, James refers to the "glorification" of the Lord (he rarely uses the term "resurrection," which underlines again his gnostic bias, though freed from classical Gnostic contexts), he speaks of His glorification as extending "down to his literal flesh and bones."[4] So intense is James's spiritual realism! And this spiritual realism includes a permanent place for Nature, both now and in the redeemed order.

It is, accordingly, vitally important to keep most of James's terms straight in relation to these two great aspects of Reality in process: the downward (creation, involution) movement, and the upward (redemption, evolution) movement. Keeping this duality of process in view—the singular form "process" is used because James sometimes stretches "creation" to cover both movements—it is possible to avoid the otherwise hopeless ambiguity and inversion of identical terms when employed by James in different contexts. This constant bi-focal frame of reference explains to the reader the, at first sight, baffling controversions of meaning in accepted philosophic terminology. "Objective," "subjective," "ultimate," "conscious," "unconscious," and many other like terms, receive, in James, such radical inversions from their more conventionalized usage as to bring the reader to utter confusion unless he bear in mind constantly the dual and dynamic duality of process inherent in James's entire metaphysics.

Nature, then, is the *terminus ad quem* for the creative movement downward, and the *terminus a quo* for the redemptive movement upward. Down and up, up and down this vast ontological process, all terms change relation to each other: "subjective" in connection with the creation-movement becomes "objective" in connection with the redemption-movement, "Effect" becomes "Cause," and so on; but it should be remembered that there is no "con-fusion" in the series going down or up, since each factor, whether Celestial-Spiritual-Natural or End-Cause-Effect or Love-Wisdom-Use, remains within its own order and, despite the relativity, retains its own integrity and identity.

We now understand why James says, in the selection on the title page fronting this chapter, that both the naturalist and the supernaturalist are "idle" in believing, the one that Nature is a "power of really conjoining" man to God, the other that Nature is "a power of really separating man from God." As usual, James occupies a position of dialectical tension between extremes. He is concerned that the actuality of Nature, albeit subservient to spiritual ends, be recognized by the exclusively idealistic school; he is equally concerned that the limited, contingent actuality of "Nature" be acknowledged by the exclusively materialistic-naturalistic thinkers. He at one and the same time forbids one to make Nature purely ideal, and at the same time denies one permission to make it absolute.

It is sufficiently apparent that James does not construct a philosophy of Nature as such. He is exclusively concentrated upon extracting its spiritual meaning as a theater of spiritual causality. James feels the importance of a spiritual view of Nature so deeply that he sets the problem with characteristic extremeness of contrast in his long article in *The North American Review* on "Faith and Science":

> Ever since the dawn of our intellectual history, two rival hypotheses in regard to man's being and destiny have striven for the mastery of the human mind; which we may name severally the religious and the sceptical hypothesis, or, in modern parlance, the spiritualist and materialist hypotheses: the one basing itself upon revelation, and having it in view as a practical result to subordinate Nature to Man; the other basing itself upon actual knowledge or experience, and having it in view as a practical result to subordinate Man to Nature. . . .
>
> At bottom, the matter disputed between Faith and Science is the measure of respect we owe to Nature.[5]

With this passage as an introduction, we shall follow our usual method of presenting the critical-negative aspect of James's thought first, and then the critical-constructive phase of his doctrine of Nature. What James says a doctrine is *not,* is always as important, both in content and in the amount of discussion, as what he says it *is.* This is peculiarly true of James, for in dealing with him we are having intellectual commerce with a thinker who is very positive even in his negations. For purposes of exposition, however, even though the negative-positive aspects of his thought are often inextricably blended even within the sentence-unit, it is possible and necessary for clarity's sake, to distinguish passages basically negative from those basically constructive.

What, therefore, is Nature *not?* Well, it certainly is not the hypostasized entity men's minds so "naturally" make of her:

> There is no such actuality as we ascribe to Nature when we give her an existence over and above her particular forms; and the sooner we disabuse ourselves of this superstition, the better, for it is the outbirth exclusively of the sensuous imagination, and fatal to a spiritual discernment of creation. . . .
> She is, in short, the realm of the indefinite, of what ecapes definition, being neither infinite nor finite, neither God nor man, neither creative nor created, but a *tertium quid,* or transient neutral quantity effectually separating between the two. . . .
> To sum up: Nature is a pure fantasy of our rudimentary intelligence, permitted by the Divine Wisdom in the interest of our eventual and perfect spiritual sanity. . . .
> That this nature of the horse has any subjectivity in itself and apart from its specific forms, that it is anything more than a mental generalization on our part by which our reason identifies all the objects that our sense presents as individual, must strike every reader as absurd. But nothing can be alleged against such a superstition, which is not true in grander measure of universal Nature regarded as having any subjective existence or reality *in se.* . . .
> In short, Nature, when philosophically regarded expresses the lowest form of the human intelligence; what in early Christian speech was wont to be denominated "the natural *mind.*"[6]

The Berkeleyan nominalism is very apparent; also, the underlined last word in James's script is a subtle touch, showing neatly his view that "Nature" is indeed to most men a state of mind—and usually, a false one! Still, there is a cure for this unphilosophic thought of Nature, even on the level of Science, if one will but meditate on the meaning of Science itself, philosophically considered:

> But the mind *is* no longer contentedly naturalistic. Science itself is the irrefragable evidence of the fact; for it is doing its unconscious best all the while to spiritualize Nature, or discharge the mind of its chronic naturalism, by resolving all existence into a mode of motion, that is, converting it from a fixed to a purely functional quantity.[7]

If James had said that Science was doing its unconscious best to "mentalize" Nature, it might have been more readily adaptable to modern parlance, though he would have been afraid of the idealistic connotations of the term. Given this "mentalization" of Nature by Science, and its conversion of Nature into a "purely functional quantity," in James's thought, we are perforce reminded of the speculations of a later generation of philosophers of science—Jeans, Eddington, Bridgman, Tennant, and others. Is not James's insight, relatively speaking throughout, the equivalent approximately of a philosophic prophecy of what has become a deep trend in contemporary thought? "Nature" converted from a "fixed to a purely functional quantity"— this is the language of the mathematico-dynamic physics of the atomic age!

Since Nature is, according to James, a "transient neutral quantity" operating between man and God, is it not accurate to say, forgetting the Swedenborgian ontologic-functional triads for the moment, that Nature is a middle term in the creation-redemption nexus, located precisely where creation-involution ceases, and redemption-evolution begins? While thinking of "middle" terms, it is helpful to remember that Spirit is the middle term in the downward movement from God to Nature, or, in Jamesian designation, from *in*-finite (God) through *fi-nite* (Man), to *in-de*-finite (Nature). On the other hand, if we anticipate James's doctrine of Spiritual Socialism for a moment, History-Society is the middle term in the return movement from *in-de-finite* Nature through *de-finite* Man, to the *in-finite* Grand Man, or the Divine-Natural-Humanity.

Nature is, then, on the Jamesian premises, obviously subservient to man. Her function is entirely "ministerial," having neither independent reality nor purpose within herself, but only pure functionality *for* Spirit:

Now Nature stands in this purely subjective or constitutional relation to man, which the marble is under to the statue, or the works of a watch to its proper uses. It constitutes him to his own consciousness merely, and so furnishes a basis for his subsequent spiritual extrication; but it no more creates or gives him spiritual being, than the marble inspires the sculptor, or the works of a watch generate its dial-plate. . . .

But this function [of keeping time] is not inherent in the watch subjectively regarded, is no way assignable to it so far as it is materially constituted, but is imposed exclusively by its objective relations to its maker. The ideal or objective being of all watches as watches is to keep time, which they never do to their own intelligence, or consciously, but to that of some superior power.[8]

Although it is undesirable to anticipate James's doctrine of the spiritual dynamics of human nature in this instead of the following chapter, there is no possibility of handling his theory of Nature without touching upon its implications for his doctrine of man. Moreover, there will be enough concepts to reckon with in the chapter on Man aside from Man's relation to Nature; therefore, the relationship of Nature to Man and Man to Nature will henceforward be considered as an organic part of the present exposition.

In a passage from *The Church of Christ Not an Ecclesiasticism,* he expresses at one and the same time what Nature is not and what she is, in terms of the purpose she serves *vis-à-vis* Man. This excerpt is the first of a good many to come in the remainder of this study which illustrates the tremendous *homo-centric* focus in James's philosophy; and this is true despite the strong theo-centric quality of his thought. God-in-Himself; Nature-in-Herself, as themes for speculation? Never, for James! But God-for-Man's sake, and Nature-for-Man's sake? Absolutely, James almost shouts from every page he ever wrote. There will be further occasion to note this homo-centricity in James's thought, even to the point of its attaining a seeming and curious type of atheism hardly distinguishable at times from Comte's "Religion of Humanity," though James's "atheism" is more profoundly religious in quality than Comte's, because the former's is theo-generated and apocalypticized as compared with the secularist, this-world-alone, positivism of Comte. There is no other religious philosopher with whom the writer is acquainted in whom such a theo-saturated system develops for about three-quarters of the way, to be capped with a doctrine in which Man is so apotheosized, in his redeemed state, as almost to "swallow up"

God, as William James puts it, for the last quarter of the journey! If there is any genuine mysticism in James, it might well be from the side of God's union-with-man rather than Man's union-with-God, so that in the final result, Man seems to come out almost on top! But we must not forget our quotation:

> God's creature must be *apparently* autonomic or self-moved, or else violate the primary condition of the Divine conjunction with it; because the Creator is life in Himself, His only true or expressive image must seem also to be life in *him*self, under penalty of renouncing such imagery. Hence the world of *Nature*, a sphere of existence in which all things are conformed to the feeling or sense of the creature, and in which the Infinite Divine Truth submits to a transitory humiliation, or succumbs to specious and fallacious appearances. The natural world has always fulfilled this initiatory function; it has never been more than the necessary floor or basis of the spiritual creation. It is the world of form or appearance in contradistinction to substance, or seeming instead of being; the world in which the phenomenon dominates the real. All its laws are amply explicable—and explicable only— on the hypothesis of its being a purely rudimentary and formative stage of human experience, of its being as it were a seminary of the true and eternal creation.[9]

Sometimes James speaks of Nature and Spirit in a way very suggestive of Schelling, but the Schellingesque quality should not blind us in the least to the fact that James's doctrine of Nature and Spirit is animated by a different motivation, and encased in a quite divergent metaphysics. The metaphysical divergences are noteworthy. To Schelling, Nature is "slumbering" Spirit, while Spirit is energized, activated, aroused Nature: thus Nature and Spirit are convertible terms in metaphysical dynamics, for Nature is Spirit dynamically visible, and Spirit is Nature invisible. Nature and Spirit culminate in The Absolute Self, not as Thought thinking itself as in Hegel, but as the "indifference point" between freedom-necessity, identity-individuality, nature-spirit, consciousness-unconsciousness. The Absolute is thus beyond personality or consciousness, is indeed a *tertium quid,* or neutral "third-somewhat."

It is quite metaphysically different with James. Nature and Spirit are in a relation, as he says in the above-quoted article on "Faith and Science," not of "continuity, but of the strictest correspondence, like that between a cause and its effect, or between a man's face and the image of that face in a glass. . . ." This view reflects Swedenborg's

doctrine of "Discrete Degrees," which doctrine in turn reflects Swedenborg's effort to overcome the sharp Cartesian dualism in European
philosophy since Descartes. Swedenborg attempts to abolish this
radical dualism of mental (or spiritual) substance and of material
substance, by a trinal monism in which the trinal aspect of
Reality is recognized (Celestial-Spiritual-Natural Worlds) with the
parallel logical principle involved of "Discrete Degrees," while the
monistic aspect is stressed by the principles of "Influx" and "Correspondence of Forms" from one world to another. This trinal monism
in Swedenborg and in James, generates in their thought a persistent
habit of triadic formulations of their doctrines. The remarkable number of triads in James's philosophy will be presented in Chapter IX.

James employs Swedenborg's triad of Love-Wisdom-Use, though
concentrating for the moment on "use" alone, in further developing
the spiritual meaning of Nature to his mind:

> In short the spirit of a thing is the end or use for which it exists.
> Thus you may take the whole range either of nature or the arts,
> and you will find everything existing for a certain use beyond
> itself, which use is the spiritual ground or justification of its
> existence. Nature is properly nothing more than the robe or
> garment of spirit. It is only the tabernacle or house of spirit,
> only the subservient instrument or means by which spirit sub-
> sists and becomes conscious. Every thing in nature, without any
> the most insignificant exception, embodies an internal use or
> capacity of operation, which constitutes its peculiar spirit. De-
> prive it of this internal use or capacity, not only actually or for
> a limited time, but potentially or for ever, and you deprive it of
> life. . . . For death, or the departure of the spirit from the body,
> means in every case the cessation of the subject's capacity of use.
> Thus nature in all its departments is merely the vehicle or minister
> of spirit.[10]

It would surprise us if James remained content with a few lyric
sentences and a cluster of abstract statements about Nature in terms
of "use." He becomes very concrete on this subject of Nature's relation to man, and reveals the acumen of his spiritualistic critique in
thoroughly specific instances as exemplified in a comparison between
animals and man:

> But if this spiritual force reside in Nature, what hinders any
> natural form being a true revelation or image of God? If, for
> example, the horse possess a spiritual substratum, why does not
> the horse image God? The reason is obvious. He is entirely un-

conscious of it. He performs incessant uses to man, but does not perform them *of himself*. His end is external to himself. The object of his actions does not fall within his own subjectivity. The spirit of universal nature is a spirit of subjection to some external power. It never manifests spontaneously, but always in obeisance to some outward constraint. Thus the horse does not spontaneously place himself in the harness. The cow does not come to your dairy, to make a spontaneous surrender of her milk. The sheep feels no spontaneous impulsion to deposit his fleece at your door. Nor does the tree inwardly shake itself in order to supply you with apples. In short there is no such thing as a spiritual horse-cow-sheep—or apple tree. . . .

No, all these performances are for the benefit of man. The whole realm of nature is destitute of a spiritual consciousness. . . . No animal is conscious of a selfhood distinct from its outward or natural limitations. No animal is capable of suicide, or the renunciation of its outer life, on the ground of its no longer fulfilling the aspiration of its inner life. Thus nature is destitute of any proper personality. The only personality it recognizes is man. To him all its uses tend. Him all its powers obey. . . . Take away man accordingly, and nature remains a clod, utterly spiritless—impersonal—dead.[11]

Keeping the melody of his thought on this theme in the same key, James asserts that Nature is not merely a servant but a friend to man, though it may often seem that the friendship is pretty well disguised:

He does not suspect the truth, but the truth is, that the slender patronage he enjoys from nature is full of compliment and friendship to him. It is because Nature means to obey with perfect obedience, that she is backward to offer supererogatory service. . . . Thus her apparent stinginess is full at bottom of a genuine friendship. She merely veils her accessory splendors for a while, in order that he may recognize a higher alliance than hers, in order that he may discern a parentage of which she herself is all unworthy, and which none of her tribes may ever aspire to know. For if man had been born on a level with nature, if he had been like the animal a creature chiefly of instinct, and therefore born into the complete knowledge and complete satisfaction of all his wants, then of course his beginning would have been as perfect as his ending, and he would have had no history, no spiritual evolution.[12]

How can man learn to read Nature aright? James drafts into service an extended metaphor to illustrate the spiritual meaning of Nature—

the figure of the mirror. He employs the figure with a brilliant display of analogical reasoning:

The summary explanation of all natural experiences, and this among the rest, is, that Nature is but an experimental world; in other words, that from her lowest pebble up to her perfected form which is the human body, she is but a *mirror* of the soul, or true creation: and it is never the function of a mirror to reflect that which inwardly or really and consciously *is*, but only that which outwardly or actually or unconsciously *appears*. In other words the mirror never reflects being as it exists to itself, or consciously, but only as it exists to others, or phenomenally. . . . If for example I should visit my glass every morning for instruction as well as information, for wisdom as well as knowledge: if I should go there not merely to ask how I *appear* to others than myself, but also to ask how I really exist to myself: I should instantly find every dictate of my consciousness belied. I should be sure to put the patch which belonged to my right cheek upon the left, and give my left whisker the trimming which every interest of equilibrium demanded only for the right. For the mirror invariably tells me that my right hand is my left, and my left hand my right, so that if I were to obey its instruction for the real truth of the case, instead of depending exclusively upon my own natural conscious-ness, I should soon exhibit as insane a picture personally, or with reference to the interests of my body, as *he* does spiritually or with reference to the interests of the soul, who follows the teach-ing of Nature in that regard, without reference to the commanding light of Revelation. . . .

By natural light therefore, *the light which the mirror herself supplies*, it is no wonder that all things within her framework appear upright and orderly and beautiful; just as in the looking glass that which is really or consciously my left hand is made to *appear* my right: whilst in reality or to the spiritual consciousness, they are the exact reverse of upright and orderly and beautiful, as we see by the inverted forms they assume when they are re-flected towards the soul, whose nearest outpost is the retina, and other apparatus constituting the needful basis of the varied life of sense.[13]

From the analogical type of argumentation, he shifts into more strictly logical analysis:

But some one will ask, Do we not see at least *by means* of this inverted image? Do we not see by virtue of a reflection of the natural world upon the retina? This question puts the cart before the horse, but I can manage to satisfy it. It is a universal truth that the natural world is altogether vivified from the spiritual one, and it is also true that this vivification takes place through certain media, which we call the senses. Thus we see, we hear, we smell, we taste, we touch, which are all experiences of natural life, by virtue of a spiritual influx into the retina, the tympanum, the olfactory and gustatory nerves, and the skin. But this influx does not traverse these various media, or pass through them: on the contrary, it is always arrested there by the exact contrariety or inversion which it encounters at the hands of Nature; and it is this very arrestation which becomes the basis of our natural subjectivity, or makes our natural experiences possible. Thus the inverted natural image on the retina is nothing more nor less than a reverberation or *contre-coup* made upon the spiritual sense by an act of natural vision: it marks the arrest and reflection, or bending back of the spiritual world upon itself, when it would otherwise pass out of its sphere, and dominate the natural one. It is therefore true to say that we see by means of this reflex natural image on the retina, thus far, namely:—that if that reflex image did not take place, it would be because there was no difference between soul and body, spirit and nature, and consequently because we were not intended to enjoy any natural life. Beyond this, it is absurdly untrue.[14]

Not being satisfied with this argument unsupported by further analysis, James engages in a wider, more philosophical description of Nature:

What, by the way, *is* nature? Popularly used, the "nature" of a thing means what the thing is *in itself,* or apart from anything else. Philosophically defined, it is the *principle of identity* in existence, forever differentiating creature from creator by stamping the one finite, subjective, conscious, the other infinite, objective, unconscious. It is, in short, the principle of *uncreation* which is logically involved in all created existence; for man's spiritual creation is by no means the very silly thing it is sometimes reported to be when it is characterized as the making him out of nothing. On the contrary, spiritual creation *is his plenary redemption out of the death and hell he is in by nature. . . .*

Nature is always to be logically taken for granted in spiritual creation, as giving the creature subjective identity, or conscious distinction from the creator; but this logical virtue is all the merit it possesses or ever will possess. Especially it must not be thought to be itself created. For the whole and sole function of nature being to constitute that supposititious realm of *uncreation, not-*

being, out of which man is logically held to be delivered by his creation, the thought of itself as created would have no other effect than to stultify this its constitutional function.[15]

The characterization of the creator as "unconscious" is surely a Schellingean touch, for the writer has not been able to find it in Swedenborg; and since James was a student of Schelling, it seems a highly probable thing that this particular idea of God as beyond "consciousness" came from the German idealist's influence upon his thought.

A bit surprisingly, after the general tenor of the preceding selections from James on Nature, he goes on to say that Nature is "metaphysical." For if Nature is mere "appearance" and actuality, how can it be meta-physical? But when we recall that "Nature" is, as contrasted with concrete objects—roses, horses, persons—an abstraction, constructed purely *in man's consciousness,* we see his meaning, so elliptically stated, when he says Nature is metaphysical:

Surely if she be taken for *all* that appears to our senses, she cannot herself be *anything* that so appears, for this would involve contradiction. In fact, she is merely the generative, constitutional subjective, or maternal principle which we by defect of understanding insist upon bringing into things in order not to account for any thing absolutely, but to account for its appearance to us. She has accordingly a purely logical or metaphysical reality with reference to everything embraced in the sphere of sense or the world of space and time. . . . But yet nature herself, though we insist upon her being the indubitable parent of all the physical reality we know, has not a particle of physical reality, but is merely taken for granted by us as the producing cause of things. Her existence, I repeat, is wholly metaphysical or unreal, having no guarantee but our logic. The brutes do not in the least recognize nature, because in the first place she does not fall under the senses, and because in the second they have no guiding and governing word connecting their understanding spiritually with God. For nature is simply the first syllabling of that uncreated word which conditions all created existence to thought; and as a word does not and cannot exist save to thought, we instinctively restrict nature to a purely logical reality.[16]

Before following James into his more inspired flights on the spiritual meaning of Nature, it seems that this is as opportune a place as any to consider his Pan-Psychism, already mentioned casually in a previous chapter. This element in his thought is important, as well as the concept of spontaneity, for its influence on the better known philosophy of his son, William James. This pan-psychistic strain is expressed by the elder James in several passages of surpassing nobility of thought and beauty of diction:

> Selfhood or identity is a composite not a simple fact. That is to say it is a fact of the strictest consciousness, implying the marriage of a common nature with a specific form. No form exists which is wholly unconscious or inanimate, though of course consciousness itself assumes infinitely diversified aspects: here a very diffuse and lethargic one, as in the mineral form of existence; there a very concentrated and energetic one, as in man: but in all its forms alike it announces the union of a common or identical substance with a specific or individual form.[1] [The index number "1" is James's, referring to a footnote which we quote in full].
>
> 1. We think the mineral existence unconscious, because it is so remote a form of consciousness from ours, that we can hardly reproduce it. But if we should accidentally fall from the roof of a house or any equal height, and be unfortunate enough to survive, we might by afterwards recalling to remembrance the sensation we felt during the fall, make an approximate of the mineral consciousness. Of course we should have known it only in inverted and most revolting form: because as our personality alienates us to the greatest possible extent from the mineral consciousness, we cannot come into the conditions of that consciousness without the utmost violence to our own. But nevertheless by translating our negative human experience into the positive mineral one, or interpreting the intense and indeed agonizing moral revolt we feel under the circumstances, by the mere experience of inertia—or abandonment to the overpowering force of gravitation—which the mineral feels, we shall be able to compass a near view of the mineral consciousness, or picture to our intelligence the state of anesthesia or drunkenness—i.e. nearly utter submergence of individual sensibility in a sense of diffused existence—which characterizes what we very absurdly call inorganic nature, or brute matter.[17]

In a book published six years earlier than *Substance and Shadow*, James chants the same idea, but with a finer lift of lyric quality. Since soul, life, and spirit were on the whole synonymous to James, one might call his doctrine Hylozoism, Pan-Vitalism, or Pan-Spiritualism, disassociating him, of course, from specifiable doctrines of other thinkers under those names:

> Gravitation, inertia, rest in space, is what all existence possesses in common. And yet the mineral which expresses this common

characteristic, is the lowest form of existence. Indeed, philosophers utterly deny life or consciousness to the mineral form, because the individual, or formal and feminine, element, is so inferior in it to the universal, or substantial and masculine element. The latter element almost swallows up the former, nearly reducing the mineral to what philosophers call a "simple substance."

But this denial is premature. Consciousness belongs to the mineral realm as truly, though not so distinctly, of course, as to the vegetable and animal. It is the most diffused or common form of consciousness, and therefore the least obvious to human apprehension. For man being the most distinct or pronounced form of life, that is to say, harbouring the universe in his private individuality, is at the utmost possible remove from communism, and hence finds it difficult to appreciate or even acknowledge a life which simply expresses that. . . . The perfect or human form is that which exactly unites or marries what is universal and what is individual, the sympathies of every well-developed man relating him to the entire universe of being. Mineral life is the first step towards this perfected life. It is the arrest of chaos. . . .

The mineral form then is the earliest or lowest evolution of the me. It is the me in an intensely inert state, in a passive state or state of rest simply. It is the me getting place or position first, in order to its subsequent experience of *growth* in the vegetable form, *motion* in the animal, and *action* in the human form. . . . Mineral life . . . being destitute as yet of sensation . . . loses itself in the womb of the common mother. But the phenomena of crystallization shew that the life-process is going on all the while not less really though invisibly, or within the still enveloping womb of Nature, so that at least very marked *tendencies* to specific form result, as we see in the characteristic differences of iron and sulphur, alum and arsenic, gold and lead, silver and copper. Were there no observable differences in these things, did they not exhibit each a different relation towards the common mineral life, which is inertia or tendency to rest, we could never have named them. . . . For life or consciousness means nothing else than the union of a common nature with a specific form.[18]

And now the really climactic portion, embedded in the above quotation from James's script, but transposed to last position for purposes of this exposition:

Originally, or in the uncreated state of man, so to speak, Creator and creature, God and man, are undistinguishable one from the other. And Nature in her earliest or fluid beginnings does exactly symbolize this indistinction. All things are then chaotically blent.

. . . And the entire scope of what we call *history* is to reduce this chaos to order, to lift up this sobbing and prostrate universe into beautiful and joyous and individual form, to train this mute and melancholy and boundless nature into the free and glorified lineaments of human personality or character.[19]

It is fascinating to see what James can do with Pan-Psychism in a freely literary rendition. Undoubtedly, when he wrote this passage, he was completely unconscious of any nameable philosophical theory, but it is nonetheless a charming example of pan-psychistic philosophy translated into prose literature:

Nature is but the echo of the soul, and images nothing therefore of the Divine creation and providence which is not primarily impressed by the soul. Your delicious English landscape, for example . . . reflects a far more evangelical lesson in these respects than the hideous jungles of Asia, or our own unsubdued forests and indolent savannas; because the humanized English *man* has first taught it so to do. Abstract this comfortable Christian English soul, who believes in nothing more soundly than a deity favourable to good cheer, prolific of everlasting cakes and ale, and your peaceful English landscape would have been by this time as ruthless and unchristian as that of Switzerland, which for the most part suggests no thoughts of Divinity but as of some huge, frowning, thunderous, overshadowing, overbearing power, eternally allied with pride and selfwill, and essentially untouched by all those blissful human sympathies and charities whose inseparable root is humility.[20]

James takes his place among the goodly company of the apostles of the universality of "Life," a company that begins with the Hylozoists of classical Greece, and continues with Leibnitz's Monads as Psychic Centers to Henry James's Pan-Psychism and Whitehead's "Organicism."

It is necessary, to a rounding off of James's doctrine of Nature, to return to the presentation of a few excerpts in which he conveys the spiritual meaning of Nature with crescendo power. He now includes space and time with Nature as ministerial to man's ascent, in and toward, his spiritual destiny:

The Divine power is primarily spiritual, and natural only by derivation from that. In other words man is the sole spiritual creature of God, and animal vegetable and mineral are his creatures only by virtue of their necessary implication in man. Thus space and time far from lying outside the Divine creation and furnishing its theatre as we suppose, fall most strictly within it, being only two most coarse or universal expressions of the absolute unity in variety, and of the infinite variety in unity, which severally animate it, and keep it eternally fresh and fragrant. In one word: space and time with all their contents are embraced in the human consciousness, and have no other function than to afford a finite basis, a fixed continent, for its superb spiritual evolution.[21]

Although James is positive about Nature's value as the realm of "identity," "constitution," "fixity," and "actuality," it is thus always in terms of her positive "priesthood" to man. He enlarged upon the concept of Nature as the servant to man in every book he wrote, returning to it again and again within any one book. Here is an example of what can be found on page after page of any of his major works. He ties his doctrine of Nature tightly to his doctrine of spiritual knowledge, or Revelation, for in Nature's inarticulateness to interpret either God, man, or herself, is to be found the most powerful argument for the need and reality of Revelation:

But if nature be nothing more than the common or ultimate bond and covering of the spiritual world, which is the universal mind of man, just as the skin is the most common or ultimate bond and covering of all the diversified kingdoms of the body: why then of course we may regard all natural phenomena only as so many graduated effects from interior spiritual causes, precisely as we regard a blush upon the skin, or a sudden pallor, as an evidence of heightened or depressed vital action. And so doubtless day and night, the succession of the seasons, birth and death, growth and decay, the subordination of mineral to vegetable, of vegetable to animal, and of all to man, *are* so many natural types, are so many ultimate symbols, of a vast and beneficent spiritual order which is inwardly shaping the universal soul of man, and which will eventually bring about the perfect reciprocal fusion or unity of each with all and all with each. But how to divine this recondite knowledge! Nature has as little consciousness of man, as the waters have of the sun and stars which irradiate their darkened and tumultuous bosom. Nature herself therefore is incapable of blabbing the secret with which she is fraught, or of proving a revelation of Divine mysteries to the soul, because she is utterly unconscious and incredulous of Divinity. She has no more comprehension of the being she images, than the looking glass has of the human substance whose various phenomenality it reflects. She is a pure surface whose depth or soul is man. . . . She has no clearly articulate speech which she does not catch up from his commanding accents. In short she knows herself truly only as the echo of his majestic personality, and shrinks from nothing so much as the pretension to lisp even a syllable of original Divine revelation. Revelation descends exclusively from the human consciousness, or from the soul of man to his senses, because man alone being the true creature of God is alone competent to reveal Him. In short the true theatre of revelation is not our mere natural or animal consciousness, but our historic or veritably human consciousness. It demands for its proper platform not merely that humble field of relations which man is under to his own body, and which constitutes what we call his *existence*, being all comprehended in the fixed quantity denominated Nature: but also and above all that superb field of relations which he is under to his own soul, or to God, and which constitutes what we properly term his *life.* . . . .[22]

Probably James's most philosophical exposition of Nature is to be found in his *The Secret of Swedenborg.* He even goes to the extent, citing Swedenborg for authority, of dividing men after death into devils and angels according to whether or not ·they held to Nature's "Absoluteness"! A truly spiritual perspective on Nature is *that* important to James's intense and radical spiritualism:

Nature accordingly does *not* involve the mind. So far indeed is it from involving the mind, that it is itself rigidly involved by the mind as the necessary subjective base of its own objective evolution; just as the marble is involved in the statue, the mother in the child, as the necessary condition of these latter's existence. In short nature has no existence save in relation to human thought, or as affording needful relief to the specific contents of our senses; and hence to talk of "the order of nature," or "the laws of nature," as if those cheap phrases expressed something more than a subjective cognition, something objective and absolute, some reality in short out of consciousness and binding upon the divine mind, is to talk childish nonsense. These terms are strictly invalid to philosophic thought, save as indicating the constancy of nature's subjection to the mind, to our mental necessities. They merely indicate the use she subserves in furnishing a hypothetical base to science, or giving it provisional flooring, foothold, fixity, during the protracted period of its spiritual infancy, or while it is still ignorant of creative order, and remains a contented dupe to the illusions of space and time. And to allow them any ontological significance therefore, any really creative virtue, is simply to shut the intellect up to the moonlight and starlight of sense, and exclude it from the fervent splendors of the sun of faith. . . .

The essential of nature is passivity or community; i.e. the predominance of substance to form, of subject to object. The essential of spirit again is activity or difference; i.e. the predominance of the formal or objective element in consciousness over its substantial or subjective element. It is obvious accordingly that the spiritual realm must be absolutely barred out of our intellectual cognizance, so long as the mind remains a prey to the illusions of our natural science, or holds nature to be a direct manifestation of divine power. . . . The fundamental difference he [Swedenborg] discovers between the good and evil spirit, or angel and devil, is that the latter confirms himself in the persuasion of nature's absoluteness, or her real universality, while the former holds her existence to be purely logical. . . . [23]

Given James's spiritualistic premises, it is entirely logical that misconception and misbelief about Nature's relation to Spirit is, philosophically speaking, "the root of all evil."

Since the natural world is "too much with us," James never wearies of expounding his doctrine of the spiritual interpretation of Nature. We find him saying, on the page following that from which the last quotation was taken, that Swedenborg's doctrine of Nature is the meaning of the title of the book—it is the "Secret" of Swedenborg:

The sole and complete meaning of nature, philosophically regarded, is, according to Swedenborg, to furnish a logical ultimate or phenomenal background to the human mind in its infancy, in order that the mind, being thus objectively mirrored to itself, might present a subjective floor or fulcrum every way apposite to the operations of the creative spirit. This, neither more nor less, is Swedenborg's philosophic secret.[24]

When men fail to get the spiritual meaning of Nature, Natural-*ism*, results, and Naturalism is no-philosophy and no-religion. This was the blight, according to James, on the philosophy and theology of his own day, whether it styled itself Rationalist or Materialist, Idealist or Transcendentalist, Orthodox or Liberal:

It is on this point precisely that the orthodox theology and philosophy signalize their inherent incapacity to furnish us with a true doctrine of Nature, or confess themselves utterly unscientific. Our popular theologians and philosophers have no idea that nature is but a correspondence by inversion of spirit, just as the foundation of a house is a correspondence by inversion of the superstructure, as the shell of a nut is an inverse correspondence of the kernel, or the outside of a glove an inverse correspondence of its inside. On the contrary, they deem the natural world to possess an independent existence, to exist for its own sake, or constitute its own end; and consequently they have declined, both classes alike, into mere Naturalism. The current theology and philosophy are both alike naturalistic, whence we now have Unitarianism as the only vital theologic doctrine extant, and Atheism or Pantheism as the only vital philosophic doctrine. We live under the Iscariot apostolate. The star of the forlorn Judas culminates at length in our ecclesiastical horizon, and we have little left to do but to burst asunder in the midst, or resolve our once soaring Divine hopes into the mere poetry and sentimentality of nature. . . . When we say that Naturalism is the disease of our current divinity and metaphysics, what do we mean to indicate by that word? . . .

Naturalism limits the reason by the senses; it accepts as final the testimony of sense affirming the identity of being and appearance, substance and shadow. . . . The consistent naturalist says in all his thought, "I *am* inwardly and spiritually what I outwardly and physically appear: that is to say, as I am naturally distinct from and disunited with all existence, so am I also spiritually distinct and disunited: and distinct and disunited existences deny unity of origin, deny that one and the same Creator could produce so many divergent creatures."

. . . Denying the unity of the soul in God, thus the unity of humanity, we split the spiritual creature up into as many conflicting and independent and selfish souls, as Nature exhibits of bodies. In short, the naturalist, instead of making nature and spirit twin aspects of one and the same consciousness, as that consciousness is viewed either subjectively or objectively: instead of seeing both the natural and spiritual universe alike included in the unity of the conscious *me* . . . gives them the reciprocal independence and obtuseness of two peas. . . .[25]

Nature's mission, then, is merely to matriculate man in the universe of Spirit. As the "floor" of the downward movement of Creation, she is also in turn the springboard from which Man, in recoil from her deterministic "principle of identity," leaps forth from her womb to commence the upward movement, thus passing from identity to "individuality," from determinism to freedom and "spontaneity," from empirical *men* to universal *Man,* from corrupt civilization to Redeemed Society:

And what Philosophy does for us—precisely what Philosophy, following the lead of Revelation, does for us in emancipating us

from the tutelage both of Natural religion and Natural science—
is, so to trace back this exuberant life of Nature, her pervasive
consciousness, her corrosive personality, her endlessly diversified
character, to the very infinitude of the Divine power as embodied
and illustrated in Man social and spontaneous. . . .[26]

In the context of this chapter, it is fitting to conclude with the most
positive tribute to the actuality of Nature in the universal Divine
economy that the writer has been able to find in an exhaustive search
throughout James's works. In this tribute to Nature, to be cited
presently, we may have a partial answer to the query raised in the
chapter on "The Doctrine of Spiritual Knowledge," in reference to that
paragraph on page 246 of *Society the Redeemed Form of Man,* where
James speaks of "the current scientific idealism is at best but a transition point between the once active but always baseless and now defunct
metaphysics of theology, and that philosophic naturalism or realism
which is even now looming in our intellectual horizon, and ready to
avouch itself the fixed immovable earth of the mind, the adamantine
rock of man's spiritual faith and hope." It is a tantalizing situation for
the expositor, because this is the only instance that the writer has been
able to find of James's applying a technical philosophical term presumably to his own position; and this is puzzling in so many ways. He
speaks of "scientific idealism" which in itself is a phrase hard to fix in
accordance with standardized philosophic usage; then he mentions
"philosophic naturalism or realism." There is, keeping in mind all the
while the various meanings given to both terms in the history of
philosophy, a tremendous difference between naturalism and realism,
and yet James speaks of them as indifferently synonymous! What this
"philosophic" Naturalism—forgetting Realism for the moment—could
mean to James is complicated even more for us by the vigor of his
attack, quoted before, on the "Naturalism" which he found in Orthodoxy, Transcendentalism, and Unitarianism alike, causing people therefore to live "under the Iscariot apostolate." And still, in the passage at
issue, he welcomes that "philosophic naturalism or realism" looming on
the intellectual horizon as the "adamantine rock" of man's "spiritual" (!) faith!

If we were to accept the selection, presently to be offered, as the
basis for interpreting James as some kind of Naturalist in philosophy,
it would be a Pyrrhic victory for Naturalism, because the application
of the term is so limited in James. Fronting Nature alone, there may be
a kind of Naturalism in James; but it must be remembered that this—

shall we say *epistemologic* naturalism?—is certainly at a great remove from James's *ontological* spiritual realism. The term "realism," in the Platonic sense of the ultimacy of the eternal Forms over their participation in substance, is readily identifiable in James's thought, as Peirce noted. Platonic realism *in re* Forms, yes; Swedenborgian spiritual realism as causation and creation in the natural world, yes; but, what could "Naturalism" mean as applied to James? We do not have a hint as to what he understood it to mean even to himself.

In the passage now to be cited may be discerned—whether we "read them into" or "read them out" of it, is really irrelevant—implications more than faintly anticipative of modern philosophies of Nature—or, it may be, of "Science"—such as Nature's being a common "field" which provides a test for the individual's perceptual veridicity, a ground for "public confirmation," and a standard for empirico-scientific "verification":

> My identity—whatsoever gives me existence to my own consciousness, enables me to recognize myself, or say *me, mine,* and by implication therefore *thee, thine*—belongs to Nature, is wholly contingent upon her sovereign will. I am conscious only by virtue of my natural senses or organization. Take that away, and what should I know? Take away my knowledge, and what basis should I have for belief? Take away both knowledge and belief, both sense and understanding, and how much of me would remain? Where in that case should I be, and what? Could I be said to be at all indeed? To be sure some philosopher in search of an anchorage, might allege that I would still have my unconscious being in God. But my unconscious being is precisely what is not my being but God's. I have not the slightest title to any being in myself but what my consciousness gives me. Unconscious being to a created one is contradictory. My consciousness is what separates me and alone separates me from God, in identifying me with Nature and Society. If consequently you take away my bodily organization, which is the sole ground of my consciousness or alone identifies me with nature and my fellow-man, you reduce me to nonentity.
> Thus it is nature which gives me identity, and in that gift insures me all my power of subsequent spiritual expansion or individuality. . . . We know or perceive natural things alone, the horse, the tree, the mountain, the cloud, the river. Take these and similar natural things away, and we should know no-thing; that is, we should not know at all. Knowledge does not inhere in me apart from my subjection to nature. . . . In knowing the rose for

example I put forth no power; so far as my proper individual force or activity is concerned, I am as helpless as the babe unborn. I cannot help knowing it. . . . All my sensible knowledge, or sensible experience of every sort, is a fact exclusively of my natural identity with, and indistinction from, every other subject of nature. . . . Were it not for this fixed basis of identity or community with other men [and Nature] to begin with, all my characteristic individuality or diversity from them . . . would be simply impossible and inconceivable.[27]

In short, James's Doctrine of the Spiritual Meaning of Nature is a complex and profound insight: for he is telling us, in essence, that Man at first identifies himself with Nature, because without Her, he could neither identify himself *to* himself or to his fellow men on the one hand, nor on the other, distinguish himself *from* God.

NOTES

1. "The Radical Dogmatics," *The Radical*, Vol. II (1867), p. 91.
2. "The Ontology of Swedenborg," *North American Review*, Vol. CV (1867), p. 111.
3. *Ibid.*, p. 117.
4. *S and S*, p. 493.
5. "Faith and Science," *The North American Review*, Vol. CI (1865), pp. 336-337.
6. *Ibid.*, pp. 349-353.
7. *Ibid.*, p. 373.
8. *Ibid.*, pp. 357-358.
9. *CCNE*, pp. 57-58.
10. *MC*, pp. 8-9.
11. *Ibid.*, pp. 9-11.
12. *LM*, Lecture on "Nature and Revelation," pp. 263-264.
13. *CLC*, pp. 44-46.
14. *Ibid.*, pp. 47-48.
15. *LR*, pp. 210-213.
16. *Ibid.*, pp. 246-247.
17. *S and S*, p. 430.
18. *CLC*, pp. 84-86.
19. *CLC*, pp. 85-86.
20. *Ibid.*, pp. 202-203.
21. *S and S*, p. 406. The concept of Nature as the servant of man is derived directly from Swedenborg, who apparently derived it from Aristotle.
22. *CLC*, pp. 194-196.
23. *S of S*, pp. 190-191.
24. *Ibid.*, pp. 191-192.
25. *CLC*, pp. 76-77, 78-80.
26. *S and S*, p. 421.
27. *S and S*, pp. 381-383.

Chapter Nine

The Doctrine of Spiritual Man

How then, does Nature evolve man? . . . Let us begin at once by frankly avowing that it will be quite impossible to do this, unless we can first establish a normal and complete distinction between man and all lower forms of existence,—unless we can prove, in other words, that human nature, instead of being the development which it is loosely supposed to be of all lower natures, is in truth their decisive arrest and confutation.

—HENRY JAMES, SR.[1]

Hence the Artist claims to be the reconciling or united term between God and man, the spiritual or infinite reality symbolized by the literal or finite God-man, the wholly incontestible son of God, the heir of all divine power majesty and glory, by whom alone God estimates the world.

—HENRY JAMES, SR.[2]

When one looks at the elder James's theory of personality in cross-section, without regard to man's origin or his ultimate destiny, it is seen to be an anticipation of Freudian theory. The sleeping Adam, the chaos of the unconscious, may be compared to the id, the concept of the proprium or self to the ego, and the conscience or social self to the superego. . . .

The adequacy of the theory is limited by the maker's own emotional constellation, but it was a great achievement for its day, and ought to be recognized as a landmark in the history of American thought.

—QUENTIN ANDERSON[3]

JAMES TOOK OCCASION in a lecture on "The Divine Man" to consider a group of concepts which developed into his general doctrine of Spiritual Man. These concepts—natural man, moral man, spiritual man—are found in this lecture by James only in embryonic form, but they constitute a constellation of ideas, or another "triad" of concepts, about which James was to write to the close of his career. The lecture entitled "The Divine Man" appeared, after its oral delivery in New York during the previous year, in *The Massachusetts Quarterly Review*, 1850, and so falls within those four years from 1846-1850 when James was acquiring his basic stock of conceptions from Sandemanianism, Swedenborgianism, and Fourierism, and trying to fuse them into a systematic philosophical expression of his own. He spent the three decades from 1850 to 1880 in a sustained literary effort to expound the ideas which he acquired during this pregnant period from 1846-1850.

Moralism and Christianity (1850), contains three lectures: "The Divine Man," "Socialism and Christianity," "Morality and the Perfect Life." These three lectures, taken together as a unit, offer a truly beautiful illustration of the dialectical pattern so inevitably associated with Fichte and Hegel, of thesis-antithesis-synthesis. The spiritual individualism of "The Divine Man" is followed by the spiritual socialism of "Socialism and Civilization," while the individualism and socialism are fused in the last lecture on "Morality and the Perfect Life." There is more sense of intellectual movement in these lectures as a unit than in any comparable span in any other of his works. They reveal plainly the record of intellectual upheaval in James at the height of his efforts to bring Swedenborg and Fourier into a fusion of some kind that would result in the construction of a philosophy of his own. After he had finished *Moralism and Christianity,* the groundwork of his philosophic superstructure was laid and completed; moreover, he never doubted his foundations from this time forward.

We are concerned specifically in this chapter with the spiritual dynamics of human personality, as viewed by James. It should be borne in mind, as we approach the investigation of his Doctrine of Spiritual Man, that James is now interested, not in man as individual or as social, but in man as man, with reference to the guiding concept of "spiritual individuality." In other words, it is a typistic, universalized, *spiritual* psychology and anthropology which he expounds. When we recall that the two great characteristics of philosophic spiritualism to James are "objectivity" and "universality," we are prepared with a proper orientation to understand his "spiritual" anthropology;

for it is obvious at once that "individuality" as spiritually defined is far from having reference to any "individual" or all individuals. One scholar of the elder James has, as we shall learn later in this chapter, explored the use to which Henry James, Jr. put the implications of his father's spiritual psychology in the creation of literary "individuals" in his novels. Given our study of James's epistemological and ontological views, however, the concept of spiritual individuality will seem, by contrast, to the reader, much more "individual" and personal than any doctrine encountered hitherto or to be encountered hereafter in James.

What *are* the dynamics of "spiritual individuality"? To answer summarily in Jamesian terms, they are variously defined by him as *Selfhood* (he often uses the Latin term *proprium*, after Swedenborg), *Personality, Conscience, Morality, Consciousness, Freedom-Spontaneity,* and finally, the spiritualized *Principle of Bi-Sexual Polarity* (this phrase is the writer's, for James gives it no covering term).

In this chapter will be considered *Personality* (with "freedom" and "Spontaneity" as sub-heads), *Selfhood* (in its "positive" aspect), *Consciousness* (with the "unconscious" as sub-head); and lastly, the *Bi-Sexual Polarity Principle,* which James variously expresses in pairs of contrasted terms, as "Adam-Eve," *"homo-vir,"* "identity-individuality," "masculine-feminine," "paternity-maternity," "substance-form." In the next chapter will be treated *Selfhood* (in its "negative" aspect), *Conscience,* and *Morality.* They are considered in relation to James's Doctrine of Spiritual Evil because of their close affiliations in his thought with the whole problem of evil.

I

That James would parallel his ontological triad of the Celestial-Spiritual-Natural worlds; and his functional triads of End-Cause-Effect and Love-Wisdom-Use; and his epistemological triad of Sensible-Rational-Spiritual knowledge—that he would parallel these triads with a psychological triad of Natural-Moral-Spiritual man is hardly an occasion for surprise. The surprise would have been if he hadn't! James's thought-structure is hierarchic, and dialectic; it is trinal monism throughout, motored by the principles of Correspondence, Influx, and the Creative-Redemptive double movement. The same structurally trichotomous schema appears in the next chapter as Physical-Moral-Spiritual evil. In his social thought it appears as Church-State-

Society, and in his philosophy of history, as Religion-Science-Philosophy.

The chief methodological and dialectical trait in James's thought, is the persistent habit of triadic formulation of his major doctrines. To cite the main examples of this characteristic is illuminating; they are arranged below in relation to the two great movements: Involution (the "downward" movement from the Divine), and Evolution (the "upward" movement, or return to the Divine). Reference to the accompanying diagram (on the following page) of these triads will make the Neo-Platonic pattern more apparent:

INVOLUTION	EVOLUTION
Triads:	Triads:
Esse-Essence-Existere	Sense-Reason-Revelation
Celestial-Spiritual-Natural	Formation-Creation-Redemption
Love-Wisdom-Use	Natural-Moral-Spiritual Man
End-Cause-Effect	Physical-Moral-Spiritual Evil
	Adam-Eve-Church
	Homo-Vir-Society
	King-Priest-Artist
	Church-State-Society
	Religion-Science-Philosophy
	Divine-Natural-Humanity.

To James, the power to evolve is itself first involved by action of the Divine Being. This concept of Involution of all that later appears in the world-process as Evolution, offers an intelligible complement to such theories as "emergent evolution" in which matter, life, mind, and Deity simply evolve in that order; or, as in Alexander's theory of Space, Time, Matter, Life, Mind, and Deity, in an evolutionary order. James's Neo-Platonic and Swedenborgian principle of Involution seems to the writer to be much profounder and more intelligible by far to philosophic consciousness. That this metaphysical doctrine of Involution-Evolution appeals to significant thinkers in every century is borne out at present by Sri Aurobindo, thought by many intelligent thinkers to be India's great living philosopher in the mid-twentieth century. To read Aurobindo's masterpiece, *The Life Divine,* is, to one who has read the senior James's works, to experience an indescribable feeling that Aurobindo and James must have corresponded and conversed with each other; so much spiritual kinship is there between the philosophies of

NEO-PLATONIC METAPHYSICS OF HENRY JAMES, SR.*

[The "Involution" triads were taken by James from Swedenborg; the "Evolution" triads were developed originally by James.]

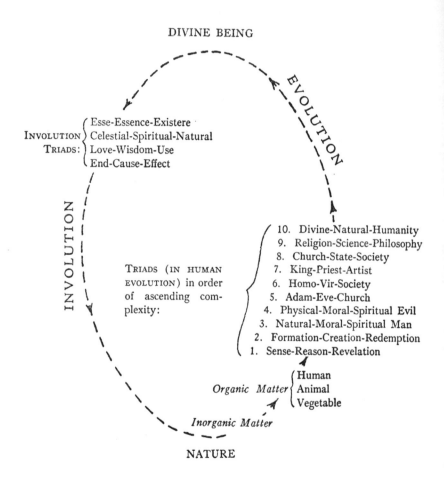

DIVINE BEING

INVOLUTION TRIADS:
{ Esse-Essence-Existere
Celestial-Spiritual-Natural
Love-Wisdom-Use
End-Cause-Effect

INVOLUTION

EVOLUTION

TRIADS (IN HUMAN EVOLUTION) in order of ascending complexity:

10. Divine-Natural-Humanity
9. Religion-Science-Philosophy
8. Church-State-Society
7. King-Priest-Artist
6. Homo-Vir-Society
5. Adam-Eve-Church
4. Physical-Moral-Spiritual Evil
3. Natural-Moral-Spiritual Man
2. Formation-Creation-Redemption
1. Sense-Reason-Revelation

Organic Matter { Human
Animal
Vegetable

Inorganic Matter

NATURE

* Diagram above, constructed by author.

NOTE: This particular type of Neo-Platonic metaphysics may be termed Trinal Monism, as distinguished from Plotinian or any other classic type. Trinal Monism, with the principles of "Correspondence" and of "Discrete Degrees," was an attempt by Swedenborg to overcome the rigid dualism of Cartesian metaphysics.

these two thinkers! The reader should be allowed to experience the remarkable similarity for himself. Aurobindo writes:

> Evolution of Life in matter supposes a previous involution of it there, unless we suppose it to be a new creation magically and unaccountably introduced into Nature. If it is that, it must either be a creation out of nothing or a result of material operations which is not accounted for by anything in the operations themselves or by any element in them which is of a kindred nature; or, conceivably, it may be a descent from above, from some supraphysical plane above the material universe. The two first suppositions can be dismissed as arbitrary conceptions [this is exactly James's position]; the last explanation is possible. . . . But this does not exclude the origin of life from Matter itself as a primary and necessary movement; for the existence of a Life-world or Life-plane above the material does not of itself lead to the emergence of Life in matter unless that Life-plane exists as a formative stage in a descent of Being through several grades or powers of itself into the Inconscience, with the result of an involution of itself with all these powers in Matter for a later evolution and emergence. (*The Life Divine*, Greystone Press, N. Y., 1949, pp. 171-172).

Again:

> The descent of the supreme Reality is in its nature a self-concealing; and in the descent there are successive levels, in the concealing successive veils. Necessarily, the revelation takes the form of an ascent; and necessarily also the ascent and the revelation are both progressive. For each successive level in the descent of the Divine is to man a stage in an ascension; each veil that hides the unkown God becomes for the God-lover and God-seeker an instrument of His unveiling. Out of the rhythmic slumber of material Nature unconscious of the Soul and the Idea that maintain the ordered activities of her energy even in her dumb and mighty material trance, the world struggles into . . . Life. . . . Out of Life it struggles upward into Mind . . . and in that awakening the universe gains the leverage it required for its supreme work, it gains self-conscious individuality. . . .
>
> For there seems to be no reason why Life should evolve out of material elements or Mind out of living form, unless we accept the Vedantic [also, Neo-Platonic and Jamesian] solution that Life is already involved in Matter and Mind in Life because in essence Matter is a form of veiled Life, Life a form of veiled Consciousness. (*Ibid.*, pp. 43-44, 45).

We should remind ourselves that the psychological triad we are about to consider, functions within the framework of the "return" or upward, redemptive, evolutionary movement. Spirit is now somewhat advanced in its first recoil from Nature and "Formation," as it now passes beyond the preliminary process of creation, on its way back to its Divine Source in God.

James exhibits his psycho-anthropology most succinctly and completely in his lecture, "The Divine Man." Here he conveys his concept of natural-man, moral-man, and spiritual- (or Divine) man. Although he is ever unsystematic and over-prodigal in his use of terms in elucidating any of his doctrines—since now he speaks in one place of "individuality, character, being, *proprium,* selfhood, personality, whatever you please to call the inmost vital fact in man"[4]—it is nonetheless impossible to miss the general correlation of "mere identity" with the natural-man, of "selfhood" and "consciousness" with the moral-man, and of "personality" and "spiritual individuality" with the spiritual-man; or, to put it in a slightly freer use of his terms: man *under* natural necessity, man *under* social constraint and self-consciousness; and man *in* the freedom and spontaneity of his spiritual estate of regeneration.

In the chapter on "The Spiritual Meaning of Nature," we saw how Nature gives man "identity" to himself; for in his very efforts to understand her, he is forced to distinguish himself from her. It is, therefore, unnecessary to expound the concept of the "natural man" here to any great extent. This man, as such, is simply a slave to "appearance" and to Nature's dictations. As for the "moral man," some exposition of "Selfhood" is requisite for a better understanding of the over-all concept of "Personality" which he applies to the "spiritual man." The concept of "selfhood" will be more fully expounded in the chapter on Evil because of its close association with that doctrine. In the present connection, "selfhood" is considered in its relation to the better comprehension of the inner evolution of the Spiritual Man.

James lays a foundation for his concept of Selfhood in his long article on "The Works of Sir William Hamilton":

> This is exactly what is involved in all organization [or selfhood], the alliance of an objective and governing nature with a subjective and obedient form. . . . It is the nature of the subject which governs his activity, which constitutes the true object of his action, and the nature of the subject is always interior to the subject's self.[5]

James then makes that abstract statement very concrete. Imagine, he says, that I am confronted by my hostess with a choice to be made between coffee or black tea: "I choose black tea. Now the action involves subject and object; I, who make the choice, am the subject; the satisfaction of my palate and, or just simply, the desire to please the hostess, is the object. The object is not black tea as Sir William Hamilton would allege; for black tea is incorporate with the action itself—*given* in the action—and clearly no action incorporates or supplies its own object any more than its own subject," for this would be to make action "deny itself."[6] The "true object" to James is "interior to the subject"; not only this, but the object, so defined, is *also* "superior" to the subject, since it governs the subject.

If we follow a loosely chronological order from his writings, we can observe varying stresses and deepening meanings as they creep into his concept of Selfhood. In *Moralism and Christianity*, he says:

Two doctrines exist in the world, that of Moralism, which affirms man's rightful subjection to nature and society; and that of the Christ, or Divine Man, which affirms man's rightful subjection only to God; and these two are so contrary one to the other as to fill the whole earth with the dust and the noise of their contention. . . .

The end of God in my creation is to impart Himself to me, to make Himself over to me with all His infinite resources of love, wisdom, and power. But in order to this end I must first exist, must first have a *quasi* selfhood, a conditional or finite existence, by the medium of which I may become introduced, as it were, to my divine bridegroom, and give myself away in an eternal espousals. . . .

All finite experience is generated of opposition. The orbit or individuality of the earth, for example, results from a perfect balance of the repellent and attractive influences of the sun, a perfect equilibrium of its centrifugal and centripetal motions. . . . Precisely similar is the genesis of man's finite experience. He becomes self-conscious, self-defined, by the experience of two opposite laws or principles inciting his activity, which laws or principles are variously named, the one external the other internal, the one public the other private, the one evil the other good, and the one infernal the other celestial.

The first of these principles is self-love. . . . The second law bears the name of charity or benevolence. . . . The operation of *either* law unchecked by the other, would be fatal to the finite consciousness: for the former would affirm the individual to the denial of the universal, while the latter would affirm the universal to the denial of the individual, and these being correlative, the denial of one is a virtual denial of both.

Man's finite selfhood or experience then demands for its perfect development an exact balance or equilibrium of these two loves, self-love and brotherly love, or charity. . . .

How then does this finite and preliminary experience of mine become elaborated? What constitutes its apparatus? Nature and Society. My experience of the natural and the moral life is what gives me a finite consciousness, a consciousness of a selfhood distinct from every other self. My relations to nature incessantly inspire the sentiment of self-love. My relations to society, or to my fellow man, as incessantly inspire the counter sentiment of charity or brotherly love. . . .

I say that the normal state of man exacts the perfectly balanced or harmonic operation of these principles. . . . And the creature cannot exhibit this perfection, this self-sufficiency, so long as either nature or society dominates him. . . .

In the first place, Nature gives me a bodily individuality, distinct from all other bodies. Then Society guarantees me an exclusive property or selfhood in this body, gives me a title to its possession good against every other individual. If it were not for the phenomenon of society or fellowship among men, if men were simply gregarious like sheep, then with their tremendous individuality they would soon exterminate each other. First, the strong would exterminate the weak, then the more strong the less strong, until you would finally get down to the solitary strongest man, dismal denizen of the unpeopled planet. . . .

Such is the constitution of the selfhood we derive from nature and society, inevitably finite or imperfect. First of all it is limited to the body, or the experience of the five senses, shut up as it were to a pin's point in space and time; and when afterwards through the fostering care of society, it becomes developed and enlarged, it still remains finite, still falls short of its rightful infinitude, of that infinitude which belongs to it by virtue of its creation.[7]

In those excerpts we can trace the evolution of James's thought step by step. Two years later, in *Lectures and Miscellanies*, he is saying the same thing, but with a note of greater philosophic mastery:

For what all over the world is the distinctive mark of manhood? It is not physical subjectivity or subjection to nature, for the vegetable is far more exclusively the subject of its physical organization, than the animal is of his. And it is not moral subjectivity, or subjection to society, for many of the animals, take the bee for example, or the ant, or the beaver, greatly excel the best of men in this respect. No, the grand distinctive trait of man is his subjection to an ideal selfhood, or his power of acting, not in obedience to either physical or social constraint, but in obedience to his own ideas of goodness, truth, and beauty. What distinguishes him from the lower existences is that his activity acknowledges an ideal end, or that his objective sphere of existence—that sphere which furnishes the end, the object, the inspiration of his action—lies within himself, within his natural subjectivity.

Accordingly if you look at the vegetable or animal existence, you will find a total destitution of this ideal subjectivity, of this subjection to an inward object. . . . Man indeed exhibits the same infirmity in so far as he is involved in the vegetable and animal existence, or so long as he is held in subjugation to the necessities of his physical and social subsistence. While food and raiment are still insecure to him, and the respect of his fellow-man unachieved, *he* also lives to a finite end, and fails to exhibit, at least in a positive manner, that true human worth which stands in the obedience of an exclusively inward and infinite object, in the obedience of ideas.

I say a "positive" manner, because man does all the while chafe under this servitude. He will not accept mere physical and moral existence, as the limit of his destiny. Instead of contenting himself like the vegetable, with the bare supply of his physical wants, or like the animal, with the added supply also of his social wants, his instincts of infinitude, his instincts of Deity, drive him to seek their *excessive* gratification, and to hurry him into vice and crime. . . .

Vice expresses his attempt to actualize his ideal and essential infinitude, without the concurrence of nature. Crime expresses his attempt to actualize it, without the concurrence of society.

Thus the very vices and crimes of man place him above nature, deny his essential finiteness, proclaim his true subjection to be to an ideal and infinite object only.[8]

With the publication three years later, in 1855, of *The Nature of Evil,* James's thought begins to dwell more on the negative concept of the *finite* selfhood, and more negatively still, he dwells on the finite selfhood as the very font and source of "spiritual evil." In the passage now to be cited, James uses "selfhood" evidently with reference to the "finite" rather than the "infinite" selfhood, but unless we keep such a distinction between the two types of selfhood constantly in mind, we are quickly led to confusion. The finite selfhood is necessary enough in itself, but it is "strictly conditional" to the emergence of the true, or infinite selfhood. James slips over into using "consciousness" as a practical synonym for the finite selfhood, but this identification is not final, for later, as we shall see when we come to consider the concept of "consciousness" in general, James, just as with the concept of selfhood, splits the concept into the finite and infinite kinds of consciousness:

> The selfhood in man, accordingly, is not absolute, but strictly finite and conditional. It is at bottom only a *quasi* or seeming selfhood, rigidly dependent upon the equilibrium of two opposing forces. These forces must be opposed, because if they were consentaneous, their accord would preclude the possibility of any middle or neutral term. . . . Hence I repeat that the existence of God's creature is conditioned upon the exact equilibrium of two opposing forces. This equilibrium furnishes the indispensable basis of the creature's consciousness, so that if you take it away, you take away not merely that consciousness, but also all that divine and infinite blessedness to which this preliminary consciousness serves as a foundation.[9]

The "two opposing forces" are variously interpreted by James as "good and evil" (moral), "truth and falsity" (intellectual), and "celestial and infernal" (spiritual); and, as he tells us on a previous page, it is not merely the opposition between these dual forces that must be recognized by the human consciousness, but also their "balance" and "exact equilibrium," because both of the extremes of each of these three pairs of "opposing forces" *define each other* to human consciousness.

James adds a footnote to the idea that man must of necessity have only *seeming* life, for if man had *real* life in himself, God would have sacrificed his god-ship at the very moment of creating man:

> Were God to create a being which could possibly exist or act independently of Himself, He would manifestly cease to be a creator the moment He became one. He might, thenceforward claim to have been a creator "once upon a time," but clearly not to be so any longer. He would have been a creator *in posse* of the creature in question, only whilst the latter was not *in esse*: the instant this event supervened, His creative relation must have ceased, or become a merely historic verity.[10]

If the finite self is only finite, and if it is the threshold only of the infinite, or spiritual, selfhood of man, it is nevertheless a marvel of creation. Eight years later than *The Nature of Evil,* James, in *Substance and Shadow,* composes a noble panegyric on this theme:

> In very truth this altogether unobtrusive fact of selfhood or natural life which we are all born to, and which we there-fore think nothing of but accept as a mere matter of course, is itself the eternal marvel of creation. We ourselves . . . can change the form of existing things; *i.e.* can convert natural forms into artificial ones. But we cannot confer life; cannot make these artificial forms self-conscious or living. We can turn a block of wood into a table, a block of stone into a statue; but our work in no wise reflects the vivacity of Nature, because we not being life in ourselves, cannot possibly communicate life to the work of our hands. We frame a beautiful effigy of life; but the effigy remains forever uninhabited, forever irresponsive to the love which fashions it; in short forever unconscious or dead.
> Now the splendor of the creative activity is, that it makes even this effigy of itself alive with the amplest life; its product being no cold inanimate statue, but a living breathing exulting person. In short the everlasting miracle is that God is able, in giving us Himself, to endow us with our own finite selfhood as well; leaving us thereby so unidentified with Himself, so utterly free and untrammelled to our own consciousness as to be able very often seriously to doubt, and not seldom permanently to deny His own existence.[11]

James wonders at the miracle, and asks how it could have happened so. Human consciousness presses for an answer. James is very positive that no answer can be more intelligible than his, not because it is his, but because it must commend itself to all thinking men. The marvel occurred because God put His very self and life into us, and this He did because Love is of the veriest essence of the Divine Being:

> And this miracle I say is utterly inexplicable upon any *datum* but that I have alleged, namely: that God is so truly infinite in love as not to shrink from shrouding His uncreated splendor in His creature's lineaments, from eternally humiliating Himself to the lowest possibilities of creaturely imbecility and iniquity, in order that the creature may thus become freely or spiritually elevated to the otherwise impracticable heights of His majestic wisdom and goodness.
> I ask no indulgence of my reader for this language. I literally mean what I say, that creation is absolutely contingent upon the Divine ability to humble Himself to the creature's level, to

diminish Himself to the creature's *natural* dimensions. Language is incapable of painting too vividly the strength of my convictions on this subject.[12]

This humbling of the Creator to the "creature's level," this diminishing of the Divine Glory to the "lowest possibilities of creaturely imbecility and iniquity, in order that the creature may thus become freely or spiritually elevated . . . to the heights of His majestic wisdom and goodness," is truly an "inversion" of the Creator's splendor, as James calls it elsewhere. Just as in his doctrine of the Spiritual Meaning of Nature, Nature or the world of physical substance is an inversion of the Divine Wisdom, so here, man is an inversion of the Divine Love.

James's convictions about God as Creator are really very empirical in quality as compared with the classical, rationalistic "proofs" of the "existence" of God in the form of the so-called ontological, cosmological, and teleological arguments. In the first place, we have seen how, on Jamesian grounds, God cannot "*ex*-ist"; in the second place, James simply looks at the empirical "creature" that is man, and inducts the dynamics of creation that must have led to this result. Anthropomorphic? James would brush the word aside as inane. What is anthropomorphism in *thought,* that one should be afraid of it, when the invisible God became the visible Lord by becoming anthropomorphic in *reality?* Contemptuous of abstract ideas as much as Berkeley, James's discourse has that quality all along which might well be designated as "Spiritual Positivism."

He would have us become immensely and "livingly" conscious of the unfathomable love and wisdom implied by our creation as he dilates upon the majestic thought:

> But obviously a love of this infinite quality implies a proportionate wisdom to carry it out. For it can never realize itself in action, save by vivifying *the nature* of the creature in a manner so absolute or thorough, as to make him seem to himself an unquestionable subject of nature, and lead him therefore instinctively to revolt at the imputation of direct creatureship. And what infinite skill or address is requisite to accomplish such a result! What an infinite wisdom, what a stupendous order, must the universe of existence exhibit, in order that the creature of God may find *himself* there without a risk of mistake or misconception; may arrive at a form of consciousness so definite and absolute, as to defy the faintest suspicion in his mind of the real

truth of the case, and leave him on the contrary so complacently self-poised as to render him an eternally fit subject of God's spiritual indwelling![13]

Both the philosophic and religious *rationale* of "selfhood" is given in two passages from *Society the Redeemed Form of Man,* in which there is first a philosophical definition of the phenomenon of "human nature," and then a warning as to its a-theistical tendencies:

Thus there is no way open to us philosophically of accounting for selfhood in the human bosom, save upon the postulate of its being the mask of an *infinite spiritual substance now imprisoned, but eventually to be set free, in our nature*: a substance whose proper energy consists in its incessantly going out of itself, or communicating itself to what is not itself, to what indeed is infinitely alien and repugnant to itself, and *dwelling there infinitely and eternally as in its very self.* That is to say, the Divine being or substance is Love, love without the least set-off or limitation of self-love, infinite or creative love in short; and it communicates itself to the creature accordingly in no voluntary or finite but in purely spontaneous or infinite measure, in a way so to speak of overwhelming *passion*: so that we practically encounter no limit to our faculty of appropriating it, but on the contrary sensibly and exquisitely feel it to be our own indisputable being, feel it to be in fact our inmost, most vital and inseparable *self,* and unhesitatingly call it *me* and *mine, you* and *yours,* cleaving to it as inmost bone of our bone, and veritable flesh of our flesh, and incontinently renouncing all things for it. . . .

If human nature, as we have seen, possess neither moral nor physical quality, save by implication, that is, be neither person nor thing: if on the contrary it be nothing else than a most powerful but invisible *Divine bond of relationship between man individual and man universal;* a bond moreover so free and elastic as safely to permit the appropriation of a private selfhood to men, and the subsequent expansion of that selfhood even to diabolic proportions: then the only philosophic obstacle to the recognition of creation as a living or spiritual work of God disappears. That is to say: the only philosophic hindrance to men's believing in God as a creator, is their inability to believe in *themselves* as created. Self-consciousness, the sentiment of personality, the feeling I have of life in myself, absolute and underived from any other save in a natural way, is so subtly and powerfully atheistic, that no matter how loyally I may be taught to insist upon creation as a mere traditional or legendary fact,

I never feel inclined personally to believe in it, save as the fruit of some profound intellectual humiliation, or hopeless inward vexation of spirit. My inward *afflatus* from this cause is so great . . . that my sense of selfhood must in some subtle exquisite way find itself wounded to death—find itself *become death in fact, the only death I am capable of believing in*—before any genuine spiritual resuscitation is at all practicable for me.[14]

What is life to *feel* is death to *believe!* Here is the conflict between natural, moral, and spiritual man all in one!

With this general theory of "selfhood" in mind, in which the "imprisoned" God within us gives us the illusion of an independent selfhood, we can understand James's preeminent concern over the "infinite" selfhood which is possible for man to see only when he causes the finite selfhood to die through his realization that it is only an illusion. In "The Divine Man," James usually calls the spiritual (divine, or infinite) selfhood, "Personality," which seems a happy term for blending man's total experience with his finite and infinite selfhoods. It is with particular reference to this lecture on the Divine Man, where he employs the term "Personality" most frequently, as he does comparatively rarely elsewhere, that we now turn.

To begin with, James discourses about the two selfhoods in man, or "composite selfhood":

But now, if personality imply the power of self-derived or spontaneous action, then it is manifest that this power supposes in the subject a composite selfhood. It supposes its subject to possess an internal or spiritual self as the end or object of the action, and an external or natural self as its means or instrument. . . . I repeat, then, that personality . . . supposes a dual or composite selfhood in the subject, a selfhood composed of two elements, one internal, spiritual, or private, the other external, natural, or public.[15]

The next step for James is to reason that the fact of a dual selfhood implies an ideal coordination beween them which will result in the infinite and spiritual selfhood, or Personality. He elucidates the meaning of "Personality" by using the Artist type of humanity as the best exemplification of what he is striving to convey. As one reads these sections of his Lecture, he detects a radical quality of apparent rebellion against Nature and Society that actually has a Nietzschean ring about it. True, Nietzsche's "tragic estheticism" and James's spiritual estheticism are quite different in various presuppositions and motivations, but there is still, untechnically speaking now, a spiritual affinity between Nietzsche's artist-superman and James's "aesthetic man." The reader will relish the flavor for himself:

> . . . We have seen that man is the only competent revelation or image of God, because man alone possesses personality. . . .
>
> But now, from the definition given of personality, it is manifest that it is to be ascribed to man only in his very inmost or highest development, and not at all in his physical or social relations. . . .
>
> Hence neither man's natural nor his moral action confers a divine or perfect personality on him. The former does not, because it displays him in subjection to nature. The latter does not, because it displays him in subjection to his fellow-man. Both the moral and natural man are imperfect. Both fail to exhibit that balanced or self-centred action, which is the exclusive basis of personality, and both alike consequently fail to express the DIVINE MAN, or accomplish the divine image in humanity. . . .
>
> Who, then, *is* the true divine man? Who of all mankind possesses personality, and thus constitutes the image of God in creation? Evidently it must be some one who unites in himself, or harmonizes, all these finite or imperfect men. For the divine man does not exclude the natural man, nor the moral man . . . nor any other phasis of humanity. These are all constituent elements of the human nature, and the perfect man is bound not to exclude but accept them, blending and reconciling all in his own infinite manhood. . . .
>
> Who, then, is the perfect or divine man, the man who actually reconciles in himself all the conflicting elements of humanity? Is any such man actually extant? If so, where shall we find him? We find him in the aesthetic man, or Artist.[16]

Preparatory to the full consideration of the concept of the "aesthetic man" should be an inquiry into James's ideas concerning "freedom" and "spontaneity," for these are the dominant characteristics in the Jamesian portrait of the Divine or Spiritual Man. The Divine, the Aesthetic, the Redeemed, the Spiritual Man—however James verbalizes one and the same idea, is a man of "Spontaneity." Freedom and spontaneity (James uses them not quite interchangeably because "spontaneity" is reserved to distinguish the highest kind of freedom, which, of course, is "spiritual" freedom): these are the essential attributes equally of Spirituality, Artistry, and Redeemed Society.

Another American thinker, Charles Sanders Peirce, was beginning to speculate on Chance ("Tychism") and Spontaneity before James died, but Peirce's "spontaneity" was weighted on the cosmological side as a theory of indeterminism, while James's was anthropological and sociological in reference. It would indeed be an attractive task to trace certain parallel *directions* of thought between James and Peirce: James's Spiritual Socialism and Peirce's "Unlimited Community," followed by Royce's "Beloved Community"; between James's Spontaneity and Peirce's "Tychism," between James's stress on the Divine Love as the supreme essence of God and Peirce's "Evolutionary Agapism." With very different presuppositions and conclusions, thinkers in a given age are often paralleling each other in the great basic trends of their thought. Regardless of technical differences, there is a much greater similarity in their mutual emphasis on the *objective*, the *generalized*, the *socialized*, between the elder James and Peirce than there is between either one of them and the individualistic William James. Subtle spiritual similarities are just as much the business of the student of cultural history to note as the often highly technical dissimilarities.

In the chapter on James's "Doctrine of Spiritual Knowledge," we observed that to him, "facts" carry *com*-pulsion upon the knowing mind, while Revelation (along with "truth" and "meaning"), yields *im*-pulsion and so choice to men's minds. Because "freedom" implies and requires growth and experience in man's life, James is opposed to intuitionalist theories of knowledge. His attack upon "intuition" might well have been treated under the chapter on knowledge; or it may now be considered in connection with the concept of "consciousness," soon to be expounded. The writer has chosen to present it here in connection with "freedom," however, because, in several places, James has associated growth in knowledge by *experience*, with the concept of freedom. Some of the lesser reviewers of James referred to him as being "intuitionist" in his philosophy, but not so Clarke, Howison, or Peirce. Just as we have not seen any good reason to call James a mystic, or a seer, so do we not see him as an advocate or practitioner of intuition-ism, in the root meaning of the word. One can have a deep sense of mystery and not be a mystic; or be a deep thinker *about* Revelation without *having* a revelation for one's self; or be a man of insight without being a man of materialized visions like Blake and Swedenborg. Just so, a man can have a strong belief in the highest and best kind of knowledge as being *within*, and yet not be an intuitionist in theory of knowledge. Who does not but admit the differences between "opinion," "knowledge," "understanding," and "wisdom" as differing levels of reaction in the growth of the human mind? Yet does not the universal recognition of these differing levels of mental apprehension give the logical quietus to any thoroughgoing intuitionism? The fact that some ideas seem to come suddenly to us as compared with others, or that our thoughts seem so deep at times that we cannot adequately express them, though we go on sometimes insisting that we "know" despite the failure in communication—such experiences are pretty much subjective. The ABC's of critical thought consist in recognizing that *subjective certainty,* whether of faith or of doubt, is *not demonstration of objective reality.* At any rate, we find James square against intuition:

> Now reason is dependent for its illumination upon experience, and consequently it cannot discern that God alone is life and the Giver of life to man, save in so far as it becomes *experimentally instructed* on that point. The reason does not live by abstract truths, but real ones. There is no such thing in God's universe as an abstraction: it is a universe exclusively of realities. It is not true abstractly, or apart from fact, that God is life and gives life to man; but *really* true, or true to fact, true, *that is, to the experience of the creature;* and so far as it is untrue to that experience, it is manifestly not true at all. Man's rational development demands, then, a theatre of experience, by means of which he may become built up and established in the truth. . . . I say so much is evident, because no one attributes to man the faculty of intuition, which is the power of growing wise without experience. Had we this power, then indeed we might know the divinest truths without the preliminary discipline of experience. But to say nothing of the utter worthlessness of such knowledge to us, were it actually possible, it is abundantly certain that our reason includes no such faculty: and this being the case, I repeat that reason must obviously remain blind to the great spiritual truth that God alone is Life . . . until such time as it shall have become experimentally taught that man is without life in himself, and consequently dependent upon God for it.[17]

In other connections, James makes it plain that his spiritual empiricism is important because it means a guarantee of man's creaturely freedom. Experience and growth, trial and error, are, as we have learned elsewhere, ways of protecting the exercise of human freedom, for if we had genuine intuition in its real, radical sense we would be God Himself. The only other alternative would be for

God to make human creatures as pure automata, in which case there would be not even "tuition" possible, much less *in*-tuition.

"Experience," however, is not itself to be confounded by any means with "Freedom." Experience as such is constituted by universal contradictions of good-and-evil, true-and-false, beautiful-and-ugly, heaven-and-hell, necessity-and-freedom. Since experience is only the means by which freedom may be distinguished in thought and practice, what, positively, is freedom itself to James? He answers, not in the customary frame of "freedom of the will," but rather, as inveterate with him, in terms of another triad:

> Three sorts of freedom or life are known to us, each of which resolutely disowns an outward origin: 1. Physical or passive freedom, of which instinct is the symbol, and which consists in doing whatsoever the heart pronounces good: *i.e.* in having all the passions and appetites of one's nature in due or normal exercise: 2. Moral or active freedom, whose symbol is will, and which consists in doing whatsoever the intellect pronounces true, even if it should contradict what the heart feels to be good: 3. Spiritual or essential freedom, whose badge is spontaneity, growing out of the reconciliation or marriage of good in the heart with truth in the understanding, and which consists accordingly in the total harmony of one's outward life with one's inward aspiration: *i.e.* in one's being precisely what one wishes to be, and seeming precisely what one is. These are the three universal modes of what we call freedom, selfhood, life, consciousness, in man; and it is obvious to a glance that each alike repugns the least outward dictation.[18]

We are only honest if we say that it is not quite so "obvious" to our "glance" as it appears to be to Mr. James's! It might seem that he has stretched the word "freedom" to cover so much that it quite loses any distinctive meaning. On the other hand, his idea has value in that it asserts freedom to hinge on something wider then the "will."

James, in his threefold concept of Freedom, has a very positive doctrine. Like End-Cause-Effect, or Love-Wisdom-Use, physical-moral-spiritual Freedom exhibits to James's thought no confusion; there is physical freedom after its kind, moral freedom according to its kind, and spiritual freedom after its kind. There is clearly, to James, an increasing quality and range of freedom as one passes up the freedom-scale. From Freedom-of-Instinct to Freedom-of-Will to Freedom-of-Spirit—this is a large and generous order of freedom in the life of man! But what about the problem of higher freedoms inhibiting the freedom of that freedom beneath its own category? James apparently senses no problem of that kind.

"Spiritual Freedom" is obviously the most significant for James, and for this type he reserves the important term of "Spontaneity," which he never uses with reference to the two lower kinds of freedom. On another occasion he becomes very concrete about spiritual freedom in a fine passage which, in its psychological depth of insight, reminds one of St. Augustine's genius for spiritual penetration of human motivation:

> With such men chastity means the literal observance of law, though the total spirit of it be habitually and foully violated. But all this is simply preposterous. True virtue or manhood is never literal or legal, but always spiritual. It stands in no amount of conformity to established usage, but only in the spirit which dictates such conformity, whether a spirit of freedom or one of self-seeking. There is no such thing as a virtuous or vicious act in itself, and apart from the temper of the actor. Man alone is virtuous or vicious, and his action is one or the other, only as it is colored by his personality. Thus chastity is not an act, it is the spirit from which every action should proceed. There is no such thing as an act of chastity, but only acts of uncleanness. All our acts are alike acts of uncleanness, until they are redeemed by that spirit of chastity which is incessantly vivifying us inwardly from God. The true marriage sentiment is first spiritual, and carnal only by derivation from that; so that the identical acts which would be unchaste when begotten of another spirit, become now the home of chastity. In truth the sentiment is so inwardly inflamed by God's spotless love: it is in its essence or origin so interior a friendship, so profound a bosom fellowship and correspondence between man and woman, that every form of its existence or outgoing is of necessity chaste. To impose outward restraints upon it: to say to it, thou shalt not do this or that: is simply to ignore its Divine genesis, and misconceive its essential innocence. It is like forbidding defilement to violets, ferocity to doves, or duplicity to sheep.[19]

The exposition has led us to a consideration of "Spontaneity." As when James says "Science" he usually means Fourierist "Social Science," so when he says "spontaneity" he means, not a doctrine of cosmological indeterminism, but rather an anthropological doctrine indicative of man's spiritual freedom. Historically, "spontaneity" has usually been associated, in philosophic nomenclature, with "freedom of the will," but James means something more than this by his "spiritual" or "spontaneous" freedom. It is a richer concept: it is a "marriage of good in the heart with truth in the understanding," with no reference to the will as such. With this marriage consummated, apparently "freedom of the will" takes care of itself by implication. James reserves his highest encomium for "spontaneity" or "spiritual freedom":

> Precisely so it is with our perfected consciousness, with our spontaneous life, with whatsoever we do from delight or attraction. Infinite and finite are so livingly united, so lovingly wedded and bedded within the periphery of our spontaneity, within all the range of our aesthetic life and action, that it is sheer nonsense to attempt a logical divorce of them, by saying where one begins and the other leaves off. The true son of God wears a garment *without seam, woven from the top throughout,* and which cannot therefore be rent or divided, one half to God, the other to Nature. You might more easily divide heat from light in the solar ray, by gazing stupidly at the sun.[20]

Quite certainly a passage in *The Church of Christ not an Ecclesiasticism* is the stellar illustration of the Jamesian theory of spontaneity:

> To sum up: the earliest or infantile stage of human development is that in which the common or natural element dominates the private or individual one; the second or moral stage is that in which the private or individual element dominates the common or natural one; the third or spontaneous stage is that in which neither element dominates the other, but each is Divinely co-ordinated and adjusted to the other. To say the same thing less abstractly: in the instinctual or animal and infantile development of man, nature controls the selfhood; the body controls the soul; the flesh controls the spirit. In the voluntary or moral and adult stage, the selfhood controls the nature; the soul controls the body; the spirit controls the flesh. In the spontaneous, spiritual and mature stage, all controversy between these things has become Divinely reconciled, the body, flesh, or nature being by its own momentum reduced to the cordial allegiance of the higher and Diviner element.
>
> The spontaneous stage of human development then is the perfected stage, or that of man's perfect subjection to Divine Love. Man is now in finished form, and the Divine Love and Wisdom can flow into him without measure.[21]

James's discussion of freedom and spontaneity is consummated in his theory of the "Artist" and "the aesthetic man." It is logical to present for our scrutiny all the chief deliverances by James on this head, and then follow with a discussion of its significance. We recall the passage in which James asked: "Who, then, *is* the true divine man?" Which question he answered by saying: "We find him in the aesthetic man, or Artist." Succeeding this announcement of the Artist as the type of the spiritual or divine Man, James develops what he means by "Artist":

But now observe that when I speak of the aesthetic man or Artist, I do not mean the man of any specific function, as the poet, painter, or musician. I mean the man of whatsoever function, who in fulfillment of it obeys his own inspiration or taste, uncontrolled either by his physical necessities or his social obligations. He alone is the Artist, whatever be his manifest vocation, whose action obeys his own internal taste or attraction, uncontrolled by necessity or duty. The action may perfectly consist both with necessity and duty . . . but these must not be its animating principles, or he sinks at once from the Artist into the artisan. . . .

The reason accordingly why the painter, the poet, the musician, and so forth, have so long monopolized the name of Artist, is, not because Art is identical with these forms of action, for it is identical with no specific forms, but simply because the poet, painter, and so forth, more than any other men, have thrown off the tyranny of nature and custom, and followed the inspirations of genius, the inspirations of beauty, in their own souls. These men to some extent have sunk the service of nature and society in the obedience of their own private attractions. They have merged the search of the good and the true in that of the beautiful, and have consequently announced a divinity as yet unannounced either in nature or society. . . . And they are kings, who reign by a *direct* unction from the Highest. But the priest is not the altar, but the servant of the altar; and the king is not the Highest, but the servant of the Highest. So painting, poetry, is not Art, but the servant and representative of Art. Art is divine, universal, infinite. . . . We do not therefore call the painter or poet, Artist, because painting or poetry is a whit more essential to Art than ditching is, but simply because the painter and poet have more frequently exhibited the life of Art by means of a hearty insubjection to nature and convention.

When, therefore, I call the divine man, or God's image in creation, by the name of Artist, the reader will not suppose me to mean the poet, painter, or any other special form of man. On the contrary, he will suppose me to mean that infinite and spiritual man whom all these finite functionaries represent indeed, but whom none of them constitutes, namely, the man who in every visible form of action acts always from his inmost self, or from attraction, and not from necessity or duty. I mean the man who is a law unto himself, and ignores all outward allegiance, whether to nature or society.[22]

The last sentence, with its Nietzschean ring, stands out particularly like a solitary eruption of a geyser in a region of unsuspected volcanic depths: "I mean the man who is a law unto himself," who "ignores all outward allegiance." In his revolt against "nature and society," James goes even further than Transcendentalist individualism, but then he encloses his individualism ultimately within his Spiritual Socialism. James is unique among the thinkers of this period in that he attempted a synthesis of the most pronounced individualism of Transcendentalist thought with a socialism which had not only affiliation with Fourierist thought, but with the social implications of Swedenborg.

The defiant tone of the last sentence above, in the passage from James, is by no means an isolated instance in the lecture on "The Divine Man." Elsewhere, for example, he speaks of the divine man as "self-centred" in action. It is not our intention to over-dramatize this kind of language, but simply to note the radical kind of spiritual individualism that can be generated within a system of thought that is finally dominated by a vision of spiritual socialism. And it should be observed here also, that James never again in his writings, speaks so vigorously and exclusively to the theme of "spiritual individuality." That he conceived a "future occasion" when he would speak again to the theme of "the aesthetic man," is evident from this selection:

The Artist, then, is the Divine Man,—the only adequate image of God in nature,—because he alone acts of himself, or finds the object of his action always *within* his own subjectivity. He is that true creature and son of God, whom God pronounces very good, and endows with the lordship of the whole earth. It would not be difficult, in the writer's estimation, to show the reason why the evolution of this man has required the whole past physical and moral experience of the race, nor yet to show how perfectly he justifies all the historic features of Christianity, standing symbolized under every fact recorded in the four gospels concerning the Lord Jesus Christ. In some other place, or at least on some future occasion, the writer will undertake these tasks.[23]

That "future occasion" never came, beyond a single lecture on "The Principle of Universality in Art" in *Lectures and Miscellanies,* two years later. This is the last time he devotes a full lecture to "Art," much less a book. This later lecture on universality in art lacks the sharp depiction of artistic man as "being a law unto himself," and attends mainly to announcing some principles of socio-aesthetic, or perhaps aesthetico-social, criticism—whichever way one chooses to put it. The remainder of James's philosophy of Art is revealed in selected passages from this later lecture:

> The sphere of Art properly so called, is the sphere of man's spontaneous productivity. I say his spontaneous productivity, in order to distinguish it on the one hand from his *natural* productivity, or that which is prompted by his physical necessities, and on the other by his moral productivity, or that which is prompted by his obligations to other men.[24]
>
> . . . For Art does not lie in copying nature. Nature only furnishes the Artist with the material by means of which to express a beauty still unexpressed in nature. He beholds in nature more than nature herself holds or is conscious of. His informing eye it is which gives her that soul of beauty, that profoundly human meaning, which alone keeps her from being burdensome to the spirit. Nature *rules* only in the young and immature, only where the sensuous imagination still predominates. . . . She is simply the platform or theatre for the revelation of that infinite and divine beauty which dwells in the soul of man, and makes itself visible in all his spontaneous action. Hence nature should never predominate in the realm of Art, but only serve. . . .
>
> It is because the inmost secret of Art does not lie within the sphere of Art, but belongs only to Life. . . . To live or to act is more than to produce: hence the technical Artist has never succeeded and never will succeed in achieving the universal empire which belongs only to Man. The poet, painter, or musician is not the perfect man, the man of destiny, the man of God, because the perfect man is so pronounced by his life or action than by his production. . . .
>
> The Artist has typified the perfect man, because in the sphere of work or production he has wrought only from ideas, or from within outwards. But he has not *been* the perfect man, because in the sphere of life he has exhibited precisely the same conflict between the ideal and the actual as other men exhibit. Some-

times he has been a morally good man, and won the commendation of society; at others he has been a morally evil man and exposed himself to its reproach. But the perfect man is above both commendation and reproach. He is neither morally good nor morally evil. . . .

It is to this sphere accordingly, the sphere of Art, that we are authorized to look for the truest emblems of the consummate man, for the clearest revelation and foretaste of that positive manhood which shall one day lift us above nature, and give us the plenary fellowship of God.

Let us embalm the Artist therefore in our regard for his prophetic worth. . . . No clergyman in the land obeys the pure inspirations of God as manifested in his own soul, but only as sanctioned by certain traditional formulas approved by his sect. No lawyer enforces the principles of absolute justice, but only so far as embodied in certain existing standards. No poet declares the whole truth that trembles upon his soul, nor any painter the ineffable beauty that dazzles his inner vision. For poet and painter, lawyer and priest, are obliged before all things to secure a living upon the earth, and yield to their inspirations only so far therefore as consists with that prime necessity.[25]

"Let us embalm the Artist": without being facetious, this is precisely what James did in the history of his later thought. He might have gone far in a philosophy of Art, but in this lecture on the principle of universality in Art, one observes the subordinate place the artist is already given as compared to the *quasi*-apotheosis in "The Divine Man." He is *now* only of "prophetic worth," but *then*, the Artist *was* and *is* the Divine Man. James never lost his high regard for Art, but it takes more and more a secondary place in his thought. All of his strongest books were written after this lecture on universality in Art, and yet in the whole eight volumes or so that he was to write from 1852-1882, there is altogether no more than a dozen or so pages with references to Art or the Artist: there are three or four pages in *Substance and Shadow* where the sculptor is compared unfavorably with the reality of *Divine* creation, and the same number of pages in *Literary Remains* in connection with the "unreality" of what is ordinarily spoken of as artistic "creation." Not only in *Literary Remains* is artistic genius *not* genuinely creative, but by a reverse implication, James denies that the Creator's activities in creation are artistic! A typical passage or two from this source underlines the humble conception of the Artist in James's mind at this time:

Now your admirers [James is addressing his reader as though the reader were a sculptor] would flatter you egregiously, if they should call your genius *creative*. They might to be sure do so in a loose, figurative way, but nothing could be so absurd if meant seriously. Artistic power is in reality the precise opposite of infinite power, and no more pregnant contrast can be imagined, for example, than between it and the power displayed in spiritual creation. It is true we talk of God as the supreme artist, thinking thereby to do him honor. But however polite and even patronizing our intention may be, we do wretchedly scant justice to the object of it, whose characteristic action, *as creative*, is necessarily one of passion, humiliation, or suffering; while that of the artist is exclusively one of action, joy, or spontaneous delight.[26]

James never lost the "tragic" quality in his theology—that is, tragic from the side of God's "imprisonment" within the "imbecility" of human nature; but it seems strange that he should have overlooked the tragic quality in the tormenting travail of the artist before he is delivered from his creative, or semi-creative, labor. True, joy comes to him after the work is completed, although even then, the most sensitive artists are haunted with the feeling of having failed to incarnate their highest vision; and this haunted feeling is an even deeper kind of tragic experience. On the other hand, is there no "joy" for God after His passion in creation, as for the artist after he has completed his piece? It really seems to us that James has posed some false contrasts in his comparison of Creator to artist, and vice-versa, though of course, any intelligent mind must heartily recognize with James the great gap between creating a being who can feel, think, act—in a word, LIVE, and an inert statue, painting, or musical score that cannot have "life" communicated to it except temporarily when man acts upon it:

But what exists in the realm of art is not real, as having an honest or inward substance behind it, but only ideal, as being the mere echo or outcome of some empty personal *afflatus*—at most, of some insubstantial personal aspiration—on the artist's part.

Thus the statue is not even a thing, but only and at best the *appearance* of a thing, cunningly wrought out of nature's substances, but wholly destitute itself of natural soul or substance, because its maker—or, as we foolishly say, its creator—has no soul or substance *of his own* to impart to it, being himself a lifeless creature still unredeemed to his own consciousness from death. And hence I maintain that it is impossible for the artist,

Pygmalion-like, to be so infatuated with self-conceit as really even to dream of endowing his statue with attributes of which he himself has as yet no perception.[27]

That was written in the last year of James's life, when the realism of approaching death evidently and naturally turned his mind to the increasing reality of God, and so to the consequent subordination of man's petty "creative" activities in art. But quite aside from his approaching death, it was really inevitable all along that the philosopher was always stronger in him than the artist; while the religious spirit that he was triumphed over artist, philosopher, and theologian alike. At the date of the above passage, his son, Henry James, Jr. had attained a high position as an artist in the world of letters; but this satisfaction to the elder James in no way disturbed his own predominant interest in spiritual philosophy.

Despite the flare-up of James's interest in the spiritual significance of Art and the Artist, Calvin and theology were deeper in his mind than Schelling and Schopenhauer, who had made James acquainted with the heady gospel of the Artist as the Divine, or Super-man. The long German tradition from Kant through Herder, Lessing, Schiller, Goethe, Heine, Schopenhauer, Schelling, and Nietzsche, to Thomas Mann in our own day, has consistently taught that the Artist is the supreme man, the type of the super-humanity. They taught that the Artist is "a law unto himself," the most powerful image available to thought and life, of creative process. Certainly, James's reading of certain of these men, started him toward a philosophy in the same direction. His dominant passion for Swedenborg cannot be advanced as a reason for the check on his speculations concerning Art, for Coleridge, Blake, and Emerson found Swedenborg, who was inartistic in his major genius, vastly stimulative to artistic theory, imagination, and aesthetic production. Even Balzac, lusty humanist and realist that he was, wrote *Seraphita* as a Swedenborgian novel. No, the reason lay in James's intellectual roots largely, and more ultimately, in his theological "temperament" as William James would call it. The sombre cast of the view that God creates in "passion and humiliation" is surely more Calvinistic in *tone* than the Faustian ego and *élan* of German Idealism's "artist" or "super-man."

It is a regrettable loss, to lovers of art and of esthetics, that James did not develop a full-blown doctrine in the direction he pioneered in "The Divine Man." He had it in him to make a genuine, if not a supreme, contribution to the Philosophy of Art. The innermost meanings involved in the relations of Art to Philosophy and Theology, or, more dynamically, the relations of Esthetic Consciousness to Religious Consciousness, is even now a comparatively virgin continent for philosophic investigation.

II

"Consciousness" is a concept in James's philosophy which has particular connotations of its own. Clearly, it has inherent affiliations both with "selfhood" and theory of knowledge. But in James it is a concept of richer timbre than either of the other two, and so demands a consideration in its own right. This richness is indicated by the fact that James often hyphenates "life-and-consciousness." Associated with the concept of "consciousness" is the sub-concept of the "unconscious," which, though suggestive of psychological implications as well as of philosophical, James did not develop very far. Sometimes it has apparently a significance beyond that of consciousness itself. We shall devote the major exposition to "consciousness" and the remainder to the "unconscious."

That "consciousness" is not exhausted in meaning within the epistemologic problem as such, is demonstated by the fact that the "problem of knowledge" arises within consciousness itself as a datum, a living fact, an ineradicable presupposition, whether consciously recognized or not. A thinker from whom James usually differed strenuously, Sir Willian Hamilton, has defined consciousness in a way which seems to do justice to James's notion of it as being so profound in its reality as to be almost equatable with life itself; for Hamilton says, in his *Metaphysics*:

> Consciousness cannot be defined: we may be ourselves fully aware what consciousness is, but we cannot without confusion convey to others a definition of what we ourselves clearly apprehend. The reason is plain: consciousness lies at the root of all knowledge.[28]

Considering the depths of the concept of consciousness in the development of phenomenology by Peirce, Brentano, Husserl, and others, one may well ask whether consciousness *is* "what we ourselves clearly apprehend"! Sir William Hamilton is, however, addressing and revealing to thought the ineffable quality in consciousness in asserting that it "lies at the root of all knowledge." As with the category of

"Life," our speculations about consciousness are chiefly assertoric judgments; our "knowledge" of consciousness is mainly analytic rather than synthetic, for both life and consciousness are surds, not as being exclusively irrational, but as having a remainder beyond the utmost "rationality" possible. It is to be borne in mind, too, that James's customary yoking of life to consciousness, is a result of his pan-psychistic doctrine. This correlation is exhibited specifically thus:

> For where involution and evolution are thus logically equal, creature and creator, object and subject, practically neutralize each other, and no logical exodus from the difficulty is either possible or conceivable. That is, creator and creature must confess themselves convertible terms, in order to creation becoming living or conscious. Created life or consciousness is possible only on one condition, which is: that creation exhibit so complete a fusion between its unconscious and conscious factors, as practically to annul their logical inequality, and so make the resultant life or consciousness one.[29]

It should be noted that consciousness is a term not precisely and exactly synonymous with Life-in-itself, but with Life-as-communicated by God to man. As for creation's exhibiting a "complete fusion between its unconscious and conscious factors," James never explains exactly what he means by his distinction between "conscious" and "unconscious"; at least, he never goes into the profound implications hinted at by such a contrast.

In reading the following citation, one is apt to think that it is a merely generalized statement of the epistemological problem, but a second reading indicates that James starts where theory of knowledge leaves off. He is speaking at a remove from theory of knowledge, because he becomes ontological in reference to mineral, vegetable, animal, and human kingdoms in a single generalization; and the last sentence especially presents his intention to go far beyond epistemology:

> Every fact of life or consciousness proceeds in other words upon the implication of a strictly conjugal tie between our sensible organization and the outlying world. It implies a complete marriage fusion or unity of these sensibly unwedded atoms, man and rose, man and water, man and sky, man and universal nature. . . .
> Every field of existence quivers with the acknowledgment of it. The mineral attests it in the phenomena of crystallization, the vegetable in the higher phenomena of sensation, the animal in the still higher ones of volition, and man in the highest of all, those

of taste or spontaneous attraction. It is the power of gravitation in the mineral, of growth in the vegetable, of motion in the animal, and of action in man. . . . You accordingly ask the philosopher to account for this stupendous marvel of Life. . . . What does the shameless fellow thereupon do? Does he instantly down upon his knees in mute because ecstatic acknowledgment of the Highest? Not a bit of it. He incontinently turns his back upon the overwhelming spectacle, and commences grubbing away like a blear-eyed mole in the mud of mere existence, to prove to you that he finds there a solution of the great mystery equally disenchanting to one's child-like adoration, and elevating to one's manly self-conceit. Life forsooth, or consciousness, is merely subject and object, the me and the not-me, in eternal correlation![30]

James next proceeds to distinguish two principal ingredient factors in consciousness, in terms of a contrast that will appear later in still other terms in the consideration of his principle of bi-sexual polarity. He sees consciousness as operating at the conjoined crossplay of finite and infinite elements:

Consciousness according to Swedenborg claims two most disproportionate generative elements;—one subjective, cosmical, passive, organic; the other objective, human, active, free. The former element gives us fixity or limitation; *identifies* us, so to speak, by relating us to the outward and finite, *i.e.* to nature. The latter element gives us freedom, which is *de*-limitation or *definition*; *individualizes* us, so to speak, by relating us to the inward and infinite, *i.e.* to God.[31]

With this, he traces how the infinite and the finite (or better, because more in the dynamism of James's thought)—the infinite-*ing* and the finit-*ing*, elements interplay in the theatre of consciousness:

This absolute or infinite (*i.e.* objective and real) element in experience . . . is what *qualifies* the experience, is what gives it natural or generic unity and so permits it to be objectively *individualized* as *man, horse, tree, stone;* while its empirical or finite element merely *quantifies* it, or gives it specific variety, and so permits it to be subjectively identified as *English*-man, *French*-man; *race*-horse, *draught*-horse; *fruit*-tree; *sand*-stone; *lime*-stone.[32]

Again, in *Christianity the Logic of Creation*, he permits himself an expansion of the same principle, but he shifts ground linguistically by using, not the substantive formulation as in the above quotation, but the present participle and adjectival forms, thus making the interplay of infinite-finite, object-subject, me and not-me, factors in consciousness even more dynamic:

> The incomparable depth and splendour of Swedenborg's genius are shewn in this, that he alone of men has ever dared to bring creation within the bounds of consciousness—within the grasp of the soul. . . . This is the fundamental distinction between his genius and that of all our other great writers, that while they, by *exteriorating* object to subject, Creator to creature, God to man, materialize man's motives, and so construct a grossly sensual Theology, and an utterly selfish Ethics; he in *interiorating* object to subject, God to man, spiritualizes man's motives, and consequently constructs a Theology which places God exclusively within the soul, and an Ethics whose sanctions lie in the demands of our endless spiritual development. . . .
>
> In a former letter I shewed you that the *me* absorbs the whole realm of the finite, the domain of sensible experience, the *outer* sphere, so to speak, of consciousness. The *not-me* equally absorbs the realm of the *infinite,* the domain of spiritual experience, or the *inner* sphere of consciousness. Consciousness forms the dividing and yet uniting line between infinite and finite. It is the hyphen which separates yet unites the object and subject, the not-me and the me. Whatsoever is on the *hither* side of consciousness, whatsoever is sensibly discerned as mineral, vegetable and animal, is finite and falls below the *me;* the me dominates it. Whatsoever is on the *thither* side of consciousness, whatsoever is spiritually discerned, as goodness, truth and beauty, in short character, is infinite and falls above the *me*. . . . Consciousness, or life, unites this higher and lower realm, giving us the *beautiful* mineral, the *graceful* shrub, the *gentle* animal, the *good* man. The grammatical adjustment of adjective and substantive is only a formula of the copulation which all life or consciousness implies between object and subject, between infinite and finite, between the not-me and the me. This is the invariable meaning of consciousness: *the copulation of an interior object with an exterior subject; the marriage of a universal substance with a specific form.* . . .
>
> According to this definition, man is the highest form of consciousness, because in him alone is the individual element proportionate to the universal. Man is the only universal form.[33]

From these premises, James deduces that man's consciousness, being the most comprehensive of any spiritual reality known, makes man a veritable microcosm:

He stands related to universal nature, on the one hand, by what he possesses in common with it, and to God on the other, by what he possesses over and above such natural community. He is related to the mineral forms of nature, by gravitation and consequent inertia: to its vegetable forms by sensation and subsequent growth: to its animal forms by volition and consequently motion; while he alone claims relationship with God, or the infinite, by what he alone possesses; namely, spontaneity, or the power of unforced individual action. . . .

The mineral form then is the earliest or lowest evolution of the me. It is the me in an intensely inert state, in a passive state or state of rest simply. It is the me getting place or position first, in order to its subsequent experience of *growth* in the vegetable form, *motion* in the animal, and *action* in the human form.[34]

Leaving this wider pan-psychistic frame of reference, and confining himself to what consciousness represents in man alone, James holds that the very existence and experience of "ego" in us, depends on consciousness; the senses themselves begin to decay when disconnected from the living consciousness:

I exist only to consciousness, only in so far as I feel myself in *universal* relations; and I LIVE, that is to say, my existence becomes beautiful and delicious to me, just in so far as these relations are relations of complete accord. . . . When the eye does not spontaneously melt into its own universe, or the realm of light, but shrinks into its bodily enclosure, it is diseased and ready to die. . . . And so of all our senses, the moment they cease to universalize the soul or *me* . . . they are diseased and prove a curse instead of a blessing. . . .[35]

The philosophic heart of James's theory of consciousness comes where he contends that, on the plane of consciousness the object-subject relationship of the plane of sense is utterly reversed. This will require further comment after the citation, for it is not only very important to an understanding of James's working presuppositions which underlie and color his entire thought-structure; it is also an extremely suggestive analysis on its own account. Ordinarily we think of ourselves as "subject," and all that is "not-me" as object, or objects. James says this is all right for the plane of "sense," but not at all for the plane of "consciousness"; in fact, the relation and terms are completely reversed. We are the "object" to the mineral, vegetable, and animal realms, and they are "subject" to us. We had our first real intimation that his thought was operating with these assumptions when, a few passages previously, he told us, though mistakenly, that the fundamental distinction of Swendenborg's genius was that he "interiorated" object to subject, "God to man." Now he carries the implications of this statement further:

> When I listen to sense, which has a very subtle and insinuating voice, I hear precisely what the philosophers hear: I hear that the distinctively *human* force in me, the soul, the self, the *me*, is subject to the natural force, is subject to my bodily limitations, or the laws of space and time: thus that I stand in the fixed relation of subject to the cat and the dog, the cockroach and the louse, and all other forms of universal life; and all these forms again in the fixed relation of *object* to me. But when I grow indignant with this sensual stuff, and listen to the voice of consciousness instead—to the voice of the soul, the reason or *true* me—I hear an exactly opposite doctrine. For the spiritual reason or consciousness tells me whenever I consult it, not that I am subject to the natural universe, but that the natural universe is properly subject to me, is in fact merely the contents of my spiritual subjectivity. It brings the natural universe, by means of the senses, within the periphery of the *me,* within the realm of conscious life: and consequently it utterly eliminates the *not-me* from the finite sphere, binding me to seek it instead in that of spiritual substance, the sphere of infinite Love and Wisdom. In other words, it identifies the *not-me* exclusively with God, thus denying me, as *subject,* any proportionate or befitting *object,* short of the immaculate Divine perfection. And in so doing, it manifestly stifles Atheism on the one hand, by proving God the sole life of the universe; while on the other hand, it sops up Atheism's younger and feebler brother, Pantheism, in yet separating God from that universe by all the breadth of our spiritual consciousness, by all the amplitude of the finite me.[36]

That passage is a philosophically intriguing instance of what a consistently hierarchical philosophy of reality, creation, knowledge, and consciousness, can do—or should we say, *must* do—in the way of inter-convertibility and inversion of all terms and relations. Every concept, term, and relation can be viewed from either end of the relation between two levels, or the relation of two levels to a third, and so on. In this manner, all terms and relations, both in an ontological sense and for purposes of philosophic discourse, are *in solution,* because they are not only operative for a given level, but are also, when applied in relation to the composite planes of being, capable of opposite meaning. Add to this the dual movement of creation and redemption,

downward and upward, involutionary and evolutionary—and one perceives the dynamism inherent in such a pattern both for reality and
for thought. Let us make all this concrete by examining the way in
which hierarchy, polarity, and the overall dual process, work out in
connection with the foregoing passage cited above.

In the sphere of "sense," Nature is objective to man and man is
subjective to nature (that is, from "natural" man's standpoint); but in
the sphere of consciousness, Nature is subjective to man and man is
objective to nature. If man be considered apart from his relation to
nature, *i.e.,* in relation now to himself, he finds himself both objective
and subjective: to sense, his body is objective and his consciousness is
subjective; but to his consciousness, consciousness is now objective and
his body properly subjective. When it comes to man's finding
any *real* Object greater than his own consciousness is to himself, that
Object can only be God as perpetual Creator-Redeemer. Certainly
God can never be objective to man sensually, except as the Lord; and
even then, though God's appearance in history as the Lord reaches to
the realm of sense, it is only as He is appropriated dynamically *within*
the order of consciousness that even that *appearance* has any meaning. Thus, though nature and his own body are thus "subjective" to
man, he himself becomes subjective *to God* on the plane of super-
consciousness; God, therefore, is, strictly speaking, the *only* Object
other than man's consciousness. Yet even God does not, in James's view,
remain purely objective to man's consciousness. He could not be more
definite on this point, for it is one of his central convictions:

> Thus the truth of creation invincibly implies that the creature
> bear a purely formal or outward and objective relation to the crea-
> tor, while the creator sustains a strictly substantial or inward and
> subjective relation to the creature.[37]
> . . . Philosophy identifies the subjective element in the creative
> equation exclusively with the Creator, and the objective element
> exclusively with the creature. That is to say: Philosophy regards
> creation not as a material or mechanical, but as a purely spiritual
> or LIVING operation of God in the created *nature;* and hence
> cannot help looking upon the Creator alone as the proper subject
> of the operation, and upon the creature alone as its proper ob-
> ject. . . . In other words creation spiritually regarded makes the
> Creator the sole and total subjective life of the creature, and the
> creature in his turn the sole and total objective life of the Crea-
> tor.[38]

We must not be misled by James's superlative-degree adverbs, such as "strictly," "solely," "exclusively," and "utterly." Not that he does not mean them as and in the context of their use but that if one took such adverbs too literally, James would seem to be "utterly" contradicting himself, when actually, if his ideas are interpreted in their given contexts, there is not a high degree of real contradiction. One reviewer complained of James's "prodigality" of statement as a habit which he "never outgrew." A little sophistication about James's adverbs saves the reader from much confusion. For example, in the last quoted passage, we read that "Philosophy identifies the subjective element in the creative equation exclusively with the Creator, and the objective element exclusively with the creature." Looking at this alone, one would conclude that God is subjective not only to Himself, but to Man; and this would be a proper inference, since the Creator is "the sole and total subjective life of the creature." This means that the whole inner life of consciousness is, though the creature be unconscious of it, God-within-him. Quite so. But, if God "sustains a strictly substantial or inward and subjective relation to the creature," God cannot be "object" to human consciousness; and if not object, how is the empirical consciousness of an individual man to separate itself on the one hand from being God, since God as objective to it is denied on Jamesian premises? James is confronted with a tight dilemma: for, on his grounds, if God's objective life consists in being the "sole and total subjective life of the creature," how is the distinction of Creator and creature maintained? Does it not destroy the metaphysical integrity of both Creator and creature: for if man's sole subjective life is the imprisoned Deity within him, how can he be *man*; and if God's sole objective life is to be in His creatures, how can He remain God? James would reply: The "Divine Man"! Even so, the problem drove him to adopt a distinction between our "conscious" and "unconscious" selves, which will be considered shortly. Meanwhile, let us see how he tries to protect the objectivity or otherness of God in line with his radical creationistic immanentalism of God as the subjective life of man:

> Were the creature anything more than a receptive form or subject of life, his creation would imply the surrender of God's own being to him, and the consequent diminution to that extent of the Creator; in which case, a perfect creation, or one commensurate with the infinite Divine Love and wisdom, must have proved

equivalent to the utter eventual absorption and extinction of Deity.[39]

William James says in his "Introduction" to *Literary Remains* that there is in his father's thought an "atheism (as we might almost call it,—that is, the swallowing up of God in Humanity) as the last result of God's achievement"; yet his father had protested against such a view as a necessary deduction by writing passages like that just cited. Still, eleven years after writing the above, James was writing to his son William, and expressing himself about this issue in language that seems to mean "almost atheism":

> Certainly you see this much to be true, that creative if it mean anything means an equation of the creative and created natures. There is just as certainly, however, no essential or absolute equality between them, so that creation if it take place at all must be purely empirical or contingent; that is to say, *must involve an experience on the creature's part which shall bring him up to level of the creator.*[40]

Maybe James would say bringing the creature "up to level" means simply being on the celestial plane *with* God, instead of "absorbing" Him; but it's a pretty thin line! The analogy, suggested before in this study, for James's doctrine seems to be that of a greater weight coming down, sending the lesser weight in the balance up accordingly, "strictly commensurate" with all the factors involved. To use awkward but significant terms, God's immanentalization in man (God's "Divine inhabitation of man," James calls it) produces a proportionate transcendentalization of man. Humanization *by* God in His incarnation as the Lord, becomes through the dynamics of the return movement, divinization *for* man. God becomes anthropo-morphic; man becomes theo-morphic, in strict ratio.

A final observation on this transvaluation of "object-subject," "objective-subjective," in James is thus possible to make: man's spiritual destiny, or the redeemed state, is itself an *object* to man's empirical consciousness as *subject* in his existential state. It is this ultimate redeemed state of society that brings us now to a consideration of James's reference to the "unconscious" self.

The "unconscious" (or "unconsciousness"), receives scanty treatment in James's works, yet the few instances in which he speaks of it are too suggestive to omit altogether from our exposition. From the quotations used in this section of the chapter, it is easy to see that, from the side of creation, "unconsciousness" is, by necessary implication, the total opposite of creation and life. It is "uncreation" and "un-life," so to speak; it is material "chaos" without form; it is the "communism" of mere identity without individuality. Yet, "unconscious" in James has two other references which carry diametrically opposite connotations; namely, (1) that our "unconscious" self or life is our "real" life hidden in God and imperceptible to the merely conscious self; and (2) that the redeemed state will remove this temporary unconsciousness of our real life by actual realization. Whether or not he means that redemption as a consummated fulfillment removes this *relative* unconsciousness of man as to his real life-in-God when he was in the finite state, or removes the need of any consciousness *absolutely,* is not made at all clear.

To exhibit "unconscious" in the first sense, as being our real life in God, an extract is taken from *The Church of Christ Not an Ecclesiasticism*:

> The internal or spiritual man, being, like the involuntary system of the body, only the *immediate* abode of Life or Deity, has no self-consciousness, and therefore generates no disease or disorder. But the natural or external man, being, like the voluntary system of the body, only the *mediate* abode of Life or Deity, is intensely self-conscious, and cannot fail therefore to generate all manner of disease and disorder, until this seeming and conscious self be brought into exact harmony with his real and unconscious one.[41]

> Man is wholly unconscious of the origin of his selfhood or freedom: in symbolic language, the *Lord God causes a deep sleep to fall on Adam, while He takes from him a rib, and of this makes a woman and brings her to the man*: he has no idea that it is an incessant Divine communication to him: on the contrary, he conceives it to be inherent in his natural organization, and as all his felicity is contingent upon it, he of necessity prizes the organization which seems its source with an altogether insane love. . . . How, then, shall God redeem man from this insanity? Evidently and only *by so subjugating self-love to neighbourly love in the universal or unconscious mind of man, as to make all the influx which descends from that mind into the individual or conscious mind attest such subjugation, and so render the latter spontaneously subject to God.*[42]

Here James identifies the "unconscious mind of man" with the "universal" mind; it is also regarded as "below" the "conscious" mind of the individual, and so, strongly akin to Jung's "collective unconscious" in contemporary psychology. Just what "universal" mind means, James does not say. He does, in a sentence subsequent to the last passage, equate "the spiritual world, or the universal mind of man," but this does not shed much light. Apparently this universal mind belongs to man as a race, or man as man abstractly—and yet, James hates abstractions. Finally, this universal, unconscious mind is obviously, on James's theory, superior to the need of consciousness, at least in the empirical and existential sense of the term.

It is very apparent to anyone who has pursued this study so far, that James is a tremendously stimulating and suggestive thinker, but a weak one in the analytical sense. His genius is predominantly synthetic rather than analytic. Apropos of this weakness, is it not a bit of intellectual irony that James is *consciously* telling us how to become *conscious* of, our *"unconscious"* universal mind? If perchance we became conscious of it we should perforce become unconscious immediately! Irony aside, however—and irony never settles anything but only sharpens the problem—it is open to speculation, aside from any conclusive data from James himself, whether he derived the notion of "unconscious mind" from elements in Schopenhauer (1788-1860), or possibly from Leibniz' theory of *petites* perceptions in Sections 21 and 23 of the *Monadology,* where the idea is certainly a foreshadowing of the development of the unconscious will in Schopenhauer. Eduard von Hartmann (1842-1906), brought out his *Philosophy of the Unconscious* in 1869, but whether or not James read it is unknown. An English translation did not come out for a considerable number of years after James's death.

It would be interesting enough to know whether James would approve of Hartmann's theory of the Unconscious as a neutral absolute in which will and idea are coordinated, thus outflanking both irrationality and rationality, both monistic subjective idealism and phenomenalism. James's "Divine Love and Wisdom" correspond to some extent with "will and idea," and there may be a genuine correspondence between Hartmann's *Unconscious* and James's absolute *Esse,* which is pure Being-as-such, being that-of-which-nothing-can-be predicated, and, therefore, beyond consciousness and so presumably unconscious. This is only speculation and offered for its suggestiveness more than for any more tangible reason.

James returns to this theme in *Society the Redeemed Form of Man.*

> Creation becomes converted in men's infirm understanding from a spiritual, or infinite and eternal, Divine life in the *unconscious nature* of the creature, which has therefore strictly public or universal issues in humanity, into a mere legal or moral administration of Divine power in the *conscious person* of the creature, having at best therefore strictly private or particular issues.[43]

This amounts to a re-affirmation of the previous statement. But is there anything in James which throws light on the second sense of the "unconscious," as indicating the annihilation of consciousness in the redeemed condition of man? What is the relation between redemption—as fulfilled—and "unconsciousness"?

Although the word "unconscious" does not appear in the passage now to be quoted, it is a strong presumption that James identifies "unconscious" with the "objective, absolute" being of man in his Creator—and for this reason: James, in the topical headings for Chapter II on the "Contents Page" of *The Secret of Swedenborg* expresses himself thus: "Consciousness according to Swedenborg, is a composite, not a simple, movement, being bound to provide the creature with subjective or conscious existence no less than objective or unconscious being." Turning to the passage referred to by this caption, we read:

> Thus creation, or the giving absolute being to things, logically involves a subordinate process of *making,* which is the giving them phenomenal or conscious form. In fact, upon this strictly incidental process of formation, the entire truth of creation philosophically pivots; for unless the creator be able to give his creature subjective identity (which is natural alienation from, or *otherness than,* himself), he will never succeed in giving him objective individuality, which is spiritual oneness with himself. . . . Thus the total truth of creation spiritually regarded hinges upon its being a reflex not a direct, a composite not a simple, a rational not an arbitrary exertion of divine power—hinges, in short, upon its supplying a subjective and phenomenal development to the creature every way commensurate with, or adequate to, the objective and absolute being he has in the creator.[44]

It must be admitted that this throws no direct illumination on the subject of "unconsciousness" as related to the redeemed destiny of man. James may have meant only that man's conscious empirical self got in the way, made him "unconscious," of his real, absolute self—and this, from *within* empirical existence; but the presumption seems strong to the writer that unconsciousness, at least, un-*self*-consciousness, will be a blessed attribute of the consummation of redemption. This is anything but Swedenborg's position, in which selfhood and self-consciousness are never transcended, but are actually prolonged eternally, whether in "hell" or in "heaven."

It might be thought that light would be forthcoming from the natural bearing this question has on the idea of Immortality in James, but after a thorough search, the writer can discover no more than about twenty-odd pages directly or indirectly related to "Immortality" in James's works, and those pages are by no means consistent; in any event, he never developed any specific doctrine of immortality. We have pursued, therefore, the concept of the "unconscious" in James as far as possible. We cannot close this section, however, without remarking the influence this germinal theory in the elder James had on his philosopher son, William James, whose theory of the "sub-conscious" in his *Psychology* is a psychological-scientific application of his father's "unconscious" as "universal mind."

It is incumbent upon us next to explore James's extraordinarily attractive theory, which, since it lacks any specific designation by James, I have ventured to call the principle of Bi-Sexual Polarity, a principle which operates by the "marriage" of a "generic substance" with a "specific form" on, and within, every level of being, and in both downward-creative and upward-redemptive movements; from God to the mineral and from the mineral back to God. This principle is the closest James ever came to a psychology, but ultimately we shall find it to be a sort of meta-psychology, or perhaps a theo-psychology.

III

It was inevitable that the poet who wrote *The Marriage of Heaven and Hell* would attract James, who wrote a short notice for *The Spirit of the Age* on "William Blake's Poems."[45] The notice, however, is insignificant for truly revealing the great principle of the "marriage" of polarities which they both, Blake and James, derived more or less from their mutual study of Swedenborg.

James's development of the bi-sexual principle as a dialectical category and a metaphysical principle of interpretation, might be called either a spiritual sexualism or a sexualized spiritualism. The phrase either way is not entirely satisfactory. At least he applies the idea in the two ways indicated by the exchanged position of the adjective and noun; in his three-cornered debate with Stephen Pearl Andrews and Horace Greeley on *Love, Marriage, and Divorce,* along with several articles in *Putnam's* and *The Atlantic Monthly,* it could quite properly be called spiritual sexualism; but in the far wider, meta-sexual applications of polarity, it would, even though he still uses sexual terms, be more precise to call it sexualized spiritualism. To cover both uses, the writer has designated the inclusive category as the Principle of Bi-Sexual Polarity.

James operates the principle from Divinity to mineral, from mineral to Divinity. We are acquainted with the "marriage" of object-subject in James's theory of knowledge; we shall come upon "marriage" as the focal word in the operation of bi-sexual polarity at every level of his discourse. The coat's "parentage," we recall, consists of the tailor and the cloth. At the other extreme, the incarnation of the Divine as the Lord in Jesus Christ is a "marriage" of God and man, of the Divine with the Human. Thus:

> It is logically in fact the very essence of the creative idea, that creation is practically a marriage of Creator and creature, whereby the creature alone spiritually *is,* or becomes infinited *in the Creator,* while the Creator alone naturally *exists,* or becomes finite, in the creature. . . . [46]

As a preface to further exposition of this subject, it is well to recall, from the chapter on "Swedenborg and James," the notice taken there of James's idea, adopted from Swedenborg, of the human father's transmitting the soul or animating principle in generation, while the mother's contribution consisted in being the passive, material receptacle for the enfleshment of the new child; also, as we noted there, this view was substantially held by Aristotle in his *On the Generation of Animals.*

The Principle of Bi-Sexual Polarity, therefore is very prominent in Swedenborg; also, the concept of "marriage" on every level of reality. He speaks, to cite only a few illustrations from *The True Christian Religion,* of "The Marriage of the Good and the True" in heaven, whence it follows "that all things that are in the whole heaven, and all that are in the whole world, are from creation nothing but a marriage of the good and the true"; moreover: "the same that was said above concerning the marriage of the good and the true, was said also concerning the Marriage of Charity and Faith, since good is of charity, and truth is of faith."[47] Not only this, but "I assure you that there is not any thing there . . . that is not from the marriage of love and wisdom in use."[48] Finally, "because there are two things which make the marriage of the Lord and the church, love and wisdom; and the Lord is love, and the church is wisdom, and wisdom is at the right hand of love. . . . But, as was said, after the wedding, the representation is changed; for then the husband represents wisdom, and the wife the love of his wisdom; but this love is not the prior love, but it is a secondary love, which the wife has from the Lord, through the wisdom of the husband."[49] The reader will have no difficulty, as we continue the exposition of James, in seeing that the basic concepts of bi-sexual polarity and "marriage" are found abundantly in Swedenborg, and that James applies them in fundamentally the same way, except that he expresses them in language colored by his study of German philosophy. For a single illustration here, it is instructive to see how James takes over directly the idea that the feminine element is "love" and the masculine, "wisdom," and yet the feminine principle gives way ultimately to the superiority of "the Lord's love," exactly as in Swedenborg above.

James extends these ideas of bi-sexual polarity and marriage throughout the total realm of existents, whether mineral, vegetable, animal, human, or Divine. In the exposition we shall follow first, the involutionary movement sweeping outwards and downwards from God in creation; then the evolutionary order from mineral back to the Divine.

James expounds the principle in terms of a "double movement"— not to be confused with the larger double movement of creation-redemption; ascribing the active, dynamical "paternal" movement to God, and the passive, statical "maternal movement" to the "fixing movement":

> Of course the reason why creation always eludes a scientific induction is, that it is primarily a process of matriculation, and the mother is naturally nearer and dearer to the child's heart than the father. Everything which exists or is formed presupposes both a visible material substance out of which—and an invisible spiritual force by which—it exists or is formed, and of which it is the unity. The former element incorporates it, gives it body, so identifying it with all other things; the latter animates it, gives it soul, so individualizing it from all other things. In other words the making of things, the giving them conscious life or form, involves of necessity a double movement: one dynamical, active, and paternal, which fecundates the thing, gives it spiritual being or soul; the other statical, passive, and maternal, which fixes the

thing, gives it material existence or body, and so promotes or serves the higher spiritual process.

Now what I say is that consciousness always identifies its subject with the mother-element in this transaction, and separates him from the father. . . . The child knows his mother without anybody's help, or instinctively; since the incessant contact he has with her leaves no obscurity upon that point. But he knows his father only upon his mother's testimony. He refuses to acknowledge anyone as lawful father, whom she does not first acknowledge as sole husband. . . .

The honor we traditionally pay to paternity over maternity is not an arbitrary thing. It grows out of the absolute necessity all human legislation has been under to reflect and promote the great truth of human destiny, which is the Divine Incarnation, or the eventual unimpeded manifestation of the infinite Divine perfection in all the forms of human nature, especially its basest forms. During the infancy of the race as of the individual of course, the law of the mother prevails over that of the father, so that at last the mind would infallibly succumb to this strong bias and sink down in abject Naturalism, were it not that the Divine Providence so guides and overrules human legislation, as gradually to mould the very mind itself of the race upon this great interior truth of its altogether Divine and infinite paternity, and its merely finite and comparatively unimportant maternity.[50]

This principle is not only true of the "Divine Incarnation," whose theater of operation is in the "historic consciousness" rather than in "Mother" Nature; it is also true of a manufactured article like a coat whose "parentage" consists of the tailor's skill and purpose as "father," imposing specific form on the undifferentiated cloth as the "mother." And if this is so in manufacture, it is much more so in the fine arts, in human parenthood, and even in the event of inspired scholarship:

The sculptor forms his statute out of the maternal marble, only by enduing the marble with the form of his own genius, investing it with the impress of his own aesthetic personality. The marble finites the statute, or imprisons it in her own unexplored womb. The genius of the sculptor animates the statute, gives it soul or ideal form, merely by *de*-fining it, so to speak, or *in*-finiting it from this maternal envelope. The mother finites the child, or wraps it away from light and life, from sight and consciousness in her own unconscious bowels: the seed of the father releases the child from this imprisonment, by animating it or giving it living soul.

The truth which the poet sings, the beauty which the painter reproduces upon the canvas, the science which the scholar patiently elaborates, lie all hopelessly entombed under any amount of actual obscuration and deformity: the penetrating aroma of the student's or artist's genius pervades their sepulchre, and awakens the mute unconscious inmates to life and form. These illustrations . . . make it plain . . . that the maternal element becomes taken up and disappears in the paternal one; or what is material substance becomes ravished—glorified—transfigured into spiritual form.[51]

This appears to be the most fitting place to relate a certain anecdote about and by Mr. James, who all along, as the discerning mind has been aware, exhibits a fine touch of humor even in discussing the profoundest themes of creation and redemption. His humor usually consists in extreme statements to nettle his reader into a violent response, favorable or unfavorable. He displayed this exuberant humor even more in conversation. M. A. DeWolfe Howe gives an account in *Memories of A Hostess,* of an anecdote told to Mrs. J. T. Fields— the "hostess" and wife of the Boston publisher of that period—by James himself, which anecdote she recorded in her diary. James narrated a witty episode to her about one of Bronson Alcott's visits to him in New York. Howe renders it as Mrs. Fields entered it in her diary:

> They got into a great battle about the premises, during which Mr. Alcott talked of the Divine paternity as relating to himself, when Mr. James broke in with, "my dear sir, you have not found your *maternity* yet. You are an egg half-hatched." To which Mr. Alcott replied, "Mr. James, you are *damaged goods* and will come up damaged goods in eternity."[52]

However it has turned out between Mr. James and Mr. Alcott in heaven, it is necessary for us to complete our "matriculation" with James's philosophy! We find that he makes the Divine Paternity the specific subject of this excerpt:

> History, it is evident, owes its supernatural character, its controlling power over Nature—whatsoever distinguishes it from mere natural growth and decay—in a word owes its strictly human and progressive quality, to the truth of man's most unequal parentage: to the fact of his being the joint and equal offspring of an infinite father (God), and a finite mother (Nature). One sees at a glance that an infinite thesis and a finite antithesis entail a

wholly unexampled synthesis; and man's destiny accordingly is never to be gauged by stupidly nor yet conceitedly ignoring its major premise: which nevertheless is what religion and science habitually do. The truest and most comprehensive formula of History is, that it is the persistent and at last successful effort of the paternal Divine element in consciousness to assert its essential primacy, and reduce the merely constitutive, or maternal natural element to its just subordination. . . . It represents the evolution of the creature's destiny, or his natural formation in the Divine image, as a graduated or composite movement, first downward or radical, giving him fixity by developing in him the intensest consciousness of community with his kind; then upward or educative, giving him the utmost spiritual expansion out of that root. Our natural history may be defined in fact to be a pure process of redemption, or spiritual formation, consisting first in giving us conscious finite maternity, but only in order that that consciousness may prove rigidly and unalterably ministerial to our conscious infinite paternity.[53]

There is James's basic philosophy of history, the philosophy of "spiritual history" it may properly be called. We shall meet it again when we come to "The Doctrine of Redemption."

Let us go now to the extreme of the creative-involutionary process, that is, to matter, using the mineral for exhibition. The mineral is the virtual beginning of the return movement of redemption-evolution, in the course of which, particularly when we come to Man, we shall find James employing new terms, and with these new terms, effecting inversions of meaning, as compared to their significance in relation to the involutionary creative movement. Here James is speaking only of the mineral realm:

Mineral life bears the same relation to vegetation and animation, that the foetus bears to fully developed bodily life. Being destitute as yet of sensation, of sensibility to outward existence, it is of course devoid of visible form or individuality, and loses itself in the womb of the common mother. But the phenomena of crystallization shew that the life-process is going on all the while not less really though invisibly, or within the still enveloping womb of Nature, so that at least very marked *tendencies* to specific form result, as we see in the characteristic differences of iron and sulphur, alum and arsenic, gold and lead, silver and copper. Were there no observable differences in these things, did they not exhibit each a different relation towards the common mineral life, which is inertia or tendency to rest, we could never have named them. But if you admit mineral differences together with a universal mineral nature, you admit mineral life or consciousness. For life or consciousness means nothing else than the union of a common nature with a specific form.[54]

. . . I hold, then, that there is no such thing as unorganized, unconscious, or dead existence; but I hold this incidentally to my main proposition, which is that all life is a form of consciousness, or a joint or composite self-knowledge, implying the union of an interior object with an exterior subject, the marriage of a vivifying succulent nature with a dependent specific form. . . . Undoubtedly, as I have already observed, the resultant form is low or high, poor or rich, exactly as the marriage is ill or well pronounced, that is, as the formal and feminine element is *freely* instead of *servilely* related to the substantial and masculine element.[55]

Already the terms and relations have changed. The "merely constitutive, or maternal element" of the creation movement is succeeded by the "formal and feminine element." Formerly, the material "substance" gave "body" and "fixation," and now the term is: the "feminine," giving the "formal" and, as we shall presently see, the "individual" element. This illustrates the necessity of keeping the reference contexts clearly in mind. This "feminine" element will become more and more important as we rise in the evolutionary scale. Obviously, there is some discontinuity of meaning here, for "feminine" is *separated* from the "maternal" aspect of the former context, instead, as we might have expected, a correlation of the two.

This meaning of "feminine" as the "individual" element in consciousness, when applied to man, is more pronounced in this statement:

The precise historic issue aimed at and accomplished is, such a thorough separation (through the activity of the Divine spirit in human nature) of the individual, spiritual, or feminine element in consciousness, from the merely common or natural and masculine element. . . . [56]

In the context of the Divine Paternity, the "spiritual" element was, by necessity of definition, "masculine." Here it is the feminine element that is spiritual. The correlation is quite opposite to our expectations. Is there any explanation of this apparent terminological inversion? There must be some root idea not as yet visible to account for this situation. We have a toehold in one word from the above, and that is "consciousness." In *Christianity the Logic of Creation* he takes us deeper into the masculine-feminine dynamics of human consciousness:

> No doubt that oxygen and hydrogen in order to form water, combine in invariably definite proportions; but this is only saying in analogous terms, that the fusion or union which the individual consciousness operates between the specific and the general, between the unitary and the universal forms, is most strictly a *marriage*-fusion or union: that is to say, that the former or limitary element in consciousness is always feminine, and the latter or universal element is always masculine, and that the secret of human destiny lies in allowing the former element the free preponderance of the latter.[57]

The contrast in usage of terms is now thoroughly established, if not as yet completely clear. There are two different orders of process and facts involved: Divine-Paternity and Nature-Maternity are of the order of "forming," "making," and creat-*ing;* masculine-natural-communist-universal and feminine-spiritual-individual-formal are of the order of "Consciousness" or crea-*tion* (or, to put it in other terms, we are now within the *redemption* movement, and James has inverted the connotations of terms as between paternal-maternal, masculine-feminine). James now applies the masculine-feminine contrast to Art:

> Thus Nature is the mother of the creature, giving him requisite finiteness or body; just as the marble may be said to be the mother of the statue, giving it visible incorporation or fixity. . . . For Art —viewed as the distinctively feminine evolution of human activity, in which freedom supplants force, or what is spiritual, individual, private, governs what is natural, common, public—makes Nature as furnishing the material in every work, purely ancillary and subservient to the Artist as furnishing its form, under penalty of defeating the work or rendering it imperfect.[58]

Here we have the utter discontinuity of any possible correlation between "maternal" and "feminine" in the same paragraph, so far at least as James is using them of two different orders of reality—"Nature" and "Consciousness."

As yet we do not know how it comes about that the feminine element in consciousness is identified by James with the individualizing, formalizing factor, and the masculine as the universalizing and communizing factor. The attempt to find the answer to this query introduces us to James's manipulation of the concepts of *homo* and *vir*. It is perhaps unnecessary but still apropos to observe at this juncture, before investigating this pair of contrasted terms, that James is nowhere dealing with sex as such. Nonetheless, he retains the sexual language even though he categorizes paternal-maternal, masculine-feminine, and later, *homo-vir* and Adam-Eve, into principles of philosophic interpretation. The masculine-feminine elements operate in consciousness, not in the two sexes conceived as empirically and physically distinguishable, but in *man as man*, in *human as human*:

> Now . . . when we are told that *"God creates man male and female"*: the *male* in this collocation being the grand cosmical or unconscious man designated by the latin word *homo,* and embracing the entire realm of physics from the lowest mineral up to the highest animal form of existence; and the *female* being the petty domestic or conscious man, designated by the Latin word *vir,* and embracing the entire realm of our free and normal historic evolution. For by this concise statement is signified that the creator endows his creature with an essentially finite genesis, or suspends his self-consciousness upon a strict equilibrium between the element of identity or universality in his nature, and that a difference or individuality exists between the element of force or necessity, and that of freedom or contingency; between the interests of the broadest humanity in short and those of the narrowest conventional virtue. And surely nothing can so effectually separate creature from creator as his subjection to this finite experience. For in the creator love and wisdom, heart and head, force and freedom, justice and mercy, universality and individuality, are one and inseparable, and it is only in the creature that the two principles are found in envenomed hostility, being held both alike in rigid abeyance to that purely empirical reconciliation with each other, which is signified by the *social* destiny of the race.
>
> Here then, at last, we have it. To be created male and female is to have a finite genesis, is to be conscious of one's self as the neutrality or indifference of two forces as wide apart as zenith and nadir, or heaven and hell.[59]

In quoting the part of the citation which touches on man's "social destiny," we allowed ourselves to anticipate the doctrine of spiritual socialism, but it is just as well to realize that, though the feminine principle of individuality, or the *vir* or domestic, conscious man is, relatively to the unconscious *homo,* superior, it is nevertheless in the long run inferior to the Divine Paternity that will resolve the antagonism between individuality-universality in the ultimate redemption of humanity. The feminine principle is therefore purely economic and provisional. But let us not anticipate this point too much because there is further exposition to be rendered as to "homo" and "vir," for James expresses this contrast even more vividly than above:

> We read accordingly the symbolic *Genesis,* that while all lower things take name from man . . . man himself (Adam or the *homo*) remains void of self-consciousness, void of moral or personal quality, remains in short wholly unvivified by the *vir,* until creation itself gives plan to redemption, or nature becomes complicated with history, in that remarkable divine intervention described as the formation of Eve or the woman out of the man's rib: by which event is symbolized of course an inward or spiritual divine fermentation in man which issues at last in his moral consciousness, or his becoming subjective as well as objective to himself. The entire mythical history amounts in philosophic import to this: that the *homo* or physical man, divinely *created,* is utterly distinct from the *vir* or moral man divinely begotten out of the other. . . .
>
> The interesting question, I repeat, then, to philosophy is . . . How is the *vir* (Eve) actually begotten of the *homo* (Adam)? How is moral life generated of mere physical existence? . . . For it is only Eve, *divinely quickened,* who brings the carnal, gross, and grovelling Adam to final and adequate self-consciousness; only the *vir* (the private specific man) who is able to mirror or reproduce the *homo* (the public generic man) to himself. The symbolic Adam is "in a deep sleep," while Eve is being divinely quickened within him. He has no suspicion that she is formed out of his own lifeless clay; that she is only his own relentless unconscious death divinely fashioned into *quasi* or conscious life; that she is but the phenomenal revelation of the most real but recognized being which he himself has exclusively in God. . . .
>
> We have the amplest warrant then to deny that moral existence, or human nature, is included in creation proper; to deny that man is God's proper creature save as *homo,* i.e. on his organic, passive, unconscious side, in which he is physically identified with mineral, vegetable, and animal existence; while as *vir,* i.e., on his free, active, or self-conscious side, in which he is morally individualized from all other existence, he is manifestly the only begotten son of God.[60]

It is important to observe the phrase above—"until creation itself give way to redemption," for this shows that the terms "masculine-homo-Adam" and "feminine-vir-Eve" represent the creation and redemption movements respectively.

Since the reference to Adam and Eve has come up, it were well to see how James states the bipolarity (his term) of *homo-vir* under the Bible names of Adam-Eve. First, there is a delightful account by James of how God came to "beget" Eve:

"And the lord God said, It is not good for man to be alone,"— he is so imbecile and unintelligent; "I will make him a suitable or enlivening helpmeet. . . . And the lord God"—still intent upon giving him such a mate—"caused a deep sleep to fall upon Adam, and while he was unconscious took from him a rib,"—which apparently was the nearest approximation he possessed to a heart— "and of this bony substance built up a woman, and brought her to the man who said, This is now bone of my bones and flesh of my flesh; she shall be called woman (Isha), because she is taken out of man (Ish)!"[61]

Probably the best approach to "Adam-Eve" is by way of a selection from *Substance and Shadow*:

Adam, before the birth of Eve, pictures to us what man is by creation merely; an eternal infant, incapable of growing in love and wisdom and power, because he is without selfhood, or personal experience; without any experience of himself, and consequently without any possibility of spiritual reaction towards— and spiritual conjunction with—his infinite source. . . .

With Eve accordingly, who symbolizes his Divinely vivified selfhood, Adam's proper personal experience begins; or the negative innocence of childhood prepares itself to be taken up into the positive innocence of ripe and wise manhood. . . . Thus the first and highest possible service which Eve renders Adam is to throw him out of Paradise: *i.e.* strip him of the innocence which he has by creation merely . . . in order finally to clothe him with the innocence which he will have by virtue of a Divine redemption of his nature, and which is one with the profoundest wisdom, or experience of selfhood. . . . In fine here lies the beginning of our social culture and discipline; of that persistent untiring devoted struggle on the part of the spiritual element in life—on the part of the WOMAN within us—to satisfy the craving of her stolid material mate after infinite delights, which is the meaning of all history, and which is Divinely prospered and fulfilled only in the social destiny of man.[62]

Again:

Human history dates from Eve. Existence dates from Adam, but life, or progress towards God, begins with Eve. . . . It is Eve, or the vivification of our natural earth by the Divine spirit, which disenchants us of our long Adamic babyhood, which emancipates us from Eden, which shews us first how full of inward death and horror is that imbecile being we have in Adam....[63]

How does Eve accomplish her magnificent role of stinging the dull and stupid Adam from "Nature" into "History," from dumbness and brute-ness into selfhood? James presents the rationale of the process, warning us at the end not to confuse "woman" with anything so empirical as a "conventional fine lady":

Eve accordingly is not slow to accept the interior guidance and guardianship of her uncouth mate; and, what is more to the purpose, she has miraculously kept that guidance and guardianship unimpaired (through all the vicissitudes of death and hell which his own nature and history have since so freely showered upon his experience), by first of all assiduously nursing him out of the mere brutal physical consciousness he was in when she met him, into a moral and rational consciousness,—and then convincing him that even this moral and rational consciousness of his to which she has brought him, is itself after all but a dim fallacious semblance of the spiritual, or infinite and eternal, manhood which she has yet to reveal to him.... It is the constant recognition of this divine worth in woman that makes man love, adore and worship her with all his heart and mind. Not the conscious individual woman, or the conventional fine lady, mind you—save in so far as these aspire to forget themselves, and become sincerely one or identical with unconscious or universal womanhood.[64]

It would be interesting, as they say at parish meetings, "to hear from the ladies." Are they willing to be adored and loved, "not as the conscious individual woman," but only as they "become sincerely one or identical with unconscious or universal womanhood"? By all evidence, Mr. and Mrs. James were very happily married; but one cannot but feel curious as to what Mrs. James felt and thought about this interpretation of woman!

What about Eve's responsibility for man's fall? Nothing of the kind, protests James contemptuously. Adam fell *up* anyway, and both responsibility and credit for it belong to Eve:

Anyone with half an eye can see, in the first place, that the death poor Adam encountered from his love to Eve was not in the least *physical*, save in so far as it implied a change in his experience, by which outward pleasure, the pleasures of sense, become altogether secondary and subservient to inward and more refined delights. In short, it was an altogether *living* or *inward* death that Adam incurred, a death in his own throbbing bosom; death to the longer predominance in his nature of its mere passive sensual instincts, which are far too exclusively animal (or paradisaic and voluptuous) to characterize God's true spiritual creature and fellow.

. . . Anyone with half an eye can see . . . that "Adam's fall," as it is called, was not that stupid lapse from the divine favor which it is vulgarly reputed to have been, but an actual rise to the normal human level out of sheer unrelieved brutality.[65]

In that interpretation of the Adam-Eve "fall," James achieves perhaps his most remarkable inversion of Calvinistic doctrine. His own theory of the Fall is so consonant with evolutionistic thought at this point that William James, with his wonted penetration of insight and elegance of expression, comments in his "Introduction" to *Literary Remains*:

The ordinary empirical ethics of evolutionary naturalism can find a perfect *permis de séjour* under the system's wings; and yet close alongside is an insistence on the need of the death of the natural man and of a supernatural redemption, more thoroughgoing than what we find in the most evangelical Protestantism. . . .

It all flowed from two perceptions, insights, convictions, whatever one pleases to call them, in its author's mind. In the first place, he felt that the individual man, as such, is nothing, but owes all he is and has to the race he inherits, and to the society into which he is born. And, secondly, he scorned to admit, even as a possibility, that the great and loving Creator, who has all the being and the power, and has brought us as far as *this*, should not bring us *through*, and *out*, into the most triumphant harmony.[66]

The reference by William James to his father's race-consciousness gives us a natural transition to the connection between the Principle of Bi-Sexual Polarity, as exhibited in human consciousness, and social redemption. We had intimations that Eve was not the end of man's evolution, however necessary a part of it. She could call up Adam from his slavery to "sense"; she could not save either him or herself from the inordinate love of the very self she had aroused. Selfhood as "moral and rational consciousness" is the greatest of boons up to a point, but unless guided by a spiritual philosophy resting upon the Divine Paternity over, in, and for all men, selfhood by the same token becomes diabolical, infernal, demoniç; it becomes the cause of the deepest of all evil as we shall learn in the next chapter. James would have us understand that, despite his high praise of Eve as "vir" in man's evolution, the very principle of selfhood is inescapably "self-ish":

> ... what conceivable ratio is there between the wholly unconscious life of mineral, vegetable, and animal, and the wholly conscious life of man? Between the blind instinctual groping of Adam, and the clear intelligent will of Eve? Between the utterly unselfish nature of the *homo,* and the utterly selfish nature of the *vir?* Between the innocence which characterizes all our distinctively *humane* tendencies and affections, and the guilt which stains all of our distinctively *virtuous* ones?[67]

He answers himself:

> Conscience then is the sovereign link or point of transition for which we have been seeking between moral and physical existence. In conscience the moral which is the individual or differential element in nature becomes disengaged from the physical, which is its strictly universal or identical element, and the conscious *vir* absorbs the unconscious *homo* in his deathless embrace, never henceforth to be reproduced save in the spiritual or regenerate lineaments of a perfect human society.[68]

But:

> It is the *final,* not the immediate, office of conscience to reveal man to himself as a unit of two forces, one infinite, the other finite; one spiritual, the other material; one specific or private, the other generic or public; so vindicating at last the sole and supreme truth of the divine natural humanity. Until this great truth is wrought out ... the moral or rational man seems of course to be the true end of the divine providence upon earth, whereas he is a strictly *mediate* end to the evolution of society. . . .[69]

James is doing here with "conscience" (which we are to consider more fully in the next chapter in connection with spiritual evil) what he did with selfhood and consciousness: there is the finite and the infinite selfhood, the ordinary and the perfected consciousness, and now, there is the mediate and the perfected conscience. James has this habit of splitting the same general concept into finite and infinite and so on, and also of using different *names, i.e.,* selfhood, consciousness, personality, conscience, as synonymous when he chooses to do so, and then making them split as has been said, between the finite and infinite factors. So it doesn't make any real difference which of the synonyms he uses; he is saying the same thing in the end.

Whether it be selfhood, consciousness, or conscience in any given context, it all amounts to the one great end of pointing up God's ultimate redemption of man:

> Now, this perfect marriage of the male and female elements in creation—this complete unification of equalization of the *homo* and the *vir*, of the cosmical and the domestic soul—manifestly appeals for its realization to the advent of a true society or fellowship among men. It is only in the race's social evolution that our absolute and contingent interests become harmonized. . . .[70]

The foregoing passage is rich with significance, for it involves essential principles in James's philosophy of the regeneration of man. Homo-Vir-Society (or Adam-Eve-Church): this triad describes for James the process of regeneration in man; and, being in the evolutionary movement of man's ascent to the Divine Humanity, it is therefore an inversion of the Wisdom-Love-Use triad of the involutionary movement of God's descent into man. That is: Adam is an image of God's Wisdom, Eve is an image of Love (sometimes called "Conscience" and "Religion"), and the Church ("Society," or sometimes, the "State") is an image of the ultimate and hidden workings of Providence, or of God, in the process of realizing man's final state of Redemption. Moreover, the process of regeneration through Adam-Eve-Church (or Homo-Vir-Society), exhibits a parallelism, though it is more implied than specifically stated by James, between individual man and universal man (Society). What happens in the individual's evolution and regeneration, is typical of all mankind in its redeemed condition; indeed, the "parallelism" tends always to merge, and finally does, into identity between man-individual and man-universal in the Divine Humanity. In sum, as will become evident in the last two chapters of this work, the process of man's redemption involves in James's thought one central, nuclear concept: God descends into Humanity, that Humanity may ascend to Divinity.

Before taking leave of *homo-vir*, we should notice what a tremendous range of meanings James can place upon this polarity-principle. The philosophic significance, as he sees it, of the bi-sexual dynamics of human consciousness, is rendered in a masterly summation:

> The *homo*, which is the fixed or cosmical and masculine element in existence, yearns towards the *vir*, which is its free or domestic

and feminine element; while the *vir* again responsively aspires to the *homo*. . . . Thus we may say that the great historic problem— the problem alike of our earliest religious and our latest philosophic culture—has been to reconcile nature and man, to fuse flesh and spirit, to wed force and freedom, to harmonize law and gospel, to marry mechanism and morals, in short permanently to unite the indefinitely great, which is the superb overbearing cosmos, with the indefinitely small, which is our humble domestic earth. . . . [71]

With one short and final quotation from James in this section of the chapter, we shall have completed the great journey from the Divine Paternity and Nature's Maternity in creation, through the masculine-femine, *homo-vir*, Adam-Eve dynamics of human consciousness and moral selfhood on the way back to ultimate redemption, when at last man will recognize that God is his father both originally and ultimately. James writes of the end of this vast pilgrimage in a single sentence which ties up almost everything that we have been studying in this section:

> Our natural history may be defined in fact to be a pure process of redemption, or spiritual formation, consisting first in giving us conscious finite maternity, but only in order that consciousness may prove rigidly and unalterably ministerial to our conscious infinite paternity.[72]

*   *   *

The Principle of Bi-Sexual Polarity is, as was previously asserted, the closest that James ever came to a psychology, and yet it is obvious that it does not resemble very much anything that we know as psychology, except Freud and Jung in one or two respects. It is a kind of meta-psychics that fits in well with his Pan-Psychism. Plainly it is not epistemology, nor ontology, yet there are epistemological and ontological elements in it. Is the term "psycho-anthropology" too labored? Does it cover enough or too much?

We have not found Sex, as such, on our great journey, but we have seen the Bi-Sexual Principle applied by James to Creation, Nature, Knowledge, Man, History, Society, and Redemption. It is certain that we now have a profounder and nobler conception of the dynamics that, in actuality, Sex does generate in human consciousness. James is one of the precious few architects of a Spiritual Philosophy of Sex.

One writer has perceived with insight and expressed with power, what he believes to be a remarkable anticipation by James of the Freudian psychology. It is heartening to find a writer who appreciates

James's dynamical theory of human consciousness as intelligently as Anderson in his article on "Henry James and the New Jerusalem." Though the article is mainly about Henry James, Jr., Anderson has devoted considerable attention to the influences of the elder James on the novelist, and in a way that may start a new cycle of Jamesian criticism in connection with the junior Henry James. Anderson says:

> Since the elder James was a theologian and a moralist it is conceivable that he stood in the same relation to the novelist as Aquinas does to Dante or Kirkegaard to Kafka.[73]

It is difficult to know what the author means in that important sentence when he calls James a "moralist." We will see in the next chapter how *anti-moralist* James is, and on the positive side, how consistently he is a philosophic and religious "spiritualist." Consequently, unless Anderson is using the term "moralist" in a quite extraordinary sense, it is hard to see its applicability to James. Anderson says: "One cannot overemphasize the importance which the elder James attached to moral energy, moral spontaneity. His universe is one of moral energies which the self-righteous man tries to arrest."[74] That is strongly stated, but is it a true use of "moral" as applied to James? This writer believes that Schneider is closer to precise depiction of James's thought when he says that his "characteristic spontaneity was not an individual trait, but a spiritual grace in which all men share."[75]

When it comes to interpreting James's spiritual philosophy in terms of psychology, Anderson has developed an interesting theory. Operating with James's concepts of "spiritual individuality" and then breaking it down into sub-concepts of "self-confrontation," "identity," the "complete parallelism between the history of mankind and the history of a given individual," and a certain parallel between James's theory of personality and Freud's, he has constructed a truly fascinating interpretation and application of James's psychology. But the writer believes that this aspect of James is more implicit than explicit, for, to quote Schneider again: James " . . . was one of the most conspicuous characters among those who cultivated individuality in extraordinary ways; he believed, however, that his characteristic spontaneity was not an individual trait. . . ."[76] Moreover, James was not, like Freud, interested at all in the biology of sex, and this fact makes a great difference in the "psychology." However this may be, there is no gainsaying that Anderson is opening up an important field of investigation.

A passage will illustrate his contribution in the interpretation of the complex elder James:

> When one looks at the elder James's theory of personality in cross-section, without regard to man's origin or his ultimate destiny, it is seen to be an anticipation of Freudian theory. The sleeping Adam, the chaos of the unconscious, may be compared to the id, the concept of the *proprium* or self to the ego, and the conscience or social self to the superego. Moreover the limiting conditions of our present consciousness are held to be self-love on the one side and brotherly love on the other. But these concepts are not, in the end, employed as we employ them. Conscience is identified with the divine love, and man has a divine assurance that Eros will triumph over Death that no modern theory would provide. It is also possible to make an analogy between the process of regeneration in James and psychoanalysis, since the whole of existence is centered in the psyche, and the divinity seated within leads us to confront our selves. In the elder James, however, this process annihilates the ego as such, and forms a society in which, as in a symphony orchestra or a colony of ants, individuals are distinguishable in function but not in character. For these reasons James's theory of personality is not separable from his theology. In fact the two are identical.
>
> The greatness of the elder James lies in the fact that he worked out a theory of consciousness which provides an account in dynamic terms of the forces which relate individuals and groups, and that this account, like modern psychology, deals with the transformation of one form of moral energy into another. The adequacy of the theory is limited by the maker's own emotional constellation, but it was a great achievement for its day, and ought to be recognized as a landmark in the history of American thought.[77]

IV

This chapter on James's Doctrine of Spiritual Man would be incomplete without certain general observations concerning the particular emphasis which he places on man's origin, function, and destiny as a creature through whom all the levels and currents of reality pass, and in whom, in a sense, they converge. This is tantamount to leading one to make a few remarks about man as "Microcosm" in James's thought, and to conclude with a magnificent passage in which he phrases the microcosmic conception of man to the music of a rich and sinewy prose.

Man as Microcosm: the conception has the dignity of a long and noble philosophic tradition, from classical Greek philosophy to Swedenborg, Lotze (1817-1881), and to James in modern times. It is not known for certain whether or not James was acquainted with Lotze's great work, *Mikrokosmos,* which came out as completed in 1864, though the English translation appeared three years after James's death. It is not known either whether James read German philosophy in the original tongue, in addition to his linguistic attainments in Hebrew, Greek, Latin, and French. In any event, the idea is embedded in Swedenborg, and developed by him into the concept of the "Grand Man." But whatever the sources, James caught the idea and expressed it in the "rich, vascular" English of the old masters:

> In short, you find no unitary animal form below the human. The lion is out of all unison with the cow, the fox with the sheep, the serpent with the dove: look where you will, diversity not unity, discord not concord, is the law of animal life. One animal preys upon another; one half of the animal kingdom lives by destroying the other half. Now man, so far as his natural form is concerned, resumes all these distinctive differences of the lower natures, and fuses them in the bosom of his own unity. He is not only devouring as the fire, and unstable as the water: he is fixed as the rock, hard as the iron, sensitive as the flower, graceful and flowing as the vine, majestic as the oak, lowly as the shrub. But especially does he reproduce in himself all the animal characteristics. He is indolent as the sloth, he is busy as the bee, he is stupid as the ox, he is provident as the beaver, he is blind as the bat, he is far-sighted as the eagle, he grovels like the mole, he soars like the lark, he is bold as the lion, timid as the fawn, cunning as the fox, artless as the sheep, venomous as the serpent, harmless as the dove: in short, all the irreconcilable antagonisms of animate nature meet and kiss one another in the unity of the human form. It perfectly melts and fuses the most obdurate contrarieties in the lap of its own universality. It is this universality of the human form which endows it with the supremacy of nature, and fits it to embosom the Divine infinitude. Because it adequately resumes in its own unity the universe of life; because it sops up, so to speak, and reproduces in its own individuality all mineral, all vegetable, and all animal forms, it claims the rightful lordship of nature, or coerces nature under its own subjection. Thus the marriage I speak of is perfectly ratified only in the human form, because in that form alone does the feminine or individual element bear any just ratio to the masculine and universal one. In short, man is

the sole measure of the universe, because he alone combines in the form of his natural individuality every conceivable character-istic of universal life. . . . He is the dazzling blossom of the universe, the peerless fruit by whose interior chemistry unripe Nature ripens all her juices to gladden the heart of creative Love. . . .

Would we be doing justice to James's profoundest current of thought if we left the above passage, confined as it is to the level of anthropology, unrelated to his theology? To man as "the sole measure of the universe," James was bound to adjoin man's "profounder life" in God:

Had I had no profounder life than that which binds me to nature and society, were I not related to God more profoundly than I am related either to my own body or to my fellow-man, I should have remained mere dove or serpent, mere horse or lion, mere sheep or tiger, to the end of the chapter: that is, I should have remained just what my spiritual association made me, a living animal with-out true freedom or selfhood, without any Divine quickening, and consequently without any power to rise above the lot of my nature.[79]

NOTES

1. Henry James, Sr., "Faith and Science," *North American Review,* Vol. CI (1865), p. 363.
2. *Moralism and Christianity,* p. 58.
3. Quentin Anderson, "Henry James and the New Jerusalem," *The Kenyon Review,* Vol. VIII (1946), pp. 524-525.
4. *MC,* p. 57.
5. "The Works of Sir William Hamilton," *Putnam's Magazine,* Vol. II (1853), p. 478.
6. *Ibid.*
7. *MC,* pp. 97, 100-101, 102-107.
8. *LM,* pp. 346-349.
9. *NE,* p. 83.
10. *NE,* note, p. 82.
11. *S and S,* pp. 82-83.
12. *Ibid.,* 83.
13. *S of S,* pp. 41-42.
14. *SRFM,* pp. 162-163; 164-166.
15. *MC,* p. 13.
16. *MC,* pp. 19, 22-23, 24-25.
17. *CLC,* pp. 24-25.
18. *S and S,* pp. 431-432.
19. *Ibid.,* pp. 514-515.
20. *Ibid.,* pp. 500-501.

21. *CCNE,* p. 86.
22. *MC,* pp. 25-27.
23. *Ibid.,* pp. 34-35.
24. *LM,* p. 102.
25. *Ibid.,* pp. 114, 126-127, 133-135.
26. *LR,* p. 338.
27. *Ibid.,* pp. 342-343.
28. Sir William Hamilton, *Metaphysics,* Vol. I, p. 191.
29. *SRFM,* pp. 260-261.
30. *S and S,* pp. 300-301.
31. "The Ontology of Swedenborg," *North American Review,* Vol. CV (1867), p. 97.
32. *Ibid.,* pp. 98-99.
33. *CLC,* pp. 81-83. When James, in the first paragraph of this quotation, speaks of Swedenborg as teaching a theology "which places God exclusively within the soul," of man, he is utterly misapprehending and misrepresenting the view of his acknowledged master, who held that God is in the human soul only by influx, as light is carried in the physical universe by rays from the sun.
34. *Ibid.,* pp. 83-84, 86.
35. *Ibid.,* p. 55.
36. *CLC,* pp. 58-59.
37. *S of S,* p. 147.
38. *SRFM,* pp. 141-142.
39. *CCNE,* pp. 53-54.
40. Ralph B. Perry, *op. cit.,* Vol. II, p. 710.
41. *CCNE,* p. 55.
42. *Ibid.,* p. 82.
43. *SRFM,* p. 144.
44. *S of S,* pp. 15-16.
45. "William Blake's Poems," *The Spirit of the Age,* Vol. I (1850), p. 113.
46. *SRFM,* p. 143.
47. *The True Christian Religion,* No. 624, p. 417.
48. *Ibid.,* No. 737, p. 492.
49. *Ibid.,* No. 748, p. 501.
50. *S and S,* pp. 494-97.
51. *Ibid.,* pp. 497-98.
52. M. A. deWolfe Howe, *Memories of a Hostess* (1922), p. 76.
53. *S and S,* pp. 463-64.
54. *CLC,* pp. 86-87.
55. *Ibid.,* pp. 92-93.
56. *S and S,* p. 424.
57. *CLC,* p. 57.
58. *S and S,* p. 465.
59. *S of S,* pp. 45-46.
60. *S of S,* pp. 148-149, 147-148.
61. *LR,* p. 258.
62. *S and S,* pp. 426-427.

63. *CLC*, p. 121.
64. *LR*, pp. 260-261, 262-263.
65. *LR*, pp. 355-356.
66. *Ibid.*, pp. 14-15.
67. *S of S*, pp. 141-142.
68. *Ibid.*, p. 154.
69. *Ibid.*, pp. 151-152.
70. *Ibid.*, p. 95.
71. *Ibid.*, p. 124.
72. *S and S*, p. 464.
73. Quentin Anderson, "Henry James and the New Jerusalem," *The Kenyon Review*, Vol. VIII (Autumn, 1946), p. 515.
74. Quentin Anderson, "The Two Henry Jameses," *Scrutiny*, Vol. XIV (Sept., 1947), p. 243.
75. Herbert W. Schneider, *A History of American Philosophy* (N. Y., 1946), pp. 301-302.
76. Herbert W. Schneider, *op. cit.*, p. 301.
77. Quentin Anderson, "Henry James and the New Jerusalem," *The Kenyon Review*, Vol. VIII (Autumn, 1946), pp. 524-525.
78. *CLC*, pp. 94-96, 97.
79. *Ibid.*, p. 125.

Chapter Ten

The Doctrine of Spiritual Evil

When we speak of inquiring into the origin of evil, we do not mean physical evil, or the evil which one SUFFERS: nor moral evil, or the evil which one DOES: but spiritual evil, or the evil which one IS.

—HENRY JAMES, SR.[1]

. . . The precise seat of spiritual evil . . . lies in the pride of moralism, or the conceit of one's moral endowments, those endowments which make a man feel that he has an absolute or independent selfhood. . . . This is original sin, the great parental fount and origin of all the evils that desolate humanity. Here lies the great mother-fallacy at whose exuberant paps cling and feed all the minor fallacies of the universe.

—HENRY JAMES, SR.[2]

The accord of moralism and religion is superficial; their discord radical. Only the deepest thinkers on both sides see that one must go.

—WILLIAM JAMES[3]

No more radical critique of liberalism has appeared in this country, though there have been many more realistic.

—HERBERT WALLACE SCHNEIDER[4]

THE GHOST OF the Genevan theocrat and the lesser ghost of Sandeman must have returned to James, whether to his "self-consciousness" or to his "unconscious," when he confronted the problem of evil. John Calvin would not agree in detail with James's doctrine of evil, but he would have recognized him as a spiritually-descended son, even though a rebellious son, in the seriousness with which James took the task of constructing a theodicy; for it is significant that James devoted an entire book to *The Nature of Evil*. It is a superb illustration of the *spiritual* continuity that often underlies radically different doctrinal formulations, that James's Doctrine of Spiritual Evil is, in its own way, as is subsequently to be exhibited, even more radical in its view than that of the great Reformist theologian.

As prefatory to an examination of this Doctrine of Spiritual Evil, it is necessary to consider two great concepts in his thought which have been reserved for treatment here because of their profound connection—in fact, a *causal* connection—with the origin and nature of evil. These concepts are "Morality" and "Conscience." The function of morality and conscience in James's spiritual dynamics, is to take man as far as a "conscience of sin," after which the "extrinsic" Redemption of man by the Lord operates to the final goal of the whole creative process, namely, the redeemed Society, or the Divine-Natural-Humanity. The Antinomianism in James might be considered a sub-concept of Morality, but in reality it is better understood as the negative aspect of his positive doctrine of Spiritual Evil—for spiritual evil is a very positive fact to James, more positive than either morality or conscience; though of course, relative to *Redemption,* spiritual evil is negative in the sense that it denies Divine efforts at saving men—though again, it is positive in its very denial. At any rate, antinomianism in James is a critique of moralism, and is in effect the negative side of the positive doctrine of spiritual evil, and so will be treated in this chapter.

I

In a general way of speaking, "Morality" in James is a highly necessary phase of man's evolution. It, like conscience, is what distinguishes man from all the lower animal existence. But it is not enough to make this mere statement of man's demarcation from the brute realm by virtue of the phenomenon of morality. What is the meaning that lies within the distinction? James tells us, in sum: the inmost meaning of morality is not in itself but in its relation to man's spirituality. James defines the difference between the two:

> The best and briefest definition of moral existence is, *the alliance of an inward subject and an outward object;* and of spiritual existence, *the alliance of an outward subject and an inward object.* Thus in moral existence what is public or universal dominates what is private or individual; whereas in spiritual existence the case is reversed, and the outward serves the inward.[5]

This distinction sounds rather familiar; in fact, it brings to mind his definition in the previous chapter of the invariable meaning of "consciousness": "The copulation of an interior object with an external subject; the marriage of a universal substance with a specific form." Thus, the conception of "consciousness" is phrased precisely the same as the conception of "spiritual existence," and the highest characteristic of both is "spiritual freedom," or "spontaneity" on that third level of freedom that we studied. James's argument to either consciousness or spiritual existence as the basic validity for his doctrines all the way along, rather than to the validity of the perceptual level or the scientific-observational level, is fundamental to a proper comprehension of his philosophy. To think otherwise is to misconceive the philosophic ground of his thought. This appeal to consciousness is plainly introspective and subjective in quality and shows the influence, through Swedenborg, of Descartes; for James never swerved from the appeal to the thinking self.

James, having defined moral existence in the abstract embodies his thought more specifically in his early lecture (1849), on "Morality and the Perfect Life." Extracting selections from this source, we get a rounded view of the direction of his mind on morality, a direction that never changed in the remainder of his intellectual career, though it received ever deepening formulation:

> The individual life in order to its perfection, exacts a perfect balance of the natural and social law, the law of self-love and the law of charity, a perfect equilibrium in other words between man's appetites and his affections or sympathies. While this balance or equilibrium is yet unattained the individual oscillates between the two extremes, now obeying this law, now obeying that. Morality expresses just this fact of oscillation. It expresses the vibratory or pendulous condition of the human individuality, preparatory to its true and immortal poise or rest in God.[6]

Therefore:

> Morality then is conditioned upon a conflict or antagonism be-
> tween nature and society, between self-love and charity, between
> my natural inclination and my social sympathies. When I prac-
> tically subject my natural inclinations or appetites to my social
> sympathies you pronounce me a good man; when I practically
> subject the latter to the former, you pronounce me an evil man.[7]

In *The Nature of Evil* James relates the operation of the "equilibrium" principle:

> All finite consciousness is conditioned upon the antagonism of good
> and evil. But *moral* consciousness, or the consciousness of a self-
> hood superior to one's physique, implies not merely the antagon-
> ism of these extremes, but also their strict equilibrium. . . . Such
> is the invariable genesis of morality. No man is good save by the
> overcoming of evil; no man wise save by the subjugation of
> falsity; no man learned save by the conquest of ignorance. I can-
> not do good save in so far as I cease to do evil; I cannot follow
> truth save in so far as I avert myself from falsity; I cannot choose
> black tea save by the simultaneous rejection of green. The equi-
> librium of these extremes is what pronounces the action mine, or
> makes it possible.[8]

A still closer analysis of morality on Jamesian tenets, of the "nature
of moral nature," so to speak, is given thus:

> What in effect I have been saying all along is, that morality is
> not a personal or specific endowment of man, but a rigidly natural
> or generic one. It is the badge, not of this, that, or the other man,
> but of all men alike, just in so far as they are men at all. It
> characterizes no special subject of human nature, but the very
> nature itself. It is indeed the essence of human nature; the logical
> *differentia* between man and the brute; being what characterizes
> him expressly as man. . . .[9]

James has gone as far as he can with anything like a positive value
for morality. On the whole he devotes more space in his writings to the
dis-positive function of morality in terms of spiritual philosophy.
Morality's greatest honor turns out to be its service as a propaedeutic
to the realization that moral distinctions, based on the principle of
selfhood, are spiritually evil. There are in his works so many statements on morality, or more strictly moral-*ism*, as the very font of spiritual evil that it is difficult to choose the most salient. The germs of
his lifelong and powerful attack on moralism, which is another way of

affirming his Doctrine of Spiritual Evil, are found in the lecture cited above, "Morality and the Perfect Life." The adjective "perfect" occurs so frequently in James when he is referring to the spiritual level of human life, that it is obvious he is a spiritual perfectionist in his religious tendency. From this plane of his spiritual perfectionism, James attacks morality and "society" (*empirical* society, not as *redeemed*) for not protecting the life of our spiritual "individuality." Society, in its historic aspect merely, should subserve our "true individuality," which in turn yields to the social state of redemption; therefore, there is no real conflict, as thus distinguished in terms, between "individuality" and the later doctrine of spiritual socialism. James understood clearly the important differences between *individual*, individual-*ism*, and individual-*ity*, distinctions too often lost sight of in most talk about "Democracy," for example. These observations help us to understand the following from "Morality and the Perfect Life":

> But . . . it is evident to you from the past rapid sketch, that society has thus far done nothing for the individual, but to deepen or intensify his moral consciousness, that is, to bring him under the law successively to his wife, his children, his relatives, his neighbors, his fellow-countrymen. The most it has done for him is to allow him a relative goodness, a goodness lying in his relations to other people. But clearly, man should be good by virtue of his creation, or his relation to the infinite God, should be good in himself, infinitely good.[10]

The individual requires the constant discipline of continuous adjustment to nature and society, if only in the end to discover that he cannot satisfy the demands of his "infinite" self in this way, for it will bring him to despair:

> The individual thus disciplined consequently, and feeling in every pulse of his soul the instinct of sovereignty, proceeds to realize it by these natural and moral methods. . . . But the more diligently he prosecutes either pursuit, that of pleasure or this of duty, the further he strays from the great quest and accumulates defeat. . . . While he seeks therefore to wring it out of the base reluctant bowels of nature and society . . . it perpetually baffles his grasp, and beats him to the dust in shame and despair.[11]

This despair is a providential means of bringing man to a realization that there is neither peace nor redemption in or for his "finite" selfhood:

Now this experience on the part of man of the utter vanity of his pursuits, of the utter inability both of nature and society to satisfy his aspiration and give him peace with himself, although bitterly painful in its transit, has yet the most indispensable uses in convincing him of his essential infinitude, and leading him to disown and reject the finite selfhood.[12]

Because James hungers after a perfect goodness rather than one based upon a comparative scale measured against other men, he asserts:

Destroy, therefore, the imperfections of our social institutions, or, what is the same thing, allow man's internal freedom a perfect outward development, and you instantly destroy all unrighteousness and all Pharisaic pride among men. In that event our mere relative or contingent good would give place to positive and universal good. No man would then appear good by the contrast of another's evil, nor any appear evil by the contrast of another's good, but every man would be positively good, good by the manifest and unlimited indwelling of the divine power. . . .

For there can be no more flagrant affront to the Divine Humanity, to God's end in creation, than for the moral life to regard itself as final.[13]

The germinal ideas are now mounted for one of the most aggressive attacks against "moralism" in the history of this long battle between spiritual religion and morality. He seems akin to Kierkegaard at this point, for the Danish thinker hated moralism *as a gospel*, with the same terrific hatred with which James hated it. In this aspect of James we can see again the antinomian influence that came from Sandemanianism. This is the chief side of James's philosophy that Sandeman permanently affected, but this tendency—antinomianism (along with anti-ecclesiasticism)—really stuck; moreover, behind Sandeman is Calvinism, for Sandeman only took to an extreme explicit statement the antinomian quality in Calvinism with its doctrine of the unqualified sovereignty of God with its corollary of double election by God of men for heaven or hell independently of any moral considerations which men might set up as effective in gaining "merit" with their Creator.

James makes it clear that he is not attacking morality as such and in its proper place, but only the pride which goes with it. This prideful moralism is actually spiritual evil, and so, nowhere do we find James speaking of morality as an evil in itself. The charge of antinomianism brought against him was at bottom quite pointless as a rule because James was not against morality *as such*, but against mora*lism* which was an un-spiritual attitude toward morality and so injuring a true morality itself; hence, a *spiritual* evil properly chargeable against the spiritual consciousness and not against morality:

> I do not complain of course that the inseparable distinction of good and evil is made too much of. No man, not an idiot, can ever fail to abhor lying, theft, adultery, and murder, as features of human conduct, nor consequently to applaud the habitual and scrupulous abnegation of these things; because our spiritual existence is conditioned upon that bipolarity of pleasure and pain and to suppose one indifferent therefore to moral distinctions is to suppose him spiritually non-existent, just as to suppose one indifferent to the distinction between pleasure and pain is to suppose him physically non-existent. In both spheres alike these things are the mere constitutional conditions of our existence, and what I quarrel with consequently is that they should not be left in that intensely subordinate plight, but become exalted by our foolish theologians and philosophers into the very sources also of our life.[14]

Having made his position entirely clear to any honest mind, James opens up the real barrage against Moralism. His sustained attack constitutes a radical indictment of the spiritual danger of relying upon morality as giving one permanent "face" or status before God. James opens the battle rather mildly as compared with his later strictures:

> It is clearly deducible then from all I have said, that I hold morality to be a transient phenomenon of humanity, or to pertain only to man's immature experience, having not only no relevancy to him as the creature of God, but imposing a positive disability upon that relation.[15]
> As Swedenborg has shown in a very complete manner, neither charity nor self-love, neither moral good nor moral evil, has its origin in the individual, but only in good or bad association. All charity, he says, is an influx into man from heavenly association; all self-love an influx into him from infernal association. Hence he says, God never attributes good nor evil to a man, never sees in him either merit or demerit. In truth, he represents God as wholly ignoring the moral man, the man who is subject either to nature or society, either to hell or heaven, and acknowledging only the Lord or perfect man, the man who subjects both hell and heaven to his own individuality, and so ensures an unimpeded intercourse between the divine and human, between the Creator and creature.[16]

It should be stated that James, whether consciously or not, is woefully misunderstanding Swedenborg; for when he asserts that, "according to Swedenborg," God "wholly ignores the moral man," it simply is *not* true, as we know from our study of the Swedish thinker, in those passages in which he upheld active moral life against the Calvinist-Sandemanian view, of Justification by Faith alone.

It appears that evil itself is to be explained for James in the light of his profound social consciousness: for both moral good and moral evil arise out of good or bad "association." Since all angels and devils are, in Swedenborgian angelology and demonology, the spirits of human souls that once lived on the earth, James's concept of "Society" stretches beyond "History," and is thus an eschatological concept; but there is no rigid partition between the historical and eschatological aspects of "Society," for those who become angels and those who become devils or satans (there is no *one* "Satan" in Swedenborg's theology) emanate a constant stream of heavenly or infernal influence upon men still living in the present type of existence. There is nothing static or individualistic about James's heaven or hell!—or, to be more precise, heavens and hells, since there is no one "place" at all known as heaven or hell, but only states of spirits in heavenly or infernal conditions in the innermost self.

The other idea to be mentioned from the above passage is the reference to the Lord or perfect man who subjects heaven and hell to his own individuality: this refers to the objective act of Redemption performed in history by the Lord, to be distinguished from "regeneration", which is man's subjective response to the Lord's redemptive mission. This whole concept will receive treatment in the next chapter on Spiritual Socialism.

Now that James has given us his wrongly-conceived "Swedenborgian" basis of thought on morality, he gives vent to an unmitigated blast on the subject, and here he uses the more precise term "moralism":

> Thus moralism is the parent of fetichism, or superstitious worship, the parent of all sensual and degrading ideas of God, the parent of all cruel and unclean and abominable worship. Leading me as it does to regard my inward self as corrupt, to distrust my heart's affections as the deadliest enmity to God, it logically prompts the crucifixion of those affections as especially well pleasing to Him, and bids me therefore offer my child to the flames, clothe my body in sackcloth and ashes, lacerate my skin, renounce the comforts and refinements of life, turn hermit or monk, forswear mar-

riage, wear lugubrious and hideous dresses that insult God's daylight, and make myself, in short, under the guise of a voluntary and mendacious humility, perfectly ulcerous with spiritual pride, a mass of *living* purulence and putridity.[17]

Morality as entirely subservient to the purposes of Spirit, is the burden of our author's theme as he again appeals to Swedenborg and interprets him for his own purposes:

Swedenborg effectually exposes this insanity, by proving that just as our physical experience has no other end than to base or matriculate our moral manhood, so our moral experiences in its turn has had no other end than to serve as a matrix or mould to our true spiritual manhood. He reduces the part morality plays in the Divine administration to a strictly educative one; its whole office being to loosen nature's remorseless grasp upon us, and so prepare us spiritually for the unimpeded Divine inhabitation. Nothing consequently can be more hurtful to the intellect than to confound the moral and spiritual consciousness in man; or make that purely phenomenal freedom which distinguishes us naturally from the brute, take the place of that most real freedom which allies us spiritually with God.[18]

James is occupied next with the results of maintaining the absoluteness of "morality"; such a view, he warns, will lead in the end to Pantheism or Atheism:

Such is the entire philosophy, as I apprehend it, of man's moral experience, or of our finite selfhood. We are endowed with moral freedom not for its own sake, or as a finality, but simply as a means to our spiritual conjunction with God. . . . Admit this end, admit that man is created for an eternal spiritual conjunction with God, and a flood of light is thrown over our moral history. Deny it, deny the normal subordination of our moral experience to a superior spiritual end, or make it its own end, and you make the divine creation a mere empiricism, so rendering the Divine Perfection itself essentially problematic. You indeed make God the author of Evil.[19]

Morality admits of no absolute justification. How can any mind of true reverence tolerate the conception of a creature of God, who is anything in-himself? For to be anything in himself, he must claim a power underived from God, and the pretension to such a power is fatal to creatureship. Accordingly, whenever a man attempts to vindicate morality unconditionally, he finds himself logically compelled to bring up in Atheism or Pantheism: at all events to deny creation in any intelligible sense of that word.[20]

The footnote James has for the index number after "word" is worth quoting also:

> Dr. Bushnell hazards a very rash and even desperate solution of the difficulty, by making God to create a number of little gods instead of men: his idea of morality being that it involves a participation of the Divine essence! See "Nature and the Supernatural," *passim*.[21]

The secular moralist as against the spiritual moralist, so to put it, is wrong in holding that civilization is based upon the finality of morality, for the teaching of the Church is counterposed to this idea:

> In the first place, if morality were absolute in its demands upon human nature, and duty constituted the Divine ideal of human action, then the teaching of the church, and the soothing ministry of its clergy at our death-beds, would be wholly out of place in civilized life. For civilization being based upon the absoluteness of the moral sentiment the instinct of self-defence or its own preservation would keep it from tolerating any influence which went to the weakening of this sentiment. But the church, at least the church in its orthodox aspect, is practically the sworn foe of the moral pretension in men. The church, so long at all events as it witnessed to man's *spiritual* life, allowed no moral differences among men to intervene between the soul and God, or complicate the gospel blessings to universal man. Its founder earned the odium of all the morally righteous men of his nation by proclaiming himself the friend of publicans and sinners, and it would be indeed difficult, nay impossible to discover why his gospel was called a gospel, if it had been addressed primarily to the special relief of those who had a conscience of sin towards God only because they had violated the law upon which their national dignity was founded.[22]

Tragically enough, the Church itself has lost sight of its great spiritual *raison d'être*:

> But all men in this day of the church's spiritual imbecility are more or less moralistic. The Unitarian or latest form of church development which represents the church in its vastated spiritual plight more faithfully than is at all agreeable to the orthodox imagination, has pushed moralism so far as to have almost openly declined, itself, into a mere school of good manners, while the orthodox congregations by a necessary reaction have been driven to contra-distinguish themselves by a gospel of fervent but puerile ritualism. Thus between the "world" and the "church" the only discernible difference is that while the former continues to be

seriously moralistic in its doctrinal beliefs as to another life, the latter grows more and more frivolously so.[23]

In the last few selections James has been speaking in effect of "spiritual evil," though he has nominally been talking about "morality" and "moralism." Since Spiritual Evil is the subject of this chapter, and since James's treatment of Morality and Conscience is only preparatory to his Doctrine of Spiritual Evil, it is time to sum up what James has been saying as a conclusion to the exposition of the concept of morality.

James's concept of morality reduces itself, in a sentence, to this: morality distinguishes man *from* the brutes; it distinguishes himself *to* his fellow-men; but in the light of spiritual religion, it has *no* distinguishing power *before* God. In fact, the more we allow ourselves to indulge the illusion that it does distinguish us to God's regard, the more we *dis*-junct ourselves from spiritual *con*junction with Him. If theology doesn't recognize this truth, it will be found that trying to solve the problem of evil will throw the whole issue into a Manichaean framework:

> Certain recent writers, ambitious to rejuvenate the old theology by giving it a *quasi* rational sanction, have labored hard to sophisticate this truth, by representing morality not as a natural but as a distinctly supernatural fact; but with no other effect than to signalize their own incompetence, since their whole labor is built upon a transparent quibble, that of confounding morality with moral goodness, so blinking moral evil out of sight. Certainly moral or voluntary goodness exists only by the antagonism of like evil; and if therefore moral good be supernatural or claim a divine source, moral evil has every right to be equally exacting. The more hardy leaders accordingly in this enterprise do not hesitate virtually to adopt the manichean hypothesis of creation, and trace back the existing evil of the creature to an "evil possibility" in the divine nature! See Dr. Bushnell's "Nature and the Supernatural."[24]

As a final passage from James on this matter of the true spiritual meaning—and dangers—of morality, we cite what contains the inner logic that will carry him on to Spiritual Socialism:

> Now if morality be as here alleged the distinctive sign of human nature, that is to say, if a man is moral, not by virtue of what he is or has in contradistinction to his fellows, but solely by virtue of what he is or has in common with all other men, it is at once obvious that the moral subject, as such, must straightway disown

every spiritual qualification, i.e. disavow any *direct* approximation to the infinite, any such approximation as does not rigidly presuppose that of his kind. He may claim to be spiritually affiliated to God, if he please, but not in his own right, and only by virtue of a previous spiritual affiliation of the race.[25]

From which it is transparently clear that James, though spiritually critical of morality, is not talking against morality as such at all. "Morality" is "the distinctive sign of human nature"; could any one have a higher conception of it, taken by itself? It is only when it leads to spiritual pride, and chokes off man's development of his spiritual consciousness, that James becomes its deadly foe. James might well be called a "three-storey" soul: natural man, moral man, spiritual man— he will have them all, but he will not let any one get in the way of any other, and especially will he not let natural and moral man get in the way of spiritual man.

* * *

The anti-moralism of James inevitably brought upon him the charge of antinomianism. In this century the charge was renewed by Ralph Barton Perry, eminent philosopher and distinguished authority on William James. It is worth while to consider a few points in Perry's article on "Religion versus Morality according to the Elder Henry James." For example:

> . . . antinomianism is a malady of excess rather than of deficiency, and the Christian has to fear it most, in the morning hours when his Christian heart is beating high.[26]

Perry continues:

> That which he attacks under the name of morality is not happiness, in the sense of a disregard of the rights or happiness of others. . . . What James condemns is a much more subtle and insidious thing. He condemns moral self-righteousness.[27]

But, says Perry, in condemning self-righteousness over one's moral virtues, James falls into a pit of his own; namely, in attacking pride in one's moral strength and in favoring humility instead, James is stumbling into an even more "dangerous form of pride":

> The most dangerous form of pride . . . is the pride of humility. It is like a quicksand in that the harder one tries to extricate one's self the more deeply one is bogged. . . . We find him condemning his self-approbation and approving his self-condemnation.[28]

The paradoxical language of James disturbs Perry, and in expressing his disturbance, he reveals that he is conscious of a profound issue involved, as William James also realized when he said, in his "Introduction" to his father's *Literary Remains*: "The accord of moralism and religion is superficial; their discord radical. Only the deepest thinkers on both sides see that one must go." Perry feels that James's view is morally and logically stultifying:

> The preliminary step toward the divine life, we are told, is to make ourselves persons; the second step is to unmake ourselves as persons. . . . It is a hard saying that the way to pass from an intermediate point to one's destination is to return to the point of departure.[29]

But is James really involved in the meaning of the "hard saying" ascribed to him in essence by Perry? The logic itself of Perry, when he describes James's position as committing him to passing from an intermediate point to one's destination only for one to find that he has returned to the "point of departure," uses a metaphor which hardly does justice to James's full and real position. As a figure of speech, it is therefore misleading for two reasons: firstly, James's thought-system as a whole is not uni-plane, but multi-plane, in its "geometry"; hence, his antinomianism must be judged with reference to all levels of his philosophy in its entirety; secondly, it implies a horizontal rather than the vertical direction of mobility involved in the metaphysical process of involution-evolution.

In sum, to use a geometric figure of speech ourselves, the graph of James's thought describes, not a line of return to point of departure, but rather a spiral which coils always upward toward the Divine Humanity; a process in which no points are fixed, and in which the tip of the spiral is an ever-growing point more in the fashion of a biological entity. The goal, then, envisaged by James in overcoming our finite, moral selfhoods is not a return to the point of departure, but a progress to the very different, spiritually speaking, point of arrival in which we are willing to lose our moral selves in order to find our infinite spiritual selves. Between the two points James traces a considerable growth and an immense change of spiritual focus.

The final point of contention by Perry with James is the distinction concerning "legal" and "spontaneous" righteousness in James's thought:

> Morality, it is argued, assumes the form of rules which are harshly imposed and abjectly obeyed, whereas the spiritual life is

one of spontaneity and freedom. . . . But because a spontaneous righteousness is better than a legal righteousness it does not follow that whatever is spontaneous is therefore better than whatever is legal.[30]

It should be apparent in general that if one is to attack James's antimoralism, he should do it in terms of James's system as a whole. His antinomianism is fairly evaluated only if held in perspective with his entire metaphysics of spiritual reality and process. James is, like St. Paul, never the gross antinomian who becomes fanatical in advocating moral irresponsibility and immoral actions that "grace might much more abound." Moreover, he is akin to St. Paul in his profound concern with the spiritual danger of self-righteousness.

II

It is indeed curious that James, with all his concern over the meaning of morality and the dangers of moralism, should not have developed a theory of "conscience" until about 1863. And even then, the idea has, in the few pages in which it appears in *Substance and Shadow*, only one meaning; namely, the "conscience of sin." Only in *The Secret of Swedenborg* does our author develop the idea of conscience to any real extent. Ordinarily James uses words of near-meaning to conscience, such as "selfhood," "moral consciousness," and "morality." Yet the treatment he gives conscience in the book indicated above is too important to by-pass, for the central meaning of the idea of "conscience of sin" will be found to be the mediating concept between the moral and spiritual consciousness; but, in addition to this somewhat negative way of speaking of conscience, James goes further and identifies conscience with "religion"; however, it should be said at once that religion itself is strictly economic to man's spiritual consciousness while on earth, and in no manner to be confused with the final consummation of man's redemption when the need for "religion" itself vanishes.

James uses the term conscience very infrequently in his earlier books, and when it does appear, it is employed with a conventional rather than with a specifically Jamesian development. In *The Nature of Evil* he devotes a few paragraphs to conscience, and a couple of brief excerpts from them will indicate that "conscience" is on its way to a Jamesian evolution that will be characteristic, and demarcated from usual connotations:

To the vulgar apprehension, conscience, or the sentiment of responsibility, instead of being the fruit and token of a spiritual declension on the part of man from the state in which he was created, becomes an original Divine endowment of the soul, and by consequence the moral life, or the life over which this sentiment presides, is practically regarded as the highest life of man. . . . But all this is puerile. Conscience is the badge of a fallen nature. It is only *after* we have eaten of the tree of knowledge of good and evil, that its voice is heard investing us with responsibility.[31]

It is impossible, however, for James not to bifurcate the concept of "conscience" as he bifurcated the concepts of selfhood, consciousness, and so on, into their finite and infinite kinds:

> Conscience, or the moral law, has two tables or aspects: one towards God, another towards man: one literal, the other spiritual; one revealing the duties we owe to our fellow-man or society, the other revealing the spirit from which these duties flow.[32]

In effect, we now have a "moral" conscience and a "spiritual" conscience, just as we had previously a "finite" and "infinite" selfhood, consciousness, and so on through all the other concepts that James has split into binary configurations.

The most important function of conscience to James is that of being a mediating concept between "morality" and "spiritual religion." He elaborates this function in terms now familiar to us:

> The interesting question, I repeat, then to philosophy is, What is the method of this hidden or spiritual divine operation? How is the *vir* (Eve) actually begotten of the *homo* (Adam)? How is moral life generated of mere physical existence? . . .
>
> Our intelligence consequently brooks no arbitrary refusal in its research after the rationale of this stupendous creative achievement. It is the urgent insatiate problem both of the world's dawning spiritual faith, and of its dawning spiritual science, to show how the *vir* becomes divinely begotten of the *homo*, how moral life is bred of physical decay, how spirit is born of flesh, or nature is quickened out of mineral, vegetable, animal into human or moral form. And the altogether sufficing solution, as it seems to me, which Swedenborg gives the problem, may be stated substantially as follows:
>
> The *vir* is begotten of the *homo* (or nature becomes spiritually vivified) exclusively through the instrumentality of conscience. . . .
>
> Conscience in its literal or subjective requirements has respect exclusively to the *homo;* and it is only as a spiritual or objective administration that it contemplates the *vir*. It is to Adam alone,

not Eve, that the prohibition to eat of the tree of knowledge is addressed. . . . Conscience *is the veritable spirit of God in the created nature, seeking to become the creature's own spirit.* . . . It is the *final,* not the immediate, office of conscience to reveal man to himself as a unit of two forces, one infinite, the other finite; one spiritual, the other material. . . .

Conscience then is the sovereign link or point of transition for which we have been seeking between moral and physical existence.[33]

The mediating flavor of the concept is not yet evident in full strength, but it is there, since is it the link between "moral and physical existence," though not the mediator between moral and spiritual consciousness.

Through page after page in *The Secret of Swedenborg* one can literally feel James's effort to formulate his idea of conscience to satisfy his every demand of thought. Before achieving his ultimate statement, James rises to a diapason of praise for conscience that is reminiscent of Kant's apostrophe to the "moral law":

Thus deeper than my intellect, deeper than my heart, deeper in fact than aught and all that I recognize as myself, or am wont to call emphatically *me,* is this dread omnipotent power of conscience which now soothes me with the voice, and nurses me with the milk of its tenderness, as the mother soothes and nurses her child, and anon scourges me with the lash of its indignation, as the father scourges his refractory heir.[34]

Thereafter he lets himself go without stint:

For conscience is *not* what it is commonly reputed to be, a mere miraculous endowment of human nature . . . liable, therefore, to all the vicissitudes of our natural genius and understanding. On the contrary, and in truth, it is *the divine natural humanity itself;* and its light, consequently, is as clear and unflickering as that of the sun at noonday, which in fact is but the servile image of its uncreated splendor.[35]

But this is largely rhetoric, for he qualifies this unrestrained praise of conscience on the next page and thereafter:

But this is only telling half the story. . . . For what conscience inevitably teaches all its earnest adepts ere long is, to give up the hopeless effort to reconcile good and evil in their own practice, and learn to identify themselves, on the contrary, with the evil principle alone, while they assign all good exclusively to

God. Thus no man of a sincere and honest intellectual make has ever set himself seriously to cultivate conscience with a view to its spiritual emoluments. . . . [36]

We suspected all along that James would bring "conscience" into line with his Philosophy of Spirit, despite his prodigal praise of conscience in its first phase as mediator between the *homo* and the *vir*. Conscience now emerges on its second level of mediation:

> The only respect it ever pays to the private votary is to convince him of sin, through a previous conviction of God's wholly *impersonal* justice or righteousness, and so divorce him from the further cultivation of a mercenary piety, while leading him to make common cause with his kind, or frankly disavow every title to the divine esteem which is not quite equally shared by publican and harlot.[37]

And next comes the identification of conscience with "religion":

> Now conscience or religion is the divinely appointed mentruum of our purgation from this sensuous mental captivity, and our consequent eventual edification in all right knowledge of the relation between man and God. . . .
>
> Thus it has always been the historic function of conscience to undermine the sensuous and merely traditional conceptions we entertain in regard to our God-ward origin and destiny, by gradually convincing us that neither the physical nor the moral man, neither Adam nor Eve, neither the *homo* nor the *vir*, has ever had any just claim to be considered God's true or spiritual creation: but only that regenerate social and aesthetic man in whom Adam and Eve, the *homo* and the *vir*, the physical and the moral man, are freed from their intrinsic oppugnancy—from their reciprocal limitations—and reproduced in perfect unity, and in whom alone consequently the divine and the human natures are completely reconciled.[38]

William James has succinctly brought together four of these terms with which we are now acquainted, and pairs them for us in a lucid exposition:

> What is self-consciousness or morality? and what is conscience or religion?—for our author uses synonymously the terms within each pair. The terminology is at first bewildering, and the metaphysical results confounding; for whilst the *stuff* of both morality and religion is, so to speak, the very energy, the very being, of God himself, yet in morality that being takes wholly, and in religion it

takes partly, the form of a lie.... To make a long story short, then, God's first product is a Nature *subject to self-consciousness or selfhood,*—that is, a Nature essentially good, as being divine, but the several members whereof *appropriate* the goodness, and egotistically and atheistically seek to identify it with their private selves. . . .

"I am nothing as substantive,—I am everything as recipient"; this is a thought in which both I and the Creator figure, but in which we figure in perfectly harmonious and truthful guise. It is accordingly the threshold of spiritual life; and instead of obstructing and striving to intercept, it welcomes and furthers all that the divine Love may have in store for every member of the created family.

The agents of the *weaning* [from the untruth of real and independent selfhood apart from God] are conscience and religion. In the philosophy before us, these faculties are considered to have no other function than that of being ministers of death to the fallacious selfhood.[39]

Since Swedenborg has little to say of conscience in his great systematic treatise, *The True Christian Religion,* it is pretty clear that James's development of the concept stems from his Calvinist-Sandemanian rooting. It has become in James a "spiritualized" Calvinism, but the parallels are striking nevertheless. Conscience in the role of the convictor of sin before God, is what any Calvinist or Sandemanian might agree with. It is fascinating to see James chant rhapsodically about conscience, as we have seen, only in the end to expound conscience as the agent of convincing us of our "spiritual" fall! The Calvinism will not die; it is simply spiritualized *via* Swedenborg. It was Emerson's lack of "conscience," in the later Jamesian sense, that irritated James:

> In short he was, as I have said before, fundamentally treacherous to civilization, without being at all aware himself of the fact. He himself, I venture to say, was peculiarly unaware of the fact. He appeared to me utterly unconscious of himself as either good or evil. He had no conscience, in fact, and lived by perception, which is an altogether lower or less spiritual faculty.[40]

A final excerpt from James on "conscience of sin" completes our indeed, we are already over the threshold—of his Doctrine of Spiritual examination of this concept and conducts us to the very threshold— Evil:

. . . How does it promote the welfare of the divine kingdom on earth, to allow serious-minded men to feel all their days a conscience of sin,—that is, a sense of poignant *self*-condemnation and self-abhorrence towards God? The entire intellectual pith and the exquisite virulence of "a conscience of sin" consists in its being a sentiment of *self*-condemnation towards God, who is traditionally held to be the outside and voluntary author of human life. . . .

The *gravamen* of the spiritual experience called conscience, is that I feel *myself* livingly implicated in the evils I do, and no longer attempt to slur them over as mere casual and natural evil deeds.[41]

With the thought that "conscience of sin" is necessary to undermine our illusion of selfhood-independent-of-God, we are more than prepared to understand James's concept of spiritual evil. Conscience of sin has a parallel function in the soul to disease in the body—it is to awaken us to the fact that our spiritual health is endangered.

In one of the most highly compressed statements of a profound idea, he expresses his conception of evil in the inevitable triadic form:

When we speak of inquiring into the origin of evil, we do not mean *physical* evil, or the evil which one SUFFERS: nor *moral* evil, or the evil which one DOES: but *spiritual* evil, or the evil which one Is.[42]

In *Society the Redeemed Form of Man,* he expands precisely the same distinctions:

What, in other words, is the origin of spiritual evil in men, or the evil which attaches to them by nature? For one rightly reasons that if the spiritual world by unduly influencing individual minds on earth ends by vitiating or corrupting human nature itself, it is important to know how so malign an influence becomes exerted by the spiritual world. We can perfectly understand how *physical* evil, or the evil which man *suffers*, originates: namely, in a want of harmony between himself and his own body. One knows too very well how *moral* evil, or the evil which man *does,* comes about: namely, from a want of free harmonic adjustment in the relations of man to man. But here is an evil incomparably deeper than both of these, because it is, in fact, their very and exclusive root: not the paltry and passing evil which under man is passive, as *pain;* nor yet the still more superficial and remedial evil in which he is active, as vice and crime; but spiritual evil, or the evil which he *is*, an evil which characterizes him in relation to his own vital consciousness, and if not removed therefore must utterly palsy his consciousness considered as a means of development to his nature.[43]

Since James has so little to say of physical and moral evil—we can "perfectly understand" the one as a "want of harmony" of a man with "his own body," and the other as a "want of free harmonic adjustment in the relations of man to man"—we need not dwell very long on it. His remarks in the quotation given above are not as cavalier as they sound taken by themselves, for James did make serious efforts to devise an adequate theory of both physical and moral evil, apparently in reply to Clarke's criticism of this lack in his (Clarke's) review-article, some years previous, of James's *The Nature of Evil*. Physical evil arises from the inharmonic adjustments that occur in the natural world of "use":

> All natural existence may be classified into forms of use; all spiritual existence into forms of power. . . . Thus the vegetable on its material side is a form of use to the animal kingdom, as giving it sustenance; while on its spiritual side it is a form of power over the mineral kingdom, as compelling it into the service of its own distinctive individuality. The animal again on its visible or corporeal side is a purely subjective implication of the human form, while on its spiritual or invisible side it furnishes the creative unity or objectivity of the vegetable world. So again man while on his natural side he furnishes a helpless platform or basis to the manifestation of God's perfection, yet as to his spiritual or individual aptitudes he compels not merely the animal but all the lower kingdoms of nature to bear resistless testimony to his power.
>
> But in thus classifying all natural existence into forms of use, and all spiritual existence into forms of power, we must not forget to observe that the use promoted by the one class is never absolutely but only relatively good, nor the power exerted by the other class absolutely but only relatively benignant. That is to say, it is good and benignant not in itself, but in opposition to something else. Thus every natural form is a form of use, but some of these uses are relatively to others good, and some evil. Some minerals nourish vegetation, others starve it. Some vegetables enrich animal life, others poison it. . . .
>
> This contrarious aspect both of nature and man has given rise . . . to a great amount of unsatisfactory speculation, because men have scarcely known how, apart from the light of Revelation, to shape their speculations in accordance with the demands of the Divine unity. . . . The mind not only rejects these puerile

cosmologies which leave the creator at war with His own creature, but . . . insists . . . that wherever we find a sphere of life antagonistic with itself, the antagonism is purely phenomenal: *i.e.* is not final, does not exist for its own sake but only in the interest of some higher unity. . . . So the good and evil attributable to vegetable forms bear reference exclusively to the difference of bearing they exert upon animal existence; while the good and evil again of animal existence attach not to the animal forms themselves, but only to the positive or negative relation they sustain to the human form.[44]

Thus the incompatibilities between "Power" and "Use" on all levels of life, and especially between one level and a higher, constitute what James calls physical good and evil—the evil which all created things, including man, *suffer* passively as pain.

James finds moral evil to proceed on the same great principle of a discrepancy between Power and Use:

The same rule holds in regard to moral existence, though the nonsensical pride we feel in ourselves habitually blinds us to the fact. I am not a bad man morally, and you a good man, by virtue of any absolute or essential difference between us, but altogether by virtue of the difference in our relation to that great unitary life of God in our nature, which we call society, fraternity, fellowship, equality. . . . But clearly if we had had no preliminary acquaintance with imperfect or finite good, good as related to evil, we should be destitute of power to appreciate or even apprehend this higher and perfect good. If we had not first suffered . . . from the experience of evil in ourselves as *morally, i.e.* finitely, constituted . . . we should have been utterly unable even to discern that ineffable Divine and infinite good which is yet to be revealed in us as socially, *i.e.* infinitely constituted. . . . [45]

And now, what about spiritual evil? This is *the* evil to James. We found, in his argument on physical and moral evil, that the interplay of the dynamics of Power and Use, Spirit and Nature, produced evil objectively apart from the individual creatures involved. And so with spiritual evil. This is a bit surprising at first, as we might have expected spiritual evil to be *in* and *of* man if any evil could be. But good and evil, spiritually speaking, do not belong to a man: they are influxes from angelic or infernal spirits and man has no property in either, and this we have seen to be utterly un-Swedenborgian. All three kinds of evil—physical, moral, and spiritual—are objectively constituted by being *in relation* to powers and uses at each level. Man

is the only known creature in whom and through whom all three
levels of good and evil operate; he is simply a microcosmic theater of
great impersonal spiritual forces. Confining ourselves entirely to the
spiritual plane now, good and evil of the spiritual kind is a bi-polarity
that functions within the category of spirit as causation and creative
power. James describes the principles underlying his conception of
spiritual good and spiritual evil, very clearly:

> For example, if we should pronounce a man spiritually good
> simply because he was morally good, or spiritually evil simply
> because he was morally evil, we should be guilty of gross ab-
> surdity, because, in reality, no human being has the slightest
> underived moral power, and it is only underived power whose
> activity confers responsibility. I have no power to injure my
> neighbor which is not derived to me from hell, or evil association,
> nor any power to refrain from injuring him which is not derived
> to me from heaven, or good association; and I am not spiritually
> chargeable, therefore, with either my moral good or evil, but
> only naturally chargeable with it. . . . I may have all the moral
> virtue that has ever inflamed human pride, and I shall not be one
> whit nearer the fountain of life. I may have all the moral infirmity
> that has ever quickened human despair, and I shall be no whit
> more remote from it. For that life surrounds human nature, as
> the waters surround the earth, bathing equally both its contrasted
> poles; and we might, with precisely the same propriety, deny to
> the ocean its measured tides, its alternate ebb and flow, as to
> the Divine life in humanity its perpetual sportive interchange and
> conjugation of brotherly love and self-love.[46]

The spiritual temper that lies behind that passage reminds one of
certain moods of the New Testament in which God's love is depicted
as James speaks of "life": God's love is super-moral; love is unfathomable and extended to all impartially, for, like the rain, it "falls on the
just and the unjust." Just so does the philosophy of spiritual realism
involve, as Anderson puts it, a conception of man as being "but a
center at which these forces (good and evil) encounter each other."[47]

As James develops further his concept of Spiritual Evil, he sees in
"Science" an instrument that is very apt to inflate human ego with a
false self-reliance that is tantamount to spiritual pride, or evil. In
a century of two World Wars, man has learned bitterly the element
of truth in what James says:

> This advancing scientific consciousness of the race has always
> been regarded as a fallen state of the mind; but it is not so

absolutely; it is so only relatively to the mental condition from which it departs. Thus measured it is no doubt a fall. If religion is bound to undergo the slow sepulture of science, with no hope of any subsequent resurrection in living or glorified form: if, in other words, science constitute the perfected form of the mind, the full measure of its expansibility: I, for one at least, have no hesitation in saying that it would have been better for the race to have remained to this day in its cradle, hearkening to the inspiration of naiad and dryad, of sea-nymph and of faun, than to have come out of it only to find its endless spiritual capacities, its capacities of spontaneous action, hopelessly stranded upon these barren rocks of science, ruthlessly imprisoned in her lifeless laws or generalizations. For if the difference between the purely religious or instinctual consciousness of the race and its growing scientific consciousness, be, as we have seen, the difference between the child and the youth, between diffidence and self-confidence; then it is extremely easy still further to see, that this subtle spiritual change which creeps over the mind of the race simply by virtue of its increasing acquaintance with itself, with its own God-given powers, can only deepen as time rolls on, until the mind becomes confirmed at last in all manner of pride and vulgar self-assertion: until its infantile and innocent sentiment of freedom, becomes hardened into one of complete unhesitating and blatant independence.

But there is no need to estimate the change exclusively in this aspect, that is, in its relation to the mental condition out of which it springs. We must view it in relation to the mental condition in which it issues or brings up; and here we shall see that what men have called a fall, is really a rise.[48]

The question has been arising in our minds: if good and evil are not attributable to man, does not this involve God ultimately as the author of evil? No, says James, because spiritual good and evil are necessary preconditions of the exercise of human freedom in maintaining equilibrium between these forces influxing into him from heaven's and hell's inhabitants; furthermore, when once the channels of communication from heavenly spirits become clogged up with a superior force of infestations from the hells, God made provision from the very start of creation for redemption also:

We have seen that the very nature of man inclines him to disturb this equilibrium, or bring himself under the bondage of the evil element. Clearly, then, whatsoever is natural to man—all that man is in himself strictly—not only gives him no help towards the permanent realization of his freedom, but actually defeats it. But if these things be so—*i.e.*, if, on the one hand, man is a proper subject of God only in so far as he is in freedom; and if, on the other hand, man's nature drive him to the destruction of this freedom; then of course it follows that God cannot make man a fitting subject of Himself, or endow him with true freedom, save in so far as He gives him redemption from the power of his own nature. *Thus, from the very necessity of the case, creation involves redemption; and until redemption is accomplished to its last fibre,* or to the literal flesh and bones of humanity, *it is premature to talk of creation being perfect.*[49]

Since "Redemption" is a major concept for consideration in the next chapter, it will not be taken up further here; it was brought in at this point only to round out James's doctrine of theodicy.

It is in *The Nature of Evil considered in a Letter to the Reverend Edward Beecher* that James enters upon his longest disquisition on evil. Beecher is having difficulties in his theodicy, as he tries to work it out minus orthodox Calvinist presuppositions. James analyzes Beecher's initial difficulty:

You represent the philosophic quest to be: *how can God be just in condemning and punishing evil?* whereas the true quest is: *how can evil even so much as get existence under the government of perfect goodness, of infinite wisdom?* . . .

You are afraid that unless we prove the damnation of the wicked to be just on the part of God, an intellectual revolt against orthodox creeds and standards must rightfully ensue on the part of all good men. He [the philosophic enquirer], on the other hand, is only afraid lest the supreme truth of the Divine existence or perfection suffer damage, from the existence of evil in the universe of creation.[50]

James follows this up with a keenly original line of thought and phraseology as he re-states the conventionalized formulations:

You talk incessantly of the "obligations of the Creator to every new-created mind," of the "claims of new-created minds," of the "rights of new-created beings," etc., etc. But if words have any meaning, moral or personal obligation is derived to the subject only from his own inward being or character. And if God be under obligation to His creature, the obligation is imposed of course by the necessity of His own perfection. . . . His [man's] claim upon the Creator is that he should image that Creator's perfection. . . . The stream cannot transcend its source, and if the Creator be good therefore, the creature will be good without any sense of merit, or if the Creator be evil, the creature will be evil without any sense of demerit.

To talk accordingly of the Creator being under any obligation to the creature, underived from His own essential perfection, is to talk very unworthily of your own excellent sense. You might with equal propriety talk of the obligation the potter is under to the clay, or the sculptor to the marble. The potter and the sculptor feel no doubt the obligation of their own genius, of their own skill, but they would be unaffectedly scandalized to find the clay and the marble taking the floor, and putting forth their extremely original views of plastic art.[51]

The sovereignty of God is the dominant note in that kind of theodicy— as might be expected from a man who is still so Calvinist in spirit and mind, however much his heart rebels against it. James's spiritualized Calvinism shows up especially in his handling of the problem of evil. In place of a physical fall we find a "spiritual" fall into the "consciousness, or conscience, of sin"; and even in regard to inheriting evil, James, in *The Nature of Evil* shows that he has by no means proceeded very far from orthodox Calvinism:

> In the first place, so far from its being true that all sin is voluntary or actual, it is not true that any sin *viewed intimately or spiritually*, is of that nature. This superficial view of sin belongs only to those who have previously lost all spiritual apprehension of their relation to God, and it is exclusively with a design to recover or restore that apprehension, that the law or conscience is given by God. . . . My moral evil, or the evil which I *do*, grows out of a deeper and spiritual evil which I *am*, but which I am unconscious of, until it is revealed to me by the light of conscience or the law. . . .
> One will cheerfully concede then to the New-School theologian, that there can be no individual or personal *imputation* of sin, which the individual person has not voluntarily and actually committed; but the existence of sin is a totally different thing from the imputation or consciousness of it. . . . Thus the personal imputation or appropriation of sin, as contingent upon law or conscience, is one thing, and belongs only to a portion of mankind. But the existence of sin, as contingent upon an alienation of heart from God, which descends to us from all our past ancestry, is a very different thing, and attaches to all mankind without exception.[52]

James would never have been burned at the stake in Geneva for those last two lines! "From all our past ancestry," and, sin as attached "to all mankind without exception"—if these concepts of the inheritability of spiritual evil and of the solidarity of all men in their sin—if these are not Calvinistic in their basic substance, what well might be?

A clear example of specifically Sandemanian influence in connection with the cure of the radical spiritual evil in man is James's treatment of "merit," in his discussion of which he maintains his consistent objectivism in all his religious thought in connection with doctrines of creation and redemption. James had no use for subjectivism in such doctrines:

> Now, manifestly, every man who cherishes a sense of *merit* towards God, on the ground of his moral or religious differences from other men, incurs this rebuke. Every man who supposes that the Holy Ghost is to be purchased by any thing he can do in the way of moral or religious obedience, affronts the inmost spirit of the law, no less than the palpable face of the gospel. The spirit of the law is a spirit of love to God and love to man, and this spirit is not to be acquired by any amount of obedience and sacrifice with a view to obtain it, but purely by the free gift of God through the redemption effected by Christ. No fancy can be so puerile, therefore, as that which leads us to think that we are going by our moral or ecclesiastical or other observances of any sort, to induce a more clement regard upon God towards us, than that which he exhibits towards all mankind.[53]

The inability to purchase redemption from spiritual evil because it is "the free gift of God," the similar inability to secure a more clement regard from God through "our moral or ecclesiastical or other observances of any sort," the ineffectuality of any of these man-initiated efforts—these all have the Sandemanian and Calvinist ring about them. There is, however, a new note combined with these, namely, the universalism, to James, of God's love "towards all mankind." Thus he retains the radical theistic realism and methodological objectivism of Calvinism, with a rebellious (though James negotiates it obliquely without express statement in the above passage) denial of what one might call the theocratic individualism of Calvinism's doctrine of election of individuals by God either to salvation or damnation. James will have only a doctrine in which God's concern is for the redemption of the race, for to James it is a libel on God to have a theory of his love in which He is involved in picking out individuals here and there for the redeemed estate. This is the theological basis of James's Spiritual Socialism and Universalistic Redemptionism.

In connection with this matter of the cure of spiritual evil, Kellogg expounds James to this effect:

> Instinct causes us to shrink from physical evil, and conscience haunts us if we give ourselves up to moral evil; but spiritual evil has this peculiarity, that the subject of it does not call it evil. . . . There is no remedy for spiritual evil but in belief. . . . As Mr. James exquisitely says: "His [Man's] belief saves him and his disbelief damns him only because the armory of the Divine Love furnishes no similar weapon capable of subduing the heart of his rebellion."[54]

The stress on "belief" is Sandemanian undoubtedly, but the significant words "belief alone," found in Sandeman, is not found in James. Since the years that he first became acquainted with the Scotch sectarian, James had been adding, through Swedenborg's influence, another element to grow alongside of, and to be the support of, belief: that is to say, "gnosis," or "knowledge of the Divine." James does not use the term "gnosis" any more than he does "spiritual socialism," but what he has left quite inexactly defined in both these instances becomes much clearer if we apply these more precise terms. This gnostic element in James shows up frequently in his idea of symbological interpretation of Biblical myths (*e.g.*, *Adam-Eve*) and in his profession of no concern over the "literal facts" of the Incarnation, Redemption, and Resurrection (James hardly mentions the latter word; his equivalent is "glorification"). It may be recalled also how, in *Substance and Shadow* he told us that belief without spiritual "knowledge" is a "house without foundations," and he spent his efforts in that book to provide those foundations. Further, in his last completed work, he demonstrates that he is a gnostic in the spiritual sense of the Greek Fathers, a seeker after "knowledge of the Divine":

> This gigantic and hopeless evil [spiritual evil] in man, then, springs from no defect of his physical nor of his moral make, but wholly from the limitation and infirmity of his finite or personal consciousness, which is a most rigid SELF-consciousness. . . . The creator himself is of course the only real or natural life of the creature—as implied in the very terms of the proposition: but how is the creature ever livingly to learn this great truth?

His creator is not the least a denizen of space and time; is not the least a visible or outward existence, so that his senses will afford him at best but a reflected or lifeless knowledge of Him. Evidently then the creature demands some other avenue to Divine knowledge than sense—some *inward* avenue, since the creator is not to be found outside of him—and this inward avenue is supplied by consciousness, or *self*-knowledge. In proportion as I come truly to know myself in all the compass of my physical, moral, and spiritual disability, do I come to a living or hearty apprehension of God's infinitude. *And in no other way.* All the bibles, all the churches, all the sacraments, all the rites and ceremonies, all the priesthoods in the land, are totally impotent to confer upon me one fibre of this living knowledge of God which is given by my life or consciousness alone; however much I doubt not they may instruct my intellect in things pertaining and subsidiary to such knowledge.[55]

"Consciousness," "learning the truth," "*inward* avenue to Divine knowledge," "self-knowledge"—the true flavor of gnostic thought is conveyed in such terms. With all James's stress on the visible Lord's incarnation in humanity and history, that alone is not sufficient for him: man must still *know* God in the depths of consciousness. In sum: since man's consciousness generates "*self*-consciouness" which is spiritual evil, the redemption of man from this evil by God must yet be realized *in* consciousness and through "knowledge of the Divine." In this fashion, James combines a consistent objectivism in his doctrines of Creation and Redemption with a dynamic concept of man's consciousness as the theater of operation for the objective acts of God in creation and redemption. Man can only *realize* these Divine actions through his own capacity for belief and divine knowledge. They are done of course by God, whether man appropriates a comprehension of them to his spiritual consciousness or not, but if man would realize them subjectively, it must be through belief and spiritual gnosis, *"and in no other way."*

Belief and spiritual gnosis as the twin cure for spiritual evil in man, brings us to the whole question of Redemption and Regeneration, which is the theme of the next and final chapter on the exposition of James's Philosophy of Spirit.

* * *

James Freeman Clarke wrote a long and able review-article on James's book, *The Nature of Evil,* in the course of which he deals with some points worth our brief consideration. After commenting that "This is a remarkable book by a remarkable man," and that "His words are not the current coin of logic, passed from hand to hand till it is worn and has lost all sharpness of impress, but they have a power of their own and a life within themselves," Clarke comes to grips with the real points at issue:

> Mr. James divides evil into physical, moral, and spiritual. . . . Physical and moral evil he presently explains away, and declares them to be no evils at all. . . . Thus physical evil, or the endurance of pain, is the necessary condition of animal life, and moral evil, or the doing what is wrong, the indispensable condition of moral life, and therefore neither of these can be really evil. It only remains, therefore, to investigate spiritual evil. . . .[56]

Clarke is fair enough in remarking James's offhand way of dismissing physical and moral evil. Probably as a result of Clarke's criticism on this head, James made the attempt to deal with physical and moral evil more fully, as we have seen in the selections from *Substance and Shadow*. When Clarke came to review this latter book, he passed over these attempts of James altogether, either because he was unimpressed or because there was so much other material in *Substance and Shadow* that he deemed more important. On James's premises, however, what else could Clarke expect in regard to physical and moral evil? James's view has at least the merit of seeing that physical and moral evil tend to destroy themselves as life is lived, and though their actuality is real enough, they demonstrate themselves to be relative and not absolute.

Clarke proceeds:

> It is not very easy to see precisely what Mr. James means by spiritual evil. Sometimes it is a purely intellectual error, and consists in the mistaken opinion that our life is our own. . . . Spiritual evil, self-hood, self-complacency, is at all events real evil. How is it to be reconciled, then, with the perfections of God? . . .
> He accounts for the origin of spiritual evil very simply. . . . We feel as if we were free and responsible. Not that we really are so, but we seem to be so. . . . We must not *believe* ourselves free, for that will be to fall into the worst, into spiritual evil. . . .
> Here, then, we have the solution of the problem. Evil comes into the world whenever man acts from himself instead of acting *as* from himself, whenever he acts as if he had a real freedom instead of acting as if he had a *quasi* freedom.[57]

After thus stating James's position in James's own language, Clarke begins his rebuttal:

> As far as we can see, neither he nor Swedenborg, whom he follows, has shown the *inevitable* origin of evil, on their own premises, but only a tendency toward it. All that would have been required, in order to have prevented the origin of all evil in the universe, was to have made man always thoroughly acquainted with the fact that his apparent freedom was only apparent, and not real. . . . No reason is given for its not having been done, and consequently the problem of evil is as much unsolved as ever. . . .
>
> By making God the only being in the universe, and man's being only apparent, and not real, he logically denies the reality of spiritual evil, as he had before denied in terms the reality of physical and moral evil. For if man, the *subject* of evil, is only an appearance not a reality, the evil which inheres in him must also be only an appearance and not a reality. But again, supposing it to be real, it exists and continues as a growth of nature, as a process unprovided for by the divine reason, as an abnormal development outside of deity. In this, also, Mr. James's theory is consequent. For a spiritual pantheism denying God's real existence in nature . . . will always virtually exclude God from the time-and-space side of the universe, and whatever goes on there will go on quite independent of him. . . .
>
> Mr. James makes the incarnation the means of introducing God, for the first time, to an acquaintance with the world of nature.[58]

From the last statement, Clarke deduces that "spiritual pantheism is really a limitation of God."

Clarke has touched, in the last sentences of the above, upon what we have noted in this study previously, namely, the residual dualism that rather drags along like a sediment at the bottom of the moving stream of James's thought. But why is the Incarnation of God, which, because it *is* God, in Swedenborg and James, and is therefore as *real* as any theology could possibly make it, to be equated therefore with pantheism? James has been at pains all along to fight off pantheism, as though conscious that his thought might be open to this charge. The illusion of "selfhood" on the part of man is necessary to James in order to give the creature "projection" from his Creator and thus avoid pantheism. The term "illusion" is what makes Clarke charge that James makes the whole realm of the finite something akin to the *Maya* of Brahmanism. Yet James insists in effect that illusion is real *as* illusion, illusion itself being necessarily a part of the very economy of the Divine in creation and redemption. This does bring him close to pantheism indeed, but if illusion has a real function as relative and not absolute, is it quite accurate to denominate James as an out-and-out pantheist? A "necessary" illusion is not altogether illusion! It is so only in a relative sense.

As a final point for us to consider in Clarke's critique, there remains, what occurred to us also, the question of how James's notion of spiritual good and evil flowing into man from God and the devils respectively, accomplishes anything more than to remove the problem of the origin of evil to them? As Clarke puts it respecting the evil in the hells, which are the societies of evil spirits:

> But the evil in *them*—whence comes it? If it comes from themselves, then they must have a life, according to this reasoning, independent of God, which is impossible. To say that it comes into them from other evil spirits is, of course, only to remove the difficulty farther off. To refer it to God he would consider blasphemy. Hence, it only remains to deny its existence altogether, and to make of it, like every other form of evil thus far, a mere negation, or the somewhat less of good.[59]

To which James might be imagined as replying: Your objection, Mr. Clarke, only goes to show how real an illusion can be, for the evil spirits in the hells are simply those who once lived on earth, but who, at the end of their earthly existence, still persisted in clinging to the idea of their possessing an independent selfhood (James's idea of complete transcendence of earthly selfhood is thoroughly un-Swedenborgian), which in turn proves that God protects man's freedom of belief even through all eternity, from all of which emerges the concept of man's freedom as involving good and evil, and is therefore the real explanation of evil, the only adequate theodicy, for men to accept.

Clarke's ultimate quarrel, then, with James must be on the grounds of an inadequate doctrine of human freedom, and it is precisely this that Clarke asserts:

> Accordingly Mr. James teaches that his [Man's] freedom is not *absolute* freedom, but *rational* freedom, or freedom in order to something else. It is not given for its own sake, but for the sake of the creature's spiritual elevation, being thus a freedom strictly in order to his eternal conjunction with God. He is free

to transcend and control his bodily appetites, but cannot become independent of God.

But this freedom is by no means a power of self-determination. And the responsibility which it implies is very limited.[60]

James would be entirely happy over that account. To him there was no such thing as the "freedom of indifference" or "absolute" freedom; and if there were, it would be meaningless, even for God. Freedom *for* and freedom *to* are the only significant kinds of freedom possible to a *creature*. Clarke would have, like Bushnell, a lot of "little gods." Finally, James would hold that freedom *for* our conjunction with God, realized subjectively through belief in, and revealed knowledge of, the illusion of our selfhoods, gives more freedom *to* our natural and moral life than any other theodicy could do. That James's belief in his self-consciousness as illusion did not prevent him from a very vital sense of freedom *from*, and yet paradoxically enough, *in* his temporary earthly existence, is very apparent in a paragraph from one of his articles:

> Unless I be superior to my passion, superior to my intellect, and superior to my brute strength, I must be their tool, and he that is the tool of these things, has not yet begun to be a man. To be the slave of passion, of knowledge, or mere physical activity, what is it but an endless headache and heartbreak? . . . The more he has of them, the more restless and unhappy they make him.[61]

*　　*　　*

The reflective reader has doubtless been reminded, by James's stress on spiritual freedom over moral law (with its distinctions between good and evil), of Nietzsche's concept, "Beyond Good and Evil." Of course, the parallelism does not extend very far beyond the basic similarity of the principle involved.

In Sri Aurobindo's *The Life Divine*, may be found an even closer parallelism to James's general concept of the provisional and temporary value of ethical distinctions. James would be overjoyed, were he to read the following:

> In other words, ethics is a stage in evolution. . . . The urge is at first non-ethical, then infra-ethical in the animal, then in the intelligent animal even anti-ethical, for it permits us to approve hurt done to others which we disapprove when done to ourselves. And just as all below us is infra-ethical, so there may be that above us whither we shall eventually arrive, which is supra-ethical, has no need of ethics. The ethical impulse and

attitude, so all-important to humanity, is a means by which it struggles out of the lower harmony and universality based on inconscience and broken up by Life into individual discords towards a higher harmony and universality based upon conscient oneness with all existences. . . .

If, then, the ethical standpoint applies only to a temporary though all-important passage from one universality to another, we cannot apply it to the total solution of the problem of the universe, but can only admit it as one element in that solution. To do otherwise is to run into the peril of falsifying all the facts of the universe, all the meaning of the evolution behind and beyond us in order to suit a temporary outlook and a half-evolved view of the utility of things. The world has three layers: infra-ethical, ethical, and supra-ethical. We have to find that which is common to all; for only so can we resolve the problem.[62]

It is entirely possible for one to agree with James that to *feel* that our life is our own, but to *believe* that it is not, is, in truth, productive of our *spiritual* freedom. If being conscious of our dependence upon the Divine Creator as He perpetually creates and recreates us, implies a theological determinism over our lives at the moral level, yet it means freedom and salvation at the spiritual level of our existence. If James disturbs our faith in the "reality" of our phenomenal life, why need that be upsetting to man's dignity, freedom, or responsibility? Does it follow that, because we learn that *God is so much more* than we thought, and is in truth our *real* life, we are *therefore so much less?* James compensates us with his vision of the ultimate "Divine Humanity" which will be to earthly humanity as "Substance is to Shadow." His conception of "Divine Humanity" is one not to be found in most European or American theological systems; in fact, the only major theology which has developed this concept, in different ways from James to be sure, is that of the present Greek Orthodox Seminary at Paris, headed by such thinkers as Bulgakov and Berdaiev.

Plentiful are the thinkers who nourish our "finite" egos; but rare are those spiritual geniuses who reveal to us our infinite selves. If such men make us realize that our empirical, this-worldly, moral selfhoods are not "Substance," but rather the "Shadow" of our real, hidden, and "unconscious" life in God, they more than repay us by limning their vision of our redeemed spiritual selfhoods in the great Redeemed Society.

NOTES

1. *The Nature of Evil,* pp. 70-71.
2. *Ibid.,* pp. 142-143.
3. William James, ed., *Literary Remains,* p. 119.
4. Herbert W. Schneider, *A History of American Philosophy,* p. 312.
5. "The Ontology of Swedenborg," *North American Review,* Vol. CV (1867), p. 97.
6. *MC,* p. 145.
7. *MC,* p. 146.
8. *NE,* pp. 79-80.
9. *S of S,* p. 93.
10. *MC,* pp. 114-115.
11. *Ibid.,* pp. 116-117.
12. *Ibid.,* p. 119.
13. *Ibid.,* pp. 153-154.
14. *CLC,* p. 262.
15. *MC,* p. 121.
16. *Ibid.,* pp. 151-152.
17. *MC,* p. 160.
18. *S and S,* p. 51.
19. *NE,* pp. 105-106.
20. *S and S,* p. 52.
21. *Ibid.*
22. *SRFM,* pp. 391-392.
23. *Ibid.,* pp. 394-395.
24. *S of S,* p. 93.
25. *Ibid.,* pp. 93-94.
26. Ralph B. Perry, "Religion versus Morality according to the Elder Henry James," *International Journal of Ethics,* Vol. XLII (1931-'32), p. 290.
27. *Ibid.,* p. 294.
28. *Ibid.*
29. *Ibid.,* pp. 296-297.
30. *Ibid.,* pp. 298-299.
31. *NE,* p. 144.
32. *Ibid.,* p. 178.
33. *S of S,* pp. 148-150; 151-152; 154.
34. *Ibid.,* p. 161.
35. *Ibid.,* p. 160.
36. *S of S,* p. 161.
37. *Ibid.,* pp. 164-165.
38. *Ibid.,* pp. 165, 166-167.
39. *LR,* pp. 20-21, 22-23.
40. *Ibid.,* p. 299.
41. *Ibid.,* pp. 268, 273.
42. *NE,* pp. 70-71.
43. *SRFM,* pp. 95-96.
44. *S and S,* pp. 142-144.
45. *Ibid.,* pp. 144-145.

46. *CLC,* note, p. 222.
47. Quentin Anderson, "Henry James and the New Jerusalem," *The Kenyon Review,* Vol. VIII (Autumn, 1946), p. 525.
48. *S and S,* pp. 57-58.
49. *CCNE,* p. 60.
50. *NE,* pp. 43-44.
51. *Ibid.,* pp. 45-47.
52. *NE,* pp. 256-258.
53. *Ibid.,* pp. 179-180.
54. Julia Kellogg, *op. cit.,* p. 27.
55. *SRFM,* pp. 96-98.
56. James F. Clarke, "James on the Theory of Evil," *Christian Examiner,* Vol. LIX (1855), p. 119.
57. *Ibid.,* pp. 131-132.
58. *Ibid.,* pp. 132-133, 135.
59. *Ibid.,* p. 129.
60. *Ibid.,* p. 120.
61. "Woman and 'The Woman's Movement'," *Putnam's Magazine,* Vol. I (1853), p. 287.
62. Sri Aurobindo, *The Life Divine* (Greystone Press, N. Y., 1949), pp. 91-92.

Chapter Eleven

The Doctrine of Redemption
or
The Divine-Natural-Humanity

*The abstract formula of our mental growth as a race . . . namely:
Religion, Science, Philosophy: would be worthless, if it did not
translate itself into the facts of our visible experience. . . . And
as this great tendency formulates itself to our apprehension in
the three intellectual symbols just cited, so of course history as
the expression of such tendency, as the product of this interior
mental evolution, must exhibit a form in exact correspondence
with them.*

*In point of fact this is what history does. History is all summed
up in the three great interests of Church, State, and Society. . . .*
                                                     —HENRY JAMES, SR.[1]

*It would be infinitely discreditable accordingly to the two factors
in creation, if their tie were anything short of a marriage tie,
i.e. if it did not claim an exclusively social sanction, or profess
to stand only in that conscious, living reconciliation of the two
otherwise irreconcilable natures which the church has always
prophesied, but which is spiritually realized only in the grand
practical truth of "the Divine NATURAL Humanity," or the advent
of that predestined perfect society, fellowship, equality of men in
heaven and on earth, which alone has power to bring nature and
spirit, the outward and the inward, the universal and particular,
the cosmos and the earth, the homo and the vir, the man and the
woman, the world and the church, into living unison. . . .*
                                                     —HENRY JAMES, SR.[2]

THAT JAMES'S THOUGHT is powerfully objective, spiritually realistic, and socially universalistic, has been steadily borne in upon us during the whole course of this book. This dominant cast of his philosophy will be seen now at its apex as we consider the entire range of his Doctrine of Redemption, or the Divine-Natural-Humanity.

In attempting an exposition of his social philosophy, it is soon recognized that a whole constellation of related concepts fall into order and receive their innermost meaning if conceived with their relevance to the nuclear concept of "Society." This constellation of concepts revolving about the master concept of "Society" in his system, comprises the substance of this chapter, and consists of the following heads, with related sub-heads in parentheses:

   I. Philosophy of History.
  II. Church and State.
 III. The State (and Democracy).
 IV. The Church (the Church in history; anti-ecclesiasticism).
  V. Religion (general philosophy of religion, miracle, sacraments, the "Word," Immortality, theology, Christology).
 VI. Redeemed and Regenerated Society (redemption, regeneration, secular socialism, spiritual socialism, Divine-Natural-Humanity).

I

The ground-plan of James's Philosophy of History is found in the first passage on the title-page of this chapter: "The abstract formula of our mental growth as a race" is "Religion, Science, Philosophy." This triadic formula for covering all the major phases of human history reminds one of Comte's triune formula for history: The Theological, the Metaphysical, and the Scientific Phases, except that the last two terms have been reversed by James, who places Science as the middle, and Philosophy, or Metaphysics, as the culminative stage.

When James says "religion is the first phase of the race's mental evolution," he means "Natural Religion," or Orthodoxy sometimes also, in which men had very sensuous ideas of Divinity and of their relations to God. This naturalistic religion extends from primitive religions right up to orthodox Christian doctrines such as that of "physical creation" in space and time, by God *ex nihilo;* or, in the notion of moral "merit" as having efficacy as a means of winning

God's propitious regard with respect to securing immortal life from Him. James does not tell us in his triune formula of his Philosophy of History that he will bring out his concept of "Spiritual Religion" as the summit of man's evolution, but it is true nevertheless, for *spiritual* Religion is to him the upper half, so to speak, of Philosophy itself. Just as James splits the concepts of selfhood, consciousness, and conscience into finite and infinite kinds, so he splits religion into "natural" and "spiritual" religion. In the present formula, then, he is speaking of only "natural" religion as being the first "phasis" of humanity's spiritual evolution.

With his triadic formula for the interpretation of history, James outlines the respective functions of Religion-Science-Philosophy in the development of man:

> Religion exacts not strictly human or creative perfection in God, because it takes Nature as given in sense, *i.e.* as a final and not as an instrumental, achievement of the Divine omnipotence; as a result, and not as a process towards a result. It looks upon Nature as a substance in her own right; as an end, not as a means to an end; as a finished gem rather than the crude ore which embeds the gem; as being herself God's true creature, rather than the purely material and maternal investiture, by which the creature becomes built up and identified to his own consciousness. Science gives her no furtherance in this career, but only impediment. Science does nothing but exalt the concept of the finite as given in sense, into that of the relative as given in reason; so completing an intellectual basis for that rich demonstration of the Infinite in the finite, and of the Absolute in the relative, which Philosophy will ultimately enact. Philosophy becomes able to throw a commanding light upon the origin of existence, only by heeding the voice of Revelation, which turns Nature from a principal into a mere accessory of the Divine creation. . . . Until Philosophy come therefore to avouch and fulfill the intellectual promise both of religion and science, the human mind will be seen on the one hand declining, under the auspices of what calls itself Positive Science, into the helpless drivel of Atheism; on the other, under the patronage of German idealism, which is what now passes for Philosophy, into the stuck-up and conceited waiting-maid of Pantheism.[3]

In another place he makes the distinctions between Religion, Science, and Philosophy in a rather different way from the above, and indicts the first two for their inability to frame a doctrine of creation. He now speaks of "Sense" as being the basis of "Faith"—the "faith," that is, of "natural" religion; but note the significant use of "faith" instead of "belief." "Belief," with its more intellectual connotations, is reserved for the true or spiritual religion, thus fusing philosophy and spiritual religion into what amounts to *gnosis*. On the level of lower, or natural religion, however:

> The sole basis of faith is sense, and sense drowns the infinite in the finite. The sole basis of science is reason, and reason drowns the absolute in the relative. Both faith and science consequently, so long as they are uncontrolled by Philosophy, are totally unable to conceive the creative infinitude, and hence to suggest any such resources in Deity as alone suffice to account for creation. They are both alike prevented from formulating any doctrine of creation. . . . [4]

Yet "faith" (or "natural religion"), is a necessary preliminary to the eventual triumph of philosophy and spiritual religion:

> The highest truths of the mind, which are those of the Divine infinity, eternity, and omnipotence, are bound first of all to seek and find ratification in the lowest plane of the mind, which is sense, under penalty of being excluded from the mental circulation altogether, or confessing themselves no organic parts of the mind. The dogmas of a purely literal or physical creation redemption and providence, house these great spiritual substances until the race is sufficiently quickened to discern them in their own lustre: so that unless our intelligence had had a preliminary initiation into the mysteries of wisdom by this rude cradling, it would have remained forever incapable of the slightest spiritual apprehension. In a word the very inmost and most celestial heights of experience in man grow out of, and are irreversibly tethered to, his lowest sensuous consciousness.[5]

As for "Science," James sees it as a "pioneer work," and men of science as "the advance corps of sappers and miners" in battering down superstitions derived from man's primordial slavery to Sense:

> The office of Science accordingly in this great work of social reconstruction, is that purely of a pioneer clearing the ground of the wild undergrowths of sense, or turning it up to the influence of light and air, and so preparing it for the endless beneficent inseminations of Philosophy. Men of science constitute the corps of sappers and miners, who . . . precede the advance of the grand army of humanity, to batter down every fortress of organized

error, bridge over every ditch of superstition, and drain off every marsh of conventional prejudice, which threatens to impede its victorious footsteps.[6]

When he comes to discuss the role of Philosophy, James, as we recall from the chapter on Spiritual Knowledge, becomes quite rhapsodical. Because he loves Philosophy most of all, however, he chides her accordingly, in reminding her that she is tied to Revelation for her true light:

> In other words, what Philosophy demands in order to her thorough extrication from the fallacies both of sense and reason, is the guiding light of Revelation. Our present so-called Philosophy has hitherto slighted this light in deference to science, or with a view to exalt the lower and more fickle authority of reason. Of set purpose indeed she allows Revelation, so full of the profoundest intellectual wealth, a purely religious significance, a merely tributary relation to natural theology. . . . In short the fault of Philosophy is a defective self-consciousness, or so low a conception of her great office as leads her not to coordinate religion and science, not to harmonize the spiritual and moral life of man, but to give the latter and lower interest absolute priority of the higher. . . . [7]

"Revelation, so full of the profoundest intellectual wealth," and Philosophy's egregious error in allowing it "a purely religious significance" —there speaks the true gnostic. History, itself, under the light of gnostical interpretation, *becomes* Philosophy. James would not be concerned over Hegel's dictum that Philosophy comes too late to influence History; with James, *History's very destiny is to realize itself in Philosophy!*

James is thoroughly evolutionistic in his Philosophy of History, for the whole history of man *is* that upward, return movement of all creation on its way back to its Divine origin, or God. The true epic of man, historically, is set and enacted within this evolving process:

> Such is the exact formula of our mental evolution as a race: Religion, Science, Philosophy. These are so many comprehensive symbols to our intelligence of the gradual development of the human form in creation; of the orderly and complete extrication of the human mind from the bondage of nature and the tyranny of custom . . . *first the blade, then the ear, and afterwards the full corn in the ear.*[8]

As James contemplates history in its institutional aspects, he posits a correlation of "Religion, Science, and Philosophy" with "Church, State, and Society." He treats of the first two—Church and State—so frequently together that it is necessary, before we examine each singly, to look at his ideas concerning them as thus bracketed together. Here, for example, is a good introduction to this subject: the term "world" is shortly to become the "State":

> "The world" represents the interests of human universality— say human *nature* in short; "the church" represents the interests of human individuality—say human *regeneration,* in short. Thus we may say that the *world* stands for the fatal side of human life, those interests of man which relate him willy-nilly to his fellow-man, and therefore place him more or less in the voluntary category, or under the rule of duty, of force, of necessity, of destiny. And *the church* on the other hand symbolizes the *free* side of human life, those interests of man which relate him primarily to his infinite source, and which exalt him therefore into the category of spontaneity, or express—all duty done and all destiny achieved—the reign thenceforth of taste, of culture, of inward attraction or delight, of immortal life in short.[9]

With the contrast of Church and the World (or State), set in terms of "freedom" and "necessity," the stage is ready for the further development of the matter. James expands this contrast into another: the Church, in the person of the Priest, represents the Divine Love on earth, while the State, in the person of the King, represents the Divine Wisdom. The correlation of freedom or spontaneity with Love, and of order and necessity with Wisdom, is grounded in Swedenborg's theology:

> . . . the Church becomes visible in its Priest, as the State does in its King. Now what I say is, that the sacerdotal office and the regal office are nothing more nor less than immature natural symbols of that Divine life in man which is only to be worthily expressed in the scientific sentiment of human society or fellowship. . . . The sanctity of the Priest represents the infinite Divine Love which is silently shaping man's nature to its own subjection; and the power of the King, who is invariably consecrated by the Priest, represents the infinite Divine Wisdom which is also secretly operative in man's nature, and which being vivified by Love, will eventually exalt him to universal dominion.[10]

Now, although James sees the Church as the genitor of the State, and the State as "wholly contingent" upon the Church for its origin, the

Church has nevertheless been yielding to the State more and more in modern times, and this, says James, is as it should be, since this development is a necessary preliminary to the advent of the true social fellowship among men when both Church and State will be unnecessary and eventually disappear. James puts this thought in slightly different ways in different books, but the basic idea follows always an identical pattern:

> Now, the Church is simply the embodiment of this revelation, and an infinite mischief accrues if you give it any other mission, or attempt to exalt it into a Divine finality . . . and if you consider it anything more, you are bound to bring up, logically, in all the obscenities of Paganism, or else in the childish frivolities of Romish and Puseyite worship, which is only Paganism deprived of its soul, and condemned to a cadaverous immortality in so-called Christian temples. The Church never was, is not, and never will be a fulfillment of the Divine end in creation, until it perfectly merge in the political State to which it has been introductory, or rather until both Church and State alike merge and disappear in the scientific society—fellowship—brotherhood—equality—of universal man.[11]

James, spiritual-social radical that he was, saw in Napoleon a force that was hurrying along the realization of the oncoming Society that he dreamed of, through the negative function of Napoleon's destruction of the actual and even symbolic power of organized Romanism:

> The State as a civil polity is wholly contingent upon the Church as an ecclesiasticism. . . . In modern Europe, just as in old Judaea, the Church no longer preserves its spiritual priority to the State. . . . The great Napoleon, animated with the spirit and armed with the prestige of the Revolution, felt so sheer a contempt for this frivolous European priesthood and its lapsed prerogative, that he did not hesitate at his coronation to snatch the coronet of the Empress Josephine from the hands of the officiating priest and place it himself on her brow; thus clearly proclaiming, by a great symbolic act infinitely beyond his own besotted thought, two things:—1. That the veil of the temple, which had hitherto shut out the people from the holy of holies, was now actually as well as typically rent; thus, that the age of types and shadows had expired by its own limitation, and that man stood henceforth face to face with spiritual substance, with eternal realities: 2. That upon whomsoever the people should confer sovereignty, they conferred sanctity as well, or that in the elect of the people, as he claimed to be, priest and king, goodness and truth, right and might, should be indissolubly blent.[12]

The State, therefore, is "stifling" the Church, but James looks forward to a time when both will disappear, to make way of course for that Spiritual Socialism which he envisages, though he never uses precisely that term. The term, coined by Schneider, is very illuminating, however, for it gives one a definite conceptual instrument by which James's doctrine can be compared, for example, to the orthodox conception of "The Kingdom of God." James's spiritualistic-socialistic commonwealth in the final state of Redemption has, though there are some similarities that could be identified, quite different connotations than a "kingdom" *under* God in the classical Christian teaching. James's Spiritual Socialism contemplates more of a society *with* God who has, through infinite love and suffering for man, practically resigned his status as a "King." Let us return now, however, to his own vision of the goal of all human history:

> For the promise is, that in Christ, or the Divine NATURAL Humanity, all men shall be made kings and priests unto God. The old Church, in claiming to be a special priesthood, and to induct only a special royalty, confesses itself recreant to its own profession. It obstinately refuses to enact this consecration of universal man . . . and it righteously invites, therefore, the contempt and indignation of the scientific mind. . . . Thus, practically, the technical State has stifled the technical Church in modern Christendom; or Kingcraft is everywhere seen putting an end to the corrupt Priestcraft which originally gave it life. . . . Of course when the Church, as a visible hierarchy, finally disappears from the earth which it defames and defaces, the State, as a visible Police, must also disappear with it, for they are strictly correlative institutions. But they will both disappear only to be reproduced in that NEW Church and State, or in that Diviner SANCTITY and POWER which shall be commensurate with man's renovated nature, and become visible in every blessed feature and fruit of universal human fellowship.[13]

In this thought on the Church and State, James resorts to the concept of a "double movement" in history as a sort of parallel, presumedly, to the great metaphysical double movement of involution-evolution, or of creation-redemption:

> The moral experience of the race necessarily involves this double or divided historic movement which we name Church and State; the former a descending or centrifugal movement by means of which the creature becomes self-convinced of his essential antagonism, as naturally constituted, to the Divine perfection: the latter

an ascending or centripetal movement, by means of which the creature acknowledges himself as such recognized antagonist of the Divine perfection, to be rightfully under law to his fellow-man. . . . The play of these two forces fills the page of human history, until they succeed at last in generating a third or grandly unitary force which we call society, in which they both willingly coalesce and disappear, and which consequently thenceforth assumes the undivided responsibility of human destiny.[14]

In the American Democracy, James sees a national polity which is the most advanced on the road to the great objective of universal fellowship:

The Church with us is of course exposed to no such coarse imperial insult [as in Europe], as the State is exposed to no such brutal revolutionary invasion. Why? Simply because our Church and State are both of them purely *social* institutions. . . . Our Church admits of all manner of sectarian diversity; our State is the fusion of all manner of national oppugnancies: because the only altar of God we recognize are the native affections of the human bosom, the only throne of God, man's scientific intelligence. . . . Occasionally some juvenescent Episcopalian, or some belated Roman Catholic convert, feels his ecclesiastical gums distending and inflaming as if dentition were going at once to ensue, and goes drooling about the streets accordingly as if the Church were still a visible power even in these latitudes. But no one listens to him because no one is quite goose enough to exchange his own flexible and fresh modern raiment for the disreputable and dilapidated duds which any Episcopal or Roman Catholic old clo' man may contrive to fish up out of our ecclesiastical Chatham streets. So also occasionally some political antiquary takes to speculating in a retrograde way, and fancies that we ought to have a government more absolute than we have; but he never can tell where such a government is to come from in these days, and so the speculation harms nobody but himself, by dwarfing him intellectually to the obsolete dimensions of his grandmother.[15]

James summarizes his thought along this line with a passage that links Protestantism and American Democracy together, in which both are disorganizing forces and disintegrative solvents of the classical Church and State:

So now, the only hindrance which our existing authorities in Church and State could offer to the new ideas, would be to patronize them, to lend them the furtherance of their adoption. . . .

The new wine of Protestantism and Democracy—the spirit of an ever-advancing humanity—would seek in that case to confine itself evermore within the old established bottles of Church and State, within the purely symbolic dimensions of priest and king. . . . Protestantism is the actual limit of the Church's elasticity,—one strain more, and it snaps into Mormonism or other downright deviltry, which reasonable people will some day be forced to sweep bodily from the earth: and the State can go no further than Democracy without going into visible extinction. In fact, all astute priests and politicians have perceived for years past that Protestantism and Democracy are not so much expansions of the old symbolic institutions of Church and State, as actual disorganizations of them. They mark the old age of those institutions, their decline into the vale of years, preparatory to their final exit from the historic scene. . . . How utterly absurd then to suppose our existing Christendom formally competent to embody the Divine spirit in humanity! This spirit seeks the infinite expansion of human nature, seeks to lift the beggar from the dunghill and to set him among princes, simply because he is man, simply because he is a living form or image of God, and hence capable of an immortal conjunction with God.[16]

Spiritual Socialism is becoming, to our understanding, something much more than a phrase!

III

In the first book acknowledged over his authorship—*What Constitutes the State* (1846), James starts his public literary career with a discussion of "The State." This lecture, given at the local Young Men's Association in Albany, contains in potentiality most of his fundamental religious and social ideas, later to be elaborated in that whole corpus of articles, lectures, essays, letters, and the dozen volumes he was to pen from this date, 1846, to the year of his death in 1882.

This lecture on the State was the first product to come out of his fermenting period, when Calvinism, Sandemanianism, Swedenborgianism, and Fourierism were jostling each other in the intellectual forum that was James's mind at that time. It is not difficult to be sensitive to these varied currents of intellectual inheritance; and it is equally easy to discern the marks of his efforts to fuse this philosophic quartette into a team productive of intellectual "harmony." Whether the result is, in the end, harmony or not is another matter; but this quartette stands in the "wings," so to speak, of *What Constitutes the State,* looking on and prompting some of the lines, though we should not understand James as a mere mechanical echo of these major influences.

At first, James distinguishes "government" from the "State" in words that, to his hearers in Albany, were vividly contemporaneous in reference:

> When a democratic president dismisses a whig postmaster merely to make room for a democrat, all the whig newspapers, from Maine to Georgia, attest the instinctive revulsion which such an abuse of power has produced in one-half of the community. And when the whig president enacted a similar feat ... all the democratic papers ... declare the instinctive revulsion which a like abuse of power has produced in the other half of the community. And thus we have the *whole* community protesting that the government is not the State itself, that offences against government merely are not necessarily social or moral offences, are not offences against humanity....
>
> Were not the State, then, something else than government and government offices—something else than King, Lords, and Commons—than the executive, the legislature, and the judiciary, society would have been from the beginning a mere anarchy, not striving by force of an indomitable instinct to hold itself together, but absolutely eager to rend itself asunder. ....[17]

He brings this line of argument to its climax in a passage reminiscent of Burke's great speeches:

> The state, then, cannot be made to mean government. It refuses to be identified with any merely political conditions which have yet been manifested on earth, or which doubtless remain to be manifested in the deathless future of the race. It disclaims all partial regards, and expresses society in some aspect in which all its members past, present, and future, stand equally included. ... In short, the term expresses the Spirit of Humanity without reference to sectional peculiarities; the spirit which, pervading all mankind alike, makes of the whole a living unity; the spirit by which the whole body, being fitly conjoined and compacted by that which every member supplies, according to the measure of its influence in him, builds itself up in immortal harmony.[18]

James manages, in the next phase of his thought, to nearly identify, for his purposes, State with Society. In his later books he demarcates more sharply between them, but not here:

> It is evident to the least reflection, that if human society is to have any permanence, is really to be a *state* at all, and not a

mere mutability, there must be some bond common to all the members. . . .

This requisite something is fitly called *the constitution* of the society. . . . It is not, however, any voluntary compact to be found written on parchment, like *Magna Charta,* or the *Constitution of the United States,* which men have made, and can therefore unmake. . . .

THE STATE then means simply the social condition peculiar to man: a condition which makes his highest life to depend upon his relations to his fellows, or which limits his enjoyment of life within the limits of his love to his brother.[19]

But *how* do man's social relations constitute the State? James grounds his concept of *social* in theology:

You will readily perceive that if the being of man lay in any thing . . . else than perfect Love, then the *social* state of man would proportionably disappear, and the tendency would be towards the individual and solitary life, instead of the social and united one. . . . Just so now the actual *unity* of man's creative source enacts the *social* state of man, making his distinctive life to be social. . . .

The fact, then, of the *essential* or *creative* unity of man alone explains, in an adequate manner, the phenomenon of his social or moral life.[20]

The last words are significant, for he has practically hyphenated the concepts "social" and "moral," and this is important because later, in accord with his anti-Moralism on the one side and the spiritualized concept of "society" on the other, James, as here, vigorously repudiates any such hyphenation:

Many people suppose that *moral* and *social* are two words for one and the same thing: whereas they express ideas exactly inversive of each other. . . . *Morality* expresses the sentiment I have of my own absoluteness, the feeling I have of a self-hood strictly independent of every other man. Society on the other hand expresses the sentiment I have of my strict unity with every other man, a unity so absolute and commanding as to stamp my moral force wholly good or wholly evil simply as it obeys or disobeys its behests.[21]

With the remainder of *What Constitutes the State,* we are not now concerned, since James goes on to speak as much about his theology of the Divine Incarnation and of Redemption as he does about the

State. One wonders if those young men in Albany ever again in their entire lifetime listened to so many ideas packed into a single lecture!

James's expansion of the State to a near-identity with Society did not satisfy him long. In later writings the State assumes a much more circumscribed role. As a final illustration of the intellectual *locus* of the State in his thought, we cite from his last completed book:

> The State has no permanent or absolute rights over the human conscience. It was never intended, as I have already shown, for any thing else than a mere *locum tenens,* a simple herald or lieutenant, to Society, while Society itself was as yet wholly unrecognized, and indeed undreamt of, as the sole intellectual truth of man's Divine-natural destiny.[22]

As we pass from James's notion of the State to the concept of "Democracy," we find him very stimulating indeed. When he deals with this idea, James handles it quite apart from the popular notion of "individual liberty," and even less in terms of "individualism." His metaphysical, objective, and societal presuppositions would incline us to expect this aloofness from the conventional conceptions usually aired in Fourth of July Orations. He devotes one lecture to Democracy, plus a Fourth of July Address at Newport in 1861, on *The Social Significance of Our Institutions.*

In the lecture on "Democracy and Its Issues," delivered in New York about 1850, he strikes out independently at once in speaking of the "Democratic idea" as a "purely negative development" in its original phase, deriving its meaning in its protest against other ideas:

> Monarchy asserts the right of one person or one family to govern others. Aristocracy asserts the right of one class of persons to govern other classes. Against these two, Democracy is a protest. It denies the claim of any one man to govern other men, and the right of any one class to govern other classes. . . .
>
> Thus the Democratic idea exhibits a purely negative development. It is revolutionary, not formative. It is born of denial. It comes into existence in the way of denying established institutions. Its office is rather to destroy the old world, than fully to reveal the new.[23]

He would not be understood as being unsanguine about the value of American institutions, but because he is a true lover of the Democratic idea, he cannot be blind to its existent shortcomings; and so, exercising his "democratic" privilege of free speech and criticism, he speaks out:

> I see in our present political attainments everything to love and admire, when I contrast them with those of the Old World, because our polity recognises on all its front, the great truth that the *true* ruler of the people, in all time, must be the *servant* of the people. But when I look to see how this truth is practically administered, I confess my enthusiasm somewhat subsides. For the ruler, when closely regarded, turns out to be the servant, not of the whole people, but a majority of them . . . as proves that the interests of the whole are not chiefly studied.
>
> Democracy, then, is still imperfectly embodied even among us. . . . But when the sentiment becomes fully acknowledged, or attracts the universal homage of mankind, it will disown our present political institutions no less than all past ones. It will disown, in fact, all merely *political* forms, and claim a purely social manifestation.[24]

Inasmuch as a true social commonwealth is the inescapable goal and implication of the Democratic idea, according to James, he expands the meaning of social-democracy negatively, in very concrete fashion with reference to England in particular.

> You see at a glance that this penury of England in all spiritual regards is owing to the simple fact that not *man,* but *English*-man, is the key-note of her aspirations. European thought generally and at best is peninsular,—that is, *almost* insular,—in that it regards European culture as constituting the probable limits of the human mind. But English thought is absolutely insular, in that it makes England the actual measure of human development. . . .
>
> I will never forget the inappreciable services she has rendered to the cause of political progress. But just as little can I be blind to the immense limitations she exhibits when measured by American humanitary ideas. She claims to be the freest of European nations; and so she is, as I have already admitted, so far as her public or political life is concerned. But viewed internally, viewed as to her *social* condition, you observe such a destitution of personal freedom and ease and courtesy among her children as distinguishes no other people, and absolutely shocks an American.[25]

In a diverting footnote, James describes the English nobleman as less "thoroughbred" than the rats which burrow in his ancestral castles:

No English nobleman can possibly be as thoroughbred as the rat which burrows in his own ancestral walls; because, let him do what he will traditionally to paralyze the human or spiritual force in him, his bare natural form perpetually prevents his lapsing into animality, by allying him with God, so forbidding him to remain the mere child of his father. The nobleman of to-day, whatever be his private vices, is vastly nearer the human type than the nobleman of five centuries ago, simply because his very nature itself is progressive, while the animal nature is not.[26]

The homely flavor of James's personal democratic feelings is expressed in words that are ever so suggestive of Walt Whitman, though the phrasing is decidedly Jamesian. He describes the "Horse-Car" as "Our True Schechinah at this Day":

I can hardly flatter myself that the frankly chaotic or *a*-cosmical aspect of our ordinary street-car has altogether escaped your enlightened notice in your visits to the city; and it will perhaps surprise you, therefore, to learn that I nevertheless continually witness so much mutual forbearance on the part of its *habitués*; so much spotless acquiescence under the rudest personal jostling and inconvenience; such a cheerful renunciation of one's strict right; such an amused deference, oftentimes, to one's invasive neighbor: in short, and as a general thing, such a heavenly self-shrinkage in order that "the neighbor," handsome or unhandsome, wholesome or unwholesome, may sit or stand at ease: that I not seldom find myself inwardly exclaiming with the patriarch: *How dreadful is this place! It is none other than the house of God, and the gate of heaven.* Undeniably on its material or sensuous side the vehicle has no claim to designation as a Bethel; but at such times on its spiritual or supersensuous side it seems to my devout sense far more alert with the holy Ghost, far more radiant and palpitating with the infinite comity and loveliness, than any the most gorgeous and brutal ecclesiastical fane that ever gloomed and stained the light of heaven.[27]

One cannot refrain from wondering if James could have maintained such idealism if he were an habitual commuter today on the New York subways, say, at five o'clock in the afternoon!

A splendid summary of his conception of both Protestantism and Democracy is found in *The Church of Christ Not an Ecclesiasticism*, and it serves as the conclusion to this section on Democracy:

In Protestantism the Church as a visible power fully disowns its authority any longer to guide human thought. In Democracy the

State as a visible power disowns its authority to guide human action. Protestantism is nothing more nor less than a proclamation of individual freedom in the spiritual sphere. Democracy is a proclamation of the same freedom in the material sphere. . . . The Church accordingly, as an authoritative Divine institution, disappears from Protestant countries, being spiritually diffused among the whole body of Christians. And the State as an authoritative Divine institution, with power to bind the popular will, disappears from Democratic countries, being equally diffused among the whole body of citizens. . . .

That emancipation from the bondage of Authority which is now so universal and irresistible a bent of the human mind, and which in its ecclesiastical aspect names itself *Protestantism,* and in its political *Democracy,* what is it but a proof that the spiritual development of Christianity is utterly fatal to all fixed ecclesiastical or political corporations, and tolerates nothing short of the universal society, fellowship or equality of men?[28]

It is more than curious that this thoroughgoing Neo-Platonic hierarchist in metaphysics, theology, epistemology, and anthropology, should be such an avowed leveller in his social philosophy—whether levelling down as in political democracy, or levelling up as in spiritual redemption! It is one of the paradoxes of this man James. Most consistent hierarchists in philosophy carry out the same principle in their political and social doctrines. Not James! He becomes the radical, equalitarian, spiritual-socialist.

IV

James is a heretic of very deep dye when he confronts the phenomena of the Church in its historic and institutional actualities. Yet he is as much concerned for the establishment of a "spiritual" Church in the hearts of men and a "Spiritual" Religion as perhaps any man has been in the history of American thought. But such is the dialectic of his spiritual philosophy that, if his ideal of a Church were to be realized, it would *be* regenerated humanity as a whole, thus transcending itself as a Church in the very moment of its realization! Church and Religion are necessary only in history. The need for both is obviated at the level of consummated Redemption, when the universal Divine-Humanity has become a reality.

For the purpose of securing James's philosophy of the Church, it is desirable that we trace the evolution of his doctrine. The order of approach suggests that we inspect his views on the Church, first in its historical, and later, in its ideal, manifestations.

In terms of the Church's inner and symbolic meaning in history, James has a large, loyal, and beautiful appreciation that could well be required reading for every priest and minister, and it would be well to make it required reading for every parish member also. James only proves again that the most violent and realistic critics of any institution are inwardly those who love it most deeply, and cherish for it the highest ideals. One senses the tremendous devotion of James to the inner significance of the church-phenomenon among men in history, and one feels it all the more when he points the mind toward the ideal, or from his premises, the *real* and spiritual Church:

> Every man in history but Jesus of Nazareth has had some pet self-righteousness, giving him a heart of hope towards God. He has been Greek or Roman, Jew or Mohammedan, Catholic or Protestant, Episcopalian or Presbyterian, Baptist or Methodist. . . . Jesus was profoundly destitute of this odious spirit. . . . In short, his bosom was the shrine of a universal love and fellowship, a love and fellowship as wide as the universe of creation, and therefore unmistakably divine. But, without the Church, this great truth could never have got to light, nor this great life found an adequate theatre of action. . . . In short, the Church has existed only to bear testimony to the supreme truth of the redemption which takes effect in the Christ: first, BY KEEPING ALIVE THE PROPHECY AND PROMISE OF HIS COMING, *until the event should take place;* and then BY KEEPING ALIVE THE MEMORY OF THAT EVENT, *until such time as its bursting and blissful meaning could be discerned in rational light.*
>
> The history of the Church, then, is the true history of creation, as embodying that redemptive process by which man has been incessantly moulding into the Divine image, or becoming reduced to the Divine subjection.[29]

No less beautifully stated is his appreciation of the meaning of the "clerical" function in human history. The language he employs arouses the reflection that this may well come from the heart of a man who felt deeply a regret that he had not found it possible to enter upon a pastoral ministry in his career:

> But, on the whole, what sweetness has baptized the clerical function in the past! What fortitude, what self-denial, what patience, what labour in season and out of season, have been the heritage of the great mass of these men! What stores of learning they

have accumulated; what splendid additions they have made to the best literature of every land; how they have enriched the sciences by their observation and studious inquiries; how they have kept the flame of patriotism aglow; how they have encouraged the generous ambition of youth, and directed it to worthy and useful ends; how they have dignified the family altar, and cherished the purity of woman, and diffused through society the charm of honest and gentle manners: all these things must be cordially acknowledged by every one competent to speak on the question. Where would be the sense of ousting such a body of men, native, as it were, and to the manor born, inheriting a grace and dignity from their time-honoured places, embalmed in the kindly reverence and goodwill of the community, only for the purpose of introducing a new and undisciplined body, honest and well-intentioned, no doubt, and in many respects intellectually well-qualified, but aggressive by the very necessity of their birth, contemptuous and insulting by the inseparable theory of their office?[30]

Words laden with such rich feeling indicate that James must have made the original decision of renouncing a public ministry at a spiritual cost to himself. Perhaps his fate in this respect was more dictated by the narrow currents of thought about him than it was by his own genius, but it is possible that, contradictory heart-and-head man that he was, he would never have found a professional ministry acceptable in any age. There is no clear answer to such speculations as these. At any rate, he was destined to preach his spiritual religion without benefit of ordination or parish. Undoubtedly by being true to himself, he actually achieved, potentially even as yet it must be admitted, a ministry more significant than any other he might have had in any branch of organized Christianity. Unrecognized though his "ministry" was in his own time, and neglected as it has been during the sixty-nine years since his passing, his really valuable spiritual insights can receive even yet their proper recognition.

Prior to a consideration of his anti-ecclesiasticism against the "visible" churches, is the necessity of examining his conception of Romanism and Protestantism as historical embodiments of the church-idea. Quite apart from the fact that his interpretation is often forced into the mould of his doctrinnaire spiritualism, some of his observations are penetrating on their own account. In *The Church of Christ Not an Ecclesiasticism,* which is his best work on the Church and from which we quote most frequently in this section, he discusses

Romanism with an intelligence and a fairness that is remarkably uncommon, even to this present day:

> I cannot, indeed, understand how any one who holds to the ecclesiastical conception of the church can for an instant deny the paramount claims of the Romish hierarchy upon his allegiance. If the Church of Christ possess of necessity an ecclesiastical constitution, or, what is the same thing, an inseparable external organization, based upon the distinction of clergy and laity, then the Roman Church is the only true church, because it alone permanently secures such an organization. Had the Protestant been as stoutly pushed *a tergo* as the Catholic has been pushed by him, and as he himself bids fair to be pushed in the future, he must long ere this have acknowledged that the only consistent ecclesiasticism is that of Rome. . . . If we want conviction on this point we have only to refer to the utter disorganization which the hierarchical idea, or the church considered as having an inseparable ecclesiastical organization, encounters at Protestant hands.[31]

This kind of thought reminds one of Dean Inge's remark in our own time, that the logical extremes of ecclesiastic theory and practice are Roman Catholicism at the theological right, and Quakerism at the theological left, with all the intermediate types being compromise positions.

James contrasts the Catholic and Protestant ecclesiasticisms in a most stimulating manner:

> The commixture of the secular element with the "religious" is precisely what differences the Protestant evolution of religion from the Catholic. . . . The Protestant church germinates in Catholicism; the Catholic church effloresces in Protestantism. . . . Thus Catholicism restricts "religion" to its priests and other emasculate orders, and allows the laity no nearness to God but what comes through their intercession; to that extent at all events keeping the laity humble and sweet, *i.e.* uncorroded by the "religious" virus, or the pretension of a peculiar sanctity towards God. And Protestantism does nothing hereupon but deny the "religious" celibacy, or proceed to make it fruitful by marrying it to the secular life, so in effect covering the whole congregation with the priestly pretension, and turning all that was before humble and sweet into flatulent and sour. In the Jewish church the Lord had respect to one person, to him who was of a contrite spirit, or felt himself none the better for the national holiness. So also in the Catholic church there was one element not unlovely,

because it was devoid of religious pretension; and this was the lay element. But Protestantism logically robs the Lord even of this delight, by exalting the layman into the clerk, or diffusing the odor of sanctity over the whole congregation: so reorganizing between herself and the world the self-same odious discrimination which Catholicism enacted within the household of faith, or between priest and layman. . . . And moreover it (Catholicism) allows this priest himself to assume only an official or representative holiness, and denies him the least personal consequence: so leaving open a clean door of escape from the spiritual peril involved in the office, to every one whose cultivated instincts avert them from it. But Protestantism remorselessly obliterates every vestige of this original Divine mercy, by denying the discrimination of priest and layman, and teaching its layman indeed to aspire to a sanctity to which the Catholic priest theoretically makes no pretension, a direct personal sanctity in the last degree revolting to truth and decency.

In Protestant countries accordingly you miss those gross outward and therefore comparatively harmless fruits, which grow out of the separation of the two elements. You see no fat lazy loafing monks, images of man's essential arrogance and imbecility: no starched demure stealthy-paced nuns, images of the lifeless womanhood engendered by such a manhood; a manhood that robs woman of her native juices, betrays her essential conjugality, falsifies her rightful maternity, leaves her teeming womb unquickened, and turns the stainless nurture of her bosom to waste. You see rather those subtler interior forms of evil which flow from the commixture of the two elements. . . . Protestant men and women, those who have any official or social consequence in the church, are apt to exhibit a high-flown religious pride, spiritual flatulence and sourness of stomach, which you do not find under the Catholic administration. . . . Our conspicuous Protestant religiosities male and female—such of them as are really animated by the spirit of Protestantism—are sweeter on the surface than in the depths.[32]

Protestantism is in much more desperate straits than Romanism unless it carry its own inner logic to the end-consequence of a redeemed Society, as envisioned by James's Spiritual Philosophy. He therefore gives us a portrait of the kind of church that should succeed Protestantism:

I need not say to you, that I look upon this end or purpose of the Divine Providence as identical with that . . . new and everlasting church, the crown and consummation of all past churches, which is constituted solely by the regenerate *nature* of her members, or a life of *spontaneous* love to God and man. . . . This church is not aristocratically constituted, like the Romish Church, nor yet democratically, like the Protestant Churches. It is not made up of clergy alone, nor of clergy and people jointly; but simply of human love and fellowship in the soul of every individual man. It is not made a church by any amount or any exactitude of ritual worship, any more than I am made a father by the number of kisses I give my children. No man can say of it, lo here! or, lo there! any more than he can limit the path of the lightning which now shines in one part of the heavens, and now in the opposite. . . .

The existing ecclesiasticisms, both Catholic and Protestant, proceed exclusively upon the *spiritual* regeneration of their members, and hence postpone our realization of the Divine beatitudes to *post mortem* states. The new church, on the contrary, by its acknowledgment of the Divine NATURAL Humanity . . . implicitly affirms the regeneration of human nature itself, and leads us to expect a realization of those beatitudes even on the earth.[33]

James's vision of the "new" church naturally raises the question: What was his attitude in general toward the "New Church" of the Swedenborgian sect? We are not surprised, given his terrific anti-ecclesiasticism, to learn that he was most denunciatory in his attacks upon this sect, which, in the name of his beloved master Swedenborg, indulged the most unspiritual comprehension of all, in organizing another visible church-body. James approved of those Anglican clergymen in the Church of England who remained within their communion, instead of becoming separatists to found a new sect. The Reverend John Clowes, first translator of Swedenborg in England, an Anglican rector of a parish in Birmingham, was one of several other Anglican clergy who brought new spiritual force from Swedenborg into their parishes without becoming disconnected from the Establishment. To separate and found a new sect was, to James, the very height of "spiritual" heresy, for it would only succeed in confining the master's influence within ever narrower limits. A page-heading in a letter contained in *Tracts for the New Times*, entitled "Swedenborg not a Swedenborgian," reminds one of George Bernard Shaw's wholesome and needed reminder that Christ was not a "Christian"! In this "Letter" to a Swedenborgian friend, James puts the whole matter in searchingly specific form:

If indeed you were *visibly distinguished* from all other men by the possession of goodness and truth, or the true faith of the Divine Humanity, then you would have some show of reason in claiming our visual acknowledgment of you as the church. . . . Dare you lay your hands on your hearts, and say that you alone of all the earth lead a good life? Thus that you alone of all the earth believe in the Lord? And if not, what a mere immodesty it is in you to flaunt the distinctive name of new church in our eyes, and stigmatize your rival corporations by that of old church! Your intellectual assent to these propositions of Swedenborg, does not constitute you a good man, nor a believer in the Lord. Why then, on the simple ground of such assent, do you challenge the world's visual recognition of you as the Lord's church? The world will say with the apostle James that it would rather see your works than your faith, rather see the spirit than the body![34]

James renews the attack on the Swedenborgians in *The Church of Christ Not an Ecclesiasticism,* which was itself written as a "Letter of Remonstrance" to a "Member of the *soi-disant* new church":

Now, what must we say of a self-styled new Church which, in face of all these palpable facts, and *while avowedly acknowledging the spiritual advent of the Christ,* does not hesitate to identify that advent with the origination of a new and senseless ecclesiasticism, so converting the literal symbols or memorials of Christ's truth into its eternal substance? This is literally, as little children say, *to play New Jerusalem.* . . . [35]

Perhaps the "most unkindest cut of all" for this sect to take from James was his statement that instead of being "new," they really showed every sign of "senility":

Accordingly, I know no sect so young that gives such unequivocal proofs of senility as your own; I know no sect so inconsiderable in point of numbers, which has already bred so many "doting questions and strifes of words." For this result I say you are indebted only to your inherent Protestantism, or the mother that bore you; for as Protestantism was not a new church, spiritually considered . . . so your more limited movement exhibits no spiritual advance upon the older Protestant sects, but only a highly rational and comfortable modification of their ritual observances.[36]

In *The New Church in the New World,* Marguerite Block has a discerning comment in regard to James's vitriolic thrusts at the Swedenborgian sect, who rather naturally expected more sympathy from

James, if not active support! But they had not taken the proper measure of the Ishmael of American religious thought; of a man who might well be called God's Terrible Radical. Marguerite Block, however, takes away some of the imposing thunder in James's letters to Swedenborgians, thus:

> This entertaining invective need not be taken too seriously. Henry James would have felt the same about any church. . . . He was the enemy of all sectarianism, which at the time was so narrow and bigoted, and his special bitterness against the New Church was merely the result of his disappointment that the followers of Swedenborg had not transcended this bigotry.[37]

Since Romanism was impossible for James; since Protestantism was working along to its necessary death; and finally, since the new sect in the name of Swedenborg was most offensive of all to him, was there anything left of the church-idea for James? He envisaged a "spiritual church" which, though not very definite as an institution—in fact, which could not exist as a visible institution—is very definite as an idea. Something of his concept of the spiritual church appeared in a previous selection, but he has something more to say about it. Of the true Church men will not, as we saw, be able to say "lo, here! or lo, there!"; it will be constituted only by a "new spirit" in the hearts of men, and in no way be associated with "particular persons, particular places, or particular rituals of worship."[38]

If there are to be no "particulars" in the Jamesian church, how may we identify it at all? Only to thought and inward vision, not by any visible sign. Official doctrines of theology? No. A paid and professional clergy? No. Public worship and cult? None is provided for by James. For the church is not even secondarily an institution for public worship:

> In all your attempts to institute a purer ritual . . . I accordingly feel a lively sympathy. But I cannot confound any such institution with the church. The church is not primarily, nor yet secondarily, an institution for public worship. Properly, it is not an institution at all. The idea of congregation is not essential to it. It owns no locality but that which inheres in upright human action. It is a most internal, or divine life in man. . . . In a word, the true visibility of the church is evinced not in any merely professional institutions, however imposing, but in a regenerate social life. . . . It is the regenerate earthly life of man, a life of complete subjection to the laws of the Divine Humanity operative

in nature, and full consequently of innocent and ennobling delights.[39]

Thus, worship, as well as doctrine and religious institutions, are swallowed up—yea, religion itself—in the redeemed Society. Granting the nobility of James's conception of the spiritual church, he nowhere tells us *how* this regenerate society is to come into consummation. It is essentially an apocalyptic idea, though James, so far as the writer can find, uses the word "apocalyptic" only once in all his books; furthermore, the apocalyptic element is blended with a kind of spiritual positivism, for this society is to be realized "on earth."

Despite his intense anti-ecclesiasticism, James had at bottom a deep understanding of and respect for the "superiority" of the Christian church over all others known to history; and with this note, we take leave of his philosophy of the Church:

> Every church on earth is doomed to perish, except the Christian church: because all but it are destitute of a philosophic basis, that is, profess no doctrine of God in nature, but only in the private soul. The Christian church is immortal because its fundamental dogma involves a doctrine of God in nature so ample and clear, as to satisfy every profoundest want of the heart and every most urgent demand of the head towards God forever.[40]

V

It is a singular fact that in James, who is a religious thinker if ever there were one, we do not have a philosopher of religion or a systematic theologian in the technical, academic, or scientific sense of those terms. His doctrines have an inner consistency and interrelatedness of their own, but at bottom, they were formulated out of the spiritual needs of a profoundly religious spirit, who seemed not to care whether they met any external requirements whatever, whether critical, systematic, or apologetical. His works read as though they were produced out of an autobiographic necessity, and for no other reason. He seems neither to have expected nor cared for response on the part of contemporary thinkers. Doubtless he would have appreciated more recognition than he received, but there is no record of his bemoaning the silence that greeted his intellectual efforts, or that he ever became bitter about it. He wrote with the same intense prodigality of thought and expression at seventy as he did at forty.

This autobiographic quality at the base of all his doctrines accounts for the gaps in what we might otherwise expect from an objective, systematic theological thinker. For example, he has little to say about "God" in any direct way. In reality he says amazingly little about the Creator. He accepted Swedenborg's basic schema of *Esse, Essence,* and *Existere* as applied to Divine Being, and deals with these concepts in a few brief paragraphs. He is mainly concerned with the Divine in His *existere* and *procedere,* as manifested in his creative activities. James is interested only in what God *does.* His philosophy might be called a theo-pragmatism and a theo-utilitarianism because of its great stress on the natural world as the realm of "use" for the power and purpose of Divine Spirit.

This emphasis upon God's activity in the natural world leads James to see a value in "miracle." He expresses himself about this topic in various ways, the most interesting of which perhaps is his idea that miracle once had value as a "scientific irritant":

> For miracle is only a brute affirmation or attestation of the creative infinitude to men's brute or undeveloped spiritual intelligence, and has been full therefore of the tenderest and most timely divine pity. That we happen to have outgrown its need at this day, and can intellectually dispense with it, has been owing not to a diminution of the creative benignity but rather to a practical enlargement of its scope, in widening the sphere of man's freedom and rationality to such an extent, as effectually to deliver him henceforth from the dominion of great names, or of routine and authority, in scientific as well as in spiritual or sacred things, and thus make him over at long last to the inspiration of the unimpeded Divine GOOD in the form of our own glorified flesh and bones. We may say in fact that without miracles as a perpetual reminder of a supersensuous life in us, the intellect must have lost its highest Divine charm, which is that of freedom, or inward inspiration, and have incontinently succumbed to the limitations of science which forever enchain it to sense. Every intellect the least spiritualized is now free to assert its just insubordination to the senses, or claim to be wholly uninspired by science. And I maintain that it owes this freedom solely to the long respect entertained among men for miracle as a distinctively Divine mode of action.[41]

As we pass from topic to topic under the general head of Religion in this section (for James does not relate these topics to each other systematically except as interpreted with reference to his own central doctrine of Creation and Redemption), the next is Theology. In his lecture on "The Old and New Theology," he compares the two types in terms already familiar: the "Old," that is, the theology of the "sects," is what he calls "Natural Religion," while the "New," or Swedenborgianized form, is "Spiritual Religion" because it spiritualizes all the old doctrines of Revelation, Creation, and Redemption. The only point that needs mention in this connection is his aversion to the term "will" as applied to God. This avoidance of "will" is doubtless directed against the Calvinist doctrine of the sovereign will of God. To James, "will" implies a limitation:

> The different bearing of the two theologies upon the divine character, is especially deserving of note. The Old theology makes creation a *voluntary* procedure on God's part, or a distinct exhibition of will, and hence makes God imperfect or finite. For will has no other fountain than want, and to feel a want in any respect is to feel so far forth insufficient to oneself, and to be insufficient to oneself is the very citadel and armory of imperfection. The New theology, on the other hand, makes creation a purely *spontaneous* procedure on the part of God. . . . Hence the New theology declares that God creates or gives being to the universe, not by his will, but by Himself. He alone it is, and not by His will, as discriminated by the Old theology from Himself, which creates or gives being to things.[42]

It is easy to see why Clarke calls James a "spiritual pantheist," despite James's vigorous rebuttal of the charge. Today he would doubtless be termed a "pan-en-theist," a term which Berdaiev nowadays has brought into use; that is, God-*in*-all, without just "being-all-that-is" without remainder. As for James's dislike of "will," it is remarkably noteworthy how he avoids the term almost completely in his discourse, even though Swedenborg uses "will," "heart," "good" and "love" as tightly interwoven and interconnected terms; for we remember that he regarded "Love" as the deeper attribute of God's Essence over that of the other attribute of "Wisdom," while "will" in man was the receptacle for receiving the Divine Love, as "intelligence" was the organ for receiving the Divine Wisdom. For this reason it has been said heretofore that James's aversion to "will" is undoubtedly motivated by his reaction against the Calvinist doctrine of the arbitrary sovereignty of God's will. An interesting parallel to this aversion to "Will" by James is his equally rare use of "liberty" in his discussion of Democracy and Society.

Regarding "sacraments," James has very little to say, except that they are strictly symbolic "memorials":

> It is true that the *old Church* has always been identified with two rites or ceremonies, *baptism* and *the holy supper*: but it is never to be forgotten for a moment that these rites are of a rigidly and inseparably MEMORIAL nature, designed to keep alive the name and memory of an absent friend till his promised return, and therefore, without one particle of vital force beyond any ordinary tombstone. . . . He who regards baptism and the eucharist as anything more than *memorials* of a Divine work effected in human nature, or as having some present cleansing and sacrificial efficacy, might quite as well spend his time in attitudinizing before Mumbo Jumbo; for he is doing nothing but hardening himself in spiritual conceit and fanaticism. These rites are two most expressive memorials and symbols of a purifying and redeeming chemistry which God is perpetually operating in the depths of human nature, or the spiritual world. . . . [43]

In thoroughgoing consistency with his Spiritual Philosophy, James considers "the Word," or Bible, as having both a "body and soul," a "literal" and a "spiritual" meaning, thus requiring a hermeneutics that will interpret the Word in both senses, the spiritual sense being, of course, the far more important. The spiritual interpretation of "The Word" in Swedenborg and James has, at times, strong similarities to Pascal's "typology" for the elucidation particularly of the Old Testament, since the New Testament contains, generally speaking, the *reality* of which the Old Testament contained only the *types*. Swedenborg spent much thought and writing on a spiritual exegesis of the Pentateuch and intended to carry his method into a consideration of the whole Bible, but James uses the principle of "spiritual" and "symbolic" interpretation of Scripture only when it suits his purpose for the issue under discussion—*e.g.*, the Adam-Eve myth, and he never attempts the role of a systematic exegete. He expresses his view of the Word:

> The method which the creative Providence uses to accomplish this necessary redemption of its conscious creature from the superstitions incident to his nativity is a purely metaphysical method, and is furnished by what is called, in old symbolic or sacred speech, the Word (of God), which we familiarly but most imperfectly appreciate as constituting the substance of our technical or formal Revelation, Religion, Regeneration. This mystical, redemptive, or regenerative Word is the sole creative

substance of the human mind, and its sole regulative form. The marvel of it is, that it is both death and life, spiritual death and natural life,—being at once the deadest, most finite letter of existence, and its living, leaping, infinite spirit. It is first altogether physical or material in form, carnal, negative, prohibitory, deadly, and death-bearing; then altogether *meta*-physical or *quasi*-spiritual, psychical, positive, inspiring, living (in short), and life-giving. Its fullest possible literal expression is what we term the Moral Law contained in the Ten Commandments, which to the unemancipated or ritual and ceremonial conscience is always *the holy of holies*. From the bosom of this fixed, dark, bitter, malignant, unyielding earth of legality it soars away, or becomes spiritually glorified, into the free lustrous heaven of human society, fellowship, or equality, shaped and eternally shaping itself to image the splendors of the creative infinitude, as these splendors become reproduced through every lurid lineament and feature of the created consciousness.[44]

James put it in less inflated rhetoric in *Christianity the Logic of Creation*:

> *Why does the Divine creation involve the necessity of a revelation?* This is only asking in other words, what is the scientific force of the *logos,* or creative WORD. . . . I do not profess myself to be an adept, but only a learner, in these sublime fields of inquiry, and I am besides subject to a painful suspicion that I do not concisely report what I clearly enough apprehend. . . .
> The entire philosophy of the creative *Word* or *logos*, is to be found in the fact that the creative *nisus* is not physical but purely spiritual: in other words, that creation is never an absolute but strictly a rational—never a wilful but strictly an orderly—procedure on the part of God, involving a due adjustment of end to means and of both to effects.[45]

On the subject of "Immortality," James is at one and the same time positively hopeful, yet tense and uneasy. All told, James does not devote much attention to the subject, probably because spiritual immortality for either heaven or hell is so explicit in all his, and Swedenborg's, thought. Immortality to James means essentially a transcendence-of-self:

> But if, as I verily believe, my existence is not the least identical with myself, but with all divine power in my nature exclusively, resurrection will assuredly follow any apparent eclipse it may undergo in myself, and I shall then at last enter upon an exist-

ence at once so broadly human and yet so unmistakably divine, as to reduce the thought of self ever after to a forgotten sound.[46]

The notion of immortality of the empirical self with its "self-consciousness" is most repugnant to James:

> I for one should distinctly prefer forfeiting my self-consciousness altogether, to being found capable, in ever so feeble a degree, of identifying myself with it [finite selfhood]. My being lies utterly outside of my*self*, lies in utterly forgetting my*self*, lies in utterly unlearning and disusing all its elaborately petty schemes and dodges now grown so transparent that a child is not deceived by them: lies in fact *in honestly identifying myself with others.* I know it will never be possible for me to do this perfectly, that is, attain to self-extinction, because being created, I can never hope actually to become Divine; but at all events I shall become through eternal years more and more intimately one in nature, and I hope in spirit, with a being who *is* thoroughly destitute of this finiting principle, that is, a being who is without selfhood save in His creatures.[47]

That passage was under a page-heading entitled "NIRVANA, or Self-Extinction, Impossible"! James rather backs his way into immortality because he cannot escape, though he does it grudgingly because he cannot become completely "Divine" which, if it were possible, would rid him forever of his "finite self." It is fruitful to observe the dialectic in James's consciousness between the mood of a would-be Buddhist with a longing for extinction of self, and, on the other hand, the spiritual imperialism which wistfully realizes that it cannot hope actually to become God Himself! No more extreme limits of spiritual temper regarding "immortality" are possible within the consciousness of either one individual man or of man in general.

A concluding passage on this topic informs us that man is not "naturally" immortal; moreover, like St. John in this respect, it declares "immortal" life to be a quality of life that it is possible to realize *now*:

> Man is not naturally immortal, and only harm is done by leading him to think himself so. By natural birth, or in himself, he is to the last degree corrupt and perishable, and though his science demonstrates any amount of order, peace, and productive power in his animal and vegetable and mineral connections, it is utterly powerless to promise himself any resurrection from the death which is latent in his own flesh and bones. To be sure science

is just as impotent to menace him with a contrary fate, because as science is functionally confined to the realm of mortal existence, it must needs confess itself a mere idiotic guesser in relation to every interest of his unseen and immortal being.[48]

Immortal life to Swedenborg always means one definite thing, and that is—soul-power, or the prevalence of a man's inward life over his outward one. It means: *the soul's exclusive power to regulate a man's outward, that is, his physical and moral, relations, and so produce an ever-growing inward and ineffable harmony between him and his creative source*: so that any man in whom this result in any sincere degree however slight is freely achieved, or his soul has learned to rule and his body to obey, has *ipso facto* entered upon immortal life; and this man only. . . .

Indeed our immortal interests, according to Swedenborg's showing, are much more nearly dependent upon our *cis-mortem* ideas and practices, than they are upon any imaginable amount of *trans-mortem* experience, were it the very happiest.[49]

To which James adds, in connection with an immortality "story" from Swedenborg which James has just related to a friend, this significant sentence: " . . . but ah! the way to believe Swedenborg!"

It is important to turn next to a consideration of James's conception of Christ. His Christology is based on the Swedenborgian doctrine that in Christ, the invisible God became the visible Lord, but not the "second person" of the orthodox Trinitarian formula. Consequently, the Incarnation is tremendously *real,* for it is literally GOD who is in-carnated and not the "only-begotten Son."

James, being the gnostic that he is, shows comparatively little interest in the "historic Jesus," for he was "dead and buried" before the Gentiles had really begun to hear of him.[50] Here again, the perennial gnostic bias exhibits itself. He is concerned only with the "philosophic value" of *the* Christ, for the New Theology views "the recorded incidents of his life, death and resurrection, not as possessing a merely historic and superficial value, but much more a philosophic value as symbols or exponents of universal truth."[51]

With his Swedenborgian principle of "spiritual" interpretation, James could take in his stride the "higher criticism" of the Scriptural Canon, which had just come to America from Germany. It is doubtful whether there were a half-dozen theological minds in this country at James's time, who were so well-prepared to face German higher criticism with such an unperturbed—nay, almost enthusiastic, manner as did James. He was saved in advance from the tragedies of many who "lost their faith" because of his free, spiritual, and profoundly philosophical method of interpreting all Biblical facts or persons, including Christ. This exemption from inner conflict over the higher criticism, is vividly exhibited in a footnote to his lecture on "The Old and the New Theology":

> Probably the highest tribute ever paid to the personality of Jesus, was that recently enacted by a distinguished German scholar, in attempting, very unsuccessfully however, to resolve the entire record of his personal history into a humanitary myth. This good man finds the evangelic facts so full of sheer *manliness*, so full of the widest human meaning and promise, that he resolves henceforth to deny them actuality, and regard them simply as a rhythmic dance of the human intellect celebrating the oncoming splendors of the race.[52]

From James's vantage, this was perfect! History gives way to Philosophy, Fact to Symbol, Individual to Race, and even Godliness to Manliness, since the very meaning of the Incarnation was God's incorporation *in* man and *of* man.

In the remainder of the exposition in this section on James's Christology, we shall consider his views on Christ's "divinity" and incarnation, reserving his treatment of Christ as the agent of redemption until the last section of this chapter, since it belongs there as the best introduction to the Doctrine of Regeneration.

With reference to Christ's birth, James occupies the orthodox position:

> I hold (perhaps more strenuously than you can at present imagine) that Christ was conceived of the Holy Ghost, that he was born of a virgin, that he lived a life of helpless humiliation and infamy in the eyes of the most reputable persons of his age and nation, while at the same time he became inwardly united with the Divine spirit to such a degree as at length to grow exanimate on his finite or maternal side, and find his literal flesh and blood becoming vivified by the infinite Love. But then I cannot conceive of these things being literally true save on one condition, which is, that nature be not the absolute and independent existence she seems; that she be in fact *the mere shadow or image of profounder realities,* projected upon the field of the sensuous understanding.[53]

However James phrases it, the value to man of the invisible God's appearance in history as the visible Lord consists in His being a type of the "universal humanity," and of the "Divine-Humanity" which will finally eventuate, as we shall see later, in his apex-concept of the "Divine-Natural-Humanity." Here we see the beginning of this process in his thought by which he extends *the* Incarnation into incarnational-*ism*:

> What a mere obscenity every great name in history confesses itself beside this spotless Judean youth, who in the thickest night of time,—unhelped by priest or ruler, by friend or neighbor, by father or mother, by brother or sister, helped, in fact, if we may so consider it, only by the dim expectant sympathy of that hungry rabble of harlots and outcasts who furnished His inglorious retinue, and still further drew upon Him the ferocious scorn of all that was devout, and honourable and powerful in His nation,—yet let in eternal daylight upon the soul, by steadfastly expanding in his private spirit to the dimensions of universal humanity, so bringing, for the first time in history, the finite human bosom into perfect experimental accord with the infinite Divine Love. For my part I am free to declare that I find the conception of any Divinity superior to this radiant human form, inexpressibly treasonable to my own manhood. . . . In short, I worship the LORD alone, the God-MAN. . . . [54]

In those words, James gives the very core of his Christology. God-hood became Christ-hood, and Christ-hood is destined to enter every human self-hood.

The Incarnation of God in Christ is utterly pivotal in James's theology. It has been observed by some that the *Incarnation* is the focal doctrinal formulation of the Anglican Communion, the *Atonement* as the central dogma of the Roman Catholic and Reformed Churches, and the *Resurrection* as the predominant doctrinal stress of the Greek Orthodox Church. In terms of such a generalization, it is plain that James is fundamentally "Anglican" in the adherence he confesses to the philosophy of incarnationalism, both special in Christ, and general in all men eventually. His secondary emphasis falls on the "glorification" aspect of the Lord's career. His tertiary emphasis is given to the Atonement, but, as we know, only in terms of "at-one-ment" of the Divine-and-Human within the Lord—not Atonement as *for* the sins of mankind, nor as *to* God. The centrality of the Incarnation is really stupendous in James; the whole body of Revelation is identified by him with the events that centered in and around the Christ's Incarnation:

The letter or body of Revelation is made up of all the personal facts recorded in the four Gospels concerning the birth, life, death, resurrection, and ascension of Jesus Christ. . . . I myself have a devout belief in the Divine Incarnation. I believe in it with such extreme good-will that I seem to myself indeed to believe in little besides. . . . For my part, believing, as I do with all my heart, the central truth of Revelation, which is the Divine Incarnation, I can see nothing in all past, in all present, and all future history, but the clearer and clearer exhibition of its resistless vitality. Indeed, the light which this deathless but discredited truth sheds upon all the otherwise inexplicable facts of modern life, and all the otherwise disheartening tendencies of modern thought, is altogether surprising to every one who seeks it. . . . [55]

To James, therefore, armored spiritually with his high doctrine of the Incarnation, there is no question of the "divinity" of Christ, as it is usually phrased. *The* problem, on James's showing, is not at all whether men can believe in the divinity of the Lord, but whether they can believe *in themselves* as recipients of divinization through an extension of the typal Incarnation of God as Lord to "universal humanity." If God submits to *humanization* of Himself, in man, then the recoil of that tremendous event must mean the *divinization* of man in God. *Humanization* of God as the incarnate Lord must obviously mean, according to the laws of spiritual dynamics, a corresponding *divinization* of man. The two processes are, says James, "strictly commensurate."

James's intense focalization of thought on the Incarnation dispenses with the orthodox Reformed and Roman Catholic stress on the Atonement. There is no need, since the Lord is the only God himself, for Him to continue a perpetual intercession, or to be perpetually "sacrificed" sacramentally on human altars, since He gave us redemption once and for all. To doubt this is to cast blasphemous doubt on the efficacy of His work, and at the same time to doubt His essential Divinity and Incarnation; for what special meaning did God's appearance in history as the Lord have, if He has to re-enact the same office continually in heaven! On such a false view of perpetual "mediation," why did He, it must be asked, leave the celestial world to appear in the natural world in the first place? To the Calvinist, Atonement means the reconciliation through Christ as Mediator, of two warring natures, the divine and the human. James will have no part of such a theory:

Every sectarian creed assumes the fact as indisputable, that an intrinsic contrariety exists between the divine and human natures. And the Christ is said to have reconciled the two by virtue of certain sufferings which he, considered as a partaker of the higher nature, submitted to endure in the lower one. . . .

. . . It is impossible to see how the suffering Christ endured can express the *reconciliation* of the two warring natures. It is simply a misuse of language to say that his human nature could be *reconciled* by the imposition of *sufferings;* and if we make the divine nature the one to be reconciled, and especially through the sufferings of the other, we not merely make the human nature the superior element in the transaction, because the immutable one, but we expressly contradict both the entire scope and the specific language of scripture, which represent man as the party to be reconciled. . . .

Precisely in so far therefore as you assume the Christ to have acted from the prompting of his divine nature, do you deny even to his own private biography the reconciliation of the two natures, leaving the human exactly *in statu quo*. The difference on this point between our modern theology and the scriptures is very significant. The latter invariably make the force of Christ's suffering whatever that force may be, dependent upon his human nature; the former upon his divine.[56]

Atonement to James means, then, what it meant to Swedenborg, an at-one-ment of God-as-invisible with the Lord-as-visible; or, again, the harmonizing of His celestial-Divine with His earthly-Human; and finally, the fusion of His "humiliation" as human with His "glorification," a consummation achieved by His Passion as the penultimate step to that great end. Thus, at-one-ment was wholly *within* the God-Lord, and not *between* two warring natures, divine and human.

Nothing more appropriate can be rendered as a conclusion to the exposition of Jamesian Christology than to cite a passage in which he is discoursing, not theologically, but in a straightforward way, giving his personal tribute to Christ:

His whole divinity lay in the fact of his having no interest apart from the welfare of universal man. . . . It is this which makes the name of Jesus more lustrous than any name in history, it is this which will ever make mankind prouder of that name than of any other, that he has absolutely no private personality, but has actually become identified to the imagination of the mass with purely humanitary or impersonal ideas. It is a name which has suggested no prisons, no gibbets, no fetters to human thought, but only the incessant softening and the final abolition of these brutalities. . . . Christ alone it appears to me among men claims this grandeur, that he grows exalted in proportion as he becomes personally abased, and is never so dishonored spiritually, as when he is honored for his own sake or personally.[57]

This consistent penchant for swallowing up the historic Jesus in the symbolical, gnostical Christ bothered James's Swedenborgian friend in London, J. J. Garth Wilkinson, who wrote:

. . . Thus I cleave to the historical, as a Romanist to his dolls; and when you talk of *the* Christ, I feel pained at the definite article, because it makes Christ Himself—the only one I know of—indefinite. . . . I cannot make History movable to please anybody; and, as to what has occurred I imagine its fact value to be inalienable. . . . The full influence of the letter is as necessary as that of the Spirit.[58]

Nearly a year later, 22 March 1850, Wilkinson wrote again to James in the same general tenor:

In your letter to me, I think you scientifically wrong in evaporating the personality of Christ in order to procure the universality of *the* Christ.[59]

There is no evidence that Wilkinson's testier sense of the historically concrete ever had any weight with James, who continued to universalize and to spiritualize the historic Jesus into *the* Christ. For James, the person of Jesus was secondary and only contributory to his symbolic, gnostical appropriation by Spiritual Philosophy as *the* Christ.

VI

With all his deep concern for "Society," James was not in his element when he tried to discuss actual and current social problems. His *forte* was not in dealing with empirical society, but with a philosophico-theological conception of the *Redeemed* Society. In the one or two instances when he did enter into debate over current social issues, he displayed his ineptitude for practical polemics and programs. Whether discussing Love, Marriage, Divorce, Crime, or Government, he would "go metaphysical," so to speak, every time. Sooner or later — and generally sooner—the metaphysics of Creation, Redemption, and the Divine-Natural-Humanity would manage to appear, no matter what the question under treatment. That is why it is really unnecessary to go into his views on these subjects in any detail. In his three-cornered debate with Horace Greeley and Stephen Pearl Andrews in the New York *Tribune* (the debate later published in pamphlet as *Love, Marriage, and Divorce*), he advocates more liberal divorce laws on the ground that easier divorce would abolish inharmonious marriages, and so clear the way for the chance to make a true, lifelong marriage. He champions greater freedom of divorce, but not of "love," (or of "free love"), because love, to him, is most binding in its nature, and presupposes the marriage-tie as its inevitable culmination.

There is no evidence that James was involved among the Swedenborgians over the fiery discussion concerning "conjugial love" and "spiritual wives," the story of which has been told by Block in *The New Church in the New World*. But he was influenced by Swedenborg's terminology in distinguishing *Conjugial Love* (Swedenborg's book by that title) from "scortatory love." Naturally James favored "conjugial love" as against the "scortatory" which was Swedenborg's term for harlotry and concupiscence; but when we say that he favored "conjugial" love, a distinction between James and Swedenborg must be brought out. By "conjugial," Swedenborg meant "spiritual affinity," not the "conjugal" bond, or marriage. Conjugiality, or spiritual affinity, might or might not exist within marriage; and in any event, the essence of the term is its reference to the harmony between spiritual mates. If this spiritual affinity did not exist in a given marriage, Swedenborg allowed, by his "Doctrine of Permission" in *Conjugial Love,* the expression, if such an affinity were found, of this spiritual love outside the marital bond.

James (in actual life generally and with reference to his view of love and marriage especially, he was really very "moral": the moral antinomian!), was clearly too moral to accept Swedenborg on this point. The idea involved in Swedenborg's doctrine of the "permission of evil" was repugnant to him; though possibly he construed Swedenborg's teaching into his (James's) plea for easier divorce laws. At all odds, Swedenborg was more realistic than James here, for Swedenborg did not approve of broken-up homes and the resultant scattering of children which he saw must be the inevitable effect if divorce were to become easier and more general.

In his argument with Greeley and Andrews, they all seem to misunderstand each other, though Andrews is the most acute logician on the subject at hand. When the debate was resumed twenty years later in 1873, between Andrews, James, and a third party who signed himself "H. Y. R.," the newcomer to the controversy penned a genial satire on James's inability to deal with the "raw edge of things," a satire that is aptly descriptive of any attempts James made to discuss current social issues, and which is well worth including here:

Henry James sits a crowned king in the realm of metaphysics. His penetration is something marvellous. His admirers become enthusiasts, and declare that he alone of living men is entitled to the name of philosopher. Time and space confess themselves mere shams, and the material universe fades out of mind under the matchless power of his analysis; the innermost mysteries of being unfold themselves, fall into order and method, and ultimate in worlds and passionate hearts as a matter of course; history is illumined, and the splendid destiny of the race is forecast with overwhelming certainty. But in the midst of all this, or perhaps because of this, one detects in him a certain inability to cope with actual affairs as they arise in the ever-shifting drama of life. His thought turns back upon itself when it comes in contact with the raw edge of things.[60]

A fitting introduction to James's views on social redemption is found in *Tracts for the New Times,* where he presents in brief the evolution of society from the family to the whole human race:

Look at the whole Providential history of human nature, at those events which separate the human life from the animal, and compel the instinctive belief of a majestic and elevating Providence in human destiny. First you see individualism in man softened by subjection to the family—and next the tribal—bond; the patriarchal order being the earliest social form known to the race. Afterwards as population increases, you see it still further mitigated by subjection to the municipal bond, the individual being brought into unity not merely with one family or tribe, but with all the families or tribes of one town. . . . And finally you see it still further modified by subjection to the national bond, which brings the individual into unity not only with all his fellow townsmen, but with all his fellow countrymen. This is our present civilization. . . . Its great final development into the unity of the race, is what remains for us to see; that development which shall make all the nations of the earth one society, or one united family, when a man shall love and serve not his own nation merely, but all the nations of the earth, when in a word his sympathies shall flow towards every brother of the race, purely according to the good that is in him. Let no good man doubt this consummation; the divine existence is thereby doubted. All history yearns for it. The whole course of Providence ensures it. Who that traces the beautiful Providential order by which the individual rises into the brother, the neighbor, and the citizen, *can* doubt that the crowning rise shall as surely be seen; that, namely, whereby the individual having already proceeded from the brother to the neighbor, and from the neighbor to the citizen, shall from the citizen rise into THE MAN,—rise into unity with all his race, giving to all men an equal regard, because all have the same divine parentage, and the same divine destiny.[61]

With this description of the evolution of human society and of its ultimate goal, we are prepared to consider the Doctrine of Spiritual Redemption, which is the climax of all of James's other doctrines. All the doctrines of Knowledge, of Creation, of Nature, of Man, of Evil, as well as all the topics of this present chapter—Philosophy of History, Church, State, and Religion with their respective sub-topics—each and every one converges in his philosophy upon the final concept of Redeemed Society, or as he sometimes puts it, The Divine-Natural Humanity.

At the very start, his distinction between "Redemption" and "Regeneration" must be fixed in mind. The former is a Divine and objective operation for humanity by the Lord; the latter is a human and subjective response to the Lord's redemption. The distinction is put very succinctly by James:

> The truth in question, when viewed on its human side, is known under the familiar name of REGENERATION; when viewed on its Divine side it is called REDEMPTION.[62]

The larger theological framework behind James's objective theory of "redemption" is found in his first published book, *What Constitutes the State*:

> The language of these paragraphs in respect to the divine Redemption will show, what the writer has no motive to conceal, that his view of the central fact of Christianity . . . differs from the one traditionally received. . . . Our creeds have doubtless served an important end in preserving the formal memory of truths, which would otherwise have been lost to the earth; but they have so obscured and degraded these great truths by vicious modes of statement, as to prevent any thing but a formal or outward acknowledgment of them. They have, for example, stated the doctrine of the Trinity as importing a trinity of *persons*—thus stultifying every rational conception of the divine

unity; and they have stated the doctrine of redemption, as importing the redemption of man *from the wrath of one of these persons through the clemency of another,* thus stultifying every rational conception of the divine *character.*[63]

Having established this approach as basic and "rational" in framing a theory of redemption, James proceeds in later works to make the most explicit statements regarding his theology of redemption, the intense objectivity of which is more than obvious; it is indeed overwhelming. For the subjective response in man, James here uses "salvation" instead of "regeneration," but they are interchangeable terms:

> Scriptually viewed, redemption is what alone makes salvation possible. It is always represented by the apostles as a necessary Divine preliminary to salvation. . . . Salvation is a subjective work, which takes place only by our own consent. . . . Redemption is an objective work, or an exclusively Divine proceeding which took place centuries before we were born. . . . Redemption is accordingly quite independent for its truth both upon our knowledge and belief. Its truth would be totally unaffected, even though no one should subsequently have been saved. . . .
>
> In the nature of things salvation cannot be compulsory, or morally obligatory. It is only spiritually obligatory, or obligatory on those who wish it. The great truth of Redemption guarantees this. For redemption implies, not the extinction of hell, but its thorough subjugation to human use, or the Divine Natural Humanity.[64]

It is evident, also, that Creation itself would have come to naught without the support of redemption:

> *Thus, from the very necessity of the case, creation involves redemption; and until redemption is accomplished to its last fibre,* or to the literal flesh and bones of humanity, *it is premature to talk of creation being perfect.*[65]

With an understanding of James's concept of Redemption, one is in a position to grasp his meaning of Regeneration. He has already told us that salvation, or regeneration, is "subjective" as being man's response to Divine redemption through the Lord. As he develops this concept of regeneration, it is not that of the individual that he stresses, though that is implied, but of Society as a whole. He thus produces his Spiritual Socialism as the result of an attempt to fuse Swedenborg's theology with Fourier's Socialism (Associationism, or Social Science).

Since James read widely in the socialist thinkers of his time—Fourier, Comte, St. Simon, Proudhon—it is advisable to consider his differences from them by way of the criticisms he levelled in their direction. Fusing Swedenborg and Fourier, spiritualism and "science," James was not content with "technical" or "secular" socialism apart from theology and Spiritual Philosophy.

In his lecture, "Socialism and Civilization in Relation to the Individual Life," James is more enthusiastic over Fourieristic Socialism, or Associationism, than he was ever to be again. But even there, he bends "Science" toward his spiritualistic philosophy in relation to the Christian-inspired hope of individual "perfection." He states the Christian hope, and then affirms that Socialism is the instrument for its consummation:

> This, I confess, is what attracts me in the programme of Socialism, the unconscious service it renders to the divine life in me, the complete inauguration and fulfillment it affords to the Christian hope of individual perfection. Christianity is a virtual denial of all mystery of Deity, and an affirmation of His essential intelligibility. It denies to Deity any mere passive or inoperative perfection, and affirms His existence exclusively within human conditions. It reveals a perfect harmony between God in His infinitude and man in his lowest natural and social debasement. . . . In short it affirms the unity of God and Man. Two things hinder the consciousness of this unity on the part of man—nature and society . . . the one by finiting his body, the other by finiting his soul. Accordingly, the Christ, or representative Divine Man, is seen warring with and subjugating both nature and society. . . .
>
> Now what is typically reported of the Christ is to be actually fulfilled in universal humanity, in every man. . . .
>
> Now Socialism alone supplies the science of this great consummation. It reveals the incessant operation of laws by which man's physical and social relations will be brought into the complete subjection of his inward or divine personality. It is the demonstration of a plenary unity between man and nature and man and man.[66]

Toward the end of the lecture, James allows his enthusiasm for Fourierism to reach full strength, but one can see that it is not an objective presentation of Fourier by any means; for, between the lines, it is easy to discern that his socialist gospel allows him a chance to square accounts with the un-social conception of Calvinism, not as to its doctrine of sin, but as to its doctrine of salvation by Divine election of individuals arbitrarily chosen by God either for salvation or damnation:

> Every one who trusts in a living and therefore active God . . . in short every one whose hope for humanity is alert, behooves to acquaint himself forthwith with the marvellous literature of Socialism, above all with the writings of CHARLES FOURIER. You will doubtless find in Fourier things of an apostolic hardness to the understanding; you will find many things to startle, many things perhaps to disgust you; but you will find vastly more both in the way of criticism and constructive science to satisfy and invigorate your understanding, while such glimpses will open on every hand of God's ravishing harmonies yet to ensue on earth, that your imagination will fairly ache with contentment, and plead to be let off.
>
> These are what you will find in Fourier, provided you have no secret interest dogging your candor and watching to betray it. Let me also tell you what you will *not* find there. You will find no such defaming thought of God as makes His glory to depend upon the antagonism of His creature's shame. You will find no allegation of an essential and eternal contrariety between man and his creative source. Whatever be FOURIER's errors and faults, this crowning and bottomless infamy by no means attaches to him. On the contrary, if the highest homage paid to Deity be that of the understanding, then FOURIER's piety may safely claim pre-eminence. For it was not a traditional piety, that piety of habit which keeps our churches open—and cheerless; nor was it a selfish piety, the piety which springs from jail-bird conceptions of Deity, and paints him as a colossal spider bestriding the web of destiny and victimizing with fell alacrity every heedless human fly that gets entangled in it. . . .[67]

In language like that James expressed his spiritual "Declaration of Independence" from the "eternal contrariety between man" and God, as found in Calvinism.

Another aspect of the Fourierist influence in James is his statement on the "Passions" on "strictly scientific" (*i.e.*, Fourierist), grounds. This is directly derived from the French thinker, who developed a doctrine of the passions as a prominent feature of his system. James's statement is important because it gives the ideological content that lies within the adjective "spontaneous," which adjective is almost always found inseparably connected with "redeemed," "regenerated," and "aesthetic" in his enumeration of the characteristics of redeemed Society:

I am not content with merely saying that a state of society which puts man in harmony with his nature, or, in equivalent terms, insures him the ample gratification of all his appetites and passions, may exist without prejudice to the interests of morality. I claim that such a state of society is absolutely *indispensable* to those interests. . . . Before attempting to prove this proposition, let me obviate a probable misconception of my meaning from the popular misuse of the word *passions*.

I use this word altogether in its scientific strictness, or as denoting certain springs or principles of action in man, certain original susceptibilities or aptitudes of human nature, bearing the names of Love, Friendship, Paternity, Ambition. These passions of man, when exempt from arbitrary compression, or left to their free development, work the most peaceful and benignant results. They are the sources or springs of all our activity, and in the exact measure of their fullness or intensity they clothe human life with beauty. . . . But these passions, when circumstances are unpropitious, especially when they are arbitrarily thwarted, assume oftentimes a morbid expression inversely proportionate to the benignity of their normal action. . . . They are all alike capable of being stung, *by the tyranny of outward circumstances,* into the most subversive action. . . . There can be no obscurity, then, upon my use of the word *passions*. I discard the vulgar use of it utterly, and confine it to its strict scientific sense, as indicating the divinely implanted springs of action in human nature. . . . A state of society which will perfectly gratify every appetite of man's body, and every want of his soul comprehended under the terms Love, Friendship, Ambition, Paternity, affords the destined and only possible fulfillment of all morality, affords indeed the indispensable basis of God's kingdom on earth. The proof of this proposition stands in the fact, that such a state of society alone meets the requirements of a perfect equality among men.[68]

From such ideas James projected his ideal of spontaneity, or "free development" of the passions, and when this ideal was eventually realized for all men, it would define the truest meaning of "equality" at the same time.

Though highly stimulated by Fourierist Socialism, James came more and more to a critical opinion of it. As always, he is no less positive in rejection than in acceptance:

Of course nothing can be easier for you than to give all this exposition of Christian truth a bad name, by calling it Socialism. . . . Besides, though Socialism is not Christianity, it is a very decided symptom of its living and active presence. Socialism . . . means some specific theory or other in regard to the *organization* of society in institutions. But Christianity means the social spirit itself, means the spirit of human love and brotherhood, the spirit of universal fellowship or equality which is yet to reign on the earth, and cover it with the manifest splendour of God. Fourier, St. Simon, and the rest, no doubt, deserve well for their attempts to embody this spirit, but we must not judge of the spirit itself from their conception of it. . . . I for my part am led to think, that the Socialists proper exhibit a very faulty conception of society. They all suppose it to be a product of purely *natural* laws. Thus their whole thought becomes absorbed in the invention of suitable gearing for society, while the crying want of the world is to be convinced of the bare *possibility* of society itself. Fourier, for example, talks of organizing society as glibly as you would talk of organizing a military company. *But where is the society which is to be organized?* The very possibility of human society yet remains to be demonstrated. . . . The Socialist conceives that society is the natural tendency of humanity. . . . The starting point of Socialism, in other words, is the goodness of human nature, and hence it inevitably violates the religious instinct in man, by denying the truth of Revelation. For Revelation affirms the intrinsic evil of human nature—theologically, the fall of man—and a consequent redemption on the part of God. I feel bound accordingly to look upon human society, human fellowship, human equality— for all these names indicate one and the same reality—not as a normal phenomenon of human nature, but only as the fruit of a most real Divine operation in humanity.[69]

Shade of John Calvin! "Revelation affirms the intrinsic evil of human nature"! Significantly, this "Letter" is dated August 24, 1855, and written therefore, not in his latter years when men sometimes revert to their youthful indoctrinations, but when James had barely passed the peak of his first enthusiasm for Socialism! The man of spiritual religion, the rationalistic supernaturalist, the sublimated Calvinist, in James, triumph over secular socialism, "science," and all forms of humanitarian utopianism.

In connection with the above passage, it is profitable to consider more at length the roots of James's ideas on Social Redemption. His statement relative to the "intrinsic evil of human nature," and his definition of man's redemption as being the "fruit of a most real, Divine operation in humanity" are so Calvinist in ideology that it is hard to distinguish it from pure Calvinism itself. There is, however, a different dialectic about these ideas in James and it is a most rewarding task to attempt to disentangle them for purposes of comparison with Calvinistic doctrine.

As we noted in our study of his Doctrine of Spiritual Evil, Adam's "fall" was a spiritual fall exclusively, unaccompanied by any physical fall involving disease, condemnation to labor, and so on. And within this "spiritual fall" itself, there is a close-knit Jamesian dialectic constructed in relation to the two ways of interpreting this fall: (1) in relation to man's moral nature, the "fall" was a fall *upwards,* because it carried him to a level of consciousness that enabled him to transcend his mere moral existence, and think of his spiritual relation to his own infinite selfhood and to God the Creator; (2) in relation to man's spiritual potentialities, the "conscience of sin" was indication of a *spiritual fall in reality,* because man learned that he had been thinking of himself more highly than he ought to think, so that when "conscience of sin" struck his soul, he became conscious of his creaturehood before the Creator. Thus, man's experience of "sin" was not of some specific evil which he *suffered,* or some specific evil which he *did,* but of the general spiritual evil which he *was,* in terms of his over-pride about his status until he was convinced of his comparative unworthiness before his Creator.

Now, for James, "conscience of sin"—which was at one and the same time a spiritual rise above morality and a spiritual fall into consciousness of creaturehood, is not conceived as being the result of some disobedience in a mythical Fall in the *past,* but consists instead of man's resistance to the great event of the *future, viz.,* the Regenerated, Divine Humanity. No man is involved in a sin committed by a real or a symbolic first man, or Adam, as in Calvinism; but a man becomes spiritually evil *originally* or from within himself, by resisting "that great unitary life of God in our nature, which we call society, fraternity, fellowship, equality, and which from the beginning of human history has been struggling to work itself . . . into final perfect and objective recognition. . . ."[70]

Thus, evil in Calvinism and in James is objective and social; but with the former it is so with reference to a past event, while with the latter it is individual and with reference to a future event; namely, the advent of the Divine-Natural-Humanity. In Calvinism, man sins collectively in Adam and is saved individually by God's election, if saved at all. In Jamesian doctrine, man sins individually in his own spiritual consciousness, and is saved collectively.

To James, accordingly, both Calvin and Fourier are, though in highly different ways, somewhat romantical in seeing "Society" as a *past* event of fact, the one pessimistically, the other optimistically. It is equally indifferent to James whether Calvin conceived society as depraved through Adam, or whether Fourier dreamed of a pure primitive society later corrupted by "civilization"; they are both wrong in positing "Society" as something given from the past; for, as James says: *"but where is the society which is to be organized?* The very possibility of human society yet remains to be demonstrated." James is therefore utterly evolutionary in his doctrine of society. "Society" simply has not, as yet, ever existed. So radical is the critique of both utopian socialism and democratic liberalism by James's spiritual realism! But James is no mere "emergent" evolutionist like Morgan and Alexander in our time, for his evolutionism is based in a prior involutionism proceeding from God in creation. Consequently, Society doesn't lift itself "by its own bootstraps" to a point higher than its origin in God, but is rather being led *via* redemption, objectively performed by the Lord, and regeneration, subjectively appropriated by man, to attain a level with God. Romantic? James would reply in substance: "No! my view is more realistic than either that of Calvinism or Fourierism because outflanking both views by not positing 'society' in the past at all, whether in a pre-corrupted or a post-corrupted state, whether 'caused' by the disobedience of the 'first man' or by 'civilization.' For what good does it do to posit a 'fall' in the past, in either the Calvinist or the Socialist meaning? In either event, our 'knowledge' of the pre-corrupted society has to be mythical. By comparison, a redeemed society in the future is simply the working out of a logic implicit in the tragic facts of empirical humanity as *is*. The future is much more real, from our actual position, and in terms of possibilities, than any past, or theory of the past, can ever be. Besides, the evolutionary order is irreversible; so why speculate on the 'corruption' which never really has yet existed, instead of looking to the future for what *can* exist. Hence, altogether I am more realistic than either Calvinism or Socialism."

On these grounds, then, James makes it clear that he is not swallowing Socialism whole, any more than he had Calvinism. His critical detachment from secularist Socialism exhibits itself very strongly in his negative remarks anent Comte's "Religion of Humanity." In the following paragraphs on Comte, James illustrates the fact that the idealist—that is, "idealist" relative to the *status quo*—is often your most penetrating realist as he levels his vision to that same *status quo!*

No man can surpass James in adjusting the mind to a realization that all such terms as "idealism" and "realism" must, especially in social philosophy, involve a searching inspection of the contexts and especially the frames of reference presupposed by their specific usage:

> I have no intellectual sympathy with the socialists so called, or those who hold that Society is a purely natural phenomenon, requiring nothing but the operation of natural laws to account for it: nor yet have I any intellectual sympathy with Comte. . . .
>
> Comte's great merit consists in his having been the first scientific intellect adequately to invoke attention to the strictly progressive nature of science. . . . His attention as a student has been arrested by the discovery that the sciences appear to be intimately concatenated, or to be developed one from another, in a regular and necessary sequence; and he has very sensibly set himself to inquiring—*whereto shall these things grow?* The Church supplied him no prognostic. Philosophy was even less suggestive. . . . "My first labour, therefore, must be to dethrone Theology and Philosophy, in order to win science a fair field, and the formula of the threefold evolution of the human understanding must be my weapon for doing this." . . . Identifying religion with the Theology of the day, or rather of a past day, he felt himself bound by the unscientific cast of that Theology, to proclaim an essential and permanent hostility between science and religion, and bade every vulgar sciolist insult, on his authority, the sacredest hope of the soul. A larger or spiritual apprehension of his theme . . . would have saved him, moreover, from the melancholy antics he is now practising *both as a theologian and philosopher.*
>
> For, alas for human frailty! Comte had no sooner demonstrated the utter evanishment of the theologic and metaphysic eras to make room for that of Positivism, than—ere the plaudits of his admirers had ceased to vibrate upon the air, or the caps they flung up had returned to earth—he set about constructing not merely a brand-new theology, but a brand-new religion as well, with creed and catechism, fast and festival, duly appointed and established; and not merely a brand-new religion either, but a brand-new Deity also, a Deity so preposterous that only the rigidly "scientific intellect" which begot Him could fail to be ashamed of Him, for He is compounded of the abstract and metaphysic unity of all God's creatures, being in fact the aggravated scum or feculence of the universal finite experience. So charmed is our new and scientific Stylites with this achievement—so intent is he upon spreading the serene and majestic tail of his own extraordinary merits before the eyes of the world—that he not

only with more than French egotism, minutely and gravely depicts the starting-point of the new cultus, in a certain erotic hallucination with which he was inspired by a certain Clotilde de Veaux, but with more than French bombast also takes every occasion publicly to subscribe himself AUGUSTE COMTE, *Fondateur de la religion de l'Humanité. . . .*

He thinks that the chief obstacle to the progress of the scientific understanding consists in the influence of the great theologic dogma of the Fall? Why? Because "this fundamental dogma, which all religions reproduce under some form or other, leads to the direct and necessary inference that man's social deterioration must keep pace with the growth of civilization." Undoubtedly, all religions claiming the dignity of a Revelation involve the idea of a Fall; but they do not therefore, as Comte alleges, necessarily imply the endless deterioration of man, for the simple reason that they all, with more or less clearness, also affirm a Divine deliverance from that catastrophe. The Fall is there to be sure, but the redemption never fails to ensue. The Christian religion especially, means nothing else than this redemption; and I really think that Comte, since he was going to set up such an egregious religion of his own, might have condescended to an accurate estimate of the system he was going to displace, at least. The founder of Christianity was, to be sure, a much humbler individual in his own estimation than the *"fondateur de la religion de l'Humanité";* but the latter is scarcely authorized entirely to overlook him. Indeed, I have a very clear presentiment, for my own part, that he will continue to exert an active influence upon human progress long after the illustrious *fondateur* shall have himself subsided into a very modest repute; the repute, possibly, of a man whose great abilities might have conferred unmixed blessing upon humanity had they not been signally vitiated by the association of an immeasurable and childish vanity.

Thus I have no philosophic sympathy with the technical Socialist.[71]

The clear historical insight James displays in his generous tribute to Comte's understanding of the growth, in sequence, of the sciences; and yet his piercing critique of Comte in the role of *fondateur de la religion de l'Humanité,* is evidence again of the fertilizing combination of Calvinistic roots and of spiritual realism *via* Swedenborg. One cannot but wish he had given his estimate of Karl Marx!

By virtue of the preliminary exposition of James's fruitful and critical contact with Socialism in its specifically Associationist form, we are thus prepared to examine his Doctrine of Spiritual Socialism entirely on its own terms.

The *adjectives* by which James qualifies the concept of the Society he envisages as the ultimate achievement and consummation of history—"redeemed, associated, regenerated, aesthetic, and spontaneous"—have all been filled with ideological content by strength of apposite quotations above, and by the accompanying exposition. Also, all the attributes of the Redeemed Society—Power, Goodness, Fellowship, Spontaneity (or Freedom)—have been traced to their roots in James's intellectual evolution. We have found also that the King, Priest, and Artist have been used by James as prefiguring types of these qualities which he projects into his vision of that Society towards which, in all literalness to James, "the whole creation moves." The King was the type of Power; the Priest, of Goodness and Fellowship; the Artist, of Spontaneity. James handles these types in a somewhat Hegelian fashion as "concrete universals," or in Pascal's sense, as belonging within the science of "Typology."

The Artist, we saw, receives the highest place in the trio of types because he embodies "livingly" the aspect of "Spontaneity" or Freedom, upon which James places the highest premium, for the reason that spontaneity represents the harmony of heart and head, love and wisdom, power and use, goodness and fellowship, individuality and sociality—a harmony not only between the members of each pair thus conceptually distinguished, but among all the pairs. The Artist, as the most satisfactory of empirically available types for the representation of what James intends for all humanity in the spiritual estate of regeneration, is the most concrete, because individuated, image we have for comprehending the otherwise highly abstract concept of Spiritual Socialism. In order to realize this fact in all its force, one short quotation, beyond those cited in the chapter on "Spiritual Man," is sufficient:

> Hence the Artist claims to be the reconciling or uniting term between God and man, the spiritual or infinite reality symbolized by the literal or finite God-man, the wholly incontestible son of God, the heir of all divine power majesty and glory, by whom alone God estimates the world.[72]

When we come to consider the *nouns* that James uses to fix the concept of Spiritual Society—nouns such as "brotherhood, equality, fellowship, universal man"—we feel the need of further exposition beyond that given to these terms thus far in our study. The concept of "equality" is given content in his Newport Address:

When I said awhile ago that an American, as such, felt himself the peer of every man of woman born, I represented my hearers as asking me whether that claim was a righteous one; whether, in fact, he whose conscience should practically ratify it in application to himself would not thereby avouch his own immodesty,—confess himself devoid of that humility which is the life of true manhood. To this question I reply promptly, No! for this excellent reason,—that the claim in question is by no means a distinctive personal claim, but a claim in behalf of every man. . . . Nothing is more common than to hear persons who are disaffected to the humane temper of our polity affecting to quote the Declaration of Independence as saying that all men are *born* equal, and under cover of that audacious forgery exposing it to ridicule. The Declaration is guilty of no such absurdity. It does not say that all men are born equal, for it is notorious that they are born under the greatest conceivable inequalities . . . but it says that, notwithstanding these inequalities, they are all *created* equal,—that is, are all equal before God, or can claim no superior merit one to another in his sight, being all alike dependent upon his power, and possessing a precisely equal claim, therefore, each with the other, to the blessings of his impartial providence. . . . No man not a fool can gainsay this, and no man not a fool, consequently, can pretend that when I urge this constitutional doctrine of human equality I have anything whatever to say of myself personally regarded, or *as discriminated from other persons,* but only as SOCIALLY regarded,—that is, as *united* with all other persons. In short, it is not a claim urged on my own behalf alone, but in behalf of every other man who is too ignorant or too debased by convention to assert it for himself.[73]

Changing ground from the argument based on the social philosophy found in the Declaration of Independence, James, as we knew he would, produces an argument from the side of Christ's divinity, the implications of which spread out from Christ's Incarnation to the eventual establishment of a society in which "the exact equality of man with man" will be universally recognized:

The truth of Christ's divinity has been hitherto found susceptible only of ecclesiastical uses. It has served to discriminate the orthodox doctrine of the Church from all its falsifications, and in this way no doubt has powerfully promoted the interests of spiritual order, the order of the human mind. But within the bounds of the natural world it has as yet only served the purpose of a broom to sweep the Church clean of the cobwebs of heresy. . . . But I, for my own part, am persuaded differently. I am persuaded that whether we believe or disbelieve, this great truth is operative under all our political and civil as well as ecclesiastical history, and forms indeed the *primum mobile* of that immense *social* agitation which is destined never to cease, but only to grow until the law of human fellowship, or of the exact equality of man with man, becomes finally realized throughout the earth.[74]

When we look at the term "fellowship," the Sandemanian roots of the concept impress the mind at once. Fellowship in the Sandemanian connotation, was a literal and concrete memory and image to James. When he penned the word "fellowship" (and "equality" also for that matter, since he usually combines the two), James must have recalled his quiet sessions with Michael Faraday; or, the Sandemanian meetings, with no paid, professional clergy, and with the opportunity for all members in rotation to hold the nominal official titles of responsibility in the congregation.

In *Society the Redeemed Form of Man*, James soars to the veriest heights of his vision:

> Neither you nor I have ever had, have now, or ever shall have, any particle of just or rational hope towards God which is based either upon any possible personal difference in us to other men, or any possible personal difference in us to ourselves in past time, but solely and wholly upon His own reconciling spirit or temper in universal man, whereby we and all men become gradually softened and refined out of our natural egotism and savagery, by being lifted out of our petty egotistic moral consciousness, and becoming gradually invested with social or race-consciousness. This is what creation, spiritually regarded, means, and all it means, not any stupid and brutal event in space and time, transcending human nature and antedating human history, but a most real and authentic life of God identical with Human nature and consubstantiate with human history: beginning with that history, animating all its movements, keeping steadfast pace with it through all its marvellous vicissitudes and revolutions, and bringing it at length to its grand triumphant climax in the coming splendors of the mystical city of God.[75]

The circle of James's thought is now complete, from the preliminary process of "Formation" in Creation, to the "mystical city of God."

Such, in short, is the true epic of Man. But we cannot leave this city without further consideration.

James's "City of God" is descendant from other great conceptions of a redeemed humanity; from Our Lord's "Kingdom of God," St. Augustine's "City of God," Leibniz' "Divine City of Spirits." In these previous conceptions the stress has been, as compared with James at least, on God as "King," or as "Monarch" in Leibniz's view. With James the emphasis is on the humanity which make up this city. What its particular relation to God will be is not made clear by James, but as for its own characteristics, he is perfectly clear. His city will be a spiritual-socialist-commonwealth, in which equality will reign between man and man. It will be no way similar to "political" democracies on earth, with their delegates and representatives, for James will have no more mediation of any kind, human or divine. James envisages the utter transcending of political democracy in favor of a spiritual social-democracy. There will be differentiation of "function," but not as to "persons."

Worriment over individual immortali-*ties* is entirely unspiritual as compared with the immortali-*ty* that appertains to all who enter the redeemed Society. Petty preoccupation over personal immortality is proof of spiritual astigmatism coincident with our unregenerated state, and is the most damning evidence of one's non-redemption from the die-hard, spiritual evil of finite selfhood. If it had been intended to secure our personal immortalities, as a prolongation of our persons as experienced in this present existence, God would have granted it outright in the first place instead of having to concern Himself about working out a method of Redemption to secure it later. James's spiritual socialism is thus radically impersonal; the individual must learn to give up all self-consciousness in favor of race-consciousness if he would pass muster for inclusion in James's version of "The City of God."

It seems at first curious that James, a spiritualistic philosopher, usually capitalizes the middle term in the Divine-NATURAL-Humanity. The cue to this apparent anomaly is best found, perhaps, in this passage:

> The existing ecclesiasticisms, both Catholic and Protestant, proceed exclusively upon the *spiritual* regeneration of their members, and hence postpone our realization of the Divine beatitudes to *post mortem* states. The new church, on the contrary, by its acknowledgement of the Divine NATURAL Humanity . . . im-

plicitly affirms the regeneration of human nature itself . . . even on the earth.[76]

Instead of stressing "spiritual," he does the diametrically opposite thing and stresses "NATURAL." In doing this, James is of course not being perverse; for if we but reflect upon his doctrine of Spiritual Creation, we recall that the very test and meaning of spiritual causation is its power to operate *in* Nature. Hence, the central significance of the Incarnation is that God came into our human nature. In the end we are redeemed *from* our nature only because God as the Lord came *into* our nature. Moreover, our nature is never to be obliterated; it is glorified and transfigured through Redemption "down to our very flesh and bones."

With this understanding, one is prepared to consider further the concept of the Divine-Natural-Humanity. Notice has been taken heretofore of James's doctrine of the Incarnation as a master principle in his theology; note was made also of the tendency in his conception of *the* Incarnation of God as the Lord, to overflow into *incarnationalism*, which becomes a general principle in his Newport Address:

> In short, we practically affirm the literal verity of the Divine Incarnation in every form of human nature, the unlimited indwelling of the infinite Godhead in every man of woman born; so turning every man by the sheer pith of his manhood into mitred priest and crowned king, or avouching ourselves finally to our own consciousness and the world's willing recognition as a faultless human society, instinct with God's unspeakable delight and approbation.[77]

In his last book, James expands the incarnational principle more definitely, and in so doing, acknowledges the non-existence of Divine incarnation in sub-human nature, at the same time affirming the incarnation of God in human nature:

> What I mean, then, by incarnation is this: that God or the Lord, meaning by that term God-man—for I am not a bit of a deist, properly so-called, and cannot for the life of me imagine the existence of a God outside of our nature, having other than essentially human attributes—is the sole substance or reality of everything embraced in the sensible universe, from its central sun to the planetary earths that encircle it, and from these again to the tiniest mineral, vegetable, and animal forms that enliven their surface. Nothing is exempt from the operation of this law but the field of self-consciousness, which not being a *thing*, or object of

sense, but on the contrary a sphere of metaphysical illusion . . . is the only possible sphere of evil in the universe, and is therefore excluded from creation altogether, being gradually absorbed and superseded by unitary or race-consciousness.

But is mineral, vegetable, and animal nature *human* nature? Unquestionably; only it is human nature with God left out. God enters human nature only through the individual conscience, confessing itself evil and false. There is no other way of his becoming incarnate in it, and so lifting us to the plenary enjoyment of his own life. The creator of man is not incarnate in mineral, vegetable, or animal, but only in man. . . .

There is but one nature, then, and that is *human* nature, so named from God's true creature, man; for mineral, vegetable, and animal are God's creatures only as involved in man. . . . [78]

Such a passage adequately accounts for the "Divine" factor in the Divine-Natural-Humanity, as indeed it does also for the other two elements.

If we add to the above quotation, however, such other thoughts as we have seen expressed by James, such as the conception that God, by His incarnation, became "exclusively imprisoned and interiorated within the soul of man," one becomes properly disturbed by the implications, especially of the word "exclusively." It may be that James, who uses that adverb so prodigally, did not think of its being taken literally; but if taken literally (as it was by his son William James and by Garth Wilkinson, who was his keenest critic), what is the result? It means that James understands the *descent* of God in *the* Incarnation and in incarnationalism generally, as being transformed, without remainder of the Divine Being, into the *ascent* of man to become the Divine Humanity, and *so becoming the new Divine Being in place of the original God,* or form of God! As William James remarked, God, on this view, is "almost swallowed up" in the divinization of Humanity; for, as this author agrees, the God who is "exclusively imprisoned" within man would seem to have to be content thereafter to identify His being "exclusively" with the distributed divine life which lives in mankind and flowers ultimately in the Divine Humanity. The object of religious reverence has shifted from God to the Divine Humanity, thus involving a curiously complex kind of atheism! James sounds essentially like Irenaeus, one of the Greek Fathers in early Christianity who was influenced by Gnosticism. Irenaeus put it succinctly enough: "God became man that man might become God."[79] It is not to our purpose here to inquire into what

Irenaeus himself meant precisely by his doctrine of the Incarnation, but it is evident that James, whether acquainted with Irenaeus' view or not, has offered substantially the same teaching as this formula conveys.

Wilkinson, who was by far the most intelligent critic that James ever had, was also disturbed by James's mystical-Gnostical tendency in his doctrine of the Divine-Natural-Humanity. It is a regrettable loss that only a very few of Wilkinson's letters to James are extant. His power as a critic, however, can be gauged by this passage from a letter to James in which he expresses himself magnificently on the theme of the Divine-Natural-Humanity:

> You would be better, not as a man, but as a consistency, if you were detached from Swedenborg. Your theory has been suggested by his collision with your mind; he has struck you hard; and in the tenderness and generosity of your constitution, you have accepted his heavy blow as polite intercourse; and founded, on your own side, not his, a friendship with his works, instead of recognizing his opposition as the main fact between you. . . .
>
> The only term common to you and Swedenborg is the *Divine Natural Humanity*. But is there any common idea between you here? I cannot find one. Swedenborg's Divine Natural is Jehovah triumphant in Jesus Christ over his infirm humanity; and over all the hells which had access to it: transforming his natural into the Divine Natural. Your Divine Natural, unless I misunderstand you, is diffused in all men, giving, or to give, them infinitude of some kind, and abolishing heavens and hells as mere preparations for the Godhead of Humanity. . . . And at last, Christ Himself seems to disappear into Humanity, as God has disappeared in Christ; and Man is all in all. You seem somehow to end with Professor Clifford, "The kingdom of man is at hand." Nothing is left to my apprehension but pananthropism, a composite form of pantheism.[80]

Wilkinson objects clearly enough to James's expansion of *the Incarnation* (which involved the only "Divine Natural" that Wilkinson knows), into the "Divine Natural *Humanity*" of James (in which the Divine is swallowed up by the Human, and "Man is all in all").

In spite of Wilkinson's penetrating critique, James was too enthralled by his vision to turn aside. He continued to express that vision in his rhapsodical prose, and who will deny that he clung to it with a touching dignity?:

It would be infinitely discreditable accordingly to the two factors [Divine and Human] in creation, if their tie were anything short of a marriage tie, i.e. if it did not claim an exclusively *social* sanction, or profess to stand only in that conscious, living reconciliation of the two otherwise irreconcilable natures [Divine and Human] which the church has always prophesied, but which is spiritually realized only in the grand practical truth of "the divine NATURAL humanity," or the advent of that predestined perfect society, fellowship, equality of men in heaven and on earth, which alone has power to bring nature and spirit, the outward and the inward, the universal and particular, the cosmos and the earth, the *homo* and the *vir*, the man and the woman, the world and the church, into living unison. . . . [81]

In those words one can see that Sandeman and Fourier, translated into a Jamesian version, have triumphed over Swedenborg!

Since James at heart was perhaps as much of a poet and prophet as he was a philosopher and theologian, it is fitting to close this presentation of his thought with his dream, pitched to lyric expression and wistful with spiritual hunger, of that "city not built with hands":

The sum of all I have been alleging is that we as a community are fully launched at length upon that metaphysic sea of being whose mystic waters float the sapphire walls of the New Jerusalem, metropolis of earth and heaven. It is not a city built of stone nor of any material rubbish, since it has no need of sun or moon to enlighten it; but its foundations are laid in the eternal wants and passions of the human heart sympathetic with God's infinitude, and its walls are the laws of man's deathless intelligence subjecting all things to his allegiance. Neither is it a city into which shall ever enter any thing that defileth, nor any thing that is contrary to nature, nor yet any thing that produceth a lie; for it is the city of God coming down to men out of the stainless heavens, and therefore full of pure unmixed blessing to human life, and there shall be no more curse.[82]

NOTES

1. *S and S,* p. 461.
2. *S of S,* p. 126.
3. *S and S,* pp. 439-440.
4. *Ibid.,* p. 437.
5. *Ibid.,* pp. 446-447.
6. *Ibid.,* pp. 444-445.
7. *Ibid.,* p. 390.
8. *Ibid.,* pp. 445-446.

9. *SRFM*, p. 19.
10. *CCNE*, pp. 80-81.
11. *Ibid.*, pp. 79-80.
12. *SSI*, Appendix, p. 42.
13. *CCNE*, pp. 122-123.
14. *S and S*, pp. 153-154.
15. *SSI*, Appendix, pp. 42-43.
16. *CLC*, pp. 208-210.
17. *WCS*, pp. 7, 11-12.
18. *Ibid.*, p. 15.
19. *Ibid.*, pp. 10, 17.
20. *Ibid.*, pp. 22, 23.
21. *S and S*, p. 137.
22. *SRFM*, p. 469.
23. *LM*, pp. 1-2.
24. *Ibid.*, pp. 6-7.
25. *SSI*, pp. 242, 239.
26. *CLC*, pp. 172-173.
27. *SRFM*, pp. 89-90.
28. *CCNE*, pp. 87-88, 87.
29. *CCNE*, pp. 65-66.
30. *Ibid.*, pp. 43-44.
31. *CCNE*, pp. 34-35.
32. *S and S*, p. 211; *passim*, p. 214.
33. *CCNE*, pp. 38-40.
34. *TNT*, p. 17.
35. *CCNE*, p. 125.
36. *Ibid.*, pp. 36-37.
37. Marguerite Block, *op. cit.*, p. 302.
38. *CCNE*, p. 11.
39. *TNT*, p. 24.
40. *S and S*, p. 230.
41. *SRFM*, pp. 178-179.
42. *LM*, pp. 152-153.
43. *CCNE*, p. 121. The theory of the sacraments as "symbolic," "spiritual," and "memorials" is taught by Swedenborg; *vide, The True Christian Religion*, Nos. 699-708, pp. 471-477.
44. *LR*, pp. 414-415.
45. *CLC*, pp. 155-156.
46. "The Reconciliation of Man Individual and Man Universal," *The Index*, Vol. VII (1876), p. 52.
47. *SRFM*, p. 362. James's yearning for self-extinction suggests readily enough a Buddhistic derivation; but there is no evidence of his having read Buddhist works directly.
48. *Ibid.*, pp. 366-367.
49. *Ibid.*, pp. 373-374.
50. *LM*, p. 162.
51. *Ibid.*, p. 161.
52. *Ibid.*, p. 165.

53. *CLC,* p. 193.
54. *Ibid.,* pp. 216-217.
55. *SSI,* Appendix, pp. 45-47.
56. *LM,* pp. 176 ff., 179.
57. *LM,* pp. 307-308.
58. Clement J. Wilkinson, *James John Garth Wilkinson,* p. 156.
59. *Ibid.,* p. 157.
60. *LMD,* p. 97.
61. *TNT,* pp. 20-21.
62. *CLC,* p. 117.
63. *WCS,* Appendix, pp. 55-56.
64. *NE,* pp. 259-261.
65. *CCNE,* p. 60.
66. *MC,* pp. 81-82, 83.
67. *Ibid.,* pp. 92-94.
68. *LM,* pp. 399 *passim,* 402.
69. *CCNE,* Letter III, pp. 95-97.
70. *S and S,* p. 145.
71. *CCNE,* pp. 101 *passim,* 107.
72. *MC,* p. 58.
73. *SSI,* pp. 244-245, in Joseph J. Blau, *op. cit.*
74. *CCNE,* pp. 94-95.
75. *SRFM,* pp. 144-145.
76. *CCNE,* pp. 39-40.
77. *SSI,* pp. 249-250, in Joseph Blau, *op. cit.*
78. *LR,* pp. 388-389, 390.
79. The resemblances of James's thought to some of the ideas of the Greek Fathers in early Christianity (and in some respects, to the concept of the "Divine Humanity" in such contemporary Greek Orthodox thinkers as Berdaiev and Bulgakov), and to the Gnostics, are really striking, and confirm the affirmation in this book of James's strong gnostical tendency.

For example, the Gnostics divided men into *hylics* ("materialists," suggesting James's "natural man"); *psychics* (suggestive of James's "moral man"); and *pneumatics* (or James's "spiritual man"). It need hardly be pointed out that the profoundest motivation to the pursuit of Philosophy to the Gnostics (and the Neo-Platonists)—and James, was the practice of *gnosis* as vision, knowledge, and experience of, the Divine, by which men attained redemption.

The Gnostic division of men into hylics, psychics, and pneumatics was an aristocratic and particularistic doctrine, since only a few could possibly qualify at the pneumatic level, and so be "redeemed." James's doctrine on the other hand, is spiritually democratic and universalistic, since he conceived that all men could and would ultimately realize the spiritual level through participation in the entity of the Divine Humanity.
80. Ralph B. Perry, *The Thought and Character of William James,* Vol. I, pp. 26-27.
81. *S of S,* p. 126.
82. *SRFM,* pp. 473-474.

Chapter Twelve

Concluding Reflections

WITH THE STRUCTURE of James's thought before one, a concluding attempt should be made to bring James as a thinker into a focus of comprehension. The kind and significance of James's contribution needs careful defining just because he is so elusive of capture in the conventional labels of philosophical or theological terms.

The first question, perhaps, that occurs to the serious student of James, is: was he a philosopher or was he fundamentally a theologian? Obviously, this is no simple alternative. A just and true perspective would involve the recognition that James was, in at least one basic respect, a genuine philosopher; while, at the same time, it should be readily admitted that in other respects he was not a philosopher. Again, it should be seen that he was in some sense a theologian, while at the same moment it should be perceived that, in the more conventional meanings of the term, he was not a theologian. Such an answer to our original question clearly requires further clarification of the aims of philosophical theology.

It appears indubitable that James was a philosopher in the *gnostical* connotation of the word as a seeker after "knowledge of the Divine." The gnostic's search is not motivated by the calm detachment which is customarily (though often very falsely!) associated with the scientist and the philosopher in the Western tradition of science and philosophy. The gnostic's quest is, on the contrary, motivated by an intense attachment to his supreme goal of individual and social "Redemption." Of course the scientist and the philosopher exhibit great attachment to their goals also, but the goals they envisage are not so personal and eschatological; that is, not so religious. The historic religions of civilized men have offered one or more, with varying degrees of stress, of three basic methods of "salvation"; namely, salvation by *good works,* salvation by *faith,* and salvation by *knowledge of the Divine* (gnosis); or, as the Hindu sages express it: *karma-yoga, bhakti-yoga* and *jñana-yoga,* respectively. None of these methods is necessarily exclusive of the others; but in James, as with the philosophical religions of Gnosticism, Neo-Platonism, and the religious philosophies of India, the prime emphasis is upon salvation by *knowledge* of the Divine. If the *motive,* which is "redemption," is religious, then the *method,* which is intellectual vision, is philosophic; that is to say, rationalistic. James, therefore, was a philosophical religionist in the gnostic meaning of the term. His concept of the Divine-Natural-Humanity, with its numerous affiliations with early Greek Fathers of the Church, with certain of the Gnostics, and with the concepts of the "Divine Humanity" and the "Divine Wisdom" (sophiology) in Greek Orthodox theology of today, stamp James unmistakably as gnostical in the cast of his thought. On the other hand, he can hardly qualify as a "philosopher of religion" in the scholastic and professional meaning of the phrase; he was not prepared either by motive, temperament, or systematic erudition, for such a role.

When it comes to the second part of our inquiry—Was James a theologian?—the reply must, as before, be based upon certain distinctions. If one intends a systematic theologian in the manner of a Calvin or a Swedenborg, the answer is clearly in the negative. He wrote about theological themes all his life, to be sure, but not as a systematic theologian develops his doctrines. In the few instances where he essayed the role of expounding definite theological concepts such as the Incarnation of God as the Lord, the Atonement, the Humiliation, and the Glorification of the Lord, it is observed at once that he is merely repeating, with varying phraseology, the teachings of Swedenborg. Such doctrines are the least original of his ideas. It can bear repeating here, that *James's originality is to be found in his attempt to fuse the Calvinist-Sandemanian-Fourierist-Swedenborgian currents in his thought, from which effort sprang his unique gnostic vision, expressed in striking triads, of man's evolution toward the Divine-Natural-Humanity.*

An interesting sub-question involved in whether James was a theologian or not, is: was James a "Christian" in his thought? Since James is very evidently less a systematic theologian than he is a religious philosopher, it is understandable that his son William James was inclined to think that his father was not "Christian" in his doctrine of the Divine-Natural-Humanity, for, like Wilkinson, he saw this view as amounting to a pantheism which issued finally as a pananthropism which in turn amounted to a virtual "atheism" in that the Divine Being Himself was "swallowed up" in the radical divinization of Humanity. But, does not the most catholic view in this matter require the recognition that there is a very complex basic issue involved: namely, the problem as to what standard is finally to be used in judging whether or not a man is "Christian" in his theological conceptions? Is one to take the New Testament as the standard? But the New Testament is in no sense a theological treatise, except perhaps in a few Pauline passages. And what about St. Paul's doctrines? Was he purely "Christian" in his views? He certainly differed in many of his interpretations from the authors of the Gospels who, again, differed considerably from each other. If it be said that the fundamental genius of Judaic Christianity was ethical rather than speculative, that might well be granted; but, judging from that viewpoint itself, how can we determine just how "Christian" are the formulas of Nicean and Chalcedonian theology, which are expressed in the concepts of Greek metaphysics? In the realm of theological construction, as also in the field of ethics, the difficulty of finding any *one* absolute standard must be admitted by any honest mind, and this admission with the assurance that such intellectual humility and honesty are more essentially Christian than any other position can really be. Probably the best way of settling this issue with regard to James, is to say that he presumably believed his thought to be as Christian, indeed, more Christian in essence than any other he knew. If Greek Fathers, some of the Gnostics, Swedenborg, and Greek Catholic theologians of today were, and are, in some sense Christian in their thought, this writer believes James to be, in a real way, Christian also. Let it be remembered that Christianity was the only religion he thought and wrote about; but, it must also be understood that in his Christianity, he went back, under the impact of Swedenborg, to theological positions differing from both the Reformed and Catholic theologians; in other words, back to the Greek mode of theological interpretation. His doctrines of God as the Lord and of *"the* Christ," for example, exhibit, whatever minor differences, a strong Docetic strain.

By way of summary in regard to this topic of James as a Christian thinker, it may be said that in superficial aspects James displays in his thinking, traits for which parallels may be found in both Roman Catholicism and Protestantism. In his conception of man as a great, organic, corporate society he has a certain spiritual kinship with the Roman Catholic stress upon the organic-social-corporate nature of the Church; in his vigorous protestations against all the moralities, theologies, and ecclesiasticisms of his day he stands forth as a Protestant of the Protestants! But these interesting, though superficial resemblances, should not blind one from realizing that the *substance* of his thoughts and beliefs places him outside any conventional or official form of either Catholicism or Protestantism. He is, under the stimulus from Swedenborg, a Greek Christian thinker incarnated in the nineteenth century.

In final perspective, James is one of the very few thinkers who have lived and thought on the North American continent, whose metaphysics is Neo-Platonic and Gnostic in its genius. Furthermore, his social philosophy is a unique doctrine standing between, or more accurately, beyond, the Calvinistic and Emersonian extremes. In reacting from the Calvinist doctrine of election to salvation for a few, and election to damnation for the majority, as well as in reacting from Emerson's doctrine of "Nature" and "*Self*-Reliance," James built a system of belief which transcended them both in its scope. To Calvin, James opposed his faith in salvation for all mankind; to Emerson's moral individualism (which William James was to revive in his own form), James proposed a spiritual universalism. Thus, both Calvinism and Emersonianism, for very different reasons, were too narrow for James's intensely social and loving spirit; and so he broadened his religious philosophy into a metaphysical-eschatological-spiritual-social-democratic universalism which embraced in its redemptive yearning, the entire race of mankind.

James would not leave out a single human soul in man's progress from the frail humanity of history to the Divine Humanity of Eternity. In behalf of that vision James, with his unique fusion of Calvinist-Sandemanian-Fourierist-Swedenborgian-Neoplatonic-Gnostic elements, tilted his philosophic lance against moralism, ecclesiasticism, orthodox Calvinism, naturalistic theism, "orthodox" theism, deism, pantheism, dualism, extreme idealism, and secularistic socialism, by developing his trinal monism and his dynamic philosophy of Spirit. To that vision James devoted, as thinker-preacher-prophet, his life and labor, his faith and thought. The result to our American philosophic inheritance is a vision of singular vitality and nobility.

Bibliography

I

BOOKS BY HENRY JAMES, SR.

1. *Remarks on the Apostolic Gospel.* 1840.

   So far as scholars on James have been able to find out, this work, included in the bibliography of James's writings in the Boston *Literary World*, XIV (Jan. 13, 1883), 9, is non-extant.

2. *What Constitutes the State.* New York: John Allen, 1846. Pp. 59.

   This is the first book acknowledged by James over his signature. The *Remarks* was unsigned.

3. *Tracts for the New Times. No. I., Letter to a Swedenborgian.* New York: John Allen, 1847. Pp. 24.

4. *Moralism and Christianity: or, Man's Experience and Destiny.* New York: Redfield, 1850. Pp. 184.

   This work contains the three basic lectures: "A Scientific Statement of the Christian Doctrine of the Lord, or Divine Man," "Socialism and Civilization in Relation to the Development of the Individual Life," and "Morality and the Perfect Life."

5. *Lectures and Miscellanies.* New York: Redfield, 1852. Pp. 442.

   Comprises six lectures: "Democracy and Its Issues," "Property as a Symbol," "The Principle of Universality in Art," and "The Old and the New Theology"—in two lectures, Parts I and II; and "The Scientific Accord of Natural and Revealed Religion."

   Added to these six lectures are ten "Miscellanies": "The Laws of Creation," "Berkeley and his Critics," "God," "Man," "Responsibility," "Morality," "A Very Long Letter," "Spiritual Rappings," "Intemperance," and "Christianity."

6. *Love, Marriage, and Divorce; A Discussion between Henry James, Horace Greeley, and Stephen Pearl Andrews.* New York: Stringer

and Townsend, 1853. Pp. 103. *Love, Marriage, and Divorce;
A Discussion between Henry James, Horace Greeley, and Stephen
Pearl Andrews. Including the final replies of Mr. Andrews, rejected
by the New York Tribune, and a subsequent discussion, occurring
twenty years later, between Mr. James and Mr. Andrews.* Boston:
Benjamin R. Tucker, Publisher, 1889.

7. *The Nature of Evil, Considered in a Letter to the Rev. Edward
Beecher, D.D., author of 'The Conflict of Ages.'* New York:
Appleton, 1855. Pp. 348.

8. *The Church of Christ not an Ecclesiasticism*: *A Letter of Remonstrance to a member of the* Soi-Disant *New Church.* New York:
Redfield, 1854. Pp. 72.

The second and enlarged edition, published in London by
W. White, appeared in 1856, with 156 pages. It is this edition
which has been used in the present study. The original was
written as a "Letter" to James John Garth Wilkinson.

9. *Christianity the Logic of Creation.* London: Wm. White, 1857.
Pp. 264. Published in New York, Appleton, 1857.
Originally written as "Letters" to Wilkinson.

10. *The Old and New Theology.* London: Longman, Green, Longman and Roberts, 1861. Pp. 197.

This book was a reprint of the two lectures on "The Old and
the New Theology" from *Lectures and Miscellanies,* combined
with *The Church of Christ not an Ecclesiasticism* (shorter American edition). Warren believes that the anonymous introduction,
obviously written by someone representing the "Broad Church"
viewpoint of Anglicanism, is "probably by some disciple of
Maurice."

11. *The Social Significance of Our Institutions*: *An Oration delivered
by Request of the Citizens of Newport, R. I., July 4, 1861.*
Boston: Ticknor and Fields, 1861. Pp. 47.

12. *Substance and Shadow*: *or, Morality and Religion in Their Relation to Life*: *An Essay on the Physics of Creation.* Boston:
Ticknor and Fields, 1863. Pp. 539.

13. *The Secret of Swedenborg*: *Being an Elucidation of his Doctrine
of the Divine Natural Humanity.* Boston: Fields, Osgood & Co.,
1869. Pp. xv + 243.

14. *Society the Redeemed Form of Man, and the Earnest of God's
Omnipotence in Human Nature*: *Affirmed in Letters to a Friend.*
Boston: Houghton, Osgood & Co., 1879. Pp. 485.

15. *The Literary Remains of the late Henry James*: Edited with an
Introduction by William James. Boston: Houghton Mifflin Co.,
1884. Pp. 471.

II
ARTICLES AND REVIEWS BY JAMES

1. "Swedenborg as a Theologian," *Massachusetts Quarterly Review*, I (1848), 293-307.
2. "Vanity Fair, or rather Becky Sharp," *The Spirit of the Age*, I (1850), 49-51. For Thackeray and James, cf. Henry James, Jr., *A Small Boy*, 87-91; and Eyre Crowe, *With Thackeray in America* (1893), 43-44, 167.
3. "William Blake's Poems," *The Spirit of the Age*, I (1850), 113.
4. "The Divine Man," *Massachusetts Quarterly Review*, III (1850), 52-67. This appeared subsequently as the first "Lecture" in *Moralism and Christianity*.
5. "Woman and the 'Woman's Movement,'" *Putnam's Monthly Magazine*, I (1853), 279-88.
6. "The Works of Sir William Hamilton," *Putnam's Magazine*, II (1853), 470-81.
7. Review of Carlyle's *Frederick the Great*, in *The Nation*, I (1865), 20-21.
8. "Miss Cobbe on Religion," *Nation*, I (1865), 249.
9. "Faith and Science," *North American Review*, CI (1865), 335-78.
10. Review of, and article on, "Stirling's *Secret of Hegel*," *North American Review*, CII (1866), 264-75.
11. Review of Horace Bushnell's *Vicarious Sacrifice*, in *The North American Review*, CII (1866), 556-71.
12. "Religion Old and New," *The Radical*, I (1866), 97-101.
13. "Emanuel Swedenborg," *Nation*, IV (1866-7), 329.
14. "The Radical Dogmatics," *The Radical*, II (1867), 84-94.
15. "Ontology of Swedenborg," *North American Review*, CV (1867), 89-123.
16. "Is Marriage Holy?" *The Atlantic Monthly*, XXV (1870), 360-68.
17. "The Woman Thou Gavest with Me," *The Atlantic Monthly*, XXV (1870), 66-72. Consists of short reviews of John Stuart Mill's *The Subjection of Women;* Horace Bushnell's *Woman Suffrage: The Reform against Nature;* and Epes Sargent's *The Woman Who Dared*.
18. "The Logic of Marriage and Murder," *The Atlantic Monthly*, XXV (1870), 744-49.
19. "Spiritualism, Old and New," *The Atlantic Monthly*, XXIX (1872), 358-62.
20. "Spiritualism: Modern Diabolism," *The Atlantic Monthly*, XXXII (1873), 219.
21. "Some Personal Recollections of Carlyle," *The Atlantic Monthly*, XLVII (1881), 593-609.
22. "Emerson," *The Atlantic Monthly*, XCIV (1904), 740-45.

III

LETTERS AND MISCELLANEOUS ITEMS BY JAMES

1. Unsigned preface of two pages, to Robert Sandeman's *Letters on Theron and Aspasio*. New York: John S. Taylor, 1838. Pp. xx + 500. Edited and prefaced by James.

2. A two-page, unsigned preface to Victor Antoine Hennequin's *Love in a Phalanstery*. New York: Dewitt & Davenport, 1848. Pp. 27. Translated from the French by James.

3. To the *Harbinger,* organ of the Brook Farm Community, James contributed, after it moved to New York City in 1847, thirty-two reviews, essays, and letters, which covered his customary topics. They include his reflections, developed more fully in his books and articles, on love and marriage, the laws of creation, the Swedenborgian sect, and the points of parallelism and convergence between Fourier's and Swedenborg's thought. The *Harbinger* ceased publication in 1849. James's contributions were signed "Y. S.," the common abbreviation of the time for "Your Servant."

4. Eleven "Letters," as Foreign Correspondent, to the New York *Tribune,* from September 3, 1855 to October 1, 1856. The captions are:
   "An American in Europe," Part I (September 3, 1855).
   "An American in Europe," Part II (September 8, 1855).
   "An American in Europe," Part III (September 22, 1855).
   "Goethe and his Morality" (January 15, 1856).
   "Christmas at London" (January 16, 1856).
   "Decay and Growth of Europe" (February 7, 1856).
   "The State of England" (March 17, 1856).
   "American Observations in Europe" (August 26, 1856).
   "Affairs in France" (September 12, 1856).
   "Affairs in France" (September 16, 1856).
   "France" (October 1, 1856).

5. Six "Letters" addressed to Francis Ellingwood Abbot, in the pages of *The Index,* VII (1876), as follows:
   "Deliverance, not Perfection, the Aim of Religion" (January 20), p. 26.
   "The Reconciliation of Man Individual with Man Universal" (February 3), p. 52.
   "Society vs. Selfhood" (February 17), p. 74.
   "Spiritual Creation" (March 23), p. 134.
   "Knowledge and Science Contrasted" (April 13), p. 172.
   "The Philosophy of the Heart" (May 18), p. 230.

6. Eighteen "Letters" to the *New Church Independent* (Chicago), from July, 1879 to August, 1881. Many of these letters are included as chapters in the essay on "Spiritual Creation," the last and unfinished work by James, included by William James in *The Literary Remains*. The rest cover the same topics more fully treated by James in his books and articles.

7. "Henry James, Sr.," an interview reported in the Boston Sunday *Herald,* April 17, 1881. A week later, April 24, 1881, in the same paper appeared a long letter in a critical tone taking the interviewer to task for some inaccurate impressions of the foregoing interview.

8. James's "Correspondence" with contemporary leaders of thought may be summarized as follows:

    a. Thirty-four letters from James to Emerson, and thirty-two from Emerson to James, at the Widener Library, Harvard University.

    b. Eight letters of William White, the English biographer of Swedenborg, to James, at the Widener Library.

    c. Letters of James to Joseph Henry, the celebrated physicist and first head of the Smithsonian Institution, at the Smithsonian Institution, Washington; and at the Houghton Library, Harvard University.

    d. Twenty-one letters by James to his Princeton friend, Parke Godwin, from 1861-1882, at the New York Public Library.

    e. For correspondence between James and J. J. Garth Wilkinson, cf. Clement Wilkinson: *John James Garth Wilkinson* (London, 1911), pp. 41-42, 48-50, 54-56, 87-89, 155-58, 180 ff. to 204. Clement Wilkinson says: "For many years the two men corresponded regularly, copiously and affectionately. The letters from London to New York have been carefully preserved . . . those from New York to London have been unfortunately with few exceptions destroyed." (Pp. 41-42.)

IV

BOOKS ON, OR WITH REFERENCE TO, JAMES, IN
CHRONOLOGICAL ORDER OF PUBLICATION.
THOSE DEVOTED EXCLUSIVELY
TO HIM ARE STARRED

*Kellogg, Julia. *The Philosophy of Henry James.* N. Y.: John W. Lovell Co., 1883, 47 pp.

Santayana, George. *Character and Opinion in the United States.* N. Y.: Scribner's Sons, 1920, 233 pp.

James, Henry (Jr.). *A Small Boy and Others.* N. Y.: Scribner & Sons, 1913, 419 pp.

---------------------------- *Notes of a Son and Brother.* N. Y.: Scribner's & Sons, 1914, pp. 515.

Emerson, E. W. *The Early Years of the Saturday Club.* N. Y.: Houghton Mifflin Co., 1918), *Cf.* chapter on "Henry James," pp. 322-333.

James, Henry (the 3rd). *The Letters of William James,* The Atlantic Monthly Press (Boston, 1920), I, 7-19. Wm. James's letters to his father may be found on pp. 60, 64, 95, 133, 218.

Howe, M. A. de Wolfe. *Memories of a Hostess.* Boston, The Atlantic Monthly Press, 1922, 74-85 pp.

Grattan, C. Hartley. *The Three Jameses.* London, Longmans, 1932, pp. 21-107.

*Warren, Austin. *The Elder Henry James.* N. Y.: MacMillan Co., 1934, x, 269 pp.

Perry, Ralph Barton. *The Thought and Character of William James,* 2 vols. Little, Brown and Co., Boston, 1935. *Cf.* pp. 3-166 in Vol. I; and, "Philosophical Correspondence between William James and his Father," in Appendix to Vol. II; pp. 705-716.

Müller, Gustav E. *Amerikanishe Philosophie,* Fromman, Stuttgart, 1936, pp. 88-94, 199, 200, 316.

Rusk, Ralph L. *The Letters of Ralph Waldo Emerson.* Columbia University, N. Y., 1939. *Cf.* Vol. VI, the "Index," p. 485, for listing of letters between Emerson and James.

Schneider, Herbert Wallace. *A History of American Philosophy.* Columbia University Press, N. Y., 1946, pp. 301-312, 318, 331-332.

Blau, Joseph. Editor, *American Philosophic Addresses, 1700-1900.* Columbia Univ. Press, N. Y., 1946, pp. 234-256.

Matthiessen, F. O. *The James Family.* N. Y.: Alfred A. Knopf Co., 1947, pp. 3-285.

Mulford, E. "Henry James, Sr.," *The Atlantic Monthly,* LV (1885), 702-05.

Orr, A. "Mr. Henry James, Senior," *The Athenaeum,* No. 2752 (1880), 113-15. A review of *Society the Redeemed Form of Man.*

Peirce, Charles Sanders. Review of *The Secret of Swedenborg,* in the *North American Review,* CX (1870), 463-68.

Perry, Ralph Barton. "Religion versus Morality according to the Elder Henry James," *International Journal of Ethics,* XLII (1932), 289-303.

------------------- "Henry James," *Dictionary of American Biography,* Vol. IX (1932), 577-79.

A review, unsigned, of *The Literary Remains of Henry James,* in the *Spectator* (London), LVIII (1885), 1237.

V

MISCELLANEOUS PERIODICAL AND NEWSPAPER ITEMS ABOUT JAMES

Bicknell. "Glimpses of a Gifted Family," *Dial,* LVI (1914), 289-91.

Edel, Leon. Review of Grattan's *The Three Jameses,* in *The Saturday Review of Literature,* IX (Nov. 12, 1932), 236.

"Henry James, Senior," Bibliography of, and tributes to, James, *The Literary World,* XIV (1883), 9-10.

"Henry James," *New-Church Independent,* XXIX (1881), 431-33.

Howells, William Dean. "Some Literary Memories of Cambridge," Part II, *Harper's Magazine,* CI (Nov., 1900), 828-31.

"In Memory of Henry James," *New-Church Independent,* XXXI (Feb., 1883), 88-89.

Ilsley, Marshall. "Letter" in praise of Henry James, Sr., in *The New Republic,* LVI (Aug. 22, 1928), 22.

Markham, Edwin. "Distinguished American Family," *Cosmopolitan,* L (Dec., 1910), 145-46.

VI

ARTICLES ON JAMES AND REVIEWS OF HIS WORKS

Albee, John. Review of *Literary Remains,* in *Journal of Speculative Philosophy,* XIX (1885), 435-37.

Anderson, Quentin. "Henry James and the New Jerusalem," *Kenyon Review,* VIII (1946), No. 4, 515-28, 532-34, 536, 538, 540-42, 565.

————————— "The Two Henry Jameses," *Scrutiny,* XIV, No. 4 (Sept., 1947), 242-51.

Baugh, Hansell. "Emerson and the Elder Henry James," *The Bookman,* LXVIII (1928), 320-22.

Clarke, James Freeman. Review of James's *The Nature of Evil,* in *Christian Examiner,* LIX (1855), 116-36.

————————— Review of *Substance and Shadow,* in *Christian Examiner,* LXXV (1863), 212-24.

Cranch, C. P. Review of *The Secret of Swedenborg,* in *Nation,* IX (1869), 436.

Galbraith, W. H. Review of *Society the Redeemed Form of Man,* in *New-Church Independent,* XXVII (1879), 229-35.

James, William. "Introduction" to *Literary Remains of the late Henry James* (Boston, 1884). Pp. 7-119.

Howells, William Dean. Review of *The Secret of Swedenborg,* in *The Atlantic Monthly,* XXIV (1869), 762-63.

Howison, George H. Review of *Society the Redeemed Form of Man,* in *Christian Register,* LVIII (No. 28, July 12, 1879), 1.

——————— Cf. James's reply to Howison in *Ibid.,* July 26; Howison's counter-reply to James in *Ibid.,* Aug. 16; James's reply to Howison's reply, *Ibid.,* Aug. 30—on first page in each case.

Kimball, W. H. "Swedenborg and Henry James," *Journal of Speculative Philosophy,* XVII (Apr., 1883), 113-30.

Lackland, C. E. "Henry James the Seer," *Journal of Speculative Philosophy,* XIX (1885), 53-60.

Larrabee, Harold A. "Henry James, Sr., '30 at Union," published in the *Union Alumni Monthly,* XV (1926), 236-47.

——————— "The Jameses: Financier, Heretic, Philosopher," *The American Scholar,* I (1932), 401-13.

——————— "Flight of Henry James the First," *New England Quarterly,* X (Dec., 1937), 774-75.

Morris, Lloyd. Review of F. O. Matthiessen's *The James Family,* in New York *Herald-Tribune* Book Review, Nov. 23, 1947, pp. 1-2.

Unsigned. Obituary account of Henry James, Sr., Boston *Evening Transcript,* Dec. 20, 1882.

Unsigned. Obituary account of Mr. Henry James, Sr., Boston *Daily Advertiser,* Dec. 20, 1882.

Perry, Ralph Barton. Review of Grattan's *The James Family* (the title was later changed from *The Three Jameses* to *The James Family*), *The Saturday Review of Literature,* X (1933-34), 749-50.

Unidentified source. A photo-portrait of Henry James, Sr., *Book Buyer,* XXI (Jan., 1901), 541.

Sechrist, Alice Spiers. "Henry James the Elder," *New-Church Messenger,* CXXXIX (Sept. 3, 1930), 203-06.

——————— Tribute to Henry James, Sr., in *The Atlantic Monthly,* LV (1885), 702-05.

Warren, Austin. "James and his Secret," *Saturday Review of Literature,* VIII (1932), 759.

——————— Review of C. Hartley Grattan's *The Three Jameses,* in *American Literature,* V (1933), 176-79.

VII

SANDEMANIANISM

Dickinson, Rodolphus. *The Miscellaneous Productions in Poetry and Prose of the late Samuel Field, Esq.* (Greenfield, Mass.: Clark & Hunt, 1818), 21-50, which is a sketch of "Christian Tenets and Practices of Sandemanians."

Fuller, Andrew. *Strictures on Sandemanianism in Twelve Letters to a Friend.* New York: Richard Scott, 1812.

Gadsby, William. *Sandemanianism Weighed in the Balance and Found Wanting. Being a Letter to Mr. William Stephen.* Manchester, England: Henry Smith, 1823. Pp. 63. A pamphlet in a bound volume of other pamphlets, entitled *Gadsby's Works.*

Glas, John. *The Works of John Glas,* in Four Volumes, Edinburgh, 1761.

Gordon, The Reverend Alexander. Article, "Robert Sandeman," *Dictionary of National Biography* (British), Vol. 50, pp. 255-56.

Hallock, G. W. "Sandemanians," *New England Magazine,* (N. S.), XIV (1896) 239-44.

Hayward, John. *The Book of Religions.* Boston: Albert Colby and Co., 1860, 126-127; 396-397.

Hornsby, John T. *John Glas: A Study in the Origins, Development, and Influence of the Glasite Movement.* An unpublished dissertation at the Library of the School of Religion at Butler University, Indianapolis, Indiana, 1936.

Langdon, Samuel. *An Impartial Examination of Mr. Robert Sandeman's Letters.* Boston, 1769. Pp. 136.

Pike, S. *An Epistolary Correspondence between S. Pike and R. Sandeman relating to the Letters on Theron and Aspasio.* London, John Olivier, 1759. Besides the *Letters,* there is also included Sandeman's work, *Some Thoughts on Christianity.*

Sandeman, Robert. *Letters on Theron and Aspasio.* New York: John S. Taylor, 1838. Pp. xx + 500. This American edition was edited and prefaced by James.

Steele, Daniel. *Antinomianism Revived, or, the Theology of the So-called Plymouth Brethren Examined and Refuted.* Boston: McDonald, Gill and Co., 1887. Pp. 266.

Walker, Williston. "Sandemanians of New England," *American Historical Association Report,* I (1902), 133-62.

"The Places of Worship of the Sandemanians in Boston," in *Publications of the Colonial Society of Massachusetts,* VI, 109-23.

"Sandemanians," *Congregational Magazine,* London, II (1819), 144.

"Theology of Sandemanians," *Eclectic Review* (London), LXVIII (1838), 519-31.

VIII

SWEDENBORG

Block, Marguerite. *The New Church in the New World.* New York: Henry Holt & Co., 1932. Pp. 464.

Coleridge, Samuel T. "Passages from the *Oeconomia Regni Animalis* and *De Cultu et Amore Dei* of Swedenborg. With Original Comments Thereon. By the late Samuel Taylor Coleridge," in *The Monthly Magazine*, V (London: June, 1841), 607-16. J. J. Garth Wilkinson's "Letter to the Editor" is appended on pp. 616-20.

Eby, Samuel C. *Swedenborg's Service to Philosophy.* Peoria, Illinois, 1891.

Emerson, Ralph Waldo. Essay on Swedenborg as "The Mystic," in *Representative Men,* Boston, 1849.

Heraud, John A. Essay on "Swedenborg," *The Monthly Magazine,* V (London: June, 1841), 441-72. Heraud was editor of this magazine.

Hite, The Reverend L. F. *Ultimate Reality.* London: the Swedenborg Society, Inc., 1936. Pp. 64. An address delivered at the International Swedenborg Congress in 1910.

.... *Swedenborg's Historical Position,* Boston, New-Church Union, 1928. Pp. 174.

Horton, Walter Marshall. *The Significance of Swedenborg for Contemporary Theology.* New York: The Swedenborg Publishing Association, 1938. Pp. 28. An address delivered in New York City in commemoration of the two hundred and fiftieth Anniversary of the birth of Swedenborg.

Kant, Immanuel. *Träume eines Geistersehers, erläutert durch Träume der Metaphysik.* (Berlin, 1921.)

Sewall, Frank. *Swedenborg and Modern Idealism.* London: James Speirs, 1902. Pp. 244.

Swedenborg, Emanuel. His chief theological works are:
  On the Worship and Love of God (1745)
  Arcana Coelestia, in 8 vols. (1756)
  The Earths in the Universe (1758)
  The New Jerusalem and its Heavenly Doctrine (1758)
  Heaven and Hell (1758)
  The Divine Love and Wisdom (1763)
  The Four Doctrines (1763)
  Divine Providence (1764)
  The Apocalypse Revealed (1766)
  Conjugial Love (1768)
  On the Intercourse between the Soul and the Body (1769)
  The True Christian Religion (1771)

Toksvig, Signe. *Emanuel Swedenborg: Scientist and Mystic* (Yale, 1948).

White, William. *Emanuel Swedenborg: His Life and Writings.* In 2 Vols., London, 1867. Cf. Vol. II, p. 653, for tribute to James.

Wilkinson, Clement J. *James John Garth Wilkinson.* London: Kegan Paul, Trench, Trübner and Co., 1911. Pp. 303. Cf., for references to, and correspondence between, James and Wilkinson: pp. 41-42, 48-50, 54-56, 87-89, 155-58, 180 ff., to 204.

Wilkinson, J. J. Garth. *Emanuel Swedenborg: A Biographical Sketch* (London, 1849).

IX

FOURIER, SOCIALISM, AND ASSOCIATIONISM

Clarke, James Freeman. "Fourierism," *Christian Examiner,* XXXVII (1844), 57-78.

Brisbane, Albert. *Association: or, a Concise Exposition of the Practical Part of Fourier's Social Science.* New York: Greeley and McElrath, 1843. Pp. 80.

Dana, Charles A. *A Lecture on Association in its Connection with Religion, delivered before the New England Fourier Society in Boston, 7 March 1844.* (Boston, 1844.) Pp. 19.

Fourier, Charles Marie François. *Oeuvres Complètes* (Paris, 1841).

Gide, Charles. *Selections from the Works of Fourier* (London, 1901).

Godwin, Parke. *A Popular View of the Doctrines of Charles Fourier.* New York: J. S. Redfield, 1844. Pp. 120.

Hempel, Charles Julius. *The True Organization of the New Church as Indicated in the Writings of Emanuel Swedenborg and Demonstrated by Charles Fourier.* New York: William Radde, 1848. Pp. 454.

Hennequin, Victor Antoine. *Love in a Phalanstery.* New York: Dewitt and Davenport, 1848. Pp. 27. Translated and prefaced by James.

Hillquit, Morris. *History of Socialism in the United States.* New York: Funk and Wagnalls, 1910. Pp. 389.

Noyes, John Humphrey. *History of American Socialisms.* Philadelphia: J. B. Lippincott & Co., 1870. Pp. 678.

Pellarin, Charles. *Life of Charles Fourier.* Translated by F. G. Shaw (New York, 1848).

X

COLLATERAL BIBLIOGRAPHY

Books

Aurobindo, Sri. *The Life Divine.* New York: Greystone Press, 1949. Pp. 1040.

Balzac, Honoré de. *Seraphita.* A "Swedenborgian novel," with Preface by George Saintsbury. New York: McKinley, Stone & MacKensie, 1915.

Berdaiev, Nicholas. *The Meaning of History*. New York: Scribner's, 1936. Pp. 224.

Blake, William. *Poems of William Blake*. Ed. by William Butler Yeats. New York: The Book League of America, Inc., 1938. Cf. especially "The Marriage of Heaven and Hell," and "Milton."

Blau, Joseph. Editor of: *American Philosophic Addresses, 1700-1900*. New York: Columbia University Press, 1946. Pp. 762.

Niebuhr, Reinhold. *The Nature and Destiny of Man: A Christian Interpretation*. New York: Charles Scribner's Sons, 1947. Cf. the chapter on "Sectarian Protestantism and the Renaissance," Vol. II, pp. 169-80, for Niebuhr's treatment of the individualist-perfectionist sects, and the social-radical-eschatological-perfectionist sects, for the light it throws on the general historical background, though not directly the roots of, James's Spiritual Socialism.

Schneider, Herbert Wallace. *Meditations in Season on the Elements of Christian Philosophy*. London and New York: Oxford University Press, 1938. See especially the meditations on "The Trinity" for the "modalism" so reminiscent of the Cappodocians among the Greek Fathers, and so similar in vein to Swedenborg's "triune God" as "Love-Wisdom-Power." Schneider's triad is Power-Love-Truth.

.... *A History of American Philosophy*. New York: Columbia University Press (1946). Pp. 646.

Temple, William. *Nature, Man, and God*. London and New York: MacMillan, 1934. Pp. 530.

COLLATERAL ARTICLES AND DISSERTATIONS

Adams, James L. *Paul Tillich's Philosophy of Culture, Science, and Religion*. University of Chicago, 1945. An unpublished doctoral dissertation.

Peirce, Benjamin. "The Conflict of Science and Religion," *Unitarian Review*, VII (1876-77), 655-66.

Pratt, James Bissett. "Religious Philosophy of William James," *Hibbert Journal*, X (1911), 225-34.

Romero, Francisco. "On Spirit and on the Spiritual Attitudes of Great Cultures." A paper, translated by Eliseo Vivas, from *Papers and Abstracts of the Second Inter-American Congress of Philosophy*, held at Columbia University, New York City, Dec. 28-31, 1947, pp. 74-90. Published by the American Philosophical Association.

Young, Frederic H. "The Conflict of Nature and Spirit, illustrated especially in Thomas Mann's *The Magic Mountain*," *Christendom*, XIII (Winter, 1948), 59-68.

Index

(*Note*: It will be observed that the great majority of entries referring to pages 1-90, indicate *sources* of James's ideas and doctrines; those entries referring to pages 91-320, indicate, in the great majority of cases, James's ideas and doctrines *themselves*. Otherwise, the Index requires no further special principle of reference.)

G.

Ghosh, Sri Aurobindo. *See* Aurobindo
Glas, John, 20-24, 35
Glasites, doctrines of, 20-24
Glorification, the, 48, 51-52, 54
Gnosticism (including gnosis, gnostic, gnostical), 65, 102, 117, 251-52, 263, 289, 294, 316 (note 79), 317-320
God, 35, 40-41, 48, 110, 117, 171, 175. *See* also Creator
God-Man. *See* Lord
Godwin, Parke, 8, 75-77, 80-84
Goethe, 101, 190
Good, 45
Gospel, 42
Grand Man, the, 60, 221
Greeley, Horace, 8-9, 72-73, 76, 204, 295
Grotius, 52

H.

Hamilton, Sir William, 103, 123-25, 170-71, 191
Harmony, 82
Harnack, Adolph, 67 (note 26)
Hartmann, Eduard von, 201
Hawthorne, Nathaniel, 74
Heart, 45
Heaven(s), 49-51, 232
Hegel, 72, 148, 165, 307
Heine, Heinrich, 190
Hell(s), 45, 49-51, 232
Helps, Arthur, 5
Hempel, Julius, 76-80, 83
Henry, Joseph, 4-5
Herder, 190
Hervey, the Rev'd John, 21
Hierarchy, 196-97
Higher Criticism, the, 289
History, origin of, 213-14; philosophy of, 260-269
Holy Spirit, the, 52-53
Homo-vir, 166, 211-18, 239, 241
Horton, Walter M., 131
Howe, M. A. DeWolfe, 207
Howison, George H., 9 (note 3), 180
Human, the, 48
Humanity, Comte's Religion of, 305-306
Humboldt, Alexander von, 29
Humiliation, the, 48
Husserl, Edmund, 191
Huxley, Thomas H., 101

I.

Idealism, 55, 58, 69, 103, 106-108, 132
Identity, principle of, 120

Illusion (of selfhood), 254-55
Immortality, 203, 287-89, 310
Incarnation, 48, 51-52, 54, 204, 206, 289-92, 312-13
Incarnationalism, 311
Indeterminism. *See* Tychism
Individualism, moral, 82, 320
Individuality, principle of, 101, 120; spiritual, 165, 202, 229
Inge, W. R., 107-108, 278
Intuition, 112, 180-81
Inversion, of terms, 143-44
Involution, 132, 143, 168-69
Irenaeus, 66 (note 26), 312-13

J.

James, Henry, Jr., 2, 5, 166, 190, 219
James, Henry, Sr.,
  biographical, 3-9
  chronology of life and works, see Preface, xiii-xiv
  divergence from Swedenborg, 61-62, 223 (note 33)
  literary style, 18-19 (note 9)
  originality, 318
  reading range, 19 (note 14)
  saneness, 79-80
  scatology, 59
  spiritual positivism, 57
  tributes to Swedenborg, 29, 33

  Note: for James's doctrines, *see* Evil, Knowledge, Nature, Man, Spirit, Redemption, Revelation, etc. *Also,* Triads. For James as gnostic, Neo-Platonist, pan-en-theist, philosopher, and theologian, *see* same, as indexed.

James, William, 1, 2, 5-6, 82, 84, 136-38, 148, 154, 180, 190, 199, 203, 215, 225, 237, 241, 312, 318-20
James, William, Sr., 3
Jeans, Sir James, 146
Jesus. *See* Christ
Jung, C. G., 201, 218
Justification, 34

K.

Kafka, Franz, 219
Kant, Immanuel, 27, 29, 30-31, 62-63, 96, 103, 120-123, 131, 190, 240
Kellogg, Mrs. Julia A., 9 (note 3), 117, 251
Kimball, W. H., 121
King-Priest-Artist, 185, 307
Kingdom of God, 267, 310
Kirkegaard, Soren, 50, 219, 230